Mission and Culture

The American Society of Missiology Series No. 48

Mission and Culture

The Louis J. Luzbetak Lectures

Edited by

Stephen B. Bevans, SVD

MKLM Library

ORBIS BOOKS

Maryknoll, New York 10545

Library of Congress Cataloging-in-Publication Data

Mission and culture : the Louis J. Luzbetak lectures / Stephen B. Bevans, editor.
    p. cm. — (The American Society of Missiology series ; no. 48)
    Includes index.
    ISBN 978-1-57075-965-9 (pbk.)
        1. Missions—Theory—Congresses. 2. Christianity and culture—Congresses. I. Bevans, Stephen B., 1944– II. Title: Louis J. Luzbetak lectures.

BV2063.M556 2012
266—dc23
                                                                2011040101

For

Roger Schroeder, SVD
co-author, collaborator, colleague—
but especially friend

Contents

Preface to the American Society of Missiology Series

The purpose of the ASM (American Society of Missiology) Series is to publish—without regard for disciplinary, national, or denominational boundaries—scholarly works of high quality and wide interest on missiological themes from the entire spectrum of scholarly pursuits relevant to Christian mission, which is always the focus of books in the Series.

By mission is meant the effort to effect passage over the boundary between faith in Jesus Christ and its absence. In this understanding of mission, the basic functions of Christian proclamation, dialogue, witness, service, worship, liberation, and nurture are of special concern. And in that context questions arise, including, How does the transition from one cultural context to another influence the shape and interaction between these dynamic functions, especially in regard to the cultural and religious plurality that comprises the global context of Christian life and mission?

The promotion of scholarly dialogue among missiologists, and among missiologists and scholars in other fields of inquiry, may involve the publication of views that some missiologists cannot accept, and with which members of the Editorial Committee themselves do not agree. Manuscripts published in the Series, accordingly, reflect the opinions of their authors and are not understood to represent the position of the American Society of Missiology or of the Editorial Committee. Selection is guided by such criteria as intrinsic worth, readability, coherence, and accessibility to a range of interested persons and not merely to experts or specialists.

The ASM Series, in collaboration with Orbis Books, seeks to publish scholarly works of high merit and wide interest on numerous aspects of missiology the scholarly study of mission. Able presentations on new and creative approaches to the practice and understanding of mission will receive close attention.

The ASM Series Committee
Jonathan J. Bonk
Angelyn Dries, OSF
Scott W. Sunquist

Abbreviations

AG   Vatican Council II, Decree on Missionary Activity, *Ad Gentes*

EN   Pope Paul VI, Apostolic Exhortation *Evangelii Nuntiandi*

LG   Vatican Council II, Dogmatic Constitution on the Church, *Lumen Gentium*

NA   Vatican Council II, Declaration on the Relationship of the Church to Non-Christian Religions, *Nostra Aetate*

Introduction

This book is a collection of scholarly lectures that probe the complex, mutually critical relationship between Christian mission and local context or culture. It is also, however, a collection that seeks to honor of the work and life of Louis J. Luzbetak (1918–2005)—member of the Society of the Divine Word (SVD), Catholic priest, missionary, cultural anthropologist, and pioneer in the field of missionary anthropology. The lectures collected here were delivered at Catholic Theological Union between 2000 and 2010 as part of the ongoing series of Louis J. Luzbetak, SVD, Lectures on Mission and Culture. The first six lectures were published as discrete pamphlets through the Chicago Center for Global Ministries. The last five have remained unpublished until now. Fr. Luzbetak attended the first five lectures before his death on March 22, 2005.

As I reflect on Fr. Luzbetak's long and rich life, what strikes me is that from the beginning to the end, he dedicated himself to reconciling several sets of seemingly opposing concerns. His greatness was not that he ever succeeded in completely reconciling them, but that he recognized that the effort was truly worth a life's dedication. It is in the context of his reconciling efforts that his great effort of bringing together "mission," on the one hand, and "culture," on the other—what this book celebrates— needs to be understood.

In a short autobiography written in 1992, entitled "My Pilgrimage in Mission,"[1] Fr. Luzbetak reminisced about his first-grade teacher, a Slovak Benedictine nun in his hometown of Joliet, Illinois, who told him over and over again, "Just do your best and God will do the rest." This is the very way that he reconciled the great theological issue of grace and nature, of the importance of human action and God's action in the world and in our lives. Fr. Luzbetak was first and foremost a man of faith. His citizenship was in heaven (Phil 3:20), as the first reading (which he chose himself) at his funeral on March 23, 2005, affirmed. In the first pages of his *magnum opus*, *The Church and Cultures*, he wrote (in italics) that "*the most important and the most desirable ingredient in a person engaged in mission is a genuine and deep spirituality.*"[2]

But this conviction that God would ultimately "do the rest" did not stop him from working hard at whatever he did, earning a doctorate in one of the most demanding academic disciplines at a renowned university (Fribourg in Germany, under the legendary Wilhelm Schmidt, SVD), writing two major books,[3] directing the Center for the Applied Research in the Apostolate (CARA), and editing one of the most important academic journals in his field, *Anthropos*. Eugene Nida, in the Foreword to the 1988 edition of *The Church and Cultures*, wrote of his "genuine scholarly humility" and the admirable balance in how he thought and what he wrote.[4]

Fr. Luzbetak's conviction of the close connection between nature and grace led him to attempt to reconcile two other seemingly opposites: faith and science. He dedicated *The Church and Cultures* to his mentor Wilhelm Schmidt, "In appreciation of his pioneering spirit in serving Faith through Science." And he loved to quote the dictum of Albert Einstein: "Science without religion is lame; religion without science is blind."[5] Fr. Luzbetak certainly saw faith as the more foundational commitment, and in many ways his faith and even his theology was very traditional, but his faith also pushed him toward the clearer understanding that only science could provide. And so he was a first-rate scientist as well as a first-rate believer. He was a Christian, a missionary, a religious, and a priest first; but he was also a leading anthropologist, an author, a researcher. For him, indeed, "science without religion is lame; religion without science is blind."

The connection between faith and science led Fr. Luzbetak to embrace the task that was to be his life's work and greatest scholarly accomplishment: the reconciliation of the scientific discipline of anthropology and the theological discipline of missiology. It was during his fieldwork in Papua New Guinea in the early 1950s that he arrived at what he described as "perhaps the most critical point"[6] in his pilgrimage in mission. There he saw the inadequacy of traditional "missionary work": the missionaries were faithful in preaching Christ, but they were not necessarily doing it in a way that people could really *understand* the message. If mission was to truly continue the work of Christ, it too needed to become incarnate in particular cultures and contexts.

As he wrote, "the Christian faith, whether in the Third World or in one's own home parish, must be expressed in terms of nothing less than one's innermost self, one's innermost premises, basic attitudes, and fundamental drives, otherwise Christianity is not authentic."[7] It was with this task in mind that Fr. Luzbetak abandoned the strictly scientific study of anthropology and devoted himself to employing anthropology to serve the church's mission. The results of this were his two great books on the church and cultures, many talks and articles advocating this, and a life lived with this conviction. Fr. Luzbetak used anthropology to make Christianity authentic, and the lectures collected here are efforts to continue his pioneering work.

A fourth set of seeming opposites to which Fr. Luzbetak devoted his life was to bridge the gaps among Christians: Protestants, Evangelicals, Catholics. "The old slogan," he wrote, "'There is much more that unites us than divides us' has been more than a mere slogan to me."[8] When the eminent Lutheran missiologist, James Scherer, heard that I had been asked to preach at Fr. Luzbetak's funeral, he sent me an e-mail saying "tell them that non-Catholics loved and appreciated him." After the closing of Divine Word Publications, which had printed the first edition of *The Church and Cultures*, the book was kept in print by an evangelical publisher, the William Carey Library.

Fr. Luzbetak was an official Catholic observer at the historic International Congress on World Evangelization at Lausanne, Switzerland, in 1974, and at the important follow-up consultation on gospel and culture at Willowbank, Bermuda, in 1978. He served as the second president—the first Catholic president—of the highly ecumenical American Society of Missiology, something by which he felt very honored. "I strongly feel," he wrote, "that the hopes for mission that I have always expressed and the dreams I have today will be impossible without such close ecumenical cooperation and mutual enrichment."[9] The contributors to this volume reflect Fr. Luzbetak's ecumenical vision and commitment. Although nine of the contributors are Catholic, all are women and men who are comfortable in ecumenical circles and have a deep ecumenical sensitivity.

The lectures collected here are presented in the order that they were delivered. I am very proud and excited to have them published together, especially as part of the American Society of Missiology Series. I want to thank the editors who accepted this book as part the series, especially Angelyn Dries, who served as chair when the book was submitted. William R. Burrows serves as current chair, and the committee members are Jonathan J. Bonk and Scott W. Sunquist. Special thanks, too, go to

Susan Perry, senior editor at Orbis, together with Orbis publisher Robert Ellsberg, for their support and for their gentle prodding to get the manuscript to them in a timely fashion. Above all I am grateful to the eleven Luzbetak lecturers from 2000 until 2010. Each lecturer has honored me, as holder of the Louis J. Luzbetak Chair of Mission and Culture, and Fr. Luzbetak himself, with their careful scholarship, vast experience, and passion for mission. I know that Fr. Luzbetak would be pleased that, through their work, his legacy of deep yet humble learning, faith-filled scientific research, and ecumenical openness continues in our own day.

Notes

1. Louis J. Luzbetak, "My Pilgrimage in Mission," *International Bulletin of Missionary Research* 16, no. 3 (1992): 124–28.

2. Louis J. Luzbetak, *The Church and Cultures: New Perspectives in Missiological Anthropology* (Maryknoll, NY: Orbis Books, 1988), 2.

3. Louis J. Luzbetak, *The Church and Cultures: An Applied Anthropology for the Religious Worker* (Techny, IL: Divine Word Publications, 1963; Pasadena, CA: William Carey Library, 1976, with several subsequent reprintings). In 1988, Fr. Luzbetak published what he called "a kind of 'Phase II' *Church and Cultures* (Luzbetak, *The Church and Cultures: New Perspectives in Missiological Anthropology*). This second book, wrote Fr. Luzbetak in its Preface, "involved a thorough rewriting to contain the many new dimensions of missiology as well as anthropology" that had taken place in the almost quarter century since the first book had been published.

4. Eugene A. Nida, ""Foreword," in *The Church and Cultures: New Perspectives*, xvi.

5. Luzbetak, *The Church and Cultures: New Perspectives*, 1. He also quoted the phrase in his speech at the Catholic Theological Union on the occasion of the inauguration of the Louis J. Luzbetak, SVD, Chair of Mission and Culture, June 30, 1998.

6. Luzbetak, "My Pilgrimage in Mission," 125.

7. Ibid.

8. Ibid., 126.

9. Ibid.

I

Inculturation as Pilgrimage

José M. de Mesa

*Using the image of pilgrimage, Dr. de Mesa presents what he has learned
about inculturation throughout a distinguished career in the Philippines.
He argues that culture should be the primary guide in the inculturation
project, especially that of Lowland Filipino culture. One develops a Filipino
theology using a "hermeneutics of appreciation." The lecture was delivered
on May 29, 2000.*

Introduction

Mount Banahaw, a dead volcano located one hundred kilometers southeast of Manila, Philippines, and rising 7,380 feet, is a national park. Blessed
with an abundance of rain and natural water because of rain clouds that
cover the peak all year round, one finds lush vegetation, giant trees with
moss and hairy vines, waterfalls and volcanic caves, gurgling brooks and
crystal clear pools on the mountain. Because nature is so profligate in
Banahaw, it has become a hidden spot for nature lovers and a secluded
place for rest and prayer.

Pilgrimage and Mount Banahaw

Mount Banahaw is also considered *the* religious center of folk religion[1]
in the Philippines where pilgrimages are made all year round, especially
during Holy Week.[2] No other mountain is inhabited and revered by as
many religious groups. Regarded as "the Holy Land" by its pilgrims,
Mount Banahaw is seen, even before the coming of Christianity, as a
power mountain whose geographical contours are regarded as having
extraordinary spiritual potency as well as the power to heal. It attracts
mystics and those who in one way or another are searching for God or

contact with the divine, for in Banahaw they look forward to experiencing "the Holy."

Pilgrims to Banahaw visit various sacred natural shrines like a river, a waterfall, the peak, a cave, or a rock called *puwesto* (from Spanish *puesto*, meaning place or position), and they are mainly mapped out by the events in the life of Jesus, suggesting that the pilgrimage is a form of solidarity with him. Thus, the term for the ritualized pilgrimage to the different shrines of Mount Banahaw is called *pamumuwesto,* literally "going to the different *puwestos.*" A parallel may be drawn between going from one *puwesto* to another and the traditional Way of the Cross, which is also a ritualized movement from one place to another.[3]

Ordinarily, pilgrims to Mount Banahaw need an experienced guide known as *pator* to go from one *puwesto* to the next. It is easy to lose one's way on the mountain. Such a *pator* or guide is one who knows all the *puwestos* of the mountain. Furthermore, more than just knowing the complex and difficult routes to the *puwestos,* the *pator* tries as much as possible to follow the prescribed rituals of *pamumuwesto,* although he is flexible enough to make changes and adaptations depending on each group he is guiding and the circumstances that they encounter. Though not expected, a good *pator* is finally one who may also explain the religious meaning of each *puwesto* and guide people in prayer at each *puwesto.*[4] It goes without saying that respect for all the *puwestos* as well as trusting and following the instructions of the *pator* are important for the success of the pilgrimage.

Pilgrimage, Guide, and Inculturation

It is this imagery of pilgrimage to Mount Banahaw and the need for a guide that I wish to explore and employ in order to present what I have learned about inculturation, specifically in the area of revelation-faith. Through this representation I hope to indicate the guidance that culture provides in efforts to inculturate the Judeo-Christian tradition; why culture should be made the primary guide in such an endeavor; how, specifically, lowland Filipino culture has guided me in my work of inculturation in the lowland Filipino context; and what I have learned from this venerable guide. Inculturation, the concern and the process of reappropriating the Judeo-Christian tradition within a particular culture, can be likened to a pilgrimage to a sacred place like Mount Banahaw. Perhaps, it is because pilgrimages are quite often living examples of inculturation itself that the elements they are made up of are good points of reference in using pilgrimage as an image.

The image of pilgrimage is rooted in Filipino Christianity, both officially as well as in folk Catholicism. There are pilgrimages officially approved and encouraged by church authorities, but there are others that are simply tolerated. The pilgrimage to Banahaw is one such undertaking. Pilgrimage refers to a religious event. The journey, like going to Mount Banahaw, is made precisely to be in touch with "the holy" on holy ground.[5] Inculturation as a pilgrimage has something to do with experiencing God, of being in touch with God, present in the midst of God's people. The representation may also be appropriate for inculturation in a more general way because for the Filipino, one of the most popular images for life in the world is "the journey of life" (*paglalakabay sa buhay*); life is likened to a pilgrimage in which attention is much more on the journey itself rather than on the destination.[6] Lastly, Vatican II also pictures the church as a pilgrim church (LG 8, 48–51; AG 2); it has not "arrived;" it is on the way as it presses forward toward its goal, which is the Reign of God. It can never say at any given moment that its situation is perfect—that nothing has to be changed, that there is no further need for any transformation.[7] The image of "pilgrim" suggests that, like the church on the way, inculturation is an ongoing process.

The Need for a "Guide"

Although no imagery can be absolutized because "every comparison limps," inculturation can still be likened to a pilgrimage to the "holy land" of one's people (where God is present and active) in order to experience "the holy" (the presence of God) among them in the way they feel, think, value, behave, and structure life. The Gospel of John reminds us that God dwells or makes God's home in the midst of God's people (see Jn 1:14). And as one needs a guide to the different *puwestos* on Mt. Banahaw, one also needs a guide to the holy aspects in the life and existence of one's people. What better guide can one get than one that, as it were, intimately "knows" this people in a favored manner: the culture. It is these features of the pilgrimage imagery that I focus on in this presentation.

Choosing the culture as guide in the pilgrimage of inculturation is a conscious decision. While culture already guides us in what we feel,

think, and do because of the enculturation process we have all under-
gone, we need to become aware of the kind of guidance it provides.
Concretely, this implies the intentional use of cultural analysis to deeply
understand people and their situations while benefiting from the "tacit
(cultural) knowledge" (M. Polanyi) we already have in comprehending
reality.[8] If deliberateness is necessary to utilize a form of social analysis to
understand what is going on in society, so it is with cultural analysis. It
will guide us to the "holy sites" (the positive aspects and elements of the
culture) and will warn us of misleading or dangerous paths as in conflicts
between the ideal patterns for behavior and actual patterns of behavior
being manifested.

Culture Is Basically Positive

Nevertheless, inculturation as pilgrimage into the land of one's people
(see 1 Pet 2:9–10) presupposes that this land is fundamentally holy. Otherwise, a pilgrimage is completely unthinkable. In paragraph 11 of *Ad Gentes*, Vatican II specifically states that leading people "to the divine light" is
done, first of all, by getting to know the people and by being in contact
with them. In this way pastoral agents who wish to proclaim the gospel can "learn" about the "treasures that a bountiful God has distributed
among the nations [peoples] of the earth." The emphatic approach rec-
ommended by the Vatican Council justifies the use of a "hermeneutics of
appreciation," an interpretation of the culture that focuses on a culture's
positive elements and aspects without falling into the trap of romanticiz-
ing it. The advice offered by M. A. C. Warren is apropos: "Our first task in
approaching another people, another culture, another religion, is to take
off our shoes, for the place we are approaching is holy. Else we may find
ourselves treading on [people's] dreams. More serious still, we may forget
that God was here before our arrival."[9] One approaches another people
with a listening heart.

Paralleling the role of the *pator* on Mount Banahaw, the indigenous
culture as guide will bring inculturation agents to the various "loci" (places,
puwestos) or areas of life and thought of Filipinos in which "the holy" can
be experienced. This includes both the issues, questions, and concerns that
Filipinos need to address, and the manner by which these issues, questions, and concerns are culturally raised and understood in an indigenous
manner as well as the way the culture proposes to address them.

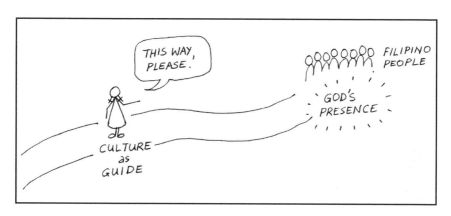

Culture is able to do this because it "knows" the whole terrain; it has knowledge of the whole, as it is an integral system. It is thus able to lead agents of inculturation through the right paths (the connections actually made by the culture itself). Showing, pointing, and warning are all learned from experience by the guide (not just from theoretical knowledge). Culture is like a tradition of time-tested experiences: culture shows the way, points out the worthwhile, and warns of dangers or pitfalls. In a context of mutual interactions between the tradition and culture, it is culture that *sensitizes* us to the tradition. It guides us in understanding the tradition and in seeing its relation to our issues, questions and concerns.

Culture will further guide by inviting inculturation agents (pilgrims) to follow the prescribed patterns of feelings, thought, values, and behavior of Filipinos to understand this people from "the inside" (emic approach). Much understanding and insight arise from such participation and subsequent reflection on it. The relevant elements the culture will explain in its own way and with its own thought and linguistic categories. Since culture is a shared gut feeling, the way we feel about reality must be considered a part of the guidance that culture gives.

The dynamic nature of culture should alert us to the fact that, while it is a good guide, it is not a perfect one. And we should not expect it to be. But its dynamism makes it a flexible guide, with plenty of experience to ensure that its flexibility does not simply turn into arbitrariness. Changes in situations and variations in experiences may require innovations beneficial to people. Cultural elements, which may have been useful in the past, may now need to be transformed for the well-being of people.

For this reason culture is to be recognized as a guide, but not a master whose dictates ought to be followed without fail. Somewhat related to this point is what Louis J. Luzbetak says about cultural conditioning. He states that "to emphasize the extent and depth of cultural conditioning is not to make human beings into automatons. We offer nothing more than guidelines for the solution of human problems. . . . Human beings are largely molded by culture and are constantly pressured by it, but never are they shackled to it."[10]

Why Culture Is the (Primary) Guide

Inculturation is realized through the mutually respectful and critical interaction of the Judeo-Christian tradition and the culture.[11] Since the interaction is mutual and it is the same Spirit at work in both, it is possible to argue that the tradition is a guide in understanding the culture, and the culture is a guide in understanding the tradition. This is true. But for the present situation of the Philippines and for methodological reasons, culture should at least be accorded the honor of being the primary guide. Allow me to spell this out.

Inculturated Theology and Recognizable Reference to Experience

Meaningful inculturated theology requires recognizable reference to the locally lived experience of people. What people ask and how they ask ought to be attended to. Historically, however, due to the dominance in the Filipino theological scene of the neoscholastic method of theologizing that absolutized the tradition in terms of immutable doctrinal formulations, reference to local experience had been largely neglected. It is undeniable that theology does not only have to deal with the demands of meaning, but also those of truth. Legitimate attention to meaningfulness does not dispense with fidelity to the Tradition. But however closely the question of meaning may be connected with that about truth, the two questions are different. The question of meaning has a certain precedence over the question of truth because only a meaningful and relevant statement can be true or false. When the relationship with actual human experience is not felt, even the significance of the truth can easily be ignored.

The rediscovery of "experience" in Filipino theologizing, which was inspired by Vatican II, first began by attending to more contemporary issues emanating from the Euro-American West rather than medieval European questions. While this restored some dynamism to the understanding of theology, it was surely inadequate. It was the explosive social situation of the sixties and the seventies, however, that forced Filipino Christians to grapple with local justice issues. What was actually happening in the country in terms of structural injustice, violation of human rights, and widespread poverty challenged theology toward relevance.

Yet something was missing. For even though "experience" in theology at least began to ring true, it was still largely interpreted both by the political Left and political Right with categories derived from outside the culture. Marxist, Leninist, and Maoist thought provided the Left a language to articulate issues involved. The capitalist and national security state frame of reference gave the Right the formulations to express its positions. The specifically cultural dimension of experience was, however, not yet considered. If we are inextricably cultural beings, then we cannot do away with the importance of culture in experience. After all, experience is not just necessarily interpreted experience but necessarily culturally interpreted experience. This was an aspect that Latin American liberation theology recognized as crucially absent in its theologizing. To one theologian (A. Echeverry) who thinks that "it is necessary to reincorporate the symbolic," "the problem with liberation theology was not being infiltrated by Marxism, but rather its inability to infiltrate grassroots logic" so that, though liberation theologians were talking about the poor and liberation, the discourse was "like a stranger to the people." Echeverry reckons that there is a "need to abandon excessive rationality and recover the subjective, which has profound dimensions in human existence."[12]

Thanks to the change in society regarding the understanding of culture from a classical to an empirical one (B. Lonergan) and the positive attitudes developed within both Catholic and Protestant churches regarding culture, culture has gained prominence in local theologizing.[13] So important a role is ascribed to culture that Paul VI's 1975 Apostolic Exhortation, *Evangelii Nuntiandi*, warns that "evangelization loses much of its force and effectiveness if it does not take into consideration the actual people to whom it is addressed, if it does not use their language, their signs and symbols, if it does not answer the questions they ask, and if it does not have an impact on their concrete life" (EN 63).

Using the culture as guide includes the pinpointing of issues, questions, and concerns that are relevant in the local situation together with the way that the culture looks at such issues, questions or concerns. For if experience is necessarily interpreted experience, we remember that it is necessarily culturally interpreted experience. So what can ensure recognizability to lived experience better than culture, which is second nature to us? As Louis Luzbetak untiringly reminds his readers, "all human beings are *cultural* beings. Jesus must be *culturally* relevant if he is really to be understood and appreciated. This is *a most obvious fact unfortunately only too often overlooked.*"[14]

The whole question of "salvation" in the Philippines, for instance, benefits from utilizing culture as guide. Prior to the renewal brought about by Vatican II, salvation was seen in terms of salvation of one's soul. It was thus that salvation was seen mainly as something that happened after this life, not something that was experienced in life. But if salvation is to be understood as genuinely human salvation and, in contrast, negative-positive experience in life as "*infirmitas-salus*," "damnation-salvation," or "*dominación-liberación*," then people who are suffering (*hirap* = suffering, difficulty, straits, burden) will surely welcome *ginhawa*. *Ginhawa* is a sense of total well-being arising from release or relief from any form of suffering (*maiahon sa hirap*).

This is also true regarding the grasp of the reality of the resurrection within the Filipino culture where ideally honor (*dangal*) is held more dearly than life. The widespread understanding of the resurrection as resuscitation, which is clearly indicated in the popular account of the passion, death, and resurrection of Jesus called the *Pasyon*, diminishes very much the relevance of this very central event in Christianity. But if the culturally significant experience of honor (*dangal*) and shame (*hiya*) become the interpretative elements for the passion, death, and resurrection of Jesus, then these will become alive for Filipinos struggling to gain some shred of honor (dignity) in the world where shame, be it in economics, politics, livelihood, profession, competition, or state of life, is constantly a threat.[15] *Pagbabangong dangal* (the raising of one's dignity or restoration of honor) makes more experiential sense within the culture.

To cite a parallel example from another setting, Sri Lankan theologian Aloysius Pieris notes, for example, how the discussion in the West of various theological positions of exclusivism, inclusivism, and pluralism vis-à-vis other religions is not pertinent in Asia. Within an Asian paradigm where the poor form a third magisterium alongside the pastoral and the academic, where a liberationist thrust is what defines the theology of religions, and where basic human communities are the social locations of such theology, the question of the uniqueness of Christ or Christianity, or of any religion does not make sense.[16]

From Translation to Reappropriation

The concern for inculturation, which was not totally absent during the time of the missionary preaching and structuring of church life that began in the second-half of the sixteenth century, has passed from the hands of "sending churches" to those of the local church. The responsibility *for* and subject *of* inculturation has shifted from foreigners to locals.

As early as the 1970s the Federation of Asian Bishops' Conferences (FABC) had already made the building up of the local church a priority. As such we can now characterize this activity as primarily one of *reappropriation* of the inherited tradition by the local Christian community into the local culture, rather than one of *translation* of the tradition as embodied by the European or American culture. This reappropriation is carried out now by the local church following the particular qualities of the cultural world-view.[17] Where the first appropriation or reception had happened mainly through translation, and this has had its own value and merit, the present one is going to occur through the rethinking or reinterpretation of the faith in indigenous categories. The structuring elements of the culture will have to give new form to this tradition. I would like to think that this is something to look forward to rather than something to be afraid of.

Today, there is even further significance to the local because of trends related to the phenomenon called "globalization" and its homogenizing tendencies.[18] More than ever, concentration on the local will be necessary if the undoubtedly soteriological issue of the cultural identity and integrity of the Filipino people is to remain viable. To Aylward Shorter the weakening of the local culture and the consequent gradual disappearance of cultural diversity "is not a mere question of nostalgic romanticism, but the perception of an injustice involving genuine cultural impoverishment and the loss of human resources."[19] Still stigmatized and devalued because of the disparagement it had experienced mainly from the Spanish and American colonial regimes, it must now also struggle against the deceptive and superficial promotion of the local by wielders of wealth and power under the catchphrase of "globalization." Emphasis on the local culture is a form of resistance in this context.[20]

The Disadvantage in Making Tradition the Primary Guide

Should the tradition be the primary focus and guide for the inculturation process, what is most likely to happen would be the "translation" of what has been highlighted by the *sending* culture, which embodies the tradition at present. This is not to underestimate the, perhaps, unintended positive effects of translation on the receiving culture, which is to provide the culture with another expressive possibility in an area of life and to give it a chance to recast the reality received in its own way.

Tradition as guide in this discussion has been operative both in official and folk understanding of Catholicism. In practice this has meant rendering in the new culture the presently prevalent interpretation of the tradition. The pre-Vatican II understanding of "truth" as propositional is a clear and long-standing example of this. Because of the preponderance of this view, the relational understanding of truth (which is closer to the biblical understanding of it) in Asia in general and in the Philippines in particular has been either obscured or marginalized.[21] This, to give a more contemporary example, is also clear with the 1994 instruction on the inculturation of liturgy where there is an insistence on the "keeping intact" the Roman rite.[22] Similar is the case with John Paul II's understanding of inculturation. For him inculturation is a matter of "how a largely pre-set tradition and institution can have the greatest possible impact on any particular cultural situation while preserving what is good in that culture." Time and again, John Paul II warns against giving culture, which to him is something thoroughly ambiguous, priority rather than the gospel.[23] The tradition has been absolutized in its Western form and expression. In which case, it is the foreign culture that would be the guide.

Part of the difficulty with giving preference to the tradition is a seeming lack of awareness that this tradition exists only within particular (cultural) traditions. And, as we are very much conscious of, the gospel is never found without its specific and concrete expression. Thus, there is a lack of critique of such embodiment of tradition in the official documents of the church. For instance, John Paul II's insistence on the communication of the gospel speaks very much of "bringing" this gospel into the culture and ensuring that the gospel "is integrated and transforms the culture." There is no mention of the tradition being purified by the workings of the Spirit in and through the culture.[24] If transformation is only deemed applicable to culture, there seems to be a tacit assumption that the tradition has no need of it. But this is not true.

John Cobb Jr. states in his book *Lay Theology*[25] the (positive) transformation of the tradition as one of the tasks of theological reflection that he encourages faith groups and churches to engage in. The tradition needs to be transformed because it is always embodied and expressed in specific cultural forms that may be themselves unchristian. Cobb, by way of an example, points out that "virtually all of Christianity to this date has been both anti-Jewish and patriarchal. These have not been superficial accretions easily set aside; they have been pervasive features of its life and thought deriving from and affecting its core doctrinal formulations as well as much of its practice."[26] Choosing, therefore, the tradition as it is presently embodied and expressed as guide to inculturation is to "inculturate" anti-Jewishness and patriarchy in the local church's life. Permit me to cite a concrete example of this anti-Jewishness that has found a new cultural expression in Filipino faith life.

The *Pabasa ng Pasyon*[27] in the Philippines is one of the most popular practices during the time of Lent. It is a folk religious practice during which a poetic account of Christ's passion is sung continuously in houses until it is finished. In the attempt to render mainly the passion of Jesus in a culturally intelligible fashion (a good example of inculturation in many ways), the author, whose creative initiative must be honored, has also given further life to anti-Semitism. Many passages echo and, at times, even exacerbate the prejudice by more than suggesting that the Jews are detestable people on account of what they have done to Jesus. Allow me to quote a few pertinent passages.

When Annas, the father-in-law of Caiaphas, the high priest at the time, speaks to the arrested Jesus, he says to him: "Here is surely revealed / your teaching as wholly deceit / wickedness without anything right / you do this / to destroy people." (*Dito'y sukat mahalata / ang aral mo'y pawang daya / walang watsto'y masasama / kaya mo ito ginawa / ang tao ay nang masira.*) (98). He also insults him thus: "You are such a base and worthless person / What? Shall we believe / in your doctrine? / Why don't you give us new instruction / you, worthless fly?" (*Tao kang hamak at mura / ano't sasampala-taya / kami sa iyong doktrina? / bakit hindi mangaral ka / bangaw na walang halaga?*) (99). Prior to being sentenced, Jesus the prisoner is described as being mocked by the Jews thus: "One by one, the Jews / slapped Christ / and spat on him, / their insults were without letup" (*Isa at isa ngang hudyo / nagsisitampat kay Kristo / at linuturang totoo, / pagmura'y di mamagkano*) (100). When Pilate asks the people their choice of prisoner to release, the *Pasyon* reports their answer: "The answer of the traitors / Pharisees and scribes / with such competing noise / release Barabbas / make Jesus suffer." (*Ang sagot ng raga sukab / pariseos at eskribas / ingay na nagtitimpalak, / ang ladaga'y si Barrabas / si Hesus ang bigyang hirap*) (125).

Pasyon commentator René Javellana says that in general we see in the popular text entitled *Casaysayan hang Pasiong Mahal m Hesukristong Pangi-noon Natin*, the Jews, represented by the figures of Herod, Judas, Scribes, and Pharisees, and leaders and their cohorts, are regarded as "antagonists of God." They are deceivers who are identified with the devil, the father of lies.[28]

A commitment to transformation forms part of being a Christian. No past or present form of Christianity is normative as such. Vatican II also insists in *Gaudium et Spes* that the gospel is never bound exclusively and indissolubly to any culture, ancient or recent (see GS 58). And because transformation is not done once and for all, this kind of commitment is aimed at the process of creative transformation rather than to any one of its products.[29]

Reappropriation Requires Fresh Cultural Categories

Reappropriation or new interpretation requires fresh categories, new perspectives that the local culture can bring or offer (especially after so long a time of Western theological categories being utilized in the local scene through the instrumentality of the English language). Otherwise, the received interpretation of the tradition can easily dominate the endeavor. This is exemplified in a way by the Tagalog translation of the Lord's Prayer, which appeared in the 1523 *Doctrina Christiana*.[30] In their choice of words the first generation missionaries, who manifested a sensitivity to the culture not unlike the attitude displayed by the Italian Jesuits Mateo Ricci, Roberto de Nobili, and Alessandro Valignano,[31] made culture their guide. In this way fresh categories for understanding the gospel became available. They could have selected other words or concepts, but what they had chosen was indicative of their approach to culture. We illustrate with four cultural elements: *Loob*, *Mauwi*, *Bigyan ng kanin*, and *Huwag iiwan*.

Moui sa amin ang pagcahari Mo.	Make Your Reign come home to us.
Ipasonod Mo ang loob Mo.	Make Your whole, most authentic and relational Self be followed.
Bigyan Ale cami ngaion nang Aming cacanin para nang saaraoarao	Give us today rice to eat.
Houag Mo caming iiwan nang di cami matalo nang tocso	Do not leave us so we are not overcome by temptation.

I can imagine that if the early missionaries used the tradition as primary guide, they would have attended, among other things, to the commonly shared explanation of these four points in the Lord's Prayer in the way these have been comprehended in Europe at that time. "*Your will be done*": The will of God as identical to what happens. The Tridentine Catholic teaching, by way of illustration, speaks of submission in all things to the divine will and pleasure, and exhorted Catholics to "remember that if by prayers and supplication we are not delivered from evil, we should endure our afflictions with patience, convinced that it is the will of God that we should endure them."[32] "*Your Kingdom come*": Since the church was considered as the kingdom of God on earth, this phrase easily led to the discourse about the establishment and spread of the church throughout the world. "*Give us this day our daily bread*" would have led to an exposition on God's support to the material life of our bodies and the spiritual life of our souls, particularly through the spiritual bread of Holy Communion; and "*Lead us not into temptation*" would have provided an occasion to talk about God's protection from harm, especially harm to our soul.[33]

Instead, other aspects of the tradition, more connected to local concerns and thought, come to the fore. With the culture as their guide, as it were, the aspects of the most authentic and relational self, the importance of going home, the significance of rice, and the value of togetherness are highlighted, and these provided new paths for theological reflection. The cultural elements underscored then act as a "searchlight" on the inherited tradition expressed in a particular cultural form and serve as fresh interpretative elements.

Thus *loob*, while including a specific reference to God's "will" that will be done, it also and more importantly incorporates the reference to God's very self and to the core of that self. So the "doing of God's will" in the vernacular rendering means "the interiorization of God's very Self and God's very nature." This certainly reminds us of the divine imperative "to be (holistically) perfect as (our) heavenly Father is perfect; to be merciful as God is merciful" (see Mt 5:48; Lk 6:30).

Mauwi, for its part, highlights the local cultural fondness for "going home," a custom that is socially, personally, and emotionally loaded for Filipinos. Filipinos manifest an almost compulsive inner desire to go home to where their families are, especially during important social occasions like Christmas, Holy Week, and the town fiesta, or on the occasion of personally significant events such as a marriage or a funeral. This is why during vacations, holidays, or special feasts, the airports and the bus stations of the country are crowded with people wanting to get a place in the particular form of transport. To present God as yearning to go home to us, as Revelation 21:3[34] does, is surely affectively effective for Filipinos. From this perspective, Jesus' desire to return home to his Father after accomplishing his mission is, for Filipinos, only to be expected.

Kanin calls our attention to the concreteness of God's providential care rather than "bread," which is generally considered by Filipinos as peripheral or secondary nourishment. When Filipinos are hungry and like to eat (as they always seem to be and do), they look for rice. Rice is the staple, and it is a very rich indigenous symbol for nourishment. Imagine the images that rice gives rise to when seen as *sinaing* (plain steamed rice), *sinangag* (fried rice), *tutong* (fire-burnt rice at the bottom of the cooking pot), *bahaw* (leftover rice), *tugaw* (rice porridge), *suman* (sticky rice), and *am* (rice broth usually given to babies). *Kanin* is daily food. And like the manna in the desert for the Israelites (see Ex 16), it has to be prepared, as it were, from day to day. It cannot be stored for the long term. Thus it connotes patient, continuous caring on the part of the giver (the one who provides and prepares). The routine association of daily rice speaks of God's participation in the ordinary.[35]

Huwag . . . iiwan reminds Filipinos of their sociability and gregariousness, of never wanting to be alone. Local sociologists note that Filipinos are not inclined to being alone. They are never alone when they are born, wedded, or buried. In general they do not want to be left alone, for to be alone for a Filipino is to be censured or ostracized. An anecdote is told of a Filipina who was in the United States for the first time as a guest of an Anglo couple. She was met at the airport and brought to the host's house. Upon arriving she was shown to the room she would be using and left alone. Instead of appreciating the gesture and feeling relieved in being alone at last, she instead cried and began asking herself what she had done wrong to be left alone.

This tendency extends even to our dead. We do not leave the corpse of our dead alone during the wake. It is our way of paying our last respects to the deceased person. I am reminded of a time several years ago when I went to a funeral parlor to pay my last respects to Salvatore Carzedda, an Italian missionary priest and alumnus of Catholic Theological Union whom I knew and who had been gunned down in cold blood.

In seeing no one was keeping watch in the room where the coffin was, I felt like cursing his Italian confreres for leaving him alone.

Huwas iiwan becomes an assurance for the Filipino when reading the tradition because God is always with us and never leaves us alone. This may be an unbearable and too imposing an image for God in other cultures, but it is a most assuring one for Filipinos: "I am with you always" and Jesus is Emmanuel (God in solidarity with us).

Reinterpreting Revelation—
Faith with Culture as My Guide

Inculturation has indeed been a pilgrimage for me in the holy land that is the Philippines and the people to which I belong. Within the intentionally limited framework of experiencing, appropriating and understanding the theological realities of revelation and faith, allow me now to illustrate from my own experience how culture has been my guide in this pilgrimage.

I had already behind me a number of years of studying and teaching revelation and faith in English with the usual European and American structure and categories of thought when it dawned on me that if I allowed culture to be my guide in the endeavor to inculturate the good news, the process of development would be faster and surer, though not in an absolute way. All those years I too had been intellectually persuaded that I understood, and understood quite well, what revelation means for Christian life and practice. Indeed, it was with a sense of accomplishment that I acknowledged that I had gone beyond the neoscholastic understanding of it (which I grew up with) and had adopted the more historical and personalistic comprehension of it as based in the Dogmatic Constitution on Divine Revelation of Vatican II and had subsequently reflected upon it.

In explaining revelation to others, I criticized the former and upheld the latter, inevitably adding an exhortation to consider the Filipino situation and culture in connection to this. Not that I preferred it to be just this way, but all that I could do at that time by way of inculturation was to make others aware of the importance and need to inculturate theology. I was at a loss myself as to how to rethink revelation-faith in a truly Filipino way. Having been conditioned to think in Western theological categories, it was not easy to move out of them. The attempts I had earlier made to convey these concepts were confined to, more or less, literal translations of the Western interpretation, albeit more contemporary. Following Western philosophical personalist categories of self-revelation and self-communication, I rendered this intimate personal "dialogue" in direct Filipino equivalents. Relativizing the inherited cultural expressions of the faith, which had strongly conditioned my own thinking, was more difficult than I thought.

Looking back, I realized that actual rethinking or reinterpretation of the tradition began when I took the situation of the country seriously. In the late seventies to the early eighties, the question of God's will became acute both situationally and culturally. Situationally, the country was faced with massive structural poverty (it still is!) and widespread violation of human rights under the martial law regime. Can such vicious and widespread suffering arising from people's inhumanity towards one another be willed by God? Culturally, the widespread popular belief is that everything happens, whether beneficial or destructive, because God wills it. Is this really God's will? Even more fundamental was another question, what kind of God do Christians believe in? In my search for the answers to these questions I saw how God's will and God's character (nature) were, within the culture itself, twin questions, intimately intertwined.[36] Gaining this insight was not possible without the specifically cultural dimension in the investigation of the issue.

The most important and most frequently used Filipino word for "will" is *loob*. God's will is God's *loob*. Already in 1523, the first translation of the Lord's Prayer had utilized, as mentioned earlier, the term for "will" in the petition, "Your will be done." To be of "bad will" was to have *masamang loob*. Conversely, to will what is good is to manifest *kagandahang-loob*.

The notion of *kagandahang-loob* comes from two concepts: *loob* and *ganda*. *Loob*, literally meaning "the within," refers to the core of one's personhood and the most authentic inner self of the Filipino which is essentially related to other selves. It is, moreover, regarded as the organizing center of human reality and the wellspring of feeling, thought, and behavior. *Loob*, as someone who synthesized the many studies on *loob* in the Philippines has shown, has many related concepts as well.[37] *Ganda* is literally beauty with a touch of charm. The culture knows of beauty that is superficial and even deceptive. But in the notion of *kagandahang-loob* it denotes a beauty that wells up from deep within the self and that which is not only ethically good, but winsomely good as well.[38] Perhaps, for Filipinos, *kagandahang-loob* is primarily "pure positivity" (Schillebeeckx) that

KAGANDAHANG-
LOOB

SINCERE
GOOD DEEDS

REVEALS

captivates and wins people over. Surely, it is a reminder of someone who "went around doing good" (see Acts 10:38). It refers to a goodness that is not cold, but rather warm, a kindness that is not enslaving, but liberating.

So what is God's *loob*? This discovery would lead me further into the inner sanctum of the culture. The essentially relational concept, *kagandahang-loob*, obviously refers to kindheartedness, benevolence, beneficence, goodness (as a specific act), and the term *loob*, when looked into more profoundly, yields a meaning equivalent to "nature," the quality not just of a relationship, but the quality of one's personhood, albeit within a relational way of thinking. *Kagandahang-loob* then is not merely a positive act in relating to others; it is the manifestation of what the person truly is deeply as shown in a specific act in a particular relationship.

This realization that *loob* is our most authentic inner self where our true worth lies led me to conceive faith as the interiorization of this divine *loob*. "To become like God" in our *loob*, in our true selves is what it means to believe. And I am reminded in connection with this of the notion of "divinization" in Eastern theological thought. Consequently, I paid greater attention to God's *kagandahang-loob* in the petition in the Lord's Prayer: "Your will (*loob*) be done." This is not merely a matter of obeying what God wants in a definite situation. More than that it is the interiorization of who God is, making God's *kagandahang-loob* as my *loob*.

I was pleasantly surprised to lately discover a similar insight in the writings of the English mystic Julian of Norwich for whom "the love of God is identical with the being of God." To her, "Love, therefore, is not something which God has or does; it is not a 'virtue' or a property of God." Nor is love something that God can decide to give here and withhold there. It cannot be uneven, or pass away. Love is, quite simply, what God is. "For Julian, love is the 'kindhood' of God rather than just the kindness of God."[39]

Culture as a Source of Interpretative Elements

It was only when I concretely attempted to reinterpret revelation and faith with Filipino categories[40] that I realized that culture could be a guide I could follow with benefit, if I allowed it. The reason was this: by attending to Filipino concerns, utilizing cultural presuppositions and following cultural thought structures, utilizing the available cultural vocabulary and taking advantage of the local cultural concepts[41] in order to respond to particular issues in the Philippines, I "felt" the goodness of the good news and was drawn by its beauty.[42] I was no longer just intellectually fascinated by it. I was personally touched by such an inculturated interpretation of revelation-faith, touched by God in and through my very own culture. Experiencing "the Holy" in and through the "burning bush" of the culture brought me to a deeper appreciation of the both the gospel and of my culture. Three realizations resulted from this experience.

Primary Aim of Inculturation:
The Experience of God

First, a conviction began to grow on me that rather than providing the endeavor of evangelization a more effective means of communication through cultural intelligibility, perhaps, the more primary aim of inculturation or contextualization is to facilitate the Christian experience of God within and through the instrumentality of the culture. Inculturation not only sensitizes us to God's active presence in the culture, but also provides a culturally intelligible and meaningful discourse (or opportunity) regarding the Christian experience of God within the culture.

To regard inculturation in this way is to broaden its vision and to root it in a more basic reality. Without detracting from the importance of inculturation for the growth of the local church as church, there is a more fundamental reality at stake—the Reign of God, a central metaphor for the way God relates to humanity and the world. God's presence can be experienced beyond the confines of the churches. In making the experience of God within and through culture the more fundamental focus of inculturation, the endeavor that is inculturation becomes Reign-of-God–centered. Such a goal is really in consonance with the thinking of the FABC of a kingdom-centered evangelization rather than a church-oriented proclamation of the gospel.[43] Within the multicultural and multireligious setting of Asia, this kind of orientation within inculturation will be much more attuned to the dialogue that the FABC wants to promote.

In addition, inculturation will provide a meaningful articulation of this experience, expressing and communicating it to others as an invitation to faith: "That which we have seen, that which we have heard, that which we have looked upon and touched with our own hands concerning the word of life, this is what we proclaim to you" (1 Jn 1:1–3). In other words, inculturation concerns itself with the most fundamental in the theological enterprise: the experience of God that is theologically grasped and expressed. With such a situation, we recapture the primary reality of the gospel as experience become message, rather than supposedly a message from heaven still in search of verification in experience.[44]

Inculturation means the discovery or experience of what God is already doing in the culture. Fr. Luzbetak, in his book *The Church and Cultures*, says that

> within culture there is a "hidden Christ," the result of God's own action and grace. Evangelization should, in fact, be built on no other foundation than on the one that God Himself in his universal love, providence and mercy (see 1 Tim 2:4) has already laid. That foundation is most clearly visible in a people's culture—in their "soul," which happens to be transmitted from generation to generation through the process of inculturation.[45]

Though this act refers quite obviously to the present culture in which Christianity already plays a significant role, it is not without basis to affirm this also of pre-Christian times in Philippine history.

Even before the missionaries arrived, the inhabitants of the Philippine Islands had experiences of God even though these were not interpreted in Christian terms. The prophet Amos reminds Israel that its exodus experience was not an exclusive prerogative. Yahweh does the same thing for other peoples as well: "Are you not like the Ethiopians to me, O people of Israel? says the Lord. Did I not bring Israel up from the land of Egypt, and the Philistines from Caphtor and the Arameans from Kir?" (Amos 9:7). Truly, our salvation history did not begin in the sixteenth century when we discovered the Spaniards, but from the very beginning of the history of our peoples.

From our present-day faith perspective, positive life-giving elements testify to divine action within the culture. They are "treasures" and their discovery by pastoral agents of the church forms a valid starting point for evangelization as the Decree on the Missionary Activity of the church, *Ad Gentes*, suggests (11). As holy places are approached respectfully during a pilgrimage, so too are people and their ways. Truly, a hermeneutics of appreciation must have a place of primacy in cultural interpretation.

The Relativity of Theological Formulations to Their Cultural Contexts

My second realization dealt with just how cultural theological formulations were and are, or how relative they were and are to their cultural contexts. Because I could express the experience of God in Jesus in our very own Filipino cultural terms, my attention was called to the European and American theological formulations I had learned as also thoroughly cultural. This new awareness led me to reconsider claims of absoluteness and immutability of theological formulations. In positing how the core of the Filipino person is understood within the culture as *loob* (the inner self, the most authentic self, the source of feelings, thoughts, and behavior), I was made aware how rationality as the distinguishing characteristic of the human being from animality was utilized to structure revelation-faith in neoscholastic theology and how Western personalist philosophy interpreted revelation-faith as a mutual *traditio personae*, the gracious divine self-gift to people and the free human entrusting of the whole self to God.

To make sense of such a relationship, Christians existing in different cultural worlds harnessed what was part and parcel of their being persons *in situ:* their cultures, their "designs for living" (Luzbetak). What was second nature to them was guiding them to make sense of God's gracious act towards them and of their openness in freedom to such initiative. I was doing the same; I was consciously making culture my guide.[46] With this in mind I even began to recognize and even appreciate the inculturation attempt of neoscholasticism.

NEOSCHOLASTIC   PERSONALIST   FILIPINO

(*Conceptual Framework*)

Rationality[47]   (Inter)subjectivity   *Loob–Kagandahang-loob*

(*Understanding of Revelation*)[48]

Revealing of Truths   Giving of Self or   *Pagpapadama–Pagsasaloob*
                                    Self-
                                    Communication[49]

The insight into the relativeness of theological formulations to the culture was only one side of the coin of my second realization. The other side of it was the insight that our culture was providing me with the clues I needed to deepen my grasp of the tradition, specifically with regard to the relationship between God and people. These cultural clues were actually serving as interpretative elements. Hence, God's action in the relationship is articulated as *pagpapadama* (making us experience; making us feel) of the divine *kagandahang-loob*, while the human response of faith is formulated as *pagsasaloob* (= making part of our *loob*) of such *kagandahang-loob*.

I must admit that I did begin rendering the notions of revelation and faith as I understood them in the historical and personalist way of the West by the use of *loob* and *kagandahang-loob*. *Loob*, after all, was the whole self for the Filipino. Did not personalist thought express "revelation" as divine self-communication? But *loob* said something more, as I understand it, than just to refer to the whole self. *Loob* is the deepest and the most authentic self. Taking my cue from John's description of God as love and Schillebeeckx's contemporary rendering of it as "pure positivity," I thought that God as *kagandahang-loob* translates the very nature of God. God is love; God is *kagandahang-loob*. That is to say, God freely and graciously acts for the well-being of people without any thought of a return of the favor. This totally gracious goodness is who God is in relation to us.

Then, in asking about how God communicates effectively God's very self, I had to turn to a most common way that Filipinos use to communicate: *pagpapadama*, that is, making someone experience, in the sense of making that someone feel what one wants to *convey*. *Pagpapadama* is both an important feature of Filipino communication patterns and indicative of the importance that Filipinos give to feelings.[50] What is truly experienced is what is really felt. *Pagpapadama*, while not devoid of the cognitive element in communication, is much more affective-intuitive. It is the kind of transaction that transpires between a mother who loves her child and the child who feels this love, or the sort of experience of lovers who feel that something is wrong with their relationship though nothing had been explicitly said. My discovery of *pagpapadama* came about by following the culture, the guide in this pilgrimage of inculturation.

Because of this Filipino penchant for making others *feel* what they want to communicate, I reinterpreted God's self-communication (the personalist expression for revelation) as *"pagpapadama ng Diyos ng Kanyang kagandahang-loob"* or God making us experience—literally, making us feel—the divine *loob* that is *maganda*: that which is truly good in the ethical sense and winsomely good in the aesthetic sense. As *loob* is the deepest and most authentic self, what God makes us experience is the divine deepest and most authentic of Godself. Still following the cue provided by the culture, faith is construed as the *"pagsasaloob ng Kagandahang-loob ng Diyos"*: the interiorization and making part of our most authentic self the very Godness of God.

The only recent use of *loob* as a key conceptual category for local theological reflection only shows how far removed we Filipino Christians have been from our culture. It was most obvious when discovered for theological purposes. But one wonders why it took so long to discover something that was with us all the time? Part of the answer, of course, lies in the fact that culture is second nature to us, and we are largely unconscious of it. As anthropologist Edward Hall has noted, "Culture hides much more than it reveals, and strangely enough what it hides, it hides most effectively from its own participants."[51] But there is also the reason that rather than dealing with our own local situations and using local cultural categories, the theological issues tackled as well as theological thought structures employed came from elsewhere. In addition theological education as well as catechesis in schools of theology, seminaries, Catholic-run universities, and schools down to the parish level are carried out, with only very few exceptions, virtually entirely in the English language. Catholicism, to mention another reason, was practically identified with Roman Catholicism in the Philippines. For many it was and, perhaps, still is not incongruous for a Catholic to identify one's religion by saying, "I am a Roman."

Inculturation Is Vernacularization

Inculturation is, to a great extent, necessarily also vernacularization. This was my third realization. Here I immediately think of the significance of rendering of the gospel into *koine* Greek in early Christianity. If language is indeed the "house of being," such rendering into the vernacular of the *fides quaerens intellectum* (*et affectum*) is a *sine qua non* and the only real way to make the gospel "at home" as the word "vernacular" suggests (*vernaculum* = born in the house). Language, of course, is not just a set of labels to identify reality but truly a way of making sense of it by interpretation.

The issue of language is important in the Philippines. "Language" had been an instrument of subjugation both of the Spaniards and of the Americans. While it is undeniable that Spanish missionaries did contribute to development of various languages in the Philippines by compiling dictionaries and writing grammars, they also symbolically subjugated these languages by making them fit Spanish, which they considered the rightful heir of the most superior language of all, Latin.[52] For what Latin was to the Roman Empire, Castilian was to the Spanish empire. Hence, it was not uncommon for missionaries to voice their praise for the native languages by comparing them to Latin and, of course, to Castilian. For Filipino languages to have some standing, they needed to be cast in Western terms. Thus, the famous *Arte y reglas de la lengua Tagala* (1610), authored by the Dominican Blancas de San José, used Latin and Castilian as the principal points of reference in the reconstruction of Tagalog grammar. In working it out, Blancas uses no Tagalog terms, giving the impression that grammar did not exist for the Tagalogs before the missionaries began to write about their language. The subtle message was that Tagalog was to defer to Castilian and be subject to it.

Today English is widely spoken in the Philippines because of the systematic efforts of the teachers of the language who came to the Philippines during the American colonial rule. Many are vocal in the country about the advantages that this development has brought. But this too was a mixed blessing. For English was used by the American military as an adjunct to its program of pacification of the natives who were against American rule. Having stolen from Filipinos the freedom that they were about to win from the Spaniards in 1898, the Americans needed to eliminate not only the armed bodily opposition, but also the nationalist sentiments that were alive in Filipino minds at that time.[53]

On both counts, language had been part of the battleground to conquer the Filipinos. If language had played such a demeaning role, surely language too will play an important part in genuine inculturation, part of which is the de-stigmatization and revaluation of the indigenous culture.

Summing Up

We have compared inculturation to a pilgrimage in order to highlight the importance of the discovery, experience, and articulation of the experience of God in the local Filipino setting. After citing the reasons for the suitability of the imagery of pilgrimage for inculturation in the Filipino context, we elaborated the need and the advantages of making the culture as guide in this pilgrimage. Aware that any given cultural understanding of the tradition arises from a mutually respectful and critical interaction between the Judeo-Christian tradition and culture, we spelled out why culture should still be regarded as the primary guide for inculturation in present-day Philippines.

In the last part of the presentation I shared my efforts at inculturating the realities of revelation and faith in the context of the God-question in the Philippines. I explained how culture guided me to discover, experience, and articulate God's *kagandahang-loob* mainly through the reality and concept of *loob* and its ramifications. Finally, I indicated and elaborated three personal realizations which emanated from this experience: namely, the more primary aim of inculturation, the cultural relativeness and resourcing of all theological formulations, and the imperative of vernacularization in inculturation.

In some ways the choice and use of the imagery of pilgrimage fail to address certain aspects of the task of inculturation. That is the way of all images: they clarify some things, but obscure others. *Omnis comparatio claudicat*, and that includes inculturation as "pilgrimage." But I hope that it, at least, highlighted certain elements of the inculturation process that are important in the local Filipino context, especially the need for a stronger appreciation and trust of culture as primary guide in the pilgrimage that is inculturation.

Notes

1. Folk religion is both window to and indicator of values arising from primal religiosity. See José M. de Mesa, "Oorspronkelijke religie en volksreligiositeit op de Filippijnen," *Wereld en Zending* 2 (1999): 46–54.

2. Vitaliano R. Gorospe, S.J., *Banahaw: Conversations with a Pilgrim to the Power Mountain* (Makati, Metro Manila: Bookmark, Inc., 1992), 16.

3. Ibid., 24.

4. Ibid., 27, 68.

5. For further information about the phenomenon of religious pilgrimage, see "Pilgrimage," in James Hastings, ed., *Encyclopaedia of Religion and Ethics*, X (Edinburgh: T & T Clark, 1926–1976), 1028.

6. For an illustration of this attitude, see the Filipino novel written by Lazaro Francisco, *Maganda Pa Ang Daigdig* (Quezon City: Ateneo de Manila University Press, 1982), 168–69. Here contrast is made between a certain Kapitan Roda who embodies a goal-oriented person and Loreto Sanchez, the central character of the story, who views life as a gift to be enjoyed and to be responsible for on the way: "Sa paglakad niya sa landas ng buhay ay hindi sa dulo ng landas nakapako ang kaniyang pananaw. Nakamasid siyang lagi sa kanyang paligid" (As she journeys through the path of life her view is not fixed on the end of the path. She is ever observant of what is around her).

7. Andrew Walls alludes to this same imagery but develops it to emphasize the universalizing factor in inculturation in contrast to the "indigenizing" factor (Andrew F. Walls, "The Gospel as Prisoner and Liberator of Culture," in *The Missionary Movement in Christian History: Studies in the Transmission of Faith* (Maryknoll, NY: Orbis Books, 1996), 7–9.

8. Scientist-philosopher Michael Polanyi contends that hunches or a certain feel for a given reality are constitutive parts of discovery. See Drusilla Scott, *Everyman Revived: The Common Sense of Michael Polanyi* (Grand Rapids, MI: William B. Eerdmans, 1995), 45–61.

9. See M. A. C. Warren, "General Introduction," in *The Primal Vision: Christian Presence and African Religion*, ed. John Taylor (Philadelphia: Fortress Press, 1963), 10.

10. Louis J. Luzbetak, SVD, *The Church and Cultures: New Perspectives in Missiological Anthropology* (Maryknoll, NY: Orbis Books, 1988), 188.

11. José M. de Mesa, "Doing Theology as Inculturation in Asia," in *New Directions in Mission and Evangelization 3: Faith and Culture,* ed. James A. Scherer and Stephen B. Bevans (Maryknoll, NY: Orbis Books, 1999), 117–33.

12. A. Echeverry, "Liberation Theology: A Necessary Revision," *Euntes* 29 (1996): 184–85.

13. See Scherer and Bevans, eds., *New Directions in Mission and Evangelization* 3, 7–11.

14. Luzbetak, *The Church and Cultures: New Perspectives*, 374.

15. José M. de Mesa, "The Resurrection in the Filipino Context," in *In Solidarity with the Culture: Studies in Theological Re-rooting* (Quezon City: Maryhill School of Theology, 1987), 102–46; see also Barbara Bowe, "Reading the Bible through Filipino Eyes," *Missiology: An International Review* 26, no. 3 (July 1998): 345–60.

16. "For our starting point is not the uniqueness of Christ or Christianity, or of any other religion. *A fortiori* such a concern would never be a hidden agenda in any inter-religious dialogue that may engage us. Furthermore, inter-religious dialogue itself is not a conscious target pursued as something desirable *per se,* as it is a luxury which the urgency of the socio-spiritual crisis in Asia would not permit" (Aloysius Pieris, "Inter-Religious Dialogue and the Theology of Religions: An Asian Paradigm," *East Asian Pastoral Review* 29, no. 4 [1992]: 366–68).

17. Stephen Bevans rightly points out that even if the primary responsibility for inculturation is in the hands of the locals, missionaries from other countries have still something valuable to contribute to the task. See Stephen B. Bevans, *Models of Contextual Theology* (Maryknoll, NY: Orbis Books, 1992), 14–15.

18. Michael Amaladoss, SJ, "Global Homogenization: Can Local Cultures Survive?" *East Asian Pastoral Review* 36, no. 4 (1999): 424–32.

19. Aylward Shorter, "Inculturation: Win or Lose the Future?" in Scherer and Bevans, eds., *New Directions in Mission and Evangelization 3*, 57–58.

20. See Peter Henriot, S.J., "Globalisation: Implications for Africa," in *Globalization and Its Victims as Seen by Its Victims*, ed. Michael Amaladoss (Delhi: ISPCK, 1999), 70.

21. José M. de Mesa, "The Quest for 'Truth' in Asia," *East Asian Pastoral Review* 35, no. 3/4 (1998): 356–65.

22. See "The Roman Liturgy and Inculturation: IVth Instruction for the Right Application of the Conciliar Constitution on Liturgy (nn. 37–40)," Congregation for Divine Worship (1994). The document insists that the Roman way of celebrating liturgy remains the main pattern. But one wonders whether calls from church authorities to highlight the universality of the church are not just an insistence on the continued translation of the Roman form of theology and worship.

23. Bevans, *Models of Contextual Theology*, 42–46.

24. Ibid., 42–46.

25. John B. Cobb Jr., *Lay Theology* (St. Louis, MO: Chalice Press, 1994), 85–112.

26. Ibid., 90–91.

27. Mariano Pilapil, *Kasaysayan ng Pasiong Mahal ni Hesukristong Panginoon Natin* (1884).

28. René B. Javellana, S.J., *Casaysayan nang Pasiong Mahal ni Jesukristong Panginoon Natin na Sucat Ipag-alab nang Puso nang Sinomang Babasa* (Quezon City: Ateneo de Manila University Press, 1988), 37.

29. Cobb, *Lay Theology*, 90–91.

30. Facsimile of the '*Doctrina Christiana*' of 1593 (Washington, DC: Library of Congress, 1947).

31. Andrew Ross, *A Vision Betrayed: The Jesuits in Japan and China, 1542–1742* (Maryknoll, NY: Orbis Books, 1994).

32. *Catechism of the Council of Trent for Parish Priests* (New York, 1934), 583.

33. Louis LaRavoire Morrow, *My Catholic Faith: A Catechism in Pictures* (Manila: The Catholic Truth Society, 1936), 17.

34. "See, the home of God is among mortals. He will dwell with them as their God; they will be his peoples, and God himself will be with them" (NRSV).

35. Masao Takenaka uses this imagery in a wider manner in his *God Is Rice* (Geneva: World Council of Churches, 1986).

36. José M. de Mesa, *Isang Maiksing Katesismo Para Sa Mga Bata (Na Dapat*

Munang Pag-aralan ng Mga Matatancla): A Study in Indigenous Catechesis (Manila: Wellspring Books, 1988), v.

37. Albert Alejo, S.J., *Tao Po! Tuloy!: Isang Landas ng Pag-unawa sa Loob ng Tao* (Quezon City: Office of Research and Publication, Ateneo de Manila University, 1990). In this book Alejo listed the various related uses and meanings of *loob*—enough to fill about sixteen pages of the book.

38. It was interesting to discover a similar concept of "beauty" among the Navajo Indians of North America. "Beauty" is central to their thought and is expressed in one of their prayers: "Beauty above me, / Beauty below me, / Beauty before me, / Beauty behind me. / May I walk in Beauty." See John D. Dadosky, "'Walking in the Beauty of the Spirit': A Phenomenological and Theological Case Study of a Navajo Blessingway Ceremony," *Mission* 6, no. 2 (1999): 199–222.

39. See Brant Pelphrey, *Christ Our Mother: Julian of Norwich* (London: Darton, Longman and Todd, 1989), 25–26.

40. de Mesa, *Isang Maiksing Katesismo Para sa Mga Bata*.

41. The points that I have mentioned are those recognized by the document, *Mysterium Ecclesiae*, of the Congregation for the Doctrine of the Faith regarding the four-fold historical conditioning of doctrinal statements by presuppositions, concerns, thought categories, and available vocabulary of a particular time and place. See José M. de Mesa and Lode L. Wostyn, *Doing Theology: Basic Realities and Processes* (Quezon City: Claretian Publications, 1990), 103.

42. When rendered "*Magandang Balita*" (Beautiful News) in Filipino, the "beauty" of the gospel is accentuated.

43. See "Journeying Together toward the Third Millennium," Statement of the Fifth Plenary Assembly of the FABC in Bandung, Indonesia, 27 July, 1990 in *For All the Peoples of Asia: Federation of Asian Bishops Conferences Documents from 1970 to 1991*, ed. Gaudencio Rosales and C. G. Arévalo (Quezon City: Claretian Publications, 1992), 280–82.

44. Edward Schillebeeckx, *Interim Report on the Books* Jesus *and* Christ (New York: Crossroad, 1981), 7–8.

45. See Luzbetak, *The Church and Cultures: New Perspectives*, 197.

46. There is something to be learned from such a cross-cultural comparison here. Understanding one's culture in contrast makes one understand one's culture better, not to mention appreciate it better.

47. In scholastic theology "intellect" is understood as the cognitive act of knowing in an immaterial way; insight, simple understanding. In its non-scholastic use it means the "ability to perceive or know" as "distinguished from feeling and will," while "affection" is seen as a quality indicating a

subjective state in response to a "stimulus" or an "emotional disposition." See Bernard Wuellner, S. J., *A Dictionary of Scholastic Philosophy*, 2nd ed. (Milwaukee, WI: Bruce, 1966), 146.

48. Note also how these three concepts, while roughly indicating the same thing of divine communication or relationship, do so in their own particular ways.

49. Commentators on the view of Vatican II regarding revelation, for instance, point to "the encounter between God and the human person," "the real exchange of personal relationship" between God and human persons, and to "God's self-disclosure and self-giving" as indications of utilizing "the profoundest existential insights of our age." See Abbot Christopher Butler, OSB, "The Constitution on Divine Revelation" and Paul S. Minear, "A Protestant Point of View," in ed. John Miller, CSC, *Vatican II: An Interfaith Appraisal* (Notre Dame, IN: University of Notre Dame Press, 1966), 44–45, 51–52, 70; Wolfgang Beinert, "Revelation," in ed. Wolfgang Beinert and Francis Schüssler Fiorenza, *Handbook of Catholic Theology* (New York: Crossroad, 1995), 601–02.

50. Melba Padilla Maggay, *Understanding Ambiguity in Filipino Communication Patterns* (Quezon City: Institute for Studies in Asian Church and Culture), 9–24.

51. As quoted in Pierre Casse, *Training for the Cross-Cultural Mind*, 2nd ed. (Washington, DC: SIETAR, 1981), 252.

52. See Vicente L. Rafael, *Contracting Colonialism: Translation and Christian Conversion in Tagalog Society under Early Spanish Rule* (Quezon City: Ateneo de Manila University Press, 1988).

53. José M. de Mesa, "The Challenge of Nationalism in the Philippines to the Church and the State in the 21st Century," *East Asian Pastoral Review* 28, no. 2 (1991): 140–42.

2

Other Beings, Postcolonially Correct

Mary Douglas[1]

Taking as a case study the Lele of the Congo, Professor Douglas argues provocatively for the need to reinterpret our ideas of gods and spirits as actually existing and operative within the world. Perhaps the Christian doctrine of angels can be of help. A postmodern consciousness makes such reinterpretation more plausible. The lecture was delivered on October 8, 2001.

It is a great honor to be invited to give this lecture at Catholic Theological Union (CTU). As a fellow anthropologist, I greatly appreciate Louis Luzbetak's achievement in making our discipline accessible to missiologists. In particular, *The Church and Cultures*,[2] since 1963 many times reprinted, much translated, and revised, relates directly to the topic of this talk, and I am especially inspired by the generous spirit of the chapter called "Integration of Culture."

Tense Relationships with Anthropologists

CTU is especially dedicated to missionary work, but I must confess that a professional bias tends to put anthropologists and missionaries at odds. The white Western anthropologist arrives in a region for the first time and soon encounters a white Western community that has been there for a long time. It would be so much nicer to be the first white person to arrive there. (Remember Saul Bellow's suave and sophisticated Rain King in a remote African region who welcomes Henderson with an apology: "I am sorry to tell you, we have been discovered!").[3] The missionaries already speak the language and know a lot about the people; moreover, they are immensely kind to the visitor. The initial stages of the anthropological enquiry are often dependent on missionary hospitality.

Two anthropologists have written books about this tension between the missionaries and their ungrateful guests. Kenelm Burridge has written with admiration and affection about what he calls "the missionary situation": "Within my working life as an anthropologist as well as outside it I have heard precious little but ill of missionaries and mission work . . . despite the help and hospitality usually accorded to anthropologists in the field, few of my colleagues have much to say in their favour."[4]

In a study of a CMS mission in Tanzania, Thomas Beidelman identifies the source of this discomfort. After all, he was wishing to study the very things the missionaries sought to eradicate. The tension was partly because of a clash of values between the Kaguru and the missionaries, "who forbade drinking, dancing, and smoking, and who frowned on many traditional beliefs" and practices, including polygyny, widow inheritance, divorce, propitiating ancestors, rainmaking—practically everything the Kaguru did. And, of course, the anthropologist would have to dance and drink with the Kaguru and attend the forbidden ceremonies. Further, as Beidelman says, with engaging frankness, their views were redolent of his own rejected past, that of the "middle class, parochial, American Midwestern background with strong German Methodist teachings."[5]

I too have experienced similar perplexities. I ought to respond to this invitation gratefully by showing missionaries in their most noble and attractive light. Regrettably, what I want to talk about may sound as if the traditional antagonism has defeated courtesy. What I am really offering to you is not a complaint against missions; it is a plea on behalf of foreign gods.

Postcolonial Charity and Ecumenism

Times have changed. In colonial days it was all right to ridicule the gods of other religions. The people might not have liked hearing their gods derided or attacked, but there was not much they could do about it. Now colonial government has faded out. Instead of control, a new spirit is abroad, of toleration, fairness, and courtesy. Our consciences afflict us for injurious words we have been wont to use. In anthropology the word "primitive" became impossible a long time ago, "tribe" is out, so is "native." And rightly so. I am here suggesting that the demand for equality and kindness to humans and animals, and the anger against orientalist and sexist bias, should be further extended. It is insulting to deny personhood to the noncorporeal beings worshiped by our friends, offensive to deny that they have any existence. It is pejorative to call their deities "false gods." Some of them may indeed be "devils," "evil spirits," or "demons," but not necessarily all. Using the contemptuous word "fetish" for their sacred objects, or "magic" for their sacraments, is as bad as calling their beliefs "superstitions" or their religious officials "witch doctors." Now that ecumenism is the order of the day, this language ought to be examined and be cleaned up, as should also the attitudes behind it.

The larger issue is whether it is consistent for Christians to attack foreign gods. Christians deplore religious intolerance directed at themselves but permit themselves to be intolerant of foreign religions. This principle might seem to attack the very roots of the missionary vocation. They have dedicated their lives to replacing falsehood by truth, and they used to consider it impossible and wrong to seek truth in pagan religions.

However, Vatican II has declared a new attitude. It has recognized that all religions are an attempt by human beings to establish contact with the ultimate mystery, beyond human explanation, that embraces our entire existence, from which we take our origin and toward which we tend.[6] The document *Nostra Aetate* pays special respect to "religions of the book," Judaism and Islam derived from the faith of Abraham, and also pays respect to Hinduism and Buddhism. It also honors the many local pagan religions, saying, "the Catholic Church rejects nothing of what is true and holy in these religions," and specifies that their conduct and doctrines "often reflect a ray of that truth which enlightens all men."[7] More recently, Pope John Paul II called for charity to other religions.[8]

This lecture is an attempt to follow these lofty injunctions. The nitty gritty is about how to speak about the foreign gods and how to treat their sacred places and objects. The pagan worshipers believe that their gods are living beings, with effective spiritual powers and energies. What should be done toward respecting their beliefs? It is an awkward question because it challenges the teachings of the sages and implicitly attacks an established range of negative attitudes. In the Bible, the Canaanite gods were ridiculed as inert blocks of wood and stone (Is 46:6–7). This would now be seen to be quite against the rubric of charity. Alternatively, foreign gods have often been credited with sinister powers. Very much alive and truly dangerous, the Mesopotamian demon was believed to intervene disruptively in human affairs. It was common in patristic writings to identify the gods of Greece and Rome with Satan. Preachers might try to avoid the topic, which should put a stop to dialogue. As Timothy Radcliffe has said, there is no preaching without dialogue.[9]

Though the Vatican may urge us to respect foreign religions, and though the missionaries themselves may sincerely want to do so, when you get close to the missionary situation, you will find some converts who do not relish this turn.[10] Indeed, the young may actually like to hear their parents and kinsfolk criticized. The new Christians may want to justify their conversion by insisting that the old gods are creations of the devil. They may derive satisfaction from telling their elders that unless the community abandons its traditional beliefs they will all go to hell. For dozens of possible reasons some people do deeply believe that their old religion was either very bad or plain nonsense. They would not be easily recruited to what charity requires between one religion and another. These would be among many delicate reasons for leaving this sensitive topic as a grey area in missiology. But it might become less sensitive if it were to be defined.

Guardian Spirits

I propose seriously that the foreign gods should be reclassified. They are thought by their worshipers to be intelligent beings with intentions and feelings. Can we not concede this much? I don't think there can be any theological objection to recognizing them in principle as part of divine creation. They could be classified as spiritual beings, under God. The Christian world is full of spiritual beings, unnumbered. The devil and the angels have always been taken for granted as part of God's creation.[11] Christian doctrine allows for good angels and bad angels. It would seem credible that good angels have been set up as a countervailing power to balance that of the devil and his minions. It would be intelligible if God had assigned angelic beings to special missions or for a long-term tutelage of the people of a valley, a kingdom, or a nation. From here it is only a small step to suppose that some of them were assigned pastoral roles, preparing their communities for the eventual encounter with Christianity. Naturally, being spiritual beings, they could only be seen in visions, and only represented by stone or metal sculptures, or by paintings. They would actually be the foreign gods that our travelers have repudiated so vehemently. The church has formally condemned the worship of angels, but paying honor to an angel or to a foreign god is not the same as worshiping and adoring. It would need close study of a foreign cult to decide whether their cult deities are regarded as independent objects of worship.

This reclassification would be only a step in aid of our being able to think and speak with more respect of other people's divinities. Classing foreign gods as angels does not imply that they are all good angels. A good guardian spirit might fail dismally in preparing a disobedient and quarrelsome people for the arrival of Christianity, and his/her priests will have been appealing to the spirit's intentions to justify their own. The principle "By their fruits you shall know them" is more difficult than it sounds. Quite certainly the angel in charge will have had difficulty in keeping the congregation on the straight and narrow path. Why should they be less stubborn and stiff-necked than the people of Israel?

To be fair, we would want to know how much of what the pagans do should count as part of their religion. For example, a major blot on the religion of the Congo Lele[12] would be their (alleged) practice of human sacrifice on the death of a chief. They try to go into hiding when a chief dies, lest they get captured and sacrificed at the funeral ceremonies. But their fear is not good evidence that human sacrifice was actually practiced. Even if it were true, we should somehow determine whether human sacrifice was, strictly speaking, part of their religion or whether it was a secular political institution.

The Development of Doctrine

In advocating a new doctrine, I may encounter challenges from those who maintain that the church cannot change its doctrines. However, if they follow John Henry Newman's theory of the development of doctrine,[13] they may concede that what may look like a change may only be a development of what the church has always taught.

This is not the place for the very interesting argument that sometimes engages anthropologists and theologians about what may count as the enduring, central principles of a culture or a religion. Newman's idea depended on being able to recognize the religion's essential unchanging core. He held that one central part of the Christian framework, if it were to be denied, would bring the rest of the doctrinal edifice down. This essential teaching is what he called "the doctrine of matter." According to that doctrine, physical matter is capable of being sacralized and blessed. The universe is not split between mind and matter; nor is it split between spirit and flesh. God who is spirit could not have become human if flesh was inherently evil; the great Christological controversies have hammered out that point. In church history, this central principle stood up against aniconic movements. The doctrine of matter consistently excludes ideal-ist philosophy; it is incompatible with a wholly spiritualized religion. It frames a view of the cosmos that can sustain the central doctrine of the incarnation. Newman considered that for the church to have weakened on the incarnation would have been a corruption of Christian doctrine.

Other changes Newman classified as enrichments, developments, or revelations of what was there already. Various theological constraints and liberties follow from the central doctrine. The incarnation governs what is acceptable in every other sphere: life, ritual, and morality. Honor for the carnal body underpins the doctrine of the resurrection of the body and the divine presence in the Eucharist. It is strongly embedded in social practice. Places, pictures, and relics may be hallowed without incurring the charge of superstition. Consistently, the church does not count sex as wrong in itself: she blesses the flesh as well as the spirit; she does not reject music, dancing, alcoholic drink, or tobacco. This is how Newman would put it all together.

Some theologians would disagree with Newman about where to lo-cate the center of Catholic doctrine: some would select the Blessed Trin-ity; others might demur again and select the mass and the Eucharist for that central place. Whatever their view, I am hoping that adding to the definition of angels is nowhere near the center. Though it would bring a big shift in the attitude to foreign gods, and a big change in missionary practice, I suggest it need not be seen as a doctrinal change at all, only as a development of the ecumenical principle on which Vatican II has taken the initiative. The present proposal would assimilate the gods in the local pagan pantheon to the class of guardian spirits under the rule of the one God. Does this encounter any special difficulties?

Monotheist Pantheons

First note that the proposal does not involve polytheism. Angels are not gods. I am asked whether there is any intermediate spot where for-eign gods could be accommodated, without inserting them into an ex-isting classification. After all, we don't know much about them, and we should not disregard their own claims to status. Their followers worship them as Gods (gods) in their own right. (Does courtesy require a capital letter?) Though they may share their divinity with other deities in a polytheistic heaven, some of them are regarded as very powerful beings. Even if it were explained to them that the local deities of small communities must expect hard times ahead, shrinking congregations, and neglected shrines, their priests may not appreciate what they are being offered. Even if it were proposed in terms of a truce, the price of an end to vilification, they might see it as a comedown for their god to be classed as an angel; so they might refuse the deal—and I would be wasting your time. Or would it matter? How do Christians feel about the deference that monotheistic Islam pays to Jesus? What other slots could there be?

Polytheism has always been a reproach in the eyes of the fiercely monotheistic religions. Polytheism is taken to be a sign of primitiveness or degeneration from an original revelation. The idea of one God is a principle of pure transcendence. It makes divinity a unique, unshareable quality. The divide it makes is not between spirit and flesh but between divinity and creaturehood. For Christianity, this divide is not negotiable. Angels are not divine, nor can humans ever be, dead or alive. This principle separates monotheism uncompromisingly from other religions.

But theological troubles lie in wait. The Trinity is the first doctrinal step necessary for the doctrine of the incarnation. Three divine persons in one God, and one of the three is God crossing the boundary and taking flesh: in the eyes of Jews and Muslims, Christianity has allowed a major breach in the pure doctrine of monotheism. Can we make a virtue of having softened the strict line? Could it be easier for us to make room for foreign gods as minor deities in our pantheon? Absolutely not; ranked polytheism is quite different—and impossible.

Many pagan religions teach that after setting up the world, a unique creator god has retired to his abode in the sky and never more intervenes directly in human lives. In some religions he provides infrastructural support to the cosmos, and for human society he protects truth and justice and the sanctity of oaths. In other religions the high god sits back and does nothing much—an "otiose deity" for whom a pantheon of minor gods, lesser spirits, and ancestors, do the intervening. Missionaries in many parts of Africa have explicitly associated this "High God" with the unique God of Judeo-Christian religions.

How does a complex pantheon emerge? African history suggests that when political units compete, problems of coordination can sometimes be solved by making alliances among their gods.[14] The Greek classicist, Marcel Detienne, has recently suggested that a pantheon of Gods may start small and grow to accompany the growth of political centralization.[15] The pagan polytheistic pantheon may often be constituted exactly as our innumerable orders of angels, and less than angels, the saints. In this perspective, what I am suggesting is only a change of label. The foreign gods, whom I hope to see promoted to the rank of angels, should feel at home in heaven.

Saints, Dead Ancestors, and the Deified Living

Thus far, the doctrinal problems have not seemed intractable. Much more difficult is the question of deified humans. To recognize them would test too severely the brittle sharp line between God and humankind that the doctrine of matter skirts around.

In many religions, no strong line separates deity from humanity; there is no doctrinal objection to deifying dead or living humans. To follow along this line would compromise the incarnational/monotheistic frame of Christian thought. It is out of the question. The doctrine of the incarnation insists on the greatness of the gulf that was crossed when God became human. This does not prevent human beings who have lived holy lives from being taken after their death into paradise, but they are just saints, not gods, nor angels. They are not the only humans in heaven. All good Christians can be there; there is no forbidden mixture of flesh and spirit that their human presence can offend.

It is different for the many religions that hold that humans can be deified after death or even in their lifetime such as the emperors of ancient Rome or the Yoruba heroes in West Africa.[16] African Protestant theologians have been for at least a century and a half in dialogue about how to assimilate their traditional hero-gods to Christian doctrine. It would be a problem for Protestants who started out with an objection to purgatory and prayers for the dead, but I do not see why Catholics would have a serious difficulty with admitting good ancestors to the communion of saints. They would have a good reason for wanting to reconcile the old religion of their converts, and this reason is what I want to supply.

In some religions the dead may be vengeful, spiteful, and dangerous for their descendants. The Christian dead are theoretically (doctrinally) harmless. They can give help but they can't hurt. Our historical fear of bad ghosts and rituals for ghost slaying suggests that there would not always be much of a difference between popular Christianity and the religions that fear the malice of their dead. But in formal Catholic doctrine, the dead cannot do any harm. They can be exorcised, and in practice the sign of the cross, a whiff of incense, or a sprinkling of blessed water has generally been enough to send off a ghost. In ancestor cults the dead are not necessarily worshiped. Some cults are aimed at keeping the ancestors away.

Ancestors are not gods. Their disqualification from being counted as saints is not that they are dead humans but that they are the wrong dead. I can see only one doctrine that would deny the revered ancestors of other religions being admitted into heaven. This is the teaching that heaven is only for baptized Christians. Not every Catholic theologian upholds it. It does not impinge at all on what Newman called the "doctrine of matter," or the incarnation, and it is not in line with the spirit of charity and ecumenism.

The project of revising our attitudes to other gods could sound un-essential, even frivolous, a mere matter of terminology. In fact, there are practical issues involved. At this stage it would help to give an in-depth case history of Christian converts who learned to despise the god of their ancestors.

Lele Christianity

What follows is based on my own experience in fieldwork among the Lele, in the Kasai district of what was then the Belgian Congo. In 1987, I paid a brief return visit[17] to the field that I had first seen nearly forty years earlier. The mission station was still at Brabanta, but of course everything around it had changed. Most pertinent to this lecture, I discovered that the Lele Christians took it for granted that the old pagan religion was the work of the devil. They believed that in its ancient rites, the Lele religious leaders, their own fathers and uncles, were paying cult to the devil, that they got their redoubtable powers of healing from him, and also that the current practitioners of the cult were much to be feared as sorcerers.

The good missionaries of the order of Oblats de Marie Immaculée had found from the start that the Lele people were highly intelligent and very receptive. The rector in charge in 1949, Father Hubert, used to visit all the villages, spending evenings around a campfire with everyone who wanted to sing and gossip with him. On these occasions, he set himself assiduously to learn all he could about their religion. He was always delighted to find, first, great theological acuity, interest, and good understanding of doctrinal issues, and second, an unexpected convergence between many pagan and Christian doctrines about God, especially sin, hell, and heaven.

I have no reason to think that he intentionally classified the Lele religion as sinful or their diviners as evil. The Lele god was on the side of health and happiness for his worshiper; the sorcerer was his opponent, consumed by malice and spite. Doctrine apart, the practice of their religion used to be dominated by antisorcery measures, techniques of detection, prevention, and cure. I can see how easily the division between the new teaching and the old would make sense in terms of the long-time accepted division between God's initiated servants (who would be the Christian priests) and the sorcerers (who would be the diviners and the whole apparatus of the cult groups).

In Central Africa, the young had a powerful incentive to convert. Lele society had a strong gerontocratic element; while the old men could have two or three wives, the young men were severely disadvantaged. They could not hope to get a wife unless an uncle died, leaving widows to be remarried. Otherwise, they might have to remain bachelors, severely restricted in esteem and influence, until they were thirty or more years old. There were just not enough women to go round. If they tried to seduce a married woman, they risked getting killed by the angry husband, and there would be no reprisals to deter him from self-help.

The missionaries arrived with a doctrine of monogamy and declared that the Belgian state would protect any couple that wished to make a Christian marriage. Polygamous marriages did not count. This was a complete break with the old system. It meant that a young lover could run away with the wife of a polygamist with impunity. Instead of punishing the seducer with an arrow in his back, the vengeful husband who tried to stop them would himself be imprisoned. Very quickly the young men and girls rushed to get baptized and make Christian marriages. But the mission saw to it that conversion was not taken lightly.

In the 1950s, the mission insisted on a long period of instruction, two or three years. During this time the catechumens stayed at the mission and repaid its hospitality and teaching by hard physical labor. They worked on the mission farms and gardens, built walls and outhouses, latrines, roads, and originally they helped to build the splendid mission house, the excellent hospital, and the schoolhouse. When eventually they had been baptized and confirmed, they went home to build houses for themselves in the Christian quarter of their village. Living together under the leadership of the catechist, they felt safer from attacks of sorcerers. When I saw it working effectively in 1949, and again in 1953, the mission school had a deservedly great reputation. The Lele were apt pupils, eager to learn and gifted for mathematics and science.

When I was in Kinshasa in 1987, my early good impressions were confirmed. I found that the Lele I had known formerly as children were now holding important positions in government and industry as well as in the university. The strong loyalty of the converts to the missionaries came as a surprise to me. I thought they had been exploited, but this was not at all their view. In the late 1960s, when civil war broke out in the aftermath of independence, bands of soldiers were looting, pillaging, and killing priests and nuns indiscriminately. The Lele living near the Brabanta mission spontaneously formed a bow-and-arrow squad to guard "their missionaries" day and night. And sure enough, not one of their missionaries was harmed in those perilous times. By 1987, the same loyalty was apparent in everything they said. In other words, this was a very successful mission station.

All the same, though the Flemish missionaries were extremely generous and hospitable in every possible way, like other anthropologists, I was not quite at ease with them. Apart from the hard labor they exacted from their catechumens, they were not severe. They did not forbid their congregations to drink, though they disapproved of certain dances they considered lewd. They communicated with the Lele in what was called a "vehicular language," *Kikongo*, and with me in French, which was a second language for them as well as for me. Partly our different ideas of Lele religion divided us. Mostly I was bothered by the way they were disturbing the balance between generations.

The missionaries did not mind breaking the power of the older men. They may have been right in thinking it was necessary for their mission. They felt it would not matter in the long run because when the old had died out and everyone alive was baptized, a new balance would be found. Meanwhile one should expect the transitional stage to be painful. They expected a long run that never came. They said the same about the danger of disrupting the social order. For a Christian community to be established, the old one had to be changed, root and branch, no matter what transitional chaos might intervene. They could not imagine that the break up of the old society might bring devastation to themselves and their work.

Let me mention two significant problems. One was the doctrine of a strongly dichotomized afterlife. As Father Hubert had noted, Lele teaching on the afterlife was very compatible with the Christian dichotomy of hell and heaven. By teaching heaven for the Christians and hell for the others, the mission utterly divided the generations. Put brutally, there was no need to pay respect to the old pagans since in the afterlife they would be in hell. I doubt that the missionaries actually taught this, but I am reporting what was being understood in the Christian quarter of the village. It may well have been a popular selection from, or distortion of, the missionaries' teaching. I heard of one Lele man who would have liked to be baptized, but his beloved wife had died, so she was presumably in hell, and as baptism would send him to heaven, he would be separated from her for all eternity. This prospect he could not endure, so he accepted the risk of going to hell himself; a risk, but not a certainty, for if he stayed in the old religion, the same doctrines would perhaps not apply.

The Lele were convinced of the wickedness of their senior relatives. The last faces they would want to see when they arrived in heaven would be those of their wicked, old uncles who, when alive, had caused them so much sorrow and in whose true repentance they had no confidence.

Lele Sorcery

The other problem was the doctrine of evil. According to the old Lele religion, the men who had been initiated into esoteric learning in various cult groups had acquired the means to kill their enemies by occult means. It was important that a whole system of related doctrines set limits to the occult danger. Some categories of people could never be accused. The idea that a child might commit sorcery was ruled out; women were not dangerous either, nor did anyone fear that adolescent boys and young men might be plotting sorcery; they were unable to do so because they had not been initiated into its secrets. In other words, knowledge of sorcery was localized in the cults. Furthermore, one did not have to worry unduly about being attacked by sorcery because an initiated senior relative could be relied on to protect his kin. This set of ideas corresponded to Christian teaching on sacramental protection against the powers of evil. In a leaky way, it institutionalized Aquinas's idea that in God's universe, evil is under control. But it was an ambiguous satisfaction: the same cults that protected the people from sorcery were run by and for the sorcerers.

On the other hand, observe that the power to accuse of sorcery, framed in this way, created a balance between young and old.[18] The young could not be accused. But they could stop the old from tyrannizing by the fear of being accused. In the Lele society, before *Pax Belgica,* there had been some equality of prestige and wealth between young and old men. The young warriors enjoyed considerable glory and wealth, and they could capture wives from enemy villages. When the Belgian colonial rule had put an end to intervillage warfare, the young men lost out; they became dependent on their old uncles and fathers. The old men unexpectedly found themselves at an advantage. The young took revenge on any elders who had quarreled with them or been too exorbitant in their demands, by laying every illness and death at their doors. The old belief in sorcery made a new kind of balance, but it was very dangerous for the old who could be hounded from their homes and forced to live rough in the forest.[19] The missionaries would not have wished the old pagans to be so disgraced and endangered, but what could they do?

Anyone involved in missionary work anywhere knows that this is not a local problem. Belief in sorcery or witchcraft is widespread in one form or another throughout the world. It puts all Christian missionaries in a dilemma. Their own doctrinal resources allow them to say that sorcery is an illusion, it does not exist, but this carries no conviction to parties who believe their kin have been murdered. Alternatively, Christian doctrine seems to make a bridge by assimilating the sorcerer's power to the power of the devil. This is the interpretation of evil that their converts would readily understand. There are two other principles that could have been invoked by Christians, a counteractive religious power in the sacraments, and a secular principle that it is wrong to punish for evil deeds that can never be proved. The missionaries would have tried them both, but I am sure that they never realized what heroic virtue would have to be required. Facing sorcery would have been heroism in the full sense of facing martyrdom in the Roman arenas. To expect their flock to live without accusing each other would be like asking them to live without justice: too much turning of the other cheek. The missionaries probably had not understood how the people articulated all their social problems in terms of the danger of sorcery. It cruelly exacerbated the division that Christianity had already deepened between the young and old men.

The missionaries had to recognize the existence of the devil, but I have no evidence that they, rather than their enthusiastic converts, had associated the old religion with devil worship and presented its sages and seers as demonic agents. Either way, this assimilation of their former just and good god to the devil had been accomplished when I returned in the 1980s. But by then the whole thing had run out of control. Christian doctrine itself was dominated by ideas of sorcery. Accusations of working for the devil flew in all directions, and the many and various restraining principles of the old religion had dissolved.

Formerly, confession of killing by sorcery was not required; the poison ordeal would exonerate or condemn the sorcerer. But Christianized sorcery added a new twist: the *sorcerer must be made to confess.* As, for some reason, exorcism would not work unless preceded by confession, with confessions being exacted by torture. A continual ferment of antisorcery cults led by Christians had culminated in a scandal reported by travelers in the early 1970s,[20] and fifteen years later it was still the talk of the day. Total disorder had arrived, bringing great sorrow and bewilderment.

The wheel had come round full circle: first the old religion was supreme. In its teaching sorcery was restrained by many other doctrines. Then the old religion was eclipsed because of the defection of the young converts to Christianity. Then other things happened beyond the borders of their country: Congolese independence was followed by civil war, economic failure, and rural destitution. These external events opened a new window for the accusatory part of the old religion, and it took over more terrifyingly than before.

By 1987, seers and diviners had arisen all over the land and, without initiation into the old cults, were claiming to be able to detect sorcerers right and left. Anyone could acquire sorcery since the demonic theory had superseded the old idea that the art took years to learn. All the constraints on who could be plausibly accused were gone. Women could be accused, and young men. Children too could be possessed by the devil; child sorcerers were regarded as dangerous as adults, and children's accusations and confessions were taken as valid. The final shock was when the missionaries themselves were accused. When I was there, one was accused of killing another by sorcery, and the patients in the mission hospital were said to be at risk from priestly sorcery. Authority was gone, and the missionaries now found themselves in a country in which the backing of the government availed them nothing. When they had once willed the social disorder that they were now witnessing, they had never expected that it would threaten their mission.

There is a happy ending to what might have been a more tragic story. The missionaries kept their heads, the steadfast loyalty of the Lele Christians prevailed, the station has not been destroyed. It flourishes, and now there is a Lele diocese, with its own bishop. But he will somehow have to deal with sorcery.

It would be wrong to claim that the missionaries could have seen what was going to happen when the young turned against the old. The long story expresses an anxiety about the missionary situation. All I can say is that events might have been less traumatic if they had tried harder to make children respect their parents. This anxiety lies behind my postcolonial concern to deal correctly with foreign gods.

It would be wrong to suggest that the missions could have turned history around simply by paying more honor to the foreign god. They could not have prevented the civil war and the devastation of the economy. It is worth remarking also that it is implausible to reclassify Njambi, their creator god, as an angel, even as a very great archangel. The great Njambi was omnipotent. The guarantor of oaths and promises, protector of the poor and innocent, the enemy of evil-doers, their Njambi is obviously the same as our God, under a foreign aspect. This is all the more reason to treat him and his ministers with deep respect.

Evil Spirits

Another element in this story is the dualism of the Lele form of Christianity, their version of a war between good and evil powers. Now and again, extreme forms of dualism emerge that formally teach that a power of evil stalks the universe, a dangerous threat to the power of good, or that the fate of humankind is in the balance while a battle rages between the powers of good and the powers of darkness. It is not Manichaeism so long as the "axis of evil" is thought to be ultimately under the power of God and so long as the victory of good is the outcome of a struggle with evil. It is a blow against monotheism to teach that the outcome is uncertain. But I am not sure that the Lele Christians thought too much about the eventual outcome; the present was quite problematic enough.

At every stage of missionary activity the Christian doctrine of evil is a major problem. The Lele case shows how in its popular forms it seriously undermines pure monotheism. The causes of sorrow and suffering link the different parts of a cosmology. Suffering demands an explanation; attributing it to the devil allows a lot of gratifying casting of blame on his alleged lieutenants. Aquinas's teaching that evil is the privation of good, not an active principle in itself, is very hard to follow because it puts a brake on blaming.

The worse thing that can happen to the missions is when fears of superhuman powers of evil become so terrifying that it is impossible for the congregation to believe in the efficacy of instituted sacraments. When God is a mere onlooker while other forces fight out the fate of human persons, the missions will eventually get drawn in. I have the notion that what the missions teach about the powers of evil is one of their most important messages. They need to know whether their congregations have for centuries been in the habit of solving social conflicts by accusing each other of wreaking their spite and envy by occult means. If fear of sorcery and witchcraft, and fear of being accused of sorcery, have been for generations the main principle of social control, then it is going to be very difficult to preach the Christian faith. This is the context in which the Christian attitude to the other gods has vital importance.

There are various ways that communities can try to live together peacefully without blaming each other for their sorrows. A community might be so keen to avoid causing conflict among its members that the members carefully avoid all confrontation. The Judeo-Christian idea of sin may be untranslatable into their language. Another way of making an end to blame is to attribute all misfortunes to demons.[21] In modern Greece, a complex interpretive framework diverts blame from persons alleged to have been possessed by a demon.[22] In that case, belief in demons is exculpatory. A community that defines its demons as harmful but capricious is presumably determined to live together without pinning responsibility for the causes of misfortune on fellow humans. Blaming dead ghosts for causing harm is another way of taking the burden of responsibility off fellow humans. Good and bad luck are also principles that serve to stop questions about misfortune getting out of hand.

Alternatively, evil can be thought to be caused by evil-minded humans who have acquired occult means of harming their neighbors, by magic, witchcraft, or sorcery, for example. This is a pernicious doctrine that sets friends against friends, neighbors against each other, ultimately destroying all trust and amity.

Development or Corruption?

Christianity and the Lele religion have met, but both religions have lost in the encounter. The old religion has no more authority, except in its techniques for identifying sorcerers. While all its essentially religious doctrines were lost, only belief in sorcery never weakened. In the 1970s and 1980s, its sages and priests were feared and hated by the young. How it goes with them now, I don't know. As for the Christian religion, it acquired knowledge of sorcery (very necessary knowledge too, a young Lele Christian told me). Newman would not have wanted to count the addition of Lele sorcery beliefs as a development of Christian doctrine. Taking Newman's criteria, in the Lele Christian case, the innovation would have to count as a corruption since it undermines the most central doctrine of all, monotheism. It insidiously inserts into this created universe another power that is all evil. It encourages a lack of faith in God's power to deal with evildoers. It contradicts all that had been written in the past against Manichaeism and other dualist heresies. It has much to do with hatred and nothing to do with love.

On Newman's criteria the old religion would also have been corrupted. It had many positive sacraments to protect and heal. It also curbed the desire to accuse. There was also a theory that outsiders were not likely either to have sorcery power or be attacked by it. This was very benign, since it exempted the anthropologist, administrators, and traders. It was a frank admission that sorcery was only due to internal feuds and hatreds. The Lele story of the origin of sorcery confirms this. Sorcery came from God. God gave it to the chief, presumably as a resource for establishing human society. But the chief's friend asked for it. It is a basic principle of Lele morals that one can deny nothing to a friend, so the chief gave it, and that is how it got out into the world. By implication, the friend wanted sorcery for wrongful purposes. One of the principal duties of initiated diviners was to protect the village from sorcerers, and their authority to detect sorcerers was also authority to dismiss some accusations. But I doubt that this was the central theme of their religious thought or their main ritual responsibility.

Newman's distinction between development and corruption depended on being able to say in what the basic original teaching consisted. For the Christian church, as I said, he identified as the central principle the idea that matter is able to be sacralized. Matter is susceptible of grace; it is capable of a union with the divine. On this foundation, the scheme of Christian belief upheld the doctrines of the incarnation, the resurrection of the body, and so on. It justified doctrines and practices that were abhorrent to religions that took a different view of matter, such as Judaism and the Gnostics.[23]

There is no inconceivable mystery in Africa about God becoming a human. If I were to try to identify the equivalent basic principle underlying the old Lele religion, it would be the fragility and desirability of peace (and this is only said from the limited knowledge of someone who could never be initiated into the men's cults). It strikes me forcibly that the central principle that gave unity to the practice of their religion was the idea that God hated conflict and injustice. This set sorcerers in opposition to religion; they must inevitably stand against their maker. Consequently the focus of the religion was on detecting and stopping them. In the afterlife, sorcerers would be in an unhappy place under the ground; their innocent victims would be in the sky with God.

Was the old Lele religion truly monotheistic? Well, not so completely as Judaism, but just as much so as Catholicism. It worshiped a single creator, a supreme God of justice who vigilantly protected the validity of oaths sworn in his name and who punished injustice, adultery, and all kinds of dishonesty. A complex pantheon of spirits mediated his will to human beings. They would have been comparable in status to the angels of Catholicism. They were localized, the spirits of the bush, spirits of the forest and rivers, and the sky. To them God had delegated various specific responsibilities, especially fertility. The spirits had animal manifestations, animals whose species each had its own territorial sphere. Certain fish and wild pigs represented spirits in the water. Birds and squirrels represented spirits in the sky and trees. Underground were burrowing animals, who shared their habitation with the spirits of the bad human dead. These ancestors also had powers to chastise the living, particularly to ensure the payment of debts and promises. They all had delegated responsibilities, taking orders from the next order of the spirit hierarchy, while free to punish intrusion into their part of the universe. Territorial intrusions were built into a web of taboos.

From this elaborate but highly consistent cosmology, the diviners had a huge array of explanations for the problem of evil. Only God and sorcerers wielded power over life and death. The spirits never killed any one. Their instruments of punishment were either sickness or failure in hunting. Divination could diagnose from the symptoms that spirits had been offended or whether sorcery was involved. Sorcery was only one of many possible causes of infertility, miscarriage, infant mortality, and other human sorrows. For the evils of sickness due to invasions of spirit-defined territory, an array of remedies was at hand. Individual sickness needed an individual history: the sick person may have provoked animosity of a dead relative or personally infringed on a prohibition.

Communal misfortunes would generally be attributed to communal offenses, such as infringement of the peace that ideally should reign in the village. Peace was the strongest barrier against sorcery. Prolonged hunting failure in the whole village might indicate a sorcerer's malevolence. But the sorcerer's wiles could never have broken through the ritual defenses of the village unless there had been a quarrel. Sorcerers' success proved the presence of sin in the village. The one sin that the spirits always punished was quarreling. The village community had to be at peace, and any signs of conflict were publicly rebuked because of the effects it would have on hunting and health. The beliefs were heartily backed by consensus. Before a hunt, there would be a general confession and rites of forgiveness.

On the practical side, this religion deserves to have been famous for its constant care for reconciliation and also for its knowledge of medicinal herbs and its work of healing the sick. On the intellectual side, its intricate religious symbolism deserves great honor. Its recursive design of God's creation at every level of existence is a marvel of speculative theology. Its way of assimilating the moral health of the village to the physical health of its members enabled it to bring pressure to bear on turbulent individuals. It taught a doctrine of symbiosis between human and animal worlds. Above all, its sturdy monotheism should be remembered. And there are other religious achievements, some of which the uninitiated could never know, some of which could be known by a more sensitive ethnography. This is undoubtedly a religion that commands deep respect. Were the missionaries afraid to learn about God's other faces? What would they have thought, fifty years ago, of the profound philosophies of personhood and experiences that are now being revealed by anthropologists and others working in neighboring areas of Congo?[24]

Would it have made any difference, in the painful crises that afflicted the missionaries and their flock, if Lele Christians had learned that their old beliefs were a deeply impressive religious synthesis? The frank answer is, No! It could not have changed anything much. It would have changed the adversarial spirit of the situation, and respect for the old diviners and the fathers and uncles who practiced the Lele religion might have reduced the destructive tension between the generations. But, in those dire times, to have recognized the splendor of the foreign pantheon would not have helped anyone, not by itself.

With the collapse of the judicial system, witchcraft beliefs would be bound to go out of control. Compare the way that European witchcraft declined of its own accord in the seventeenth century. Several explanations are offered by historians. One attributes the decline in witchcraft beliefs to the growth of science and the prestige of its alternative explanations. This is weak because it supposes the two kinds of belief to be competing and treats the questions as a matter of intellectual grasp. I prefer the explanation of Barbara Shapiro, historian of the seventeenth century. She holds that the development of the judicial system, with stricter standards of evidence and proof, combined with an increasing reluctance among judges and juries to convict. Together these three factors brought about the end of witch persecution in England. "As Englishmen became more concerned with and had available to them more critical standards which they could apply, witch trials evaporated rather quickly."[25]

When there is no personal advantage (revenge, or compensation) from making accusations, people are not going to lose time on it. If accusations cannot be lodged, or if accused witches cannot be convicted and penalized, the belief becomes impotent, and for lack of application, it will eventually fade, only to linger in nursery stories and old wives' tales. The breakdown of law and order in the Congo would have the opposite effect: when any flimsy justification for accusations will do, and it costs nothing to accuse, and when public opinion can readily be mustered to condemn a suspect without formal trial, then witch accusers are unfettered.

Conclusion: Speaking Ill of Foreign Gods

The need to think anew about the pagan religions is created by current, secular demands. It would be in the spirit of postcolonial correctness to take a more respectful attitude. To this end, I have proposed that the high gods of foreign religions be assimilated to the Christian God and that the lesser gods and spirits be redefined as spiritual beings, as their worshipers believe them to be, created by the one God and serving him. They could be classified as angels, with a special mission to care for and guide their people until they can meet Christianity.

Newman based his idea of the development of Christian doctrine on the centrality of two fundamental principles: monotheism and the incarnation. This suggests a program for comparing foreign religions on these crucial doctrines. I have picked out particular topics that related to what he called the doctrine of matter: the relation between divine and nondivine beings, to the hereafter, to sin, to authority, and above all, to God's omnipotence. The attitude to suffering and misfortune is the main diagnostic question. Dual principles, a God of goodness in conflict with a God of evil, the old Manichean heresy, is incompatible with a Catholic view of God's unique and total power. At this point assimilation is impossible. The argument is supported by a case history of Christians persecuting sorcerers.

But it is possible that the Lele sorcery crisis of the 1970s could have been less destructive if the missions had held a fairer opinion of the foreign god and his acolytes. Reduced antagonism to the foreign cult might have brought other advantages. With a less adversarial tradition, missionaries might have rejoiced in the peace-loving religion of the Lele. They might have made as many old converts as young. They could have modified the pains of the generational cleavage instead of increasing them. Respecting the other religion, knowing it better, the missionaries would have rejoiced to find it was so near to theirs. In conversation the Lele might have found not reversal but completion. Christianity might have brought fulfillment not a harsh breach with the past.

Their old religion is not a subject the Lele care to learn about since they have been taught to repudiate it, lock, stock, and barrel. I am not sure that there is any one left who remembers it, but as I glimpsed it in the 1950s before it was given over entirely to antisorcery techniques, it was an intellectually and emotionally satisfying system.

The argument works the other way round. The very lack of public esteem that, according to the anthropologists, was encountered by the missions in the 1980s and 1990s would have sapped their confidence. Their situation in any region of the world is now more like it would have been for the Jesuits in seventeenth-century China, or for the Little Brothers of

Charles de Foucauld among the Muslims in our day: a powerful foreign context that they cannot but respect. A passive mission of demonstrating a Christian way of life may be the postcolonial form. They are no longer the emissaries of great empires; they no longer have power and authority behind them. Stripping off their authority, the missionaries of the future can still do their work as an unobtrusive presence, willing to teach and dialogue.

A parallel, in reverse, has happened in the anthropology of religion. Anthropologists used to try to eliminate themselves from the scene they were depicting. In the interests of objectivity they practiced elaborate contortions; no fly on the wall could distance itself more completely. Their writing (I should say "our writing") grafted what was called "the ethnographic present" seamlessly on the past. But now the fieldworker's stance is frankly engaged in the present.

The new anthropologists are not primarily recording a remembered religion: in this generation they are undergoing initiation, falling into trances, dancing ecstatically with the spirits, actually performing healing rites themselves.[26] They know the spirits by name, they know where they live, and they call them to join the rituals. The spirits travel a long way when they are called, and on arrival they make their presence manifest. They have their individual likes and dislikes, and they choose their own friends. Just reading about them is unnerving. They are not in any way inert. They send their human colleagues into joyful trances, and they really do cure—of course not always. In the old days it was easy to be superior and dismiss these effects as the result of suggestion. "Suggestion" itself is now being examined scientifically.

In the old days it was ridiculous to expect the anthropologist to believe in the foreign gods. But now it is hard not to believe in their presences. A development of doctrine in favor of the foreign gods might smooth the path of conversion. It would probably slow things down for the mission station, but it would relieve the tension of the missionary vocation. Timothy Radcliffe, the Dominican, justifies the case for taking seriously the beliefs of other religions: "[T]he final challenge is dialogue with those who have seen another face of God, members of other faiths. We should be attentive to them, learn from them, dialogue with them.[27]

Notes

1. I need to thank many friends for their help and advice, starting with Joseph Carola, Sebastian Cody, Maurice Couve de Murville, Valeer Neckebrouck, Adam Kuper, Bart Pattyn, and John Peel, to whom I am very grateful for taking trouble to comment very profoundly.

2. Louis J. Luzbetak, *The Church and Cultures: New Perspectives in Missiological Anthropology* (Maryknoll, NY: Orbis Books, 1988).

3. Saul Bellow, *Henderson the Rain King* (New York: Viking Press, 1959).

4. Kenelm Burridge, *In the Way: A Study of Christian Missionary Endeavours* (Vancouver: University of British Columbia Press, 1991), x.

5. Thomas O. Beidelman, *Colonial Evangelism: A Socio-historical History of an East African Mission at the Grass Roots* (Bloomington: Indiana University Press, 1982), xii, xvi. "CMS" refers to the Anglican (Evangelical) Church Mission Society.

6. See Vatican Council II, Declaration on the Relationship of the Church to Non-Christian Religions (*Nostra Aetate*), 1. I warmly thank Archbishop Maurice Couve de Murville for drawing my attention to these statements that have caused me to revise my original Luzbetak Lecture.

7. *Nostra Aetate*, 2.

8. John Paul II, Encyclical Letter *Redemptoris Missio*, 31.

9. See Timothy Radcliffe, *I Call You Friends* (New York: Continuum, 2001), 75.

10. This was pointed out to me in the discussion after the Luzbetak Lecture.

11. Karl Rahner, "Angels," in *The Concise* Sacramentum Mundi, ed. Karl Rahner (London: Burns and Oates, 1975), 4–13.

12. Mary Douglas, *The Lele of Kasai* (Oxford: Oxford University Press for the International African Institute, 1963).

13. John Henry Newman, *The Development of Christian Doctrine* (London: Longmans, 1949 [1845, 1878]).

14. Robin Horton, "A Definition of Religion," in *Patterns of Thought: Essays on Magic, Religion and Science* (Cambridge: Cambridge University Press, 1993), chap. 1.

15. Marcel Detienne, "Du Polythéisme in Général," *Classical Philology* 81, no. 1 (1986): 47–55.

16. J. D. Y. Peel, *Encountering Religion: The Making of the Yoruba* (Bloomington: Indiana University Press, 2000).

17. Mary Douglas, "Sorcery Accusations Unleashed: The Lele Revisited, 1987," *Africa* 69, no. 2 (1999): 176–93.

18. Mary Douglas, "Techniques of Sorcery Control in Central Africa," in *Witchcraft and Sorcery in East Africa*, ed. John Middleton and E. H. Winter (London: Routledge, 1963), 123–43.

19. I have described cases of this in *The Lele of the Kasai*.

20. Pierre Ndolamb Ngokwey, "Le Désenchantement Enchanteur, ou, d'un Mouvement Religieux à l'Autre," *Cahiers de CEDAF*, 8 (Brussels: Centre d'Etudes et de Documentations Africaines, 1978).

21. Mary Douglas, "Demonology in Robertson Smith's Theory of Religion," in *William Robertson Smith: Essays in Reassessment*, ed. William Johnstone, *JOTSS* 189 (Sheffield: Sheffield Academic Press, 1995), 274–92.

22. Charles Stewart, *Demons and the Devil: Moral Imagination in Modern Greek Culture* (Princeton, NJ: Princeton University Press, 1991).

23. Newman, *The Development of Christian Doctrine*, 375–76.

24. Eric de Rosny, *Les Yeux de ma Chévre* (Paris: Plon, 1981); Eric de Rosny, *La Nuit, les Yeux Ouverts* (Paris: Editions du Seuil, 1996); Meinrad P. Hebga, *Sorcellerie et Prière de Déliverance* (Paris: Présence Africaine, 1982).

25. Barbara J. Shapiro, *Probability and Certainty in Seventeenth Century England* (Princeton, NJ: Princeton University Press, 1983), 197.

26. Roy Willis, *Some Spirits Heal, Others Only Dance* (Oxford: Berg Publishers, 1999).

27. Radcliffe, *I Call You Friends*, 63.

3

Anthropology and Mission: The Incarnational Connection

Darrell L. Whiteman

Dr. Whiteman begins the lecture with a historical overview of the relationship between anthropology and mission. He then proceeds to discuss the importance of anthropology for mission and concludes with the proposal that the doctrine of the incarnation is the most appropriate doctrine for understanding the nature of missionary activity. The lecture was delivered on May 5, 2003.

"Good missionaries have always been good 'anthropologists,'" is the opening line of Eugene Nida's classic text, *Customs and Cultures: Anthropology for Christian Missions*, published a half century ago.[1] In this address I will explore why Nida's comment is so profoundly true and why anthropology still has an important role to play in twenty-first century Christian mission.[2]

God's mission to the world in the present era of globalization takes on forms that are very different from yesterday's missionary activity in the heyday of colonialism. In fact, appropriate forms of mission today are so different from yesterday that some people believe that because we are becoming a global village we no longer need the insights from anthropology that help us understand and appreciate cultural differences. The erroneous assumption is that the world is quickly melding into a homogeneous global village with capitalism as its economic engine and English as its language of discourse. But this is not happening, at least not very quickly. Cultural diversity is heightened, not flattened, and so I will argue that the present era of mission needs insights from anthropology as much, if not more, than any previous period of missionary activity.[3] Moreover, I'll propose that there are biblical and theological reasons for maintaining a close connection between anthropology and mission. We'll begin with a historical overview of the relationship between anthropology and mission, proceed to discussing the importance of anthropology for mission, and conclude with a discussion of the incarnation as a model for mission and why anthropology, therefore, has an important role to play in mission today.

In the Beginning:
The Emergence of Anthropology as a Discipline

Anthropology began as armchair social philosophers in the mid-nineteenth century speculated on the origin of human beings, their religion, and their culture. Evolutionary thought was in the air, and belief in human progress was undaunted. The Enlightenment that followed on the heels of the Reformation and Counter-Reformation in the sixteenth and seventeenth centuries created an intellectual climate of religious skepticism. The divine role in the creation of human society and its institutions was now questioned. Culture was seen as contingent rather than absolute, historically created rather than eternal, and humanly designed and managed instead of divinely given.[4] With advances in exploration of the globe and the colonization of exotic places in the world, the sheer enormity of human and cultural diversity called for some kind of "scientific" explanation.

Anthropologists rose to the occasion. Literalist interpretations of biblical explanations for the origin and diversity of human beings were increasingly called into question. Early anthropology was driven by an evolutionary paradigm that conjectured that human societies, including religion, marriage, kinship, and other aspects of culture, evolved from homogeneous to heterogeneous, from simple to complex.[5] Within this evolutionary framework, anthropologists attempted to make sense out of the bewildering and exotic diversity of peoples and their cultures being discovered around the world.

For example, Edward B. Tylor (1832–1917), recognized today as the founding father of anthropology, partly because he occupied the first chair of anthropology at Oxford, developed a scheme where he proposed that religion evolved from initial animism, which is the belief in spirits, to polytheism, and eventually to monotheism. Tylor had no personal use for religion and in fact derided theologians. As a product of the Enlightenment, he was convinced that through rational thought, "primitive" people would evolve into civilized people. Lewis Henry Morgan developed a universal evolutionary scheme that put humanity on three rungs of the evolutionary ladder: savages, barbarians, and civilized.[6] James G. Frazer argued that human beings progressed from belief in magic, to belief in religion, and eventually to science. E. B. Tylor's 1871 book, *Primitive Culture*, gave us the first definition of the concept of culture in English, and although it was a static unilinear view of culture, it nevertheless helped establish the concept and the beginnings of scientific anthropology.

Missionary Contributions to Anthropology

It is important to remember that the early anthropologists drew data for their speculative theories initially from explorers and travelers and later, missionaries, not from first-hand encounters with "the natives." They would not have deigned to get themselves dirty by doing firsthand fieldwork, which did not come fully into anthropology until the 1920s and 1930s.[7] Instead, they sat in the comfort of their Victorian studies, reading the reports of others' initial contact with non-Western peoples. The journals of explorers like Captain James Cook in the Pacific provided the grist for their intellectual mill. E. B. Tylor and Lewis Henry Morgan, among others, corresponded with missionaries, inquiring about the people among whom they lived and outlining areas of research for missionaries to pursue. It is noteworthy that anthropologists have been loath to recognize the great debt they owe to missionaries, not only in the early stages of anthropology's development, but even today as missionaries provide hospitality, vocabulary lists, and other aids to fledging anthropologists in the field. It is arguable that the discipline of anthropology would not have emerged without its heavy reliance upon ethnographic data provided by missionaries. Despite the fact that there was little application of anthropology to mission during this period, it is ironic that much of the ethnographic data used by anthropologists to spin their theoretical designs came from missionaries.

This nineteenth-century use of missionary writing began a long stream of missionary ethnographic contributions, which was anticipated several centuries earlier by Catholic missionary ethnographers such as Bartolomé de Las Casas (1484–1566) and Bernardino de Sahagun (1499–1590) in Latin America, Joseph-François Lafitau (1681–1746) and Gabriel Sagard (c.1590–c.1650) in North America, Matteo Ricci (1552–1610) in China, and Roberto de Nobili (1577–1656) in India.[8]

To demonstrate how anthropologists like Tylor and Morgan stimulated missionaries' ethnographic research, let us look briefly at the writing of missionaries in Melanesia. Lewis Henry Morgan, author of *Systems of Consanguinity and Affinity in the Human Family*,[9] sent his kinship questionnaire all over the world to missionaries, asking them to fill in the data and send it back to him. One of his contacts was Lorimer Fison (1832–1907), the Australian Wesleyan missionary in Fiji, who got hooked on anthropology and developed a deep appreciation for how it helped him to understand the Fijian worldview and the changing Fijian society under Western contact.[10] Fison corresponded with Robert H. Codrington (1830–1922), an Anglican missionary with the Melanesian Mission in the Solomon Islands and New Hebrides who then also became an ethnographer, writing a book on Melanesian languages and producing his landmark book, *The Melanesians: Studies in Their Anthropology and Folklore*.[11] Codrington's work influenced another Melanesian Mission missionary, Charles E. Fox (1878–1977), who wrote an important ethnography entitled *The Threshold of the Pacific: An Account of the Social Organization, Magic, and Religion of the People of San Cristoval in the Solomon Islands*.[12] Several other Anglican missionaries of the Melanesian Mission made significant ethnographic contributions, including Alfred Penny (1845–1935), A. I. Hopkins (1869–1943), and Walter Ivens (1871–1939).[13]

Although the Melanesian Mission is outstanding and unusual for the number of missionaries who made ethnographic contributions to anthropology, other missionaries should also be noted as well. For example, John Batchelor (1854–1944), an Anglican missionary among the Ainu of Japan for twenty years, reduced their language to writing, translated the entire Bible, and planted a church. He wrote *Ainu Life and Lore*.[14] Maurice Leenhardt (1878–1954), the French Protestant missionary to New Caledonia (1902–1927), wrote the classic *Do Kamo: Person and Myth in the Melanesian World*.[15] "The author of one of the finest anthropological monographs yet written," according to Evans-Pritchard, was Henri Alexandre Junod (1863–1934) of the Swiss Romande Mission, who published *The Life of a South African Tribe* in 1912.[16] *Behind Mud Walls*, a pioneer work in Indian anthropology, was written by William Wiser (1890–1961) and Charlotte Wiser (1892–1981), Presbyterian missionaries in India.[17]

We cannot leave this topic of missionary contributions to anthropology without mentioning the substantial contribution made by Fr. Wilhelm Schmidt (1868–1954). Although never a field missionary himself, as a trainer of missionaries he nevertheless encouraged and organized members of his own Society of the Divine Word and others to produce carefully researched ethnographies of the people among whom they worked. He himself produced more than 650 publications. In 1906, he founded the ethnological journal *Anthropos* as a venue for publishing the many ethnographic reports he received from missionaries, and later he established the Anthropos Institute as a center for anthropological research.[18] Luzbetak, who studied with Schmidt, says,

> To him, ethnology was a pure *Geisteswissenschaft* and a strictly historical field. As a scholar who believed in the purity of his discipline, he would not allow the journal [*Anthropos*] or his [Anthropos] Institute to depart from this concept, insisting that concentration on strictly scientific, rather than applied, ethnology would assure the needed respect of the world of science.[19]

This list of missionary contributions to anthropology, both ethnographic and theoretical, could go on and on, but space does not permit.[20] The point I want to emphasize is the significant contributions missionaries have made to the field of anthropology, and I think today there is more acceptance of that fact in mainstream anthropology. For example, in November 2003, at the annual meeting of the American Anthropological Association in Chicago there was a symposium entitled "Homage to the Missionary Anthropologists." Presentations were made by many of us who are missiological anthropologists, but the secular anthropologists also made contributions to this symposium.

One reason early missionaries were able to make substantial contributions to ethnography as well as anthropological theory is because they knew much more about the people with whom they were living and about whom they were writing than did anthropologists who sat in the comfort of their Victorian studies and theorized about how societies had evolved over time. Charles Taber captures well the mood and situation of anthropologists of this early era and their relationship to missionaries. He notes,

> The first explicit interaction between missionaries and anthropologists occurred in the 1860s, when missionaries served as sources of field data for the earliest anthropological theorists, who were

armchair scholars. This represented a significant advance over the prior situation in which anthropologists merely used as grist for their mills whatever data they could glean haphazardly from missionary and other writings. But anthropologists such as Edward B. Tylor actively corresponded with missionaries, asking them specific questions and suggesting specific lines of inquiry. The anthropologists involved had no personal experience of the exotic,[21] little or no respect for the persons and cultures of the "primitive" world they theorized about, and little or no sympathy with the religious aims of the missionaries whose data they were using.[22]

Anthropology's Early Interest in Solving Human Problems

After slavery was abolished in Britain in 1807 and the Emancipation Act of 1833 was passed, those in the abolitionist movement turned their attention to the general welfare of native peoples within the British Empire. In 1838, an Aborigines Protection Society was founded in London. The society had not been established for very long when a serious division arose about the proper way to protect aborigines. One of the factions associated with missionaries argued that the best way to protect aborigines was to bestow the benefits of Western civilization on them. The more academically inclined faction wanted to study the natives first as a way to raise their standards of living and protect them. This faction left the Aborigines Protection Society and founded the Ethnological Society of London in 1843. They envisioned a marriage between scholarly study and humanitarian interests. In 1856, Sir B. C. Brodie wrote in the *Journal of the Ethnological Society*,

> Ethnology is now generally recognized as having the strongest claims in our attention, not merely as it tends to gratify the curiosity of those who love to look into Nature's works, but also as being of great practical importance, especially in this country, whose numerous colonies and extensive commerce bring it into contact with so many varieties of the human species differing in their physical and moral qualities both from each other and from ourselves.[23]

It did not take long for the Ethnological Society to also experience division within its ranks. The debate was over the slavery question and whether or not human beings were one or more species. In 1863, the divergent group who believed there was more than one species of human beings left the Ethnological Society and formed the Anthropological Society of London. The new society was very successful and within four years had a total of 706 members, in contrast to the Ethnological Society that never grew to more than 107 members. Members of the Anthropological Society of London while believing in the inequality of races, nevertheless championed the use of anthropology for practical, humanitarian causes. While wanting to be scientific and academic, they nevertheless believed that applied anthropology was ultimately more important. In 1866, the society published *Popular Magazine of Anthropology*, noting, "Anthropology, independently of its scientific interest and importance, may and should become an applied science, aiding in the solution of the painful problems which human society and modern civilization proffer, and tending to the bettering of the conditions of man in the aggregate all over the world."[24]

Conrad Reining has called this period of the 1860s, "A Lost Period of Applied Anthropology."[25] It is interesting to note that the earliest call for using anthropology in the service of mission was made during this same period by George Harris in an address to the Manchester Anthropological Society, Monday, September 28, 1868. Harris notes,

> If the information communicated by missionaries is valuable to anthropologists in the pursuit of their studies, I venture to assert that the study of anthropology, if correctly and comprehensively considered, is of no less value to missionaries in pursuit of their arduous and often perplexing undertaking.... Anthropologists and missionaries ought, therefore, instead of ever opposing each other, to be always the closest allies, and should derive important aid from each other's efforts.[26]

Members of the London Anthropological Society had heady confidence in anthropology's ability to be both scientific and hence dispassionate, as well as very practical with almost limitless potential for bettering humanity. But the Anthropological Society with its focus on applying anthropology to human problems was not embraced without controversy. Two groups in particular opposed the anthropologists at this time. One was made up of evangelicals whose literal interpretation of the biblical stories of the Garden of Eden and the Flood caused them to affirm that all of humanity was one, not diverse species, and that there were not moral or physical inequalities inherent in the human race. The second group who opposed anthropologists was composed of political liberals whose commitment to social justice caused them to object to the notion of the inequality of human beings. The Anthropological Society of London after eight years of existence fell on hard times, and its members combined again with the Ethnological Society in 1871. Thomas Huxley took the lead in creating a new organization out of the old ones, and the Anthropological Institute of Great Britain and Ireland was formed in 1871. Huxley did much to establish the new discipline of anthropology as a respectable science and in the process moved away from the previous emphasis on application of anthropological knowledge to ameliorating human problems.

For the next thirty years, the focus was on getting anthropology accepted as an academic discipline in universities, and the practical value of anthropology was rarely mentioned. In 1883, E. B. Tylor was appointed as the first professor of anthropology at Oxford, and the next year a separate section for anthropology was created in the British Association for the Advancement of Science. The first faculty position of anthropology in the United States was established at Columbia University with Franz Boas in 1890. Certainly, in this era there was no one advocating that anthropology and mission could benefit one another, neither anthropologists nor missionaries.

From 1870 onward, the subject matter of anthropology became increasingly more esoteric, and those in the field avoided applying anthropology to everyday problems. It was during this time frame that anthropologists began to earn their reputation as peddlers of the exotic whose study is of no earthly good. James G. Frazer, author of the popular book *The Golden Bough*,[27] is characteristic of this era when he claimed that anthropology should not be concerned with application and instead should focus on studying preliterate people in order to illustrate the history and evolution of society. The early anthropologists' interests were in the past, their research was centered on the evolution of society.

The diagram on the next page attempts to show the various strands of anthropologists and missionaries as they have converged and diverged over time. It includes key players and events but is far from exhaustive. Some of the events and persons in the twentieth century in this diagram will be discussed below.

The Ambivalent Relationship between Anthropology and Mission

The relationship between anthropology and mission has been an ambivalent one for over a hundred years.[28] Committed to the doctrine of cultural relativism, most anthropologists view religion only as an epiphenomenon of culture, as a mere reflection of society.[29] They therefore conclude that Christianity is no different than other religions. It is simply a cultural by-product; it is human made, they argue, not God given. Because there are so few anthropologists with personal Christian faith, it is not surprising that a fair amount of antagonism toward missionaries has come from anthropologists. For example, in his presidential address to the American Anthropological Association in 1976, Walter Goldschmidt declared, "Missionaries are in many ways our opposites; they believe in original sin, the moral depravity of uncivilized man, and the evil of native customs. Because they wish to change the people we wish to study, we view them as spoilers."[30] This lack of appreciation for or understanding of missionaries by anthropologists has been well documented and discussed by Robert Priest in a provocative article in *Current Anthropology* entitled, "Missionary Positions: Christian, Modernist, Postmodernist."[31]

Anthropologists have frequently stereotyped missionaries as narrow-minded destroyers of culture. And, unfortunately, some missionaries must confess, "guilty as charged," but the preponderance of evidence demonstrates that missionaries have often contributed to the preservation of languages and cultures more than to their destruction.[32] Lamin Sanneh has argued persuasively that through Bible translation into vernacular languages, missionaries have done much to preserve rather than destroy indigenous cultures.[33]

If anthropologists have been suspicious of missionaries, missionaries in turn have been slow to show appreciation for the insights that anthropology has to offer them. In 1978 Paul Hiebert described the relationship between missions and anthropology as a love/hate relationship. In 1985,

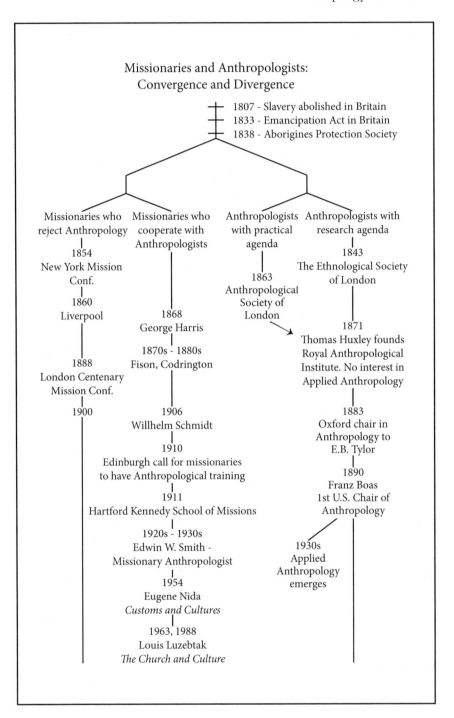

Missionaries and Anthropologists:
Convergence and Divergence

1807 - Slavery abolished in Britain
1833 - Emancipation Act in Britain
1838 - Aborigines Protection Society

Missionaries who reject Anthropology
1854
New York Mission Conf.
1860
Liverpool
1888
London Centenary Mission Conf.
1900

Missionaries who cooperate with Anthropologists
1868
George Harris
1870s - 1880s
Fison, Codrington
1906
Willhelm Schmidt
1910
Edinburgh call for missionaries to have Anthropological training
1911
Hartford Kennedy School of Missions
1920s - 1930s
Edwin W. Smith -
Missionary Anthropologist
1954
Eugene Nida
Customs and Cultures
1963, 1988
Louis Luzebtak
The Church and Culture

Anthropologists with practical agenda
1863
Anthropological Society of London
1930s
Applied Anthropology emerges

Anthropologists with research agenda
1843
The Ethnological Society of London
1871
Thomas Huxley founds Royal Anthropological Institute. No interest in Applied Anthropology
1883
Oxford chair in Anthropology to E.B. Tylor
1890
Franz Boas
1st U.S. Chair of Anthropology

Louis Luzbetak called for a better understanding and a closer cooperation between the two antagonistic groups of anthropologists and missionaries, and offered some practical suggestions as to how this could come about. In 1991, Kenelm Burridge, who is more sympathetic and understanding of missionaries than are most anthropologists, documented this long history of ambivalence between anthropologists and missionaries, and notes the significant ethnographic contributions many missionaries have made.[34]

A Turning of the Tide in Anthropology and Mission

At the beginning of the twentieth century, anthropology as a discipline was becoming established and was recovering from its obsession with evolutionary thought. Other theories were advanced to explain the diversity of human beings and their cultures. In reaction to the nineteenth-century evolutionary schemes, several different theories of cultural diffusion were pressed into explaining cultural diversity. The devastation left by World War I and the expansion of colonialism called for the application of anthropology to human problems. For example, in 1921, proposals were made for the establishment of a School of Applied Anthropology in Great Britain, suggesting that "the anthropological point of view should permeate the whole body of the people" and that the lack of this "was the cause of our present troubles."[35]

In 1929, Bronislaw Malinowski published an article in the journal *Africa* entitled "Practical Anthropology." He noted at the time the huge gap between the theoretical concerns of anthropology and the practical interests of colonial administrators and missionaries. Writing from the African context, Malinowski notes,

> Now I think the gap is artificial and of great prejudice to either side. The practical man should be asked to state his needs as regards knowledge on savage law, economics, customs, and institutions; he would then stimulate the scientific anthropologist to a most fruitful line of research and thus receive information without which he often gropes in the dark. The anthropologist, on the other hand, must move towards a direct study of indigenous institutions as they now exist and work. He must also become more concerned in the anthropology of the changing African, and in the anthropology of

contact of white and coloured, of European culture and primitive tribal life.[36]

Despite the colonial tone of his words, Malinowski was calling for anthropologists to study people as they are now, undergoing change from the impact of colonialism and to stop pursuing a speculative anthropology that seeks to reconstruct the lives and cultures of people from a bygone era. In contrast to this salvage anthropology,[37] Malinowski was calling for the creation of a new kind of anthropology, which would later come to be called applied anthropology. Malinowski, perhaps more than any other anthropologist in Britain, helped to popularize anthropology and get it into the hands of nonprofessional laypeople. From the London School of Economics, Malinowski trained a generation of anthropologists who slowly took up his challenge and conducted research that was helpful in the context of changing cultures under colonial influence. Later post-modern critiques of anthropology would be very critical of anthropology's cozy relationship with colonialism.

Applied anthropology emerged in the 1930s, both in Britain and the United States. American anthropologists such as Robert Redfield, Ralph Linton, Melville Herskovits, and Margaret Mead sought to merge practical anthropology and academic anthropology while at the same time distancing themselves from missionaries and their concerns. Postmodern anthropology would later attempt to "expose" both anthropology and mission for having an agenda.

Malinowski began calling for the practical use of anthropology as early as 1929 and in 1938 argued that the time had come to make anthropology practical:

The anthropologist with all his highly vaunted technique of field work, his scientific acumen, and his humanistic outlook, has so far kept aloof from the fierce battle of opinions about the future and the welfare of native races. In the heated arguments between those who want to "keep the native in his place" and those who want to "secure him a place in the sun," the anthropologist has so far taken no active part. Does this mean that knowledge serves merely to blind us to the reality of human interests and vital issues? The science that claims to understand culture and to have the clue to racial problems must not remain silent on the drama of culture conflict and of racial clash. . . .

Anthropology must become an applied science. Every student of scientific history knows that science is born of its applications.[38]

Bronislaw Malinowski did much to take anthropology beyond the academy and into the real world. His theory of functionalism, which is sometimes maligned by people critical of the church growth movement, was a helpful schema for understanding how change introduced into one part of a culture would impact all other aspects of the society. As a theory, Malinowski's functionalism is not particularly fruitful, but as a guide for research and for interpreting the impact of one culture on another. it is excellent. This perspective would become very important for colonial administrators and, of course, for missionaries.

Missionaries after the turn of the century also started to get in touch with the value of anthropology for their work. Ecumenical mission conferences were held in New York in 1854, Liverpool in 1860, and in 1888, the Centenary Conference on Protestant Missions was held at Exeter Hall in London, with sixteen hundred representatives from fifty-three mission societies. Over this thirty-year period, the missionary movement had grown statistically in a remarkable way, but it had also become more paternalistic, with more vested interests. There is little evidence of either awareness of or need for anthropological insight coming out of these conferences.

But Edinburgh 1910 was a different story. The report of the commission was a large series of nine volumes, with one devoted completely to the preparation of missionaries (volume 5). The importance of understanding the cultures and customs of the people to whom missionaries go was stressed from this time onwards. Edinburgh is important because it shows that missionaries were struggling with all the points of criticism that anthropologists would make, long before they ever started to speak on the matter. One of the features of this conference was the recognition of the fact of sociocultural change as well as the need to move beyond ethnocentric evaluations of cultural differences. The call for anthropological training of missionaries was clearly sounded at Edinburgh. The report says,

It is, therefore, clear that the missionary needs to know far more than the mere manners and customs of the race to which he is sent; he ought to be versed in the genius of the people, that which has made them the people they are; and to sympathise so truly with the good which they have evolved, that he may be able to aid the national leaders reverently to build up a Christian civilisation after their own kind, not after the European kind.[39]

Edinburgh differs from other missionary conferences because it was the first time that a particular voice was heard. Both the speakers at the conference and the reports that had come in from all over the world articulated what many missionaries were feeling very strongly, namely, a need for better education of the religion and the values of the people among whom they were working. They were beginning to realize that sympathy was not enough, that empathy and understanding were required, and that their evangelism would be far more effective if it took place within a worldview other than their own.

The leading advocate for applying anthropological insights to mission was Edwin G. Smith (1876–1957). Smith, born of missionary parents of the Primitive Methodist Mission in South Africa, served as a missionary in Zambia among the Baila-Batonga people from 1902 to 1915. Although he often thought of himself as an amateur anthropologist he nevertheless was held in high esteem by contemporary anthropologists of his day. He was a member of the Royal Anthropological Institute of Great Britain from 1909 until his death in 1957, and he served as president from 1933 to 1935, the first and only missionary to do so. He contributed substantially to anthropology[40] and wrote frequently in the *International Review of Missions*. In 1924, in an article entitled "Social Anthropology and Missionary Work" Smith argues that, "the science of social anthropology [should be] recognized as an essential discipline in the training of missionaries."[41] He goes on to note that we need to understand people from their point of view, not just our own, if mission work is to be effective. He notes in language characteristic of his time that "a study of social anthropology will lead the young missionary to look at things always from the native's point of view, and this will save him from making serious blunders. Tact is not enough; nor is love. . . . Tact needs to be based on knowledge; love there can hardly be without understanding."[42]

Ten years later in his 1934 Presidential Address to the Royal Anthropological Institute entitled "Anthropology and the Practical Man," Smith connected his Christian faith and missionary work with his anthropological perspective. He notes,

> I think that too often missionaries have regarded themselves as agents of European civilization and have thought it part of their duty to spread the use of English language, English clothing, English music—the whole gamut of our culture. They have confounded Christianity with western Civilization. In my view this is a mistaken view of the Christian mission. I am convinced that essential elements in Christian belief and practice are of universal value—that in other words, there are fundamental needs of the human soul that Christ alone can satisfy. But in the Christianity that we know there are unessential elements, accretions which it has taken on from its European environment and which it is not part of the Christian missionary's duty to propagate.[43]

Smith goes on to note, in language that is similar to contemporary discussions of contextualization, that Christianity must take on appropriate cultural forms in each culture it encounters. And then with a spirit of optimism he claims,

> Here and there in the field academically trained anthropologists are to be found on the [mission] staffs. Some of us will not be content until such qualified persons are at work in every mission area and every missionary has had some anthropological training. In short, there are signs that the modern missionary is becoming anthropologically minded, without being any the less zealous in his religious duties.[44]

I believe Edwin Smith's optimism was premature, for today many, if not most missionaries, are not anthropologically minded, even though we see there was a call for this as far back as Edinburgh 1910.

Another early advocate for connecting anthropology and mission was Henri Philippe Junod, missionary in South Africa and son of the missionary ethnographer Henri A. Junod mentioned above. Writing in 1935, he says, "I wish anthropologists would realize what they owe to missionary work. Many scientists do acknowledge this debt, but others forget the contribution of missionaries to science itself. It is not accidental if missionaries have sometimes proved to be the best anthropologists…" He then bemoans the fact that "Mission policy, however, has had too little to do with anthropology."[45] He goes on to say,

I believe that anthropology can help us greatly. It can widen our views, it can open our eyes, it can teach us to understand, it can improve our educational policy and point out to us the dangers of the way. But we are not here to preserve native custom as a curio for some African museum. We are dealing with the realities of the present.[46]

Missionary anthropologists like Edwin W. Smith and Henri Junod had more impact on European missionaries from mainline denominations than on American evangelical missionaries. The first post–World War II era anthropology book written by a missionary in the United States was *The Missionary and Anthropology: An Introduction to the Study of Primitive Man for Missionaries* by Gordon Hedderly Smith, published in 1945.[47] This is a very inadequate book, drawing too much on E. B. Tylor and John Lubbock, nineteenth-century evolutionary anthropologists. Smith argues for the importance of anthropological training as part and parcel of missionary preparation, but given the shortcomings of this book, it is not surprising that it had limited influence.

During the 1940s and continuing well beyond the end of World War II, Wheaton College in Wheaton, Illinois, became a center for preparing missionaries. The distinguished and popular Russian-born Dr. Alexander Grigolia developed a strong anthropology major and course program, and he was succeeded at Wheaton by a series of young anthropology instructors committed both to providing balanced undergraduate anthropological training and teaching the conceptual and practical tools required for effective communication across cultural boundaries. Perhaps the most famous anthropology major from Wheaton was the renowned evangelist Billy Graham, who graduated from Wheaton in 1943 and who had chosen anthropology partly because of an interest in becoming a missionary.[48] Graham drew on anthropological concepts for his evangelistic ministry. Wheaton students, such as Charles Kraft, Henry Bradley, and William Merrifield (class of 1953), would all go on to make important contributions to missiological anthropology. As of 1953, Wheaton had graduated over two hundred majors in anthropology, many of whom were serving or were destined to work as missionaries.

As Wheaton College's anthropology program waned in the early 1960s, Bethel College in St. Paul, Minnesota, began to establish a program in anthropology for training Christian missionaries, practitioners in development and other applied fields, and academics. Building on an already strong sociology department under the guidance of David Moberg, Claude Stipe established the anthropology program that became part of a blended department of sociology and anthropology. Soon linguistics was added, and the department became known as the Department of Anthropology, Sociology, and Linguistics. Some of the key professors during this time period were Thomas Correll, Don Larson, William Smalley, Ken Gowdy, and Paul Wiebe. This team added James Hurd in the early 1980s. The department attracted a relatively small number of majors, but the graduates of this program during this era created careers of distinction. The anthropology graduates included Thomas Headland, Michael Rynkiewich, Stephen Ybarro, Richard Swanson, and Douglas Magnuson. Between 1986 and 1988, all but Ken Gowdy and James Hurd took early retirement or left for other opportunities. Today the Department of Anthropology and Sociology has a major in sociocultural studies with four "tracks" that allow a student to specialize in anthropology, sociology, cross-cultural missions, or urban studies. The program attracts almost seventy majors a year (around 60 percent in the anthropology and cross-cultural tracks, 20 percent in sociology, and 20 percent in urban studies). The faculty consists of three anthropologists (Harley Schreck, James Hurd, and Jennell Paris Williams) and two sociologists (Samuel Zalanga and Curtis De Young).

The Kennedy School of Missions of Hartford Seminary[49] was the equivalent graduate program where anthropology was taught and used in the advanced training of Protestant missionaries. Edwin W. Smith, upon his retirement in 1939, was a visiting lecturer of African anthropology and history at Hartford until 1943, and Paul Leser served as professor of anthropology. Charles Taber, and Charles Kraft, two well-known anthropologically trained missiologists, received their Ph.D. degrees from Hartford before it closed the mission program in the mid 1960s, reflecting the decline in missionaries being sent by mainline Protestant mission boards. As the Kennedy School of Missions at Hartford was folding, Schools of World Mission with an emphasis on applying anthropological insights in missiology and employing trained professional anthropologists on their faculty opened at Fuller Theological Seminary in 1965, Trinity Evangelical Divinity School in 1969, and Asbury Theological Seminary in 1983.

A high-water mark in the history of anthropology and mission came in 1954 with the publication of Eugene Nida's *Customs and Cultures: Anthropology for Christian Missions.* Although Nida's Ph.D. is in linguistics more than in anthropology, as a translation consultant for the American Bible Society, Nida traveled widely, working in some two hundred languages in seventy-five countries. From this vast experience Nida saw first hand the problems and challenges faced by missionaries and translators, and his anthropological perspective enabled him to make keen observations and write copious notes from which *Customs and Cultures* was written in a brief six-week period while Nida was in Brazil between translation workshops. *Customs and Cultures* is conceptually so rich and well grounded anthropologically that it is still used today in colleges and seminaries, although many of his illustrations are dated, especially those from pre–Vatican II Latin America. Nevertheless, I have had students tell me they wished they had read Nida's book before they had sallied forth into cross-cultural ministry.

The Journal *Practical Anthropology*

One index that an academic field is reaching maturity is when a journal in that field is published. This was the case with missionary anthropology and the publication of *Practical Anthropology*.

Malinowski's article entitled "Practical Anthropology" published in 1929 was a call for anthropology to move beyond the sterile confines of academia and enter the world where cultures were clashing with one another, where colonialism was impacting indigenous cultures. Malinowski was not a man of faith, so it is perhaps ironic that his call for a practical anthropology was a harbinger of the practical application of anthropology to mission work.

It is interesting to note that following World War II and the proliferation of Protestant evangelical missionaries and the beginning of the decline of colonialism, a new journal titled *Practical Anthropology* was launched in 1953. Its humble beginning began when Robert B. Taylor, anthropology instructor at Wheaton College, prepared and distributed two initial issues to test the level of interest in a journal on applications of anthropology in Christian thought and practice. The response was favorable, mainly among those interested in cross-cultural communication of the Christian message.

At Wheaton, Taylor typed the mimeograph masters and had them reproduced by the college copy center. Both at Wheaton in 1953–54 and in Eugene, Oregon, in 1954–56, he continued to develop the journal, keeping the subscription cost at $1.00 per year by doing all the work with the help of his wife, Floris, except for the mimeographing and, later, multilithing. Within a few years there were 250 subscribers. During these years of development, the project was helped along, perhaps indispensably, by the counsel and writing of articles by William Smalley, William Reyburn, Marie Fetzer Reyburn, Eugene Nida, and James O. Buswell III. When Taylor left the University of Oregon campus for doctoral field research, William Smalley became editor, and *Practical Anthropology* developed into a journal primarily for missionaries and Bible translators needing the insights from anthropology and wanting a forum where they could share their ideas and their anthropologically informed experiences of mission in the field. This conformed to a vision Smalley had held for some time for just such a publication, and, with the help of others, he built effectively on the journal Taylor turned over to him to realize this vision.

Practical Anthropology ran for nineteen years, continuing as an outlet for anthropologically minded missiologists like Nida, Smalley, Loewen, the Reyburns, and Charles Taber, all of who were committed to cross-cultural mission and Bible translation. The pages of the early editions of this journal are full of stories and examples of how anthropology can illuminate the cross-cultural complexities of effective mission work. It is interesting to read letters to the editor wishing that the readers had had this kind of anthropological insight when they began their missionary careers. For example, Herbert Greig writing from Batouri, Cameroun, lamented, "If only I had *this* before I went to Africa, *what* a difference it would have made. With regret I look back upon the embarrassments and the lost opportunities, and would like to save others from like mistakes."[50]

After nineteen consecutive years of publishing six issues a year, in 1973, *Practical Anthropology* ceased publication and merged into *Missiology*, the journal of the American Society of Missiology. At this time, there were over three thousand subscribers to *Practical Anthropology,*[51] indicating the tremendous growth this journal underwent in a relatively short span of time. The need for insights from anthropology applied to the problems of cross-cultural mission was significant, and *Practical Anthropology* responded with timely helpful articles. The last editor of *Practical Anthropology*, Charles Taber noted,

From the beginning, PA took for its scope the entire field of cross-cultural communication, viewed from an anthropological perspective. Its potential audience included anyone interested in such communication, especially of the Christian gospel. Such concepts as ethnocentrism, cultural relativity, accommodation, identification, and so forth were introduced and discussed, and their implications for Christian mission explored. We believe that PA has served an important function and has been helpful to many by making *practical* applications of *anthropology* to their work in all parts of the world.[52]

The first editor of *Missiology* for six years was anthropologist Alan Tippett from Fuller Theological Seminary's School of World Mission. He promised to continue the emphases in *Practical Anthropology* in the new journal *Missiology*.[53] And I, as an anthropologist and the fourth editor of *Missiology*, from 1989 to 2003, also kept the *Practical Anthropology* legacy alive. William Smalley captured the best of *Practical Anthropology* in two books entitled *Readings in Missionary Anthropology* and *Readings in Missionary Anthropology II*.[54]

At the time that *Practical Anthropology* was launched in 1953, the common understanding among most Bible translators and missionaries was that if we could just get the scriptures into indigenous peoples' languages, then they would come to think like us in the West. And so anthropology was pressed into the service of Bible translation and other aspects of mission. It would not be until the 1970s that we would come to appreciate the importance of contextualization and to realize that people in different cultures should not only *not* come to think like us once they have the Bible in their own language, but that they should have the mind of Christ within their *own* culture. This new insight would usher in the field of ethnotheology[55] and contextualization.[56]

The Contribution of Roman Catholics to Missiological Anthropology

While evangelical missionaries, anthropologists, and Bible translators were writing in the pages of *Practical Anthropology*, Roman Catholic missionaries were being introduced to the writing of Fr. Louis Luzbetak, in whose name this lecture series is given. Luzbetak, trained in anthropology under the famous Wilhelm Schmidt, differed from his mentor in believing that anthropology should be applied to and integrated with mission instead of being a separate enterprise. In the midst of his mission and fieldwork in New Guinea, Luzbetak came to the conclusion that academic anthropology needed to be better connected with mission. He notes,

> I became so convinced of the importance of cultural anthropology for the mission of the church, and so frustrated was I by the fact that so little attention was being given to the relation between faith and culture, that I was determined to do everything in my power not to return to my original specialization but rather to devote all my energy in the future to the application of anthropology to mission.[57]

Luzbetak sketched out his ideas in an essay entitled "Toward an Applied Missionary Anthropology" in 1958 and then delivered on his promise with the publication of *The Church and Cultures: An Applied Anthropology for the Religious Worker*.[58] This work was met with enthusiasm by missionaries in the field and by missionary anthropologists. I remember reading the second printing (1970) as a graduate student in anthropology, and saying to myself, "This is exactly what I want to do with my life— make anthropology understandable and useful for the missionary enterprise." After two printings with Divine Word Publications, William Carey Library reprinted the book four more times. Luzbetak's ecumenical spirit spilled over into Protestant missionary circles, hungry for deeper understanding of how anthropology could relate to mission. Then, twenty-five years after the original publication of *The Church and Cultures*, Luzbetak published his *magnum opus*, a complete revision of *The Church and Cultures* with a new subtitle: "*New Perspectives in Missiological Anthropology*" which as of today has sold seventy-five hundred copies.[59] In his lavish review of this book, Charles Taber rightfully calls Luzbetak the dean of living missiological anthropologists and says that *The Church and Cultures* "is one of the most significant missiological books of the last quarter of this century."[60] Luzbetak's subtitle, "New Perspectives in Missiological Anthropology" breaks new ground conceptually, by moving us beyond *missionary* anthropology tied to the previous era of colonial missions, to *missiological* anthropology that is more appropriate for the present age of global Christianity.

Several other Catholic anthropologists have made significant contributions from anthropology to mission. First is Gerald Arbuckle, a Marist priest from New Zealand who has written and lectured widely. Applying anthropological insights to the church, Arbuckle has focused especially on inculturation and the refounding of religious communities. His popular books *Earthing the Gospel: An Inculturation Handbook for Pastoral Workers* and *Refounding the Church: Dissent for Leadership* capture much of his anthropological insight for mission.[61]

Another significant Catholic missiological anthropologist is Aylward Shorter, a British missionary of Africa, who studied under E. E. Evans-Pritchard at Oxford. Drawing on his extensive mission work in East Africa, Shorter has brought to bear anthropological insights on the church in Africa, notably in his *African Culture and the Christian Church: An Introduction to Social and Pastoral Anthropology*, and *Jesus and the Witchdoctor*. Shorter's more theological work is *Toward a Theology of Inculturation*.[62]

Anthony Gittins is a third Catholic missiological anthropologist of note. A priest of the Congregation of the Holy Spirit, Gittins was trained at Edinburgh, has had mission experience in West Africa, and is presently teaching at Catholic Theological Union in Chicago. His book *Mende Religion* is an in-depth anthropological study of the belief system of the Mende in Sierra Leone. His other works, which draw on his anthropological perspective, include *Gifts and Strangers*, *Bread for the Journey*, *Life and Death Matters: The Practice of Inculturation in Africa*, and *Ministry at the Margins*.[63] Finally, anthropologist Stephen Fuchs, SVD, has published extensively from his experience in India, contributing substantially to Catholic missiological anthropology.[64]

Three other books, these written by evangelical missiological anthropologists, have become important landmarks on the road of anthropology's journey in the service of mission. Marvin Mayers, with a Ph.D. in anthropology from the University of Chicago and experience in Guatemala with Wycliffe Bible Translators, was professor of anthropology at Wheaton College when he wrote *Christianity Confronts Culture: A Strategy for Cross-Cultural Evangelism*.[65] Combining anthropological theory with missiological case studies, this book has gone through ten printings of twelve thousand copies.

Charles Kraft, trained in anthropology at Wheaton College and Hartford Seminary's Kennedy School of Missions, broke new ground with his monumental *Christianity in Culture* published by Orbis Books.[66] Today

Kraft's book has sold twenty thousand copies, but it was not initially welcomed with open arms by the more conservative fundamentalist wing of the missionary enterprise. One particularly vicious attack on Kraft was a book entitled *Is Charles Kraft an Evangelical?*[67] Kraft was castigated for his anthropological perspective on mission, but he clearly demonstrated how much our culture shapes and influences our theologizing and how so often the form of Christianity communicated by the missionary does not connect deeply with the culture of the receptor.

The third important book that connects anthropology with mission is Paul Hiebert's *Anthropological Insights for Missionaries* published in 1985.[68] In its eighteenth printing with over forty-eight thousand copies sold, this may be one of the most widely read missiological anthropology books in print today. Paul Hiebert, who died in 2007, has been the most prolific writer among evangelical missiological anthropologists and his work on epistemology and mission has broken new ground for missiology.[69]

The Under-Utilization of Anthropology in Mission

As we have seen, there is a growing contribution of and appreciation for anthropological insights and perspectives applied to mission. But despite this, and despite the significant books and key players, the application of anthropology to the missionary enterprise is still rather insignificant. Of the thousands of anthropologists, less than one percent would call themselves Christian, and even fewer have used their professional anthropology in the service of the church and mission. In 1989 I founded the Network of Christian Anthropologists, and we gather each year at the annual meeting of the American Anthropological Association. There we discuss the challenges of relating anthropology to Christian faith and to mission. I'm pleased to report that we have over a hundred people in our network. These are small gains in a world where anthropology and mission, or should I say anthropologists and missionaries, have more often than not been enemies instead of colleagues.

Nevertheless, the number of North American missionaries, both Protestant and Catholic, who have any kind of training in anthropology is very small. Over a thirteen-year period, I worked with the Southern Baptist Foreign Mission Board and helped train about three thousand of their five thousand missionaries. My two-day intensive crash course on anthropological insights for crossing cultural barriers with the gospel was frequently met with an astonished comment like, "Why have I never heard this anthropological perspective before? Here I am, six weeks away from getting on an airplane to fly off and spend the rest of my life ministering to people in a different culture, and I've never heard anything like this." Eugene Nida once said to me in the mid-1990s that he thought missionaries were more poorly trained today in the area of cross-cultural understanding than at any previous period of mission history.

Anthropology and the Training of Non-Western Missionaries

Moreover, as the center of gravity for the Christian church moves south and east, the number of European and North American missionaries is declining as the number of non-Western missionaries is increasing.[70] For example, in 2003, there were over ten thousand Korean missionaries found all over the globe. In 2010, that number increased to twenty thousand Korean missionaries serving in 169 countries.[71] As part of their missionary training and orientation, they seldom if ever are introduced to the insights of anthropology that would help them discover the nature of their cross-cultural interaction and ministry.[72] And because Korea is one of the most homogeneous societies in the world, Korean missionaries easily confuse Christianity with their Korean cultural patterns of worship, so their converts are led to believe that to become a Christian, one must also adopt Korean culture. If we Americans are guilty of wrapping the gospel in the American flag, then Koreans metaphorically wrap the gospel in kimchi (a potent symbol of their culture). This pattern of confusing the gospel with one's culture is being repeated throughout the non-Western world, and missionaries from these cultures are making the *same* mistakes that Western missionaries made in the age of colonialism when the gospel was first brought to their cultures. There is a growing literature on the training and problems of non-Western missionaries. For example, William Taylor's edited volume *Internationalising Missionary Training* focuses on training non-Western missionaries. In *Too Valuable to Lose* the problem of attrition of missionaries from Korea, Brazil, and Ghana, along with missionaries from some Western countries, is discussed. The journal *Training for Cross-Cultural Ministries*, that ran from 1990 to 2001, also features the training of non-Western missionaries.[73]

So the need for training missionaries from the West as well as training non-Western missionaries in cross-cultural understanding has never been greater, especially in this age of "the coming of global Christianity," as Philip Jenkins puts it in his book, *The Next Christendom*.[74]

Why Anthropology Has Not Caught on among Missionaries

Given this long rich history of anthropology's interaction with mission, the wealth of information published in books and journals on how anthropological insights can inform mission practice, and the establishing of significant schools of world mission for training, one can only wonder why anthropology has not caught on more among missionaries? Why are so many missionaries, Protestant and Catholic, Western and non-Western, unaware of the value of anthropology for their work and ministry? I have been pondering this question for many years, and a few ideas come to mind.

First, one's theology influences greatly one's appreciation of culture. Missionaries who see human beings and their cultures as totally depraved, will be slow to see any reason why they ought to understand the webs of meaning behind the behavior and customs of the people among whom they live. They will see their "cultural mandate" as bringing change to the culture, but unfortunately it is usually change in the direction of the missionary's culture more than toward the kingdom of God. In contrast, a missionary who has a strong theology of creation, and sees God's prevenient grace at work in the lives of people and their cultures, will more likely desire to understand cross-cultural differences and will therefore be more open to the insights from anthropology.

Another reason missionaries have not taken anthropology more seriously is because they are in too much of a hurry. Either their eschatology tells them that Christ's return is imminent, and therefore it would be a waste of time to study in depth the language and culture of the people, or they are on a fast timetable to plant so many churches, or baptize so many converts, so they really don't have time to bother with all this anthropological stuff. Jon Kirby, however, argues, that in the present age of mission and the world church, language and culture learning are more important than ever and in fact are forms of ministry themselves.[75]

A third reason missionaries don't take anthropology seriously is that they see it as concerned, if not consumed, with the exotic, and so they perceive it to not be of much practical value. There have been too few missiological anthropologists to function as cultural brokers and bridge builders between the missionary enterprise and the anthropology academy. Pragmatic missionaries don't want to waste their valuable ministry time on something that they believe will yield few dividends.

Another reason I believe anthropology is not taken more seriously is because fewer and fewer missionaries are spending a lifetime among a people. The average length of time for a "career" missionary is now seven years. If one is not intending to spend ten to twenty-five years in a culture, it is easier to conclude that one can "get by" with very little linguistic and cultural knowledge, and so who needs anthropology?

Of course, all these reasons for not taking anthropology more seriously are also contributing factors that lead to missionary ineffectiveness and burnout. For example, just understanding the phenomenon of culture shock would have saved many missionary careers, but without having a framework for understanding the source of culture shock, many have concluded in their depths of despair and depression that they must not have been called to these people after all. An enormous challenge remains to give missionaries from every culture a sense of curiosity for cultural differences, an appreciation for the insights that anthropology can provide, and a determination to pursue cross-cultural understanding when in their busyness they don't feel they have time.

Connecting the Gospel to Culture:
How Anthropology Can Help

In 1999, I spent part of my sabbatical in Paraguay, one of the poorest countries in South America. There I encountered the phrase, "Paraguayans speak in Spanish, but think in Guarani." Guarani is the language spoken by the indigenous people of this region before the Spanish Conquest, and it is still alive and well today. I immediately asked, "In what language do Paraguayans worship and read the Bible?" The answer was "Spanish, not Guarani." In other words, Christianity is expressed through the medium of Spanish rather than in the heart language of Guarani. More recently, I learned that when the Jesuits came to this area in the seventeenth century, they asked for the local name of the highest God in the Guarani cosmology and were given a name for God that they used instead of the Spanish *Dios*. Only recently has an anthropologist researching the Guarani cosmology learned that the Guarani had a god that was higher than the god whose name they gave to the Jesuits, but that god was so high in the sky that no name was given to it. In other words, here was the unknown god, alive and well in the Guarani cosmology, but because the missionaries did not adequately research and understand the Guarani cosmology, the Christian God they introduced was confined to a subordinate position to the unknown god of the Guarani.

The missionaries also searched for a word that they could use to convey the meaning of baptism. It was not easy, but they came up with a term they thought captured the essence of baptism for the Guarani. Anthropological investigation, hundreds of years later, discovered that the term used for baptism meant, "becoming Spanish." Mistakes like this could be avoided if missionaries were properly trained in anthropological methods of research and if they had an anthropological perspective to help them cope with and understand cultural differences.

There are many other "horror stories" that could be told of missionary mistakes made because of a lack of cross-cultural understanding and the absence of an anthropological perspective. Nevertheless, let me briefly note seven areas in which I believe anthropology can help us connect the gospel to culture:

1. Anthropology deals with people in all dimensions of their existence—socially, culturally, and ecologically. Anthropology takes a holistic approach to studying human beings.
2. Anthropology deals with people's actual behavior, as well as what they say, how they think, and how they feel. It is a behavioral science, and a dose of realism is good in any ministry.
3. Anthropology seeks to generalize about human behavior and looks for cross-cultural universals and patterns. This gives us a greater appreciation for distinguishing what is unique to one culture and what is more characteristic of all human beings.
4. Anthropology uses an approach to research called "participant observation" that is particularly useful for cross-cultural ministry. It gives us tools for knowing how to discover deeper cultural understanding while living with the people we serve.

5. Anthropology focuses on the elements in human interaction that relate to communication. It helps us appreciate the need to learn in depth the language of the people, and to recognize that most communication is more nonverbal than verbal.

6. Anthropology helps us distinguish between cultural forms and their meanings. This is particularly important when we want to communicate Christian meanings in forms that are appropriate for the culture of the receptors of our message.

7. Anthropology focuses on how cultures change. Missionaries by definition should be agents of change, but too often the change we introduce is disruptive and counterproductive. We need to understand thoroughly the cultural dynamics of the society in which we serve.

This is a brief list of why cross-cultural witnesses should incorporate anthropological training into their preparation for ministry and why they should use anthropological insights as part and parcel of their ministry.

The Incarnational Connection

I now come at last to what I call the incarnational connection between anthropology and mission. I have argued above that for reasons of pragmatism and efficiency, anthropology should inform mission, but there are also important theological reasons for doing so. The incarnation is our model for cross-cultural ministry and the biblical reason why anthropology needs to inform mission. As a theological concept, the incarnation is about God becoming human, but in the mystery of the incarnation, God did not become a generic human being. God became Jesus the Jew, shaped and molded by first-century Roman-occupied, Palestinian Jewish culture. This meant that Jesus spoke Aramaic with the low prestige accent spoken around Galilee. He avoided eating pork and other foods prohibited by the Torah. He believed the earth was flat and the center of the universe with the sun revolving around it. Jesus did not know that germs cause disease because germs would not be "discovered" for at least 1,870 years. In other words Jesus was thoroughly shaped by his Jewish culture at that particular time and in this particular location. The God of the universe was manifest through Jesus who was embedded in this particular culture. For as Philippians 2:6–8 says,

He always had the nature of God, but he did not think that by force he should try to remain or become equal with God. Instead of this, of his own free will he gave up all he had, and took the nature of a servant. He became like a human being and appeared in human likeness. He was humble and walked the path of obedience all the way to death—his death on the cross.

In his whimsical style Ogden Nash once wrote, "How odd of God, to choose the Jews." But God *did* choose the Jews at a particular point in time to reveal something about God's character. John Donne, in his *Holy Sonnet* has written, "T'was much that man was made like God, long before. / But that God should be made like man, much more."

In the preface to Jesuit John Haughey's book, *The Conspiracy of God: The Holy Spirit in Us* we read,

> With justification, the author points out that in the past we have given in to the tendency to present the mystery of Jesus in terms of a Divine Theophany—God coming to us under human appearance rather than *from among* us in the mystery of the Incarnation. We must meet the authentic Jesus, a man among men, conditioned by the relativity of time and space as men always are.[76]

The incarnation tells us something important about God. God chose an imperfect culture with its limitations for making known God's supreme revelation. From the beginning of humanity, God has been reaching out to human beings embedded in their different cultures. And God's plan for the salvation of the world has been to use ordinary human beings, like ourselves, to reach others who are immersed in a culture different from our own. The incarnation tells us that God is not afraid of using culture to communicate with us. S. D. Gordon once said, "Jesus is God spelling himself out in a language that man can understand."[77] This language that human beings can understand is the language of human culture. The incarnation shows us that God has taken both humanity and culture seriously. So the incarnation tells us something about God's nature. It also becomes a model for ministry in our own time. In the same way that God entered Jewish culture in the person of Jesus, we must be willing to enter the culture of the people among whom we serve, to speak their language, to adjust our lifestyle to theirs, to understand their worldview and religious values, and to laugh and weep with them.

But how do we do that in cultures that are so different from our own? We cannot go back into the womb and be born again in another culture. This is where the power of anthropological insight comes to bear on our ministry. I submit that without the insight of anthropology, which helps us understand and appreciate cultural differences, we will automatically revert to our ethnocentric mode of interpretation and behavior. We will fall into the cultural trap of assuming that what works well for ministry in our own culture will also work well in a different culture, but it seldom does. We will tend to assume erroneously that all human beings see the world essentially the same as we do, but they seldom do. We will likely believe that cultural differences are not that significant since we are all human beings created in God's image.

But cultural differences *are* significant, very significant, for theological reasons as much as anthropological ones. The various cultures of the world are gifts of God's grace. We get a picture of the biblical importance of cultural diversity in Revelation 7:9. John writes, "After this I looked, and there was an enormous crowd—no one could count all the people! They were from every race, tribe, nation, and language, and they stood in front of the throne and of the Lamb, dressed in white robes and holding branches in their hands" (Rev 7:9).

One may ask, how did John know this? How did he draw his conclusion that this crowd around the throne of God was so diverse? He must have seen the many cultural and linguistic differences apparent among the people. So, the image we get here is one of unity in cultural diversity, not cultural uniformity. The absence of diversity is not unity. It is uniformity. In fact, you can't have unity without diversity. The chaos of Babel was redeemed at Pentecost and will be expressed around the throne of God someday. People from every ethnolinguistic group will surround the throne of God, worshipping God, not in English, or even English as a second language, but in their own language shaped by their own worldview and culture. The view we get of the kingdom of God is a multicultural view, not one of ethnic uniformity. Cultural diversity around the throne of God is united in praise to God as the Lord of Life, but it is expressed through a diversity of languages, cultures, and worldviews. We can count on hearing about 6,809 languages around that throne.[78] One of the things we admire most about the gospel is its ability to speak within the worldview of every culture. And this to me is the empirical proof of its authenticity.

The same process of incarnation, of God becoming a human being, occurs every time the gospel crosses a new cultural, linguistic, or religious frontier. If the mission of God was achieved by the incarnation of Jesus, and Jesus in turn said to his disciples and to us, "As the Father has sent me into the world so send I you into the world" (John 20:21), then what does this mean for a model of mission, of cross-cultural ministry? I think we can assume that we are bound to work within the limitations of the cultural forms of the people to whom we are sent. This is not rigid or static because culture changes, but it means we start with the confines and limitations imposed by their culture, as well as opportunities. We start with where people are, embedded in their culture, because this is where God started with us in order to transform us into what God wants us to become. When we take the incarnation seriously as a model for mission, it frequently means downward mobility. Incarnation for Jesus led to crucifixion, and this means for us that there will be many things in our life that we will have to die to—our biases and prejudices, our lifestyle, our agenda of what we want to do for God, maybe for some of us even our physical life. When we take the incarnation seriously in ministry it means we bow at the cross in humility before we wave the flag of patriotism. The incarnation as a model for mission means we must give up our own cultural compulsives and preferences, and we must not insist that the cultural expression of the gospel in another culture be the same as it is in our own.

Incarnational identification with the people among whom we live and serve does not mean we try to "go native." Try as we might, we can't. We cannot go native because our parents weren't "native." That is, we already have been shaped and molded by another culture, so we can never completely rid ourselves of it. And we don't need to. Pathetic attempts to "go native" are often met with disgust by those we are trying to impress. Moreover, if we were to succeed in "going native," then we would no longer be a conduit for ideas and values from outside the culture that come with the gospel. I must admit that in over thirty years of studying missionaries I have yet to find anyone who "went too far." We normally have the opposite problem of not going far enough in our attempts to identify with the people.

So, what does it mean to be incarnational in our approach to cultural differences? It frequently means at least the following eight practices:

1. We start with people where they are, embedded in their culture, and this frequently requires downward mobility on our part.
2. We take their culture seriously, for this is the context in which life has meaning for them.
3. We approach them as learners, as children, anxious to see the world from their perspective.
4. We are forced to be humble, for in their world of culture we have not yet learned the acquired knowledge to interpret experience and generate social behavior.
5. We must lay aside our own cultural ethnocentricism, our positions of prestige and power.
6. We will be very vulnerable; our defenses will have to go, and we'll have to rely more on the Holy Spirit than our own knowledge and experience.
7. We make every effort to identify with people where they are, by living among them, loving them, and learning from them.
8. We discover, from the inside, how Christ is the answer to the questions they ask, and to their needs that they feel.

Conclusion

In summary and conclusion we have seen how over the past century or more anthropology has slowly been appropriated by mission for service in the kingdom of God. And we have briefly discussed the contribution that missionaries have made to the field of anthropology. Today, some of us perhaps understand the value of anthropological insights for mission better than we ever have, because of the missiological and anthropological research and writing that have transpired over the past century. But we continue in a situation where the majority of missionaries, both Western and non-Western, are still largely uninformed by anthropological insights. Without cross-cultural understanding, we will miss the richness of other cultures, for one who knows only one culture, knows no culture.[79] There is a wonderful Kikuyu proverb from Kenya that captures the blinding ethnocentricism that comes from knowing only one culture. It says, "He who does not travel, believes his mother is the world's best cook." With proper anthropological training, missioners can overcome their ethnocentricism and feast on a smorgasbord of cross-cultural experience prepared by many good cooks.

I have argued in this lecture that the incarnation as a model for cross-cultural ministry helps us make the important connection between anthropology and mission. I want to close this presentation on anthropology, mission, and incarnation with an ancient Chinese poem that captures the essence of the incarnation.

> Go to the people,
> Live among them,
> Learn from them,
> Love them.
> Start with what they know,
> Build on what they have.

This is the incarnational way of doing and being in mission, but we need the insights of anthropology, the humility of Christ, and the empowerment of the Holy Spirit, to be in mission in this way.

Notes

1. Eugene A. Nida, *Customs and Cultures: Anthropology for Christian Missions* (New York: Harper & Row, 1954).

2. I owe many thanks to those who have read and reviewed this presentation as well as those who have helped me discover valuable research leads. They include Julee Bellar, Steve Bevans, Dean Gilliland, Harriet Hill, Mike Rynkiewich, Harley Schrek, Wilbert Shenk, Charles Taber, and Robert Taylor.

3. See Darrell L. Whiteman, "The Role of the Behavioral Sciences in Missiological Education," in *Missiological Education for the 21st Century: The Book, the Circle, and the Sandals*, ed. J. Dudley Woodbury, Charles van Engen, and Edgar J. Elliston (Maryknoll, NY: Orbis Books, 1996), 133–43.

4. Charles Taber, *To Understand the World, to Save the World: The Interface between Missiology and Social Science* (Harrisburg, PA: Trinity Press, 2000), 18.

5. Herbert Spencer, *The Study of Sociology* (New York: Appleton, 1873).

6. Lewis Henry Morgan, *Ancient Society* (New York: World Publishing, 1877).

7. Not wanting to perpetuate the myth that all early anthropologists were only armchair theorists, it should be noted that there were a few anthropologists

in this early era who did fieldwork, such as H. C. Haddon, W. H. R. Rivers (1864–1922), and C. G. Seligman in the Torres Strait Expedition of 1898; Baldwin Spencer's work among the Arunta of Central Australia in the mid-1890s; and Franz Boas (1858–1942) among the Eskimo (1883–84) and thirteen times among the Northwest Coast Native Americans between 1886 and 1931. It was Bronislaw Malinowski's fieldwork in the Trobriand Islands (1914–18) that would bring fieldwork into the mainstream of anthropological research.

8. Books by or about these early missionary ethnographers include the following: for Las Casas: Lewis Hanke, *Bartolomé de las Casas* (The Hague: Martinus Nijhof, 1951); Helen Parish and H. R. Wagner, *The Life and Writings of Bartolomé de las Casas* (Albuquerque: University of New Mexico Press, 1967); Gustavo Gutiérrez, *Las Casas: In Search of the Poor of Jesus Christ* (Maryknoll, NY: Orbis Books, 1993); for Sahagun: Bernardino de Sahagun, *General History of the Things Seen of New Spain: Florentine Codex*, trans. Arthur J. O. Anderson and Charles E. Dibble (Salt Lake City: School of American Research, University of Utah, 1950–82); for Sagard: Gabriel Thédat Sagard, *Le Grand Voyage du pays des Hurons situé en l'Amerique vers la mer douce, es derniers confines de la Nouvelle France dite Canada* (Paris: Emile Chevalier, Tross, 1632 [1865]); Gabriel Thédat Sagard, *The Long Journey to the Country of the Hurons,* ed. and with an introduction by George M. Wrong; trans. H. H. Langton (Toronto: Champlain Society, 1939); for Ricci: Jonathan D. Spence, *The Memory Palace of Matteo Ricci* (New York: Viking Penguin, 1984); for De Nobili: Savarimuthu Rajamanickam, *Robert De Nobili on Indian Customs* (Palayamkottai, India: De Nobili Research Institute, St. Xavier's College, 1972); Savarimuthu Rajamanickam, *The First Oriental Scholar* (Tirunelveli, India: De Nobili Research Institute, 1972); Savarimuthu Rajamanickam, *Roberto De Nobili on Adaptation* (Palayamkottai, India: De Nobili Research Institute, 1971).

9. Lewis Henry Morgan, *Systems of Consanguinity and Affinity in the Human Family* (Washington, DC: Smithsonian Institution, 1871).

10. Lorimer Fison, *Tales from Old Fiji* (London: Alexander Moring, 1907).

11. Robert H. Codrington, *The Melanesians: Studies in Their Anthropology and Folklore* (Oxford: Clarendon Press, 1891).

12. Charles E. Fox, *The Threshold of the Pacific: An Account of the Social Organisation, Magic and Religion of the Peoples of San Cristoval in the Solomon Islands* (London: Kegan Paul, Trench, Trubner, 1924).

13. Alfred Penny, *Ten Years in Melanesia* (London: Wells Gardner, Darton, 1887); A. I. Hopkins, *In the Isles of King Solomon: Twenty-five Years among the Primitive Solomon Islanders* (London: Seely, Service, 1928); Walter G. Ivens, *Melanesians of the Southeast Solomon Islands* (London: Kegan Paul, Trench,

Trubner, 1927); Walter G. Ivens, *The Island Builders of the Pacific* (London: Seely, Service, 1930).

14. John Batchelor, *Ainu Life and Lore: Echoes of a Departing Race* (Tokyo: Kyobunkwan, 1927 [reprint: New York: Johnson Reprint, 1971]).

15. Maurice Leenhardt, *Do Kamo: Person and Myth in the Melanesian World* (Chicago: University of Chicago Press, 1947, 1979).

16. E. E. Evans-Pritchard, *Social Anthropology and Other Essays* (New York: The Free Press, 1964), 114. Henri Alexandre Junod, *The Life of a South African Tribe*, 2 vols. (New Hyde Park, NY: University Books, 1962 [1912]).

17. William Wiser and Charlotte Wiser, *Behind Mud Walls* (New York: R. R. Smith, 1930; rev. ed., Berkeley: University of California Press, 1971).

18. Ernest Brandewie, *When Giants Walked the Earth: The Life and Times of Wilhelm Schmidt, SVD* (Fribourg, Switzerland: University Press, 1990); Louis Luzbetak, "Wilhelm Schmidt, S.V.D. 1868–1954: Priest, Linguist, Ethnologist," in *Mission Legacies: Biographical Studies of Leaders of the Modern Missionary Movement*, ed. Gerald H. Anderson et al. (Maryknoll, NY: Orbis Books, 1994), 475–85.

19. Luzbetak, "Wilhelm Schmidt," 478.

20. See Kenelm Burridge, *In the Way: A Study of Christian Missionary Endeavours* (Vancouver: University of British Columbia Press, 1991), esp. chap. 7 and appendix; Charles Taber, *The World Is Too Much with Us: "Culture" in Modern Protestant Mission* (Macon, GA: Mercer University Press, 1991), 150–55.

21. This is a slight overstatement because, as noted above, there were some early anthropologists who did in fact have some firsthand field experience with the people about whom they wrote. Even Morgan spent time with the Iroquois (see Marvin Harris, *The Rise of Anthropological Theory* [New York: Thomas Y. Crowell, 1968], 169). This statement is most true of James G. Frazer and Herbert Spencer, but less true of A. C. Haddon, W. H. R. Rivers, C. G. Seligman, Baldwin Spencer, Franz Boas, and others who in fact did do research among the people about whom they wrote.

22. Taber, *To Understand the World*, 95.

23. Sir B. C. Brodie, "Address," *Journal of the Ethnological Society* 4 (1856): 294–95.

24. *Popular Magazine of Anthropology* (1866): 6.

25. Conrad Reining, "A Lost Period of Applied Anthropology," *American Anthropologist* 64 (1962): 593–600.

26. George Harris, *On Foreign Missions in Connection with Civilization and Anthropology* (London: Bell and Daldy, 1868), 4–5.

27. James G. Frazer, *The Golden Bough*, 2 vols. (London: Macmillan, 1890).

28. Paul G. Hiebert, "Missions and Anthropology: A Love/Hate Relationship," *Missiology: An International Review* 6 (1978): 165–80; Claude Stipe,

"Anthrpologists versus Missionaries," *Current Anthropology* 21 (1980): 165–68; Louis J. Luzbetak, "Prospects for a Better Understanding and Closer Cooperation between Anthropologists and Missionaries," in *Missionaries, Anthropologists, and Cultural Change*, Studies in Third World Societies, no. 25, ed. Darrell L. Whiteman (Williamsburg, VA: College of William and Mary, 1985), 1–53; Vinson H. Sutlive, Jr., "Anthropologists and Missionaries: Eternal Enemies or Colleagues in Disguise?" in Whiteman, ed., *Missionaries, Anthropologists, and Cultural Change*, 55–99; Frank A. Salamone, Guest Editor, *Missionaries and Anthropologists*, Part II, Studies in Third World Societies, no. 26 (Williamsburg, VA: College of William and Mary, 1985); Sjaak van der Geest, "Anthropologists and Missionaries: Brothers under the Skin," *Man* 25 (1990): 588–601; Burridge, *In the Way*; Robert J. Priest, "Missionary Positions: Christian, Modernist, Postmodernist," *Current Anthropology* 42 (2001): 29–70.

29. Emile Durkheim, *The Elementary Forms of Religious Life*, trans. J. W. Stain (London: Allen & Unwin, 1912, 1915).

30. Walter Goldschmidt, "Anthropology and the Coming Crisis: An Autoethnographic Appraisal," *American Anthropologist* 79, no. 2 (1977): 296. In this statement Goldschmidt ignores the fact that anthropologists also "spoil" when they enter a culture to study it, and that anthropologists also have a mission. For example, see Bruce Knauft, *Genealogies for the Present in Cultural Anthropology* (New York: Routledge, 1996). Knauft, a postmodern anthropologist with evangelistic zeal, calls for the need of passion and clear mission in anthropology.

31. See Priest, "Missionary Positions"; see also Stipe, "Anthropologists versus Missionaries"; Sutlive, "Anthropologists and Missionaries"; Salamone, *Missionaries and Anthropologists*; Roland Bonsen, Hans Marks, and Jelle Miedema, eds., *The Ambiguity of Rapprochement: Reflections of Anthropologists on Their Controversial Relationship with Missionaries* (Nijmegen, The Netherlands: Focaal, 1990); van der Geest, "Anthropologists and Missionaries."

32. Darrell L. Whiteman, "Does Christianity Destroy Cultures?: An Interview with Cultural Anthropologist Darrell Whiteman, *Heartbeat* 23 (Summer 2002): 1–8.

33. Lamin Sanneh, *Translating the Message: The Missionary Impact on Culture* (Maryknoll, NY: Orbis Books, 1989).

34. For references, see note 28 above.

35. N. J. E. Peake, "Discussion," *Man* 21, no. 103 (1921): 174.

36. "Practical Anthropology," *Africa* 2 (1929): 23–24. Reprinted in *Applied Anthropology: Readings in the Uses of the Science of Man*, ed. James A. Clifton (Boston: Houghton Mifflin, 1970), 13.

37. "Salvage" anthropologists were trying to collect the last remnants of

traditional culture, especially among Native Americans, before the onslaught of Euro-American culture would destroy it.

38. Bronislaw Malinowski, *Methods of Study of Culture Contact*, Memorandum 15, International African Institute (London: Oxford University Press, 1939), x.

39. World Missionary Conference, Edinburgh, *The Preparation of Missionaries*, Report of Commission V (Edinburgh: Oliphant, Anderson & Ferrier, 1910), 170.

40. Edwin W. Smith, *Handbook of the Ila Language* (London: Oxford University Press, 1907); Edwin W. Smith, "Anthropology and the Practical Man," Presidential Address, *Journal of the Royal Anthropological Institute* 64 (1934): xiii–xxxvii.

41. Edwin W. Smith, "Social Anthropology and Missionary Work," *International Review of Missions* 13, no. 52 (1924): 519.

42. Smith, "Social Anthropology and Missionary Work," 522–23.

43. Smith, "Anthropology and the Practical Man," xxvi–xxvii.

44. Ibid., xxix.

45. Henri Philippe Junod, "Anthropology and Missionary Education," *International Review of Missions* 24, no. 94 (1935): 217.

46. Junod, "Anthropology and Missionary Education," 228.

47. Gordon Hedderly Smith, *The Missionary and Anthropology: An Introduction to the Study of Primitive Man for Missionaries* (Chicago: Moody Press, 1945).

48. Billy Graham, *Just As I Am: The Autobiography of Billy Graham* (San Francisco: HarperSanFrancisco, 1997), 64–65.

49. The Kennedy School of Missions was a direct response to Edinburgh 1910, and especially the Report of Commission V on the preparation of missionaries, which was chaired by W. Douglas McKenzie, president of Hartford Seminary. Attending the Edinburgh Conference was Mrs. John Stewart Kennedy, who, when approached by Hartford Seminary, agreed to give $500,000 toward the new School of Missions. The school was named in memory of her late husband, John Stewart Kennedy of New York. See Curtis Manning Geer, *The Hartford Seminary 1834–1934* (Hartford, CT: Case, Lockwood & Brainard, 1934), 202–18.

50. Herbert Grieg, "Letters to the Editor," *Practical Anthropology* 4, no. 5 (1957): 204.

51. Wilbert R. Shenk and George R. Hunsberger, *The American Society of Missiology: The First Quarter Century* (Decatur, GA: American Society of Missiology, 1998), 17.

52. Charles Taber, "Change and Continuity: Guest Editorial," *Missiology: An International Review* 1, no. 1 (1973): 7.

53. Alan Tippet, "Missiology: 'For Such a Time as This!'—Editorial," *Missiology: An International Review* 1, no. 1 (1973): 15–22.

54. William A. Smalley, ed., *Readings in Missionary Anthropology* (Tarrytown, NY: Practical Anthropology, 1967); William A. Smalley, ed., *Readings in Missionary Anthropology II*, enlarged 1978 ed. (Pasadena, CA: William Carey Library, 1978).

55.. Charles H. Kraft, "Toward a Christian Ethnotheology," in *God, Man and Church Growth: A Festschrift in Honor of Donald Anderson McGavran*, ed. Alan R. Tippett (Grand Rapids, MI: William B. Eerdmans, 1973), 109–26.

56. Darrell L. Whiteman, "Contextualization: The Theory, the Gap, the Challenge," *International Bulletin of Missionary Research* 21 (January, 1997): 2–7. Reprinted in James A. Scherer and Stephen B. Bevans, eds., *New Directions in Mission and Evangelization 3: Faith and Culture* (Maryknoll, NY: Orbis Books, 1999), 42–53.

57. Louis J. Luzbetak, "My Pilgrimage in Mission," *International Bulletin of Missionary Research* 16 (July 1992): 125.

58. Louis J. Luzbetak, "Toward an Applied Missionary Anthropology," *Anthropological Quarterly* 34 (1958): 165–76; Louis J. Luzbetak, *The Church and Cultures: An Applied Anthropology for the Religious Worker* (Techny, IL: Divine Word Publications, 1963).

59. Louis J. Luzbetak, *The Church and Cultures: New Perspectives in Missiological Anthropology* (Maryknoll, NY: Orbis Books, 1988).

60. Charles Taber, review of *The Church and Cultures: New Perspectives in Missiological Anthropology*, *Missiology: An International Review* 18, no. 1 (1990): 104.

61. Gerald A. Arbuckle, *Earthing the Gospel: An Inculturation Handbook for Pastoral Workers* (Maryknoll, NY: Orbis Books, 1990); Gerald A. Arbuckle, *Refounding the Church: Dissent for Leadership* (Maryknoll, NY: Orbis Books, 1993).

62. Aylward Shorter, *African Culture and the Christian Church: An Introduction to Social and Pastoral Anthropology* (Maryknoll, NY: Orbis Books, 1974); Aylward Shorter, *Jesus and the Witchdoctor* (Maryknoll, NY: Orbis Books, 1985); Aylward Shorter, *Toward a Theology of Inculturation* (Maryknoll, NY: Orbis Books, 1988).

63. Anthony J. Gittins, *Mende Religion: Aspects of Belief and Thought in Sierra Leone*, Studia Instituti Anthropos, vol. 41 (Nettetal, Germany: Steyler Verlag—Wort und Werk, 1987); Anthony J. Gittins, *Gifts and Strangers: Meeting the Challenge of Inculturation* (New York: Paulist Press, 1989); Anthony J. Gittins, *Bread for the Journey: The Mission of Transformation and the Transformation of Mission*, American Society of Missiology Series, no. 17 (Maryknoll, NY: Orbis Books, 1993); Anthony J. Gittins, ed., *Life and Death Matters: The Practice*

of Inculturation in Africa (Nettetal, Germany: Steyler Verlag, 2000); Anthony J. Gittins, *Ministry at the Margins: Strategy and Spirituality for Mission* (Maryknoll, NY: Orbis Books, 2002).

64. Stephen Fuchs, *Rebellious Prophets: A Study of Messianic Movements in Indian Religions* (New York: Asia Publishing House, 1965); Stephen Fuchs, *The Aboriginal Tribes of India* (New York: St. Martin's Press, 1977).

65. Marvin K. Mayers, *Christianity Confronts Culture: A Strategy for Cross-Cultural Evangelism* (Grand Rapids, MI: Zondervan, 1974).

66. Charles H. Kraft, *Christianity in Culture: A Study in Dynamic Biblical Theologizing in Cross-Cultural Perspective*, rev. 25th anniv. ed. (Maryknoll, NY: Orbis Books, 1979, 2005).

67. Edward N. Gross, *Is Charles Kraft an Evangelical? A Critique of Christianity in Culture* (Philadelphia, PA: Christian Beacon Press, 1985).

68. Paul G. Hiebert, *Anthropological Insights for Missionaries* (Grand Rapids, MI: Baker Books, 1985).

69. Paul G. Hiebert, *Missiological Implications of Epistemological Shifts: Affirming Truth in a Modern/Postmodern World*, Christian Mission and Modern Culture Series (Harrisburg, PA: Trinity Press, 1999). Two books by Paul Hiebert were published posthumously. *Transforming Worldviews: An Anthropological Understanding of How People Change* (Grand Rapids, MI: Baker Academic, 2008). *The Gospel in Human Contexts: Anthropological Explorations for Contemporary Missions* (Grand Rapids, MI: Baker Academic, 2009).

70. Larry Pate, *From Every People: A Handbook of Two-Thirds World Missions with Directory, Histories, and Analysis* (Monrovia, CA: MARC, 1989).

71. Steve S. C. Moon, "The Recent Korean Missionary Movement: A Record of Growth, and More Growth Needed," *International Bulletin of Missionary Research* 27, no. 1 (January 2003): 11–17. Insook Jeong, "Statistic of Missionaries in Various Nations as of 2009 [electronic version] Korean World Mission Association *(KWMA) Newsletter* 17, no. 58 (March 19, 2010): 4.

72. See Hyung Keun Choi, "Preparing Korean Missionaries for Cross-Cultural Effectiveness" (Ph.D. diss., Asbury Theological Seminary, 2000).

73. William D. Taylor, ed., *Internationalising Missionary Training: A Global Perspective* (Exeter, UK: Paternoster Press; Grand Rapids, MI: Baker Book House, 1991); William D. Taylor, *Too Valuable to Lose: Exploring the Causes and Cures of Missionary Attrition* (Pasadena, CA: William Carey Library, 1997); David Harley, *Preparing to Serve: Training for Cross-Cultural Mission* (Pasadena, CA: William Carey Library, 1995); Wilma Davie, "Anthropology in Missions Training," *Training for Cross-Cultural Ministries* 1 (2000): 6–7.

74. Philip Jenkins, *The Next Christendom: The Coming of Global Christianity* (New York: Oxford University Press, 2002).

75. Jon P. Kirby, "Language and Culture Learning IS Conversion . . . IS Ministry: Toward a Theological Rationale for Language and Culture Learning as a Part of Missionary Formation in a Cross-cultural Context," *Missiology: An International Review* 23, no. 2 (1995): 131–43.

76. John C. Haughey, *The Conspiracy of God: The Holy Spirit in Us* (Garden City, NY: Doubleday Image Books, 1973), 7.

77. S. D. Gordon, *Quiet Talks about Jesus, 1: The Purpose of Jesus' Coming*, part 1 (New York: A. C. Armstrong, 1906), 13.

78. Barbara F. Grimes, ed., *Ethnologue: Languages of the World*, 14th ed. (Dallas, TX: SIL, 2000); see http://www.ethnologue.com.

79. David W. Augsburger, *Pastoral Counseling across Cultures* (Philadelphia, PA: Westminster Press, 1986), 18.

4

Inculturation in Africa—
The Way Forward

Aylward Shorter, M.Afr.

In this lecture, Aylward Shorter insists that inculturation is a process that is much more involved with the deeper structures of culture than with mere textual expression. In a second move, he proposes that the way forward in the process of inculturation involves the development of an "ascending Christology," in which the reality of Christ is recognized in the daily experience of African life. Fr. Shorter delivered his lecture on October 6, 2003.

The Nature and Place of
Culture in Evangelization

Louis J. Luzbetak has spoken from time to time of the Vienna school of the legacy of Pater Wilhelm Schmidt.[1] Continuing that tradition, Father Luzbetak's own legacy is to have bequeathed to missionaries the first comprehensive introduction to missiological anthropology and its methods. I believe the message of that handbook is summed up in his words: "The Gospel must be preached to human beings as human beings."[2]

Culture is an attribute of human beings in their diversity, a fact that was more clearly realized in the mid-twentieth century than at any previous time, due to the development of global communication. The link between culture and the gospel as a way of life was emphasized in several documents of the Second Vatican Council, particularly in the magnificent chapter on the particular church in the decree on the church's missionary activity and in the Pastoral Constitution on the Church in the Modern World.[3] Pope Paul VI's synodal exhortation on evangelization in 1975 explicitly addressed the evangelization of culture, an evangelization that was to be profoundly "anthropological" and not superficially semantic.[4] To this cultural understanding of evangelization, Pope John Paul II has added many insights of his own, not least in his letter of 1982 to the Pontifical Council for Culture, when he wrote the memorable words: "A faith which does not become culture is a faith which has not been fully received, not thoroughly thought through, not fully lived out."[5]

Culture is basically a system of meaningful forms that, as Father Luzbetak says, provides human beings with a "shared design for living."[6] It is a set of images, collectively inherited and experienced, that enable human beings to relate to one another in community and to the world in which they live, intellectually, emotionally, and behaviorally. Furthermore, this inheritance gives them a collective identity. Modern anthropologists, in their definitions of culture, stress the importance of ideas or meanings and their influence on human behavior. They also speak of the social control of perception through culture, the fact that we "half create what we perceive."[7] However, they also note the ability of human individuals to "invent" or "reinvent" their culture by appropriating and applying its forms adaptively. Human beings are enculturated in their own society by learning to "play the game of culture," as it were. Culture is thus a historical tradition into which human beings enter, a tradition that usually takes its origins in the interface of a human society with a given physical environment, the interaction of a people and their land.

It is noteworthy that anthropologists have an inclusive understanding of culture. For them, it is the prism through which the human individual perceives and confronts every aspect of experience. It is not confined to the interest of an elite in fine art, music, and literature, for example. It is not the kind of antiquarian interest that an African theologian has labeled "indigenism," the luxury of a concern with the past for its own sake, rather than as an inspiration for a contemporary renaissance, the reinterpretation of ancient forms for the purpose of serving present and future needs.[8]

In the very mild and low-key controversy between the protagonists of the theological terms "inculturation" and "contextualization," Father Luzbetak, with his anthropological training, has opted—along with the majority of Catholic theologians, and the church's own magisterial pronouncements—for the discourse of "culture" rather than of "context." For the anthropological missiologist, the term "culture" does not exclude the political and socioeconomic levels, but rather embraces all the possible cultural levels as well as a multitude of subcultures and microcultures that are legitimate objects of missionary evangelization in the modern world.[9] Anthropologists may be pardoned for feeling that "context" is too vague a term to refer to a basic attribute of humanity, although they readily understand the preference for the discourse of "context" in places where, as happened recently in South Africa, traditional culture was used by a minority regime to hold back the education and social development of the majority.

Culture is not only dynamic, but it is also relational. It is objectively relative, a category of interaction. Although the belief in, and corresponding fear of, cultural relativism is still rife in academic and theological circles, it remains a fact of experience that people of differing cultures communicate and exchange meaningful cultural forms with one another. They can do this not because they break through the barriers of mutually exclusive philosophies or categories of thought, but because cultural language is basically imaginative. Missionary evangelization is able to ride the waves of intercultural contact, because the psychology of the Christian faith is as, John Henry Newman demonstrated, a question of rendering the person of Jesus Christ and the primary symbols of the gospel imaginatively credible to people.[10]

Having reminded ourselves, therefore, of the nature of culture and its relevance to evangelization, I propose now to examine the prospects for African ethnic cultures in an era of globalization and the possibility of global forms of culture developing. After this, I wish to contrast nonverbal with textual emphases in inculturation and then go on to discuss inculturation as an encounter of the gospel with whole cultures. An example of this is provided by the construction of an ascending Christology through the biblical transformation of an African organic universe. This raises the question of the place of the gospel in the African reinvention of culture and leads to a discussion of other forms of ascending Christology, notably in the African urban situation. Finally, I try to draw some conclusions for a future of inculturation that lies firmly in African hands.

The Ethnic Cultures of Africa
in an Era of Globalization

Although sub-Saharan Africa is culturally extremely fragmented, the historic interaction of its ethnic cultures was providentially a preparation for the Christian gospel. At the religious level, there was a truly amazing sharing of beliefs, rituals, and institutions over very wide areas; a sharing that often crossed the frontiers of language and of physical and social ecology. This mutual experience has been sufficiently documented by historians to make the hypothesis of a unified African religion already acceptable in a real sense. However, it was not only in the religious sphere that cultural interaction took place. Anthropologists and missionaries have instinctively recognized the existence of regional groupings of ethnic cultures that share similarities of language, imagery, and organizational structure, however difficult it may be in practice to define the boundaries of such regions.

Colonial governments that made administrative use of traditional authorities and institutions often opposed the desire of missionaries to promote the development of ethnic cultures and to wean them from dehumanizing social practices such as domestic slavery or the denial of liberty to women. It even took some time before they challenged the missionary monopoly of formal education. Although they were ultimately responsible for politicizing African ethnic differences, colonial authorities had a vested interest in maintaining the cultural status quo, and they employed government anthropologists to codify customary law and to set native tradition "in concrete," as it were. Missionaries had a truer understanding of the dynamic character of ethnic cultures. Although, there was plenty of room for racialist prejudice or paternalism, missionaries generally cultivated a positive appreciation of African culture. In spite of the bad name so frequently given to them nowadays, many missionaries were as full of praise for the virtues and endowments of their people as any anthropologist participant observer.[11]

An outstanding example of this is provided by Joseph Dupont (1850–1930), the first Catholic bishop of what are now Zambia and Malawi.[12] Dupont, known to his contemporaries as *Moto Moto*, "Man of Fire," fell in love with the Bemba people at first sight. He admired their open, fearless character, their intelligence, and their fine physique. As a former soldier who had fought in the Franco-Prussian War, Dupont admired the courage and discipline of the Bemba warriors. Not only did he learn the Bemba language, he also entered into the game of internal Bemba politics, and he tried always to meet Bemba expectations of him as healer, prophet, and even magician. He prayed successfully to divert threatening locust swarms. He accompanied the young men on hunting expeditions, during which he taught them the Catholic catechism. And in 1898, when the local paramount died, he accepted the role of successor and protector of the chiefdom. Small wonder that *Moto Moto* is now inseparably part of Bemba tradition and folklore, and that Catholicism is solidly established in Bembaland.

Anthropology, it has been said, is a form of "after-ology," an *a posteriori* reinterpretation of cultural experience. Missionaries, like anthropologists, reflect on their experience of other cultures, discerning structures in order to understand them, and they have taught their African successors to do the same. Structuring of one kind or another is a necessity of systematic knowledge, whatever postmodern critics have to say. However, structural analysis can suggest that the boundaries of ethnic cultures are too hard and fast. As we have seen, history shows them to have been relatively permeable and changeable. In contemporary Africa, the scale and rapidity of cultural interaction has been aggravated by urbanization, population mobility, and the global ecumene, the latter being sustained by a relentless cultural bombardment from the electronic media, a "cumulative colonization" of Africa by the first world.

African inculturation has never been a simple dialogue between the gospel and a pristine rural culture, and this is even less so today, when multicultural situations and experiences are becoming more and more common. At the time of the nineteenth-century antimodernist controversy, it was said that history was the "hair shirt" of theology. Today, urbanization is the "hair shirt" of inculturation; and urbanization—it must be remembered—is a social process that transcends the physical limits of the city. However, without denying the impact of the global cultural flow on urban life or the reality of urban cultural forms, the proverbial urban cultural melting pot is remarkably elusive. The city continues to be an encounter of cultures that retain their essential identity. It is an organization of diversity, not the replication of uniformity. It is an "Irish stew" of recognizable ingredients rather than an anonymous fusion of alloyed metal. The urgency of inculturation in the city is to find an acceptable means of cultural interaction promoting a cultural dialogue of life that enhances humanity and mutual human respect.

The Possibility of a Global Culture

A well-known British anthropologist recently suggested that if there were such a thing as an anthropological index of forbidden books, Samuel P. Huntington's *The Clash of Civilizations and the Remaking of*

World Order should be placed on it.[13] Needless to say, no anthropologist really believes such an index to be desirable, least of all Jonathan Benthall, who made the suggestion. The anachronism was employed to give force to his radical criticism of Huntington. According to Benthall, not only is Huntington's concept of civilization, as the highest unit of analysis below the human species, borrowed from the now outmoded philosopher of history, Arnold Toynbee, but other objections can be raised against his theory. Huntington downplays race, and though he may be right to do the same for secularism, it is surely questionable to equate fundamentalism with authentic religious revival. Worse than this, he completely overlooks the massive growth of global Christianity in the southern hemisphere, while pursuing his thesis that Mohammed will "win out" in the third world.[14]

Although in Huntington's panorama, civilizations simply turn out to be a set of mutually antagonistic tribes, his depiction of Western civilization has no coherence. It is identified with its worst political ideologies as well as its better ones. While he believes the West to be the most powerful civilization, Huntington questions its pretensions to universality, even when these are manifested by the promotion of human rights and genuine democracy. This is scarcely surprising, in view of his prophecy of confrontation and his picture of Western cultural heterogeneity. However, *pace* Benthall, one does not have to espouse Huntington's theories in order to agree with his conclusion that a universal, homogeneous culture is not likely to be imposed on the world by the West, whether Christian or post-Christian.

Ulf Hannerz, the Swedish anthropologist, is a self-confessed postmodernist, but his vision for humanity is infinitely more subtle than that of Huntington.[15] Without denying the force of the global flow, he prefers to observe culture at a microanthropological level. He concentrates on local forms of life, the small-scale everyday activities of ordinary people. This is the real locus of culture, and it has nothing to do with McLuhanite technological determinism or the homogeneous "global village." What is offered to Africa by the global *ecumene* at this level is far from homogeneous. Moreover, Africans are able to reconstruct their cultures selectively. Popular culture draws from many sources and frequently operates on its own terms. In the end, the survival of autonomous and bounded local cultures is a matter of degree, not a question of life or death. What is taking place is the creative response that Hannerz calls "Créolization." Such a picture corresponds with the experience of the urban apostolate in Africa today. Ordinary African town dwellers, especially the youth, appear to be overwhelmed by Euro-American television culture but are in practice creating a popular culture that has many continuities with tradition.

The documents of the Second Vatican Council speak of new and more universal forms of culture that are coming into existence.[16] While this is undoubtedly true as far as it goes, some Catholic theologians have gone further and have predicted the demise of local cultures under the impact of a universal civilization with roots in the Christian West.[17] This is little more than a return to the mid–twentieth-century prophecies of Arnold Toynbee and Christopher Dawson.

Africa's cultural fragmentation is certainly undergoing a measure of rationalization. Some languages and cultures prove not to be viable. Rather than disappear, they tend to coalesce and to take new forms in the light of modern social developments. The process, which was started as a colonial administrative necessity and a matter of missionary pastoral strategy, continues under sociopolitical forces that characterize the independent African state, its early expansion, and current retraction. But it is not the emergence of a Western cultural analogue. Not only is the creation of a rational technical society in Africa unlikely to succeed, but even its future in the West has been deemed by some to be uncertain.[18] Meanwhile in Africa "there lives the dearest freshness deep down things" (to quote the poet Hopkins).[19] African resilience, solidarity, and social creativity continue. Africa may be economically moribund, but its peoples live in happiness and dignity despite the poverty and austerity of their surroundings, and their populations continue to grow in number.

The logic of inculturation defies the replication of uniformity. Instead, it demands the recognition of cultural diversity and the development of a culturally pluriform church. In this, it is being nothing less than realistic. Cultural diversity is a fact of life. It is not doomed to extinction. To be Catholic means to establish a unity in diversity, to love people—as God loves them—in their difference, to accept the prospect of Christian pluriformity. As Pedro Arrupe pointed out at the 1977 Synod of Bishops, failure to do this poses a much greater danger to ecclesial unity than to accept the diversification and local creativity implied by inculturation.[20]

Non-Verbal Inculturation
versus Textual Emphasis

The faster interplay and closer interaction between African languages and cultures, on the one hand, and between them and an asymmetrical global agenda, on the other, makes inculturation an even more urgent concern for Christians. Respect for human cultures demands that they be taken seriously as working systems of meaningful forms—as genuine designs for living. They should not be approached in a piecemeal fashion in which cultural components are taken out of their own milieu and inserted into an alien context. It was perhaps inevitable that the earliest efforts at inculturation should be liturgical, even Eucharistic. Liturgy is an obvious and highly visible facet of Christian life. It was the first concern of the Second Vatican Council, even before the bishops gave their attention to the nature of the church and the relevance of culture. The first recommendations of the Council for liturgical renewal in the so-called mission countries were to insert elements of local culture into the church's sacramental rites. These recommendations were—perhaps understandably—more concerned with the authenticity and relevance of the restored liturgical rites themselves than with the transformation of local cultures by the gospel. In this and, in virtually all the liturgical renewal that followed, there was an overriding preoccupation with the written text.

Granted that scriptures and liturgical books have occupied an all-important place in the traditions of the Western church, and that written texts offer a guarantee of liturgical authenticity that cannot be denied, it must nevertheless be acknowledged that problems arise when such traditions encounter the nonliterate, or most recently literate, cultures of Africa as well as new forms of popular culture in which literacy does not necessarily hold a position of importance. Bible societies and biblical associations in Africa are confronted by the perennial problem of how to communicate the message of the Bible to the illiterate masses. Even when literacy is linked to baptism, there can be a decline in literacy among the baptized.

The popularity of the first African Eucharistic rites owed nothing to the adopted texts. The Ndzon Melen Mass or Cameroon rite started out in 1968 with the texts of the Tridentine Roman Missal and went on to use the 1969 missal and the new lectionary of Pope Paul VI. Its African character did not depend on a text, but rather on the music and choreography of the Beti village reconciliation assembly on which the rite was based. This was a spectacular audio-visual performance that was innately African and participatory.[21] It also corresponded to Paul VI's own vision of an "African Christianity."

When Paul VI came to Kampala in 1969 to close the first meeting of the Symposium of Episcopal Conferences of Africa and Madagascar (SECAM), his speech contained an intriguing set of alternatives. "Must the Church," he asked, "be European, Latin, Oriental . . . or must she be African?"[22] Many of the pope's hearers concluded that he was offering Africa the possibility of her own liturgical rite. Such a possibility was aired at the African Synod of 1994, in either the form of a full-blown African rite, or a special African liturgical region of the Roman Rite. These hopes were unequivocally dashed by Pope John Paul II in the synodal exhortation *Ecclesia in Africa*.[23] That this had not been Paul VI's meaning is borne out by his continuing remarks at Kampala. He went on to speak of the "tongue, the style, the genius and the culture" of Africa as a mode of manifesting the one faith. And he concluded with the oft-quoted words "And in this sense, you may, and you must, have an African Christianity."

The African character of the Ndzon Melen Mass was entirely due to its style, its genius, and its cultural mode of manifestation. The same is true of the Zaire Mass that first appeared in 1974. Its texts were far less important than its musical setting, characteristic dance, vestments, and locally inspired liturgical art. The Zaire Mass offered an audio-visual package that was authentically African and immediately popular. Although, as Raymond Moloney remarked, the Zaire Mass did not textually "break the mould of the Roman Rite," its texts were submitted to a Roman scrutiny, lasting thirteen years.[24] During all this time, the rite remained immensely popular and was celebrated publicly in Zaire and privately in some other African countries. It even inspired projects for a Eucharistic rite in neighboring Tanzania.[25] When it was officially accepted as a legitimate variant of the Roman Rite, it was already a *fait accompli* of inculturation, which the new legal status did little or nothing to enhance.

The same conclusion must be drawn from ordinary Sunday celebrations in African parishes that are liturgically active. Musical creativity and performance, dancing by children and adults, dramatizations of the scripture readings, morality plays that enhance the homily, processions of the Word, and offerings, exuberant gestures of peace giving, colorful costumes, vestments, and decorations, completely relativize the written word on the pages of the Roman Missal. To the liturgical purist, it may be a matter of regret that the Eucharistic prayer is buried beneath a morass of cultural externals and contingencies, but these are not amenable to textual criticism. They belong to a cultural event, a manifestation of the performing arts of Africa, and this is the present and future shape of African liturgical inculturation. Some commentators dismiss drumming, drama, and dance as entirely superficial—at best an early stage of inculturation, at worst a substitute for the genuine article.[26] This is to misjudge them as meaningful forms that open on to an entire nexus or web of cultural meanings.

A draft appendix to the new Roman Missal for English-speaking Africa makes this very point.[27] Certain features are constant in African celebrations: the extensive use of symbols, gestures, and words. People are renewed and strengthened in their identity and their sense of belonging by means of story, song, music, and dance. The Sunday Eucharistic celebration cannot do otherwise than make use of these cultural riches if there is to be full and active liturgical participation.

Another fact has to be noted in this connection. It is that the Catholic Church in Africa is not unaffected by the meteoric rise of Pentecostalism in the continent. Catholic charismatic practice rejoins much that is typical of African traditional celebration and tends to confirm and strengthen it.

The Encounter of the Gospel with Whole Cultures

This approach to liturgical inculturation leans more toward an encounter between gospel and culture than does mere textual creativity, and such an encounter is the essence and justification of inculturation. A superficial and piecemeal process by which the Roman liturgy is garnished with souvenirs of African culture does not constitute such an encounter. But a truly African celebration of the Roman Rite in which the African element is primarily nonverbal may open a doorway onto a whole view of life and way of thought that is authentically African. Inculturation is basically the encounter between the gospel of Jesus Christ, on the one hand, and whole cultures on the other. The gospel illuminates and transforms culture, while culture reexpresses and even—to a certain extent—reinterprets the gospel. We may expect to find such an encounter in the process of theological reformulation, particularly when it takes the form of homiletics and catechetics.

More than two decades have elapsed since the publication of Thomas Christensen's brilliant exposition of *An African Tree of Life*.[28] This consisted in the Christian transformation of the organic universe of a remote rural people, the Gbaya of the Cameroon-Central African frontier. As such, it is a classic of uncomplicated, one to one, inculturation, which may now be a thing of the past. Christensen's interpretation, however, did not monopolize Gbaya culture, and it remains a *locus classicus* for understanding the meaning of such an encounter.

A semiotic analysis of the structure of Gbaya signs revealed that the root-symbol of the Gbaya is the *soré* tree. The whole web of meaning that underlies Gbaya culture is centered on this ordinary little tree, called by them "the cool thing." A branch from this tree is used ritually to overcome the threat of death in cases of bloodfeud or the breaking of taboos that entail the sanction of death. It helps them cope with their consciousness of sin and takes them through the threat of death into a new life. It is therefore very much "a tree of life." Both Christensen and the Gbaya saw in the *soré* an analogy with the cross of Christ as the means of salvation in Christianity. They therefore interpreted the whole *soré* symbolic complex in the light of a Christian theology of the cross.

The association of *soré* with the crucified Jesus was first made by Gbaya Christian preachers themselves. It was a search for theological meaning evoked by evangelization. This led to the reflection that if *soré* is so important to the Gbaya, what does Jesus Christ have to do with *soré*? The answer is that the cross is the link. It is the symbol of all that God has done for us in and through Jesus. The cross is thus the fulfilment of *soré*, transforming and enhancing its meaning.

Christensen examined all the life contexts in which *soré* played a role. These included ritual meals and sacrifices, purification in life-crisis rituals, blood pacts, marriage, dancing, hunting, conflict resolution, justice and peace, vows, promises, exorcisms, funerals, prophecy, and house moving. He then examined biblical and patristic tree symbolism and particularly the tree of life image as applied to the cross. This reached a climax in the thirteenth-century writings of St. Bonaventure.

When the Gbaya *soré* meanings are applied to the cross of Jesus, they bring a metaphorical newness to Christian teaching but are themselves transcended by the reality of salvation wrought by Christ. The Gbaya believe that God is at work in *soré*. The application, therefore, of this symbol to Jesus draws attention to his divinity. *Soré* is the symbol of life and the transmission of life through the covenant of love that is marriage. It is therefore an apt symbol of the love of God revealed in Jesus Christ, the Word of life. The use of *soré* in the washing rituals at Gbaya funerals is the means by which the bereaved return to normal life. Christensen shows their relevance to the "water of life" in Christian baptism. The prominence of *soré* in meals of reconciliation lends itself to a Eucharistic application with the "Bread of Life." Many parallels can therefore be found between Gbaya culture and Christian salvation theology. Moreover, this Christian transformation of Gbaya culture sets the scene for particular Gbaya inculturations of the image of Jesus himself and of the Christian sacraments.

Maia Green, an anthropologist working among Pogoro Catholics in southern Tanzania, records another and more recent example of an African theology. The Pogoro people are massively Catholic, but in spite of authoritarian church structures and official moral conservatism, they have developed their own theological nuances. Traditionally, Pogoro women engender power through the management of fertility at puberty rituals and the removal of death pollution at funerals. These roles have inspired a popular female religiosity focused on the Blessed Virgin Mary as the compassionate and bereaved mother of Jesus.[29] Without any doubt, there are many more such instances of fruitful encounter between gospel and culture in contemporary Africa, that are—as yet—unrecorded.

Ascending Christology— Transforming the African Organic Universe

African ethnic religions are typically "religions of nature." That does not mean that they are nature religions, in which natural phenomena, as such, are objects of worship. It means that created nature offers both an explanation of the Divine and at the same time the means of contact with divine reality. In African religion, the physical environment is not only sacred, but also constitutes an organic universe. In other words, nature is biologically continuous with humanity, and it connects human beings with the world of spirit. Christensen's inculturation of the Gbaya organic universe is what Monika Hellwig has called "an ascending Christology."[30] Christ has ascended through all the spheres and "has placed all things under his feet" (Eph 1:22). In other words, by becoming human and through the mystery of his death and resurrection, Christ has brought about a cosmic rebirth. In this new world order, humanity and created nature—which is the setting of human life—have been reattached to

God. The physical environment can therefore speak to us not only about God the Creator, but also about the redemption wrought for us by Christ.

About twenty years before Christensen's book appeared, I published the results of a homiletic experiment among the Kimbu people of southern Tanzania in which I applied the Kimbu choric story format to a series of Sunday sermons.[31] Through this means, I explored the possibilities of dialogue between biblical themes and certain aspects of the Kimbu organic universe. The most ambitious of these homilies was one that used the solar symbolism that the Kimbu apply to God and that developed it with reference to biblical solar symbolism and the New Testament salvation themes of light and darkness. Although even thirty years ago the Kimbu region was not culturally homogeneous, the Kimbu organic universe corresponded to a fairly general perception of people then living there. My experiment was, therefore, another classic example of ascending Christology, which had yet to submit to the "hair shirt" of urbanization and the far-reaching social processes of population mobility.

The Place of the Gospel in the African Reinvention of Culture

What then is the *modus operandi* of inculturation in the rapidly changing Africa described at the beginning of this lecture? We can draw three conclusions so far: (1) Africans are reinventing culture in the forms of ordinary life, even though these are influenced by the global flow of ideas and values; (2) more attention is to be paid to forms and style than to the formulation of hard and fast texts; and (3) a genuine encounter must take place between the gospel and these forms of life, taken as a whole. A useful precedent was set in the 1970s with the production of a religious education syllabus for secondary schools in eastern Africa.[32] The Gaba Syllabus was one of the most impressive and far-reaching religious education programs ever attempted in Africa. Even this experiment placed too much reliance on a text and not enough emphasis on the training and talents of the teachers who used it. In Uganda, it continued in use for a long time, and it influenced further developments in religious education in Kenya, Tanzania, and Zambia, as well as in other African countries. The syllabus, which was called *Christian Living Today*, was the product of a series of international and ecumenical workshops that aimed at producing material for the final two years of senior secondary school or sixth form college—in effect, for young adults. The visible product was an attractive two-volume classroom text that could be used by both pupils and teachers.

What is relevant for our discussion here is not the text itself and its inevitable limitations over the course of time but the method that it employed. To begin with, the syllabus was addressed to educated young men and women from all over East and Central Africa and it did so in their own cultural setting, their own form of life and expectations of life. It was not tied to any particular ethnic tradition, though it made reference to many such traditions, and to the interaction taking place between them. Rather, it concentrated on the shared subcultures of youth and the emerging professional classes of Africa that these pupils were being prepared to join. There was no particular emphasis on the transient culture of the secondary school. Rather, the emphasis was on the adult community for which the school served as a threshold. The syllabus did not offer its readers a blueprint for Christian living or a ready-made formula for Christian life in contemporary Africa. Instead of such a recipe, it offered a list of ingredients, out of which African young adults could construct their own culture.

The Gaba syllabus was thematic. It took fifteen general life themes, beginning with that of sociocultural change. Within these themes, it analyzed the contemporary situation, the structural changes taking place, the continuities with the past, and the relevance of Africa's cultural heritage. Then it examined the historical experiences of Christianity in the region and deepened its findings in the light of biblical revelation. Through this method, it offered the pupil a range of Christian understandings as well as a series of moral choices and alternatives. Finally, it was left to the students to make their own cultural and theological synthesis, individually and in shared discussion. It was up to them to reinvent their culture in this changing situation. They were the ones who had to discover their identity as Africans and Christians. The syllabus gave them the tools, the materials, and the orientations, but the faith response was their own.

My suggestion is that the church should operate like this syllabus at all levels of society, offering people the ingredients for a synthesis of their own making. The church can help in their cultural reeducation, reminding them of cultural continuities with the past, as well as of cultural possibilities in the future. Pastors can point out the congruence between this changing culture and the gospel of Jesus Christ. It is up to the people of

Africa, in their own cultural situations, to discern the features of a Christ that is both human and divine, in other words, to formulate and to live their own ascending Christology.

An objection that is frequently raised in this kind of discussion is that inculturation has always taken place throughout church history without it having to be a self-conscious process. The apostles did not write or speak about inculturation. The early Christians felt no need of a council for culture. Even though there was ongoing debate about disengagement from Jewish religious culture, and Paul could air his acquaintance with minor Greek poets when addressing the academics of the Areopagus, there was no conscious or systematic dialogue with the cultures of Greece and Rome. Even the polemics of the Apologist Fathers of the second and third centuries were a somewhat one-sided Christian manipulation of the classical heritage. The ongoing inculturation of the gospel in the early church did not depend on such academic feats. It was a subconscious process that was taken for granted at the time but that could be delineated centuries later by modern patristic scholars such as Jaroslav Pelikan.[33]

For ourselves, in our time, inculturation has to be a self-conscious process. There are several reasons for this. One is that culture is a twentieth-century discovery. We can no longer be satisfied with the classicist conception of a universal monoculture, especially after the historical collapse of Christendom and the kaleidoscopic spectacle of rapidly changing cultures in varying relationships. More persuasive still are the consequences of decolonization. We are still just emerging from a colonial era in which Western colonial powers made assumptions about a cultural superiority that gave them the right to dominate and undermine the cultures of others. Christian missionaries adopted the same assumptions all too easily, placing the evangelization process in jeopardy and risking a very real alienation of Christianity in the African continent. Inculturation has to become a conscious program, a necessity of pastoral planning, if we are not to slip back mindlessly into old attitudes on the part of evangelizers and evangelized. We have to ensure that evangelization takes place in a human manner.

Another objection to the contemporary concern with inculturation is that it is impossible in a situation of secularism. This is not the case. Africans have never been innoculated against secularism, now or in the past. It is true that Western post-Christian secularism is especially intractable, not because of indifference, but because of its overt hostility to the church. The latter is associated in many people's minds with painful childhood memories, for example, or with the countercultural discipline of celibacy for priests and religious that contradicts the supreme value of modern secular society, which is the individual's right to the pleasures of sex. Africa has yet to reach this stage. Yet even if it does, experience shows that in such cases of hostility, human values can be uncovered in popular culture that offer genuine elements of divine truth or "seeds of the gospel," and that dialogue is possible.[34]

Ascending Christology in the African Urban Parish

I have long upheld the argument that the parish is the essential vehicle for inculturation in Africa. This is eminently true, even when it wears the "hair shirt" of urbanization. For more than twenty years, I have been associated with a densely populated slum parish in the Eastlands of Nairobi City, the capital of Kenya. Out of a church-going population of around seven thousand, some fifteen hundred parishioners are members of base communities that assist the parish pastoral team to animate the pastoral self-care of the parish. The primary experience of these communities, on which all else is based, is that of the weekly meeting. These meetings are focused on the Bible and its interpretation, especially its application to the people's own life situations. They are helped in this task by a networking team of visitors or specialist animators from the parish level. These are called in Swahili *wakolezaji*, "those who give flavor to food." They are, in other words, the "salt" of the parish.

With their help and using a weekly reading of the Bible, the base communities of the parish begin to understand the humanity of Jesus from their own experience of being human. Jesus is their "Brother," and in their concern for social justice and in their compassion for the poor, the sick, and the stranger, they celebrate the compassion and healing activity of Jesus. Through this understanding, they learn what it means to be human, while living in the inhuman conditions of the slum and squatter areas of the parish. Once again, they fashion an ascending Christology. From the humanity of Jesus, they rise to an intuition of his divinity that illuminates and reinterprets their urban way of life.

This experience does not, however, begin and end with meetings of the base communities. It extends to the entire community of celebration focused on the parish center. The base communities are the core of a participatory and collaborative parish structure. They coordinate the liturgical and other activities of a multiethnic population. They help parishioners to transcend the human frontiers of language and culture, and to integrate their cultural contributions within the parish celebrations, dramatizations, and festivities. They bring their cultural insights to bear on the Christian initiation of children and adults and on the great liturgies of Holy Week, Eastertide, and Pentecost. They contribute music, dance, and drama to these occasions and facilitate the participation of all, even those who are not members of the base communities. All these activities are the self-conscious fruit of discussion, debate, and planning in the parish. People become aware of the possibilities from the *wakolezaji* and from the sharing that takes place within and between the base communities, but the synthesis is ultimately their own.

What we are witnessing, therefore, in the activities of such a parish, is the realization, in a lived urban setting, of the method of the Gaba Syllabus. The church offers the ingredients, cultural and biblical, as well as the required flavor, but the recipe belongs to those who do the actual cooking. Even in the modern urban situation, inculturation can be brewed in an African pot! This is a form of inculturation that obeys the criteria already identified in this lecture: the need to address the levels of ordinary human life, the emphasis on forms and styles—in this case widely shared among different ethnic traditions—and the discernment of an ascending Christology from a whole spectrum of life—a genuine encounter of gospel and culture.

The Future of Inculturation in African Hands

Inculturation comes from below. This is how it is taking place in Africa today and how it will continue to take place. Inculturation is in the hands of the African people. They are carrying it forward without the need for a blueprint handed down to them from above, let alone from the outside. Once given self-confidence and the understanding and opportunity to inculturate the gospel, they are fully equipped by their faith to carry it forward. Leadership is needed to stimulate their initiative, to give them this self-confidence, and to provide the opportunity in parish life. Inculturation, as Pedro Arrupe reminded us in 1978, is a creative process. It results in a "new creation," a new way of being Christian and living the gospel. Therefore creativity is at a premium. Creative people must be hunted out and creative talents nurtured. In Africa, this means primarily music, dance, poetry, and drama. There is need for a penetrating discernment, a thorough appropriation of both culture and gospel, as Pope Paul VI pointed out in *Evangelii Nuntiandi*. This is not a mere question of verbal translation.

Inculturation also requires a sensitivity to achievements in other communities and particular churches—the ability to learn from their example and their insights. One must be strongly aware of the tradition of faith that goes back to the earthly Jesus and the many forms it has taken throughout the history of the church. Above all, the African practitioner of inculturation has to eschew all piecemeal "pick and mix" approaches. Even in the postmodern situation, Christians are still confronted by whole cultural systems and the challenge to reinvent them so that they can be transformed by the gospel of Christ. Culture, like language, is the organization of diversity. Everyone, knowingly and unknowingly, participates in the ongoing invention of language. Likewise, all may contribute to an ongoing Christian design for living in postmodern Africa.

Conclusion

Planning a Sunday liturgy in an African parish or rehearsing a Bible play with an African youth group teaches one a great deal about the future of inculturation in Africa and the methods it is likely to employ. The ideas that are shared emerge from an encounter between faith and the experience of real life. Contemporary life and culture are used to discover meaning in the symbols of the liturgy and in the stories of the Bible. They are the hermeneutical tools. Everything is focused on a local form of life, on everyday life as it is lived in a real community, an actual neighborhood. The method is far from sophisticated, but it respects the cultural forms it invokes, their multiplicity, mutuality, and meaning. "Créolization" may be regarded as an ugly word, but it suggests the paradoxical heterogeneity and simplicity of the process. At times, the mixture takes a linguistic form, like Créole itself, which is a simplified and Africanized form of French. In the Nairobi slum parish mentioned above, the Kenyan slum language, known as *Sheng*, reflects the intercultural exchanges that take place there as well as the impact of global influences. It was a shock when I heard it used in church for the first time, but I reflected afterwards that this was part of the creative reinvention of African culture and that it epitomized the contemporary process of inculturation in Africa.

Notes

1. For example, Louis J. Luzbetak, *The Church and Cultures* (Maryknoll, NY: Orbis Books, 1988), 61–63.

2. Ibid., 44.

3. AG 22; GS 53, 58.

4. Pope Paul VI, Apostolic Exhortation, *Evangelii Nuntiandi*, 63.

5. Pope John Paul II, Address to the Italian National Congress of the Ecclesial Movement for Cultural Commitment, January 16, 1982, *L'Osservatore Romano*, English ed. (June 28, 1982): 1–8.

6. Luzbetak, *The Church and Cultures*, 156.

7. William Wordsworth, "Tintern Abbey," in *A Choice of Wordsworth's Verse*, ed. R. S. Thomas (London: Faber and Faber), 24.

8. See Jean-Marc Ela, *Ma Foi d'Africain* (Paris: Editions Karthala); English ed. *My Faith as an African*, trans. John Pairman Brown and Susan Perry (Maryknoll, NY: Orbis Books, 1988).

9. Gerald A. Arbuckle, *Earthing the Gospel: A Handbook of Inculturation* (Maryknoll, NY: Orbis Books, 1990), 18.

10. John Henry Newman, *An Essay in Aid of a Grammar of Assent* (1870; reprint Notre Dame, IN: University of Notre Dame Press, 1979).

11. Two examples are the missionary bishops Adolphe Lechaptois in Tanzania and Joseph Dupont in Zambia-Malawi.

12. See Henri Pineau, *Evêque-Roi des Brigands: Monseigneur Joseph Dupont Premier Vicaire Apostolique du Nyassa 1850–1930* (Paris: Missionaries of Africa, 1937).

13. Jonathan Benthall, "Imagined Civilizations?" *Anthropology Today* 18, no. 6 (December 2002): 1–2; Samuel P. Huntington, *The Clash of Civilizations and the Remaking of World Order* (New York: Simon and Schuster, 1996).

14. Philip Jenkins, *The Next Christendom—The Coming of Global Christianity* (New York: Oxford University Press, 2002).

15. Ulf Hannerz, *Cultural Complexity: Studies in the Social Organization of Meaning* (New York: Columbia University Press, 1992).

16. See, for example, GS 54.

17. Joseph Cardinal Ratzinger, "In the Encounter of Christianity and Religions, Syncretism Is Not the Goal," *L'Osservatore Romano* 17, no. 26 (April 1995): 5–8.

18. Serge Latouche, "What the West Can Learn from Africa," Interview, *Zenit.org*, Venice, Italy, October 5, 2002.

19. Gerard Manley Hopkins, "God's Grandeur," *Collected Poems* (Oxford: Oxford University Press, 1949), 70.

20. Pedro Arrupe, *African Ecclesial Review* 20, no. 1 (1978): 32–33.

21. P. Abega, "Liturgical Adaptation," in *Christianity in Independent Africa*, ed. E. Fashole-Luke et al. (London: Rex Collings, 1978), 597–605. The author of this lecture assisted at the Ndzon Melen Mass in Yaounde in 1972.

22. Paul VI, Kampala Address, in *Modern Missionary Documents and Africa*, ed. R. Hickey (Dublin: Dominican Publications, 1982), 203.

23. Pope John Paul II, *Ecclesia in Africa*, 59.

24. Raymond Moloney, "The Zairean Mass and Inculturation," *Worship* 62, no. 5 (1988): 433–42.

25. Tanzania National Committee for Cultural Research, *Mtindo wa Ibada ya Misa kwa Nchi ya Tanzania*, mimeographed, Eldoret, Kenya, 1977.

26. See Namibian Catholic Archbishop Bonifatius Haushiku in a *New York Times* article by Alan Cowell, May 1, 1994, quoted in Jenkins, *The Next Christendom*, 115.

27. "Working Draft Special Appendix" (unpublished manuscript). I am grateful to Rev. Rinaldo Ronzani, MCCJ, for sharing this draft with me.

28. Thomas Christensen, *An African Tree of Life* (Maryknoll, NY: Orbis Books, 1990).

29. Maia Green, *Priests, Witches and Power: Popular Christianity after Mission in Southern Tanzania* (Cambridge: Cambridge University Press, 2003).

30. Monica Hellwig, "Christologies Emerging from Small Christian Communities," in *Small Christian Communities: Imagining Future Church*, ed. Robert S. Pelton (Notre Dame, IN: University of Notre Dame Press, 1997), 27–34.

31. Aylward Shorter, "Form and Content in the African Sermon: An Experiment," *African Ecclesiastical Review* 11, no. 3 (1969): 265–79.

32. Richard Kiley et al., *Christian Living Today*, 2 vols. (London: Geoffrey Chapman, 1974).

33. Jaroslav Pelikan, *Jesus through the Centuries: His Place in the History of Culture* (New Haven, CT: Yale University Press, 1985).

34. Bishops' Conference of England and Wales, *Reflections* (photocopy, 1993).

5

Anthropology, Mission, and the African Woman

Linda E. Thomas

Speaking from her perspective as an African American woman and trained anthropologist, Dr. Linda Thomas suggests that a Lucan rather than a Matthean perspective is more appropriate for doing mission today. Rather than going and converting (Mt 28), Christians are called to be with people and receive from them (Lk 9–10). It is with this more open stance that Christians participate best in the missio Dei. *Dr. Thomas's lecture was delivered on October 25, 2004.*

I thank you for inviting me, a theologian of African descent and a woman, to speak about our Christian tradition of "proclaiming the gospel in 'distant' lands." I pray that the spirit of transformation and liberation will be present as we spend time together this afternoon.

I come to the task of understanding and analyzing mission from a hermeneutic of plurality.[1] With thanks to scholars such as Louis Luzbetak, who started to pave the way, I am glad to see academia increasingly coming around to embrace or at least be more honest about the ways context, cultural and otherwise, influences our work as scholars.

I work from my many contexts, and thus I consider myself a multidisciplined scholar. I approach this project first from my social location. I am a black woman, living in a country infused with racism, classism, sexism, and heterosexism. Generations long ago and now have suffered, resisted, and overcome centuries of atrocities still done by mostly men in the Western Christian tradition in the name of God or *missio Dei.*

I work as a black woman but with the juxtaposition of being an African American Christian woman ordained in the United Methodist

Church. I am called to the *missio Dei*, to evangelize, to witness to Christ's presence. I work necessarily from a place of tension and complexity: a hermeneutic of plurality.

Adding to the list, I approach the work as an African American ordained Christian theologian in the womanist tradition. Enough said—almost. I am also an anthropologist.

In this lecture, I use an ethnographic methodology to examine what second-, third-, fourth-, and fifth-generation African Christians have to say about mission on their continent. *Missio Dei* so often comes from what we know as the "Great Commission" (Mt 28:16–20)—words, by the way, that do not appear in the passage itself. The Great Commission, as interpreted in the West, commands Christians to go all over the world telling people about their God and teaching Western ways.

This approach to entering a new community, culture, or religion does not work with my approach to anthropology and mission. Rather, the method I use, both for understanding *missio Dei* and conducting research, better fits with Luke's version of *missio Dei* (Lk 9:1–9, 10:1–10). Here, Jesus sends the disciples out but not with an agenda of telling about Jesus. No, he sends his disciples with no bag, no food, not much at all. Jesus sends them out not to call people to receive Christ. Quite contrarily, Jesus sends them to stand both hungry and tired at the door of the stranger with the hope that the good people of the house or the street will receive them, feed them, and save the disciples from the elements.

This is the approach I take as a theologian trained in anthropology. In my work, I am missionized, a concept to which I will return later in this lecture. I come to the persons and communities and diaries and songs of Africans in order to listen. As an anthropologist, I cannot be a community member; I am a guest, privileged to privilege the voices of Africans and their histories of Christian mission. I look not to the colonists or the European priests. I look to the people who did not need to file reports detailing how many persons they baptized. I listen closely for the voices that can save me and you from repeating the inexcusable violence that so dominates what we call *missio Dei*. Let us be missionized this day.

I rely on sources whose voice respects the pluralities and dynamism of African religiosity, culture, and philosophy. More specifically, I privilege those voices that for far too long have not and are not yet given the authority due them. We will be missionized today by the voices of African women.

Critical liberation theology and, may I dare say, Jesus speak theological truth to power from the street, the AIDS clinic, the battlefield—all those places we see on mission advertisements, on glossy fundraising posters, all those places we can pretend are "over there."

My training and my experience of the spirit of God compel me to give authority to the voices and experiences of those trapped by structures that cause perpetual poverty and pervasive oppression. (Last time I checked, that's who Jesus was. He did not reach down to the poor; he was poor—a subtle difference overlooked for millennia.) Today, the statisticians tell us that African women are at the top—the top of the list of the bottom, that is. Of the United Nations' list of most impoverished nations and people, women across the continent of Africa top the list of the most poor, the least educated, and those with the least access to power—political, domestic, economic, social, and simply the power to turn on a light bulb.

As Cameroonian theologian Louise Tappa puts it, the African woman "incarnates the mass of the poor and the oppressed."[2] How right she is. Fifty-eight percent of women living in sub-Saharan Africa have HIV/AIDS. Forty percent of the pregnant women in Botswana have been infected with HIV and/or are living with full-blown AIDS.[3] In some countries, the ratio of infection in girls and boys is as high as 6:1—with six girls infected for every boy.

During the civil war in Liberia, men raped at least 40 percent of the women in Liberia. According to the United Nations, rape and sexual slavery have been among the most common war crimes. Women who became pregnant as a result were frequently turned to the street, rejected by their husbands, and ostracized by their families.[4] The World Health Organization (WHO) launched a major program to reach thousands of women in North Darfur in an effort to learn the extent of rape crimes. Every single girl or woman had been raped by a man—often men—or they knew someone who had been raped. WHO reports rape as a crime of terror and states that no girl or woman is safe.

WHO has named the rates of death while giving childbirth an "invisible epidemic." In Africa, and elsewhere, women are one hundred times more likely to die in childbirth than in wealthy countries like the United States. And even this startling number is unrealistic as WHO reports that only 50 percent of deaths during childbirth are reported.

Tappa recognizes the Jesus of the gospels not as a man reaching down to help "those poor people." Instead, she proclaims that Jesus is one of "those poor people," one of "those African women."

The spirit of Jesus is the same spirit of African women. In their most radical suffering is where God may be found. Tappa states, "I believe that when [the African] woman has really come to understand the message of liberation that Jesus bears, she will be able to take her brothers by the hand and lead them to the way of liberation that is ours."[5] To whom do we listen, to whom do we look to missionize us? Today we must listen to the women of Africa in order that we, too, might be liberated and saved from the historical malpractice of the *missio Dei*.

Liberation Defined

Let me speak plainly. Christians—well intended for the most part—have jacked up (pardon me), they have erred sometimes, to understand and devote their lives to the *missio Dei*. A close reading of just about any classical theology, so-called orthodox theology, supports the notion of *missio Dei* as being one of telling, curing, saving, doing something to people who believe differently about the cosmos and all that is in it. At the end of the day, historical *missio Dei*—and one trip to Google.com will indicate that "historical" includes yesterday and right now—has been about telling others that we have the keys to the kin-dom. They have got to get on board with the program, and we can teach "them." All we need are a few Bibles, some guns, sexually transmitted diseases, Western social structures, education, proper clothing, oppressive sexual mores, and patriarchal church structures.

When I listen to those whose continent has been cut up by well-intended Christian men, chopped apart in ways that cause famine, I hear movement. I hear the spirit of African women—no less than the spirit of God—moving out from under the systemic poverty, sexism, and racism that were planted inside the missionizing churches. I hear a movement. I've witnessed it in South Africa—a movement of liberation.

Today, the only *missio Dei* must have liberation at its core. It is, of course, the message in which our scriptures are soaked. Biblically, from Isaiah to Luke to Revelation, the history of the people of God tells of a God who liberates. Using Trinitarian language, liberation is the work of the spirit. The spirit creates, liberates, and sustains. *Ruach* never stops making something new or making something happen. The question at hand is who among us will slow down enough to listen to this good news, or who among us will sit at the feet of the women of Sudan, of Chad, or of Uganda or of Nigeria to hear their good news?

The good news must identify most plainly with liberation. The spirit liberates; that's her vocation. She liberates from unjust situations and systems. Unjust situations and systems try to contain the unruly spirit and her people. Such systems and structures erect barriers and perpetuate violence toward women. They deny that women's bodies reflect the image of God, that humanity's essential power is to create, to generate, to produce/reproduce. Unjust situations and systems cannot contain the indwelling spirit.

In Hebrew, she is *Ruach*, the God who continually creates life anew. According to the priestly tradition, all it took was her breath to call the cosmos into being. The creeds name her the Giver of Life, in Greek *Zoopoion*, the "Maker," the "Poet" of Life. In Greek, *pneuma*, spirit, is the source of Jesus' power to restore life; indeed, *pneuma* resurrected him. When he expired and breathed his last, the *Spiritus*, in Latin, inspired his dry bones by conspiring with him. This spirit, the liberator, has and does exterminate the situations and systems that fear new creation brought about by conspiracy. This spirit of God "keeps going and going and going," overturning tables (often in the temples) and healing on the Sabbath (in spite of our erected churches). This is scary stuff for any neatly packaged evangelistic mission trip.

The spirit demands liberation, and she lives in us. Ghanaian theologian Mercy Amba Odoyoye sees clearly and writes, "All limitations to the fullness of life envisaged in the Christ Event ought to be completely uprooted."[6] She appropriates to her context these words that Jesus appropriated from Isaiah. Let us receive, be missionized, by the African woman whose breath speaks these words of liberative *missio Dei*:

> The poor will hear good news.
> Those who are depressed will feel the comfort that
>   stimulates action;
> Those who are oppressed will be encouraged and
>   enabled to free themselves
>
> Abilities rather than disabilities will be what counts [sic].
> All who are blind to their own and others' oppression
>   will come to new insights

And God will pardon all at the jubilee.
It will be a new beginning for all.
That is liberation.[7]

The Concept of the African Woman

The spirit that is God is the same spirit that blends herself within our tissues and tendons to wrap up her life with ours. The transcendent spirit that creates heaven and earth is also immanent, indwelling, and indivisible in our midst. The immanent spirit is multicultural, multivalent, and multi-faceted. This makes the spirit allusive, hard to define, and very unconventional. Situations and systems that prefer a restrictive order would do well to learn that the spirit is not monomorphic. She moves from person to person, dwelling with the chaff and the wheat. The spirit is not interested in monopoly, monotony, or monogamy—metaphorically speaking.

As a womanist anthropologist, I witness the plurality of the spirit across vastly different social contexts. I witness the plurality of the spirit in the grand variety of African women. There is no monolithic African woman. Kenyan ethicist Nyambura J. Njoroge writes, "African women theologians have acknowledged that there is nothing like 'the African Woman': rather there are broad influences in Africa that condition women's lives with varying degrees of success."[8] The spirit dwells in African women but does not control or constrict the person or power of any African woman. Indeed, spirit and body conspire to create diversity.

The *missio Dei* must not only understand but also honor the *imago Dei* made manifest across the diverse cultures of Africa. All African women are made in the image of God. In the words of the African women theologians and ethicists in the Circle of Concerned African Women, the *missio Dei* is best fulfilled when it examines "the socio-economic and political situation in Africa through women's experiences."[9] Thus my approach to missiology recognizes that the transcendent spirit finds expression, creatively and immanently, in the vast array of beliefs, customs, and ways of living among African women. Likewise, the transcendent spirit knows intimately that economic, political, and social systems and situations oppress African women and do violence to the *imago Dei* that is each African woman. Oppression of African women is "transgeographical."[10] Oppression of African women is the oppression of God's own image and energy.

Fashioning a Theory for a Womanist Approach to Mission

A womanist approach to mission employs Alice Walker's definition of "womanist" in her text *In Search of Our Mothers' Gardens*. That definition, laid out in four parts, suggests that a womanist is both "bold and audacious," as well as "courageous and willful." Womanists know what it takes to have their voices heard in a culture and religious environment that does not want to hear the truth a womanist has to tell. A womanist appreciates the variety of life in our world and also sees that "nature" is created. It is a construct with power. A womanist loves her whole body as it bears the image of God; she owns her sexuality. A womanist expresses freely a range of emotional feelings and chooses intentionally to live as a relational being. With all she has to do, a womanist loves herself enough to make it a priority to take care of herself. Finally, womanism is different from feminism. In the words of Walker, "womanist is to feminist as purple to lavender."[11]

Theologian Dwight Hopkins claims that "Walker's four-part definition contains aspects of (1) tradition; (2) community; (3) self, nature, and the Spirit; and (4) criticism of white feminism."[12] In this sense, a womanist is one who recognizes that she is created in the image of God (i.e., the *imago Dei*). Once she is conscious of her positive relationship to the divine, she celebrates this by taking the good news of liberation to others (i.e., the *missio Dei*).

A womanist theologian, then, privileges the voices and gives authority to the perspective and experience of women of African descent. This lecture focuses on African women as they are some of the most impoverished and powerful women in our world. The approach to mission is to be missionized, to listen to the testimony, to witness the spirit of God in action, and to resist the desire to proclaim, tell, or contest. We must be saved by these women and through their experience as the hands and feet of the Lord in whose name we have forcibly baptized. These women know a thing or two about insurrection, resurrection, and life everlasting. They survive and subvert systems with wisdom and courage that "shock and awe." My role as a womanist theologian and anthropologist, then, is to release the voices of those whose stories are untold.

The Suppression of African Women's Voices

Diverse African women denounce the daily experience of systematic oppression. Scholars in the Circle of Concerned African Women call for resistance and proclaim liberation. In the introduction of their book *Groaning in Faith: African Women in the Household of God*, Musimbi R. A. Kanyoro and Nyambura J. Njoroge write, "In the deep pain of exclusion, domination and marginalization, we have the voices of wise women urging us to speak out and tell our stories, for which we alone hold the copyright."[13]

Kanyoro and Njoroge's book brings the voices of African women in East and Southern Africa to the public sphere so that others will come to know the "double reality of pain and faith experienced on the African continent."[14] African culture and Christian religion live in relationship, a relationship that is often tenuous and sometimes salvific. Secular and sacred influence one another. On paper, that may sound like a positive movement toward syncretism in the best sense of the word. The authors expose the double edge of the culture/religion dynamic: like attracts like. "Non-liberating cultural values, which are oppressive to women," meet "like" notions in religion to increase rhetoric that restricts, represses, and reinforces systems that do violence to the *imago Dei* of African women.[15] Too often, the combined power structures preach and teach the historically entrenched notion that women's *imago Dei* is a bit dimmer than men's.

The *imago Dei* of African women will not allow such destructive teaching to remain. The spirit, *imago Dei*, embodied in African women supplies the power to proclaim a different version of the good news—that any oppressive religious and cultural system or situation is simply wrong.

As outlined earlier, this is where the spirit transcendent and immanent does her work. African women gather to contest, conjure, conspire, and call on the spirit of God who has already started the work. Kanyoro and Njoroge offer a collection of stories of African women acting to insurrect, resurrect, inspire, in spite of what missionaries in union with culture teach.

Women can look elsewhere for the good news—to Isaiah, Jesus, and African scholar Mercy Amba Odoyoye. There is power—the power that created the heavens and earth, the power of the spirit that dwells inextricably in her people in the prophecy. The Word promises that the poor will finally hear good news, that the oppressed will free themselves, that oppressors will find a new way, and that it is time for the jubilee. That is the kind of good news that Kanyoro and Njoroge claim can inspire "new ways of relating," give power to refuse to accept "oppression and indignity," and give birth to faith communities, *koinonia*—*koinonia* African style.[16]

African Scholars' Reflections about Missionaries and the Impact of Christian Missions on Africa

Let us hear now some voices of African persons who tell us the history and experience of Christian mission. We begin with a story I first heard from Archbishop Desmond Tutu, a third generation African Christian, and heard again recently from Randall Robinson, an African American lawyer, author, and former head of TransAfrica. Pay attention because it is a short story. "When the missionaries came to us, we had the land and they had the Bibles. We reverently bowed our heads to pray. When we concluded our prayer and looked up, we had the Bibles, and the missionaries had the land."

This parable tells the truth the way parables tend to do—by shocking listeners from their comfort zone and rousing the cozy out of tradition. I find myself amazed at the resistance toward listening to the truth in such narratives. In many Christian communities this parable would be considered exaggeration—created only for shock value, dismissed as angry hyperbole, and simply fictional. Last time I checked, the Jesus of parables and the parables of Jesus met more than a fair share of resistance. The power of narrative is the way a story can speak the truth to power. In the rich tradition of African American literature, fiction most certainly tells the truth.

Our question then is what does the painful past reveal about the ecclesiastical tendency to systematically oppress the *imago Dei* expressed differently from the image/idol created in the minds and from the contexts of the missionaries? What would happen if we truly, truly listened and considered the narrative and the authoritative word that trumps our own. As I suggested early on in this lecture, the time has come for us to listen. Christian missionizers simply talk too much. For a decade or so in scholarly circles, it has been quite in vogue to talk (ironically) about the need to listen and to care about the voices of the other, in this case, African persons. How, though, do we actually listen, as happened that first Pentecost, if our goal is to tell, proclaim, and call African persons to realize that our way is the only way? Ultimately, and this travels far beyond the field of mission, we who wield Christian mission theories and practice do not listen with the intent of being transformed and changed ourselves by what the "other" has to say. The history of Christian mission provides vivid evidence of the way that listening rarely equals structural transformation. More plainly, the history of Christian mission provides vivid evidence that what we call listening is a way we talk a good story.

If we are listening with an agenda, with firm resolve and definite conviction, we cannot honestly call that listening, can we? Perhaps we need to listen in order to be missionized.

Let us listen to the words of the late Ogbu U. Kalu, a third-generation Nigerian Christian, who, until his untimely death in 2009, was the Henry Winters Luce Professor of World Christianity and Mission at McCormick Theological Seminary here in Chicago. Kalu's seminal article, "Church Presence in Africa: A Historical Analysis of the Evangelization Process," clearly locates the problem in "missionary history." Kalu writes, "Missionary history was and still is being written by missionaries and their protégés who have swallowed missionary ideology hook, line, and sinker. Missionary history is propagandist and unanalytical."[17] Already we hear a harsh critique of one who received many benefits from the mission movement but who knows personally the costs exacted. Kalu argues that missionary history produced a literary genre that "focused on how the Gospel came" to different parts of Africa but "ignored the socioeconomic and political background of the host communities."[18] Moreover, Kalu asserts that "the history of Christianity in Africa is not only what missionaries did or did not do but also what Africans thought about what was going on and how they responded."[19]

It is this second point that offers a concrete lesson for those undertaking a liberative mission approach. According to Kalu, such an approach "should analyze the inner dynamics of the evangelization process, perceiving that process as an encounter between viable cosmologies and cultures. This method rejects European Christianity as the starting point of African church history. On the contrary, Africa and its cultures constitute the starting point."[20]

A third lesson is to acknowledge and appreciate the "alive universe" of various African peoples. For example, anthropologist R. S. Rattray does a remarkable job in describing the Ghanaian Ashanti religion and culture depicted in the Ashanti cosmology.[21] He presents a vibrant cosmology with an elaborate social order. When missionary history overlooks or discounts these worldviews and cosmologies, the history is misleading if not fictitious. Kalu also contends that "missionaries came not only with various European and American cultural values but with an identifiable ideology characteristic of their age."[22] While in *The Responsible Church and Foreign Mission*, Beyerhaus and Lefever contend that missionary goals and aims differed, Kalu describes a unified ideology at the beginning of the missionary enterprise.[23] He writes, "Though the Portuguese pretended to be looking for a mythical kingdom of Prester John and were inspired by the scientific advances of the Renaissance, their main aim was economic, and their view of Africans was racist."[24]

Finally, Kalu advances a salient point that is especially noteworthy for those who desire to learn from past mistakes. He says,

> missionaries came [to Africa] with an amazing degree of confidence in the supremacy of Christianity and the European social and economic order. They came with the certainty that they were obeying the Great Command to go into all the world, baptizing and making disciples of all nations. Such a sense of certainty often produced hard-headed insensitivity toward indigenous cultures.[25]

Is it possible to fulfill the Great Commission and yet have sensitivity toward and respect of indigenous cultures? Yes, it is if one loses his/her own cultural confidence and claims only the faithfulness to the gospel. Now the question is, is this even possible?

Musa Dube of Botswana thinks not. She writes from her own hermeneutic of plurality. Dube is an African Christian woman who is a New Testament scholar and identifies herself as postcolonial and feminist. Through these multiple dimensions, she finds clarity. She argues convincingly that imperialism is in play whenever a dominant nation imposes economic, political, and cultural institutions upon foreign ones. Dube contends that mission is an imported cultural institution and as such "it is important to determine whether its strategies advocate power relations that resonate with the model of liberating interdependence or embrace a model consistent with imperialistic impositions."[26] The bold and audacious character of womanist theology and the critical eye of anthropology lead me to argue that mission cannot escape imperialist tendencies. In other words, mission as we know it bears a striking resemblance to imperialist imposition.

Mercy Amba Oduyoye examines missionaries' inability to understand that only those who practice indigenous religions and rituals can make a judgment about their modification or their usefulness. Africans themselves have the ultimate responsibility for evaluating their use.[27] As I hear this African woman scholar who trained at Cambridge University speak, I believe that perhaps we could come closer together if the missionizers would turn around their mission and listen to the breath, wind, and spirit that speaks through the language, culture, and religion, of African persons—who, by the way, are created in the very image of what is most holy.

Returning to the Lucan Model of Mission

If we listen to Jesus instruct his disciples, we do not even need to bring Jesus into the conversation. In Luke's account, the disciples embark on a very radical—and far more Jesus-like mission. They go out as beggars; they have nothing to give. They are neither teachers nor proselytizers. They go out to encounter God's kin-dom in ways quite unorthodox. The disciples can only hope that someone in the street or in a house will receive them in mercy and with grace. The disciples have to rely on others.

The disciples do not bring God to others; no introduction is necessary. God's image greets them at the door; the Word comes to them when a stranger outside the gate says, "I have some extra bread if you're hungry." The disciples' work has nothing to do with changing others and everything to do with changing themselves. We do not create the kin-dom; we receive it when we are invited in just as we are, accepted by the *imago Dei* of a stranger who offers to wash our dirty feet.

We do not build the kin-dom by convincing African women to give up honoring ancestors. We glimpse the kin-dom when we listen to the Word spoken through and see the image of God in women living in Africa. The *missio Dei* is in our midst precisely when we forget our bag with Jesus in it.

In the parabolic way Jesus prefers to teach, the disciples go to new towns and meet new people not to change but to be changed, not to tell but to listen, not with power but helpless. Jesus' approach to *missio Dei* is far less complicated and far more demanding. We have to live an ethic of *koinonia*—welcoming, receiving, and experiencing the Word and cherishing the *imago Dei* in people with whom we do not particularly have anything in common.

We receive a glimpse of the very *missio Dei* from the pluralities of *imago Dei* and multiple expressions of spirit offered by women of African descent. We experience "mission possible."

Conclusion

In this lecture, I have examined mission from the hermeneutic of plurality. My social location as an African American womanist anthropologist informs my understanding of the *missio Dei*. Most importantly, my understanding of the gospel necessitates that I open myself to be missionized as I stand present with others, particularly African women, to understand the amazing way that God in Jesus Christ works in the world. My understanding of the gospel means that I bring a liberation approach to mission as structures impact negatively the lives of African women who are made in God's image. Second-, third-, fourth-, and fifth-generation African scholars have raised their voices to say that mission has to take away its imperialism, and I submit that perhaps the best thing that the *missio Dei* can do is to influence governments and churches in the first world to be missionized by the liberating work of Jesus Christ made known to us in the poor, and particularly, African women.

Notes

1. I want to express thanks to my research assistant, Jamie Jazdzyk, for conceptualizing the notion of "plural" in her conversation with my lecture.

2. Louise Tappa, "The Christ-Event from the Viewpoint of African Women: A Protestant Perspective," in *With Passion and Compassion: Third World Women Doing Theology*, ed. Virginia Fabella and Mercy Amba Odoyoye (Maryknoll, NY: Orbis Books, 1988), 33.

3. Jodi L. Jacobson, Executive Director, the Center for Health and Gender Equity, "Women, HIV, and the Global Gag Rule: The Dis-Integration of US Global Aids Funding," press release, February 25, 2003.

4. Afrol news report, March 3, 2004, http://www.afrol.com.

5. Tappa, "The Christ-Event from the Viewpoint of African Women," 33.

6. Mercy Amba Odoyoye, *Daughters of Anowa: African Women and Patriarchy* (Maryknoll, NY: Orbis Books, 1997), 4.

7. Ibid., 4.

8. Nyambura J. Njoroge, *Kiama Kia Ngo: An African Christian Feminist Ethic of Resistance and Transformation* (Legon, Ghana: Legon Theological Studies Series Project in collaboration with Asempa Publishers, 2000), 126.

9. Ibid.

10. Irma McClaurin, "Introduction: Forging a Theory, Politics, Praxis, and Poetics of Black Feminist Anthropology," in *Black Feminist Anthropology: Theory, Politics, Praxis, and Poetics*, ed. Irma McClaurin (New Brunswick, NJ: Rutgers University Press, 2001), 9.

11. Alice Walker, *In Search of Our Mother's Gardens: Womanist Prose* (New York: Harcourt Brace Jovanovich, 1983), xi.

12. Dwight Hopkins, *Introducing Black Theology of Liberation* (Maryknoll, NY: Orbis Books, 1999), 130.

13. Musimbi R. A. Kanyoro and N. J. Njoroge, "Introduction," in *Groaning in Faith: African Women in the Household of God*, ed. Musimbi R. A. Kanyoro and N. J. Njoroge (Nairobi, Kenya: Acton Publishers, 1996), xii.

14. Ibid., xiii.

15. Ibid.

16. Ibid.

17. Ogbu U. Kalu, "Church Presence in Africa: A Historical Analysis of the Evangelization Process," in *African Theology en Route*, ed. Kofi Appiah-Kubi and Sergio Torres (Maryknoll, NY: Orbis Books, 1981), 13.

18. Ibid., 14.

19. Ibid.

20. Ibid.

21. Robert Sutherland Rattray, *Ashanti* (Oxford: Clarendon Press, 1923; reprint Westport, CT: Greenwood/African Universities Press, 1969).

22. Kalu, "Church Presence in Africa," 17.

23. P. Beyerhaus and H. Lefever, *The Responsible Church and the Foreign Mission* (London: World Dominion Press, 1964).

24. Kalu, "Church Presence in Africa," 17.

25. Ibid., 18.

26. Musa W. Dube, *Postcolonial Feminist Interpretation of the Bible* (St. Louis, MO: Chalice Press, 2000), 128.

27. Mercy Amba Oduyoye, "Women and Ritual in Africa," in *The Will to Arise: Women, Tradition, and the Church in Africa*, ed. Mercy Amba Odoyoye and Musimbi R. A. Kanyoro (Maryknoll, NY: Orbis Books, 1992), 9–10.

6

The Universal in the Local: Power, Piety, and Paradox in the Formation of Missionary Community

Anthony J. Gittins, CSSp

Making use of sociologists' distinction between the "Church of Piety" and the "Church of Power," Professor Gittins argues that one can see this played out in the distinction between gospel/faith and culture, and the universal and the local. Both aspects are needed, but a certain "preferential option" needs to be given for the second term in all three. The implication for mission is that, while the gospel needs by all means to be proclaimed, it must be proclaimed with attention to the people *with whom it is shared. In this way, mission participates in the vulnerable, loving, wholly incarnate God of Jesus Christ. The lecture was delivered on December 5, 2005.*

Introduction

Many think that theology (read missiology) is a mere science or rhetoric, whereas it is a living experience and practice. Everyone now endeavors to be eminent and distinguished in the world, but no one is willing to learn to be pious. Everyone wishes very much to be a servant of Christ, but no one wishes to be his follower. But a true servant must be Christ's follower.[1]

Written four hundred years ago by Johannes Arndt, this is my point of departure and arrival. It is from his book, *True Christianity*, and it articulates a critical theme that virtually all reform movements before and since have tried to recapture. It is a theme that echoes in the theology, anthropology, and life of Louis Luzbetak, whom we honor again in this lecture. Arndt was a Lutheran and a pietist—a word with some unfortunate connotations; yet without piety, Christianity is a scandal.

Arndt wrote in critical times, but crisis is the red thread running throughout Christian history, and true piety is a measure of Christianity's resilience and renewal. If we look at other crises that preceded and produced the sixteenth-century Reformation and Arndt's challenging reminder, we might discover some wisdom that can help us better respond to the crisis that undoubtedly characterizes the present moment in the church at both universal and local levels. My ideas are specifically intended to stimulate your thought and action as pious followers of Christ, at Catholic Theological Union and beyond. I am not a historian, so my readings may seem a little quirky, and I approach theology from the perspective of the social sciences, so there may be some unfamiliar emphases. My hope is that at least some light will show through my interpretative lenses.

If missiology is a form of practical theology, it challenges every Christian to attend to, to assert, and to a renewal of praxis: in other words, to careful study, considered judgment, and ongoing conversion. As we struggle to interpret God's revelation in a confusing and ambiguous world—with its oil-and-water of militarism and reconciliation, secularism and religious pluralism, authoritarianism and peace-making—Santayana's aphorism, that those who fail to learn from history are doomed to repeat its mistakes, lurks accusingly. So let's look back in order to look forward, scroll through the pages of Christian history, and identify the sin and the grace that mark our path. But first let me say a word about procedure.

The disciplines of theology and cultural anthropology are intensely concerned with humanity. Yet, in a world savaged by genocide and xenophobia, scarred by vindictiveness and injustice, and seared by innocent suffering and a silent deity, where is the conversation between them? Despite their common commitment to interpreting human experience, theologians and anthropologists are largely unknown or widely irrelevant, not only to most people beyond the academy, but also to each other. Louis Luzbetak was one of a still pitifully small number of advocates of vigorous interdisciplinary scholarship and authentic missionary engagement. There is no acceptable reason for such paucity, and our very faith cries out for a more positive response to the need. Another well-respected but nontheologian anthropologist asserts that "Christianity is able to question its own messianic and universalizing learnings *from within*. It has led to forms of post-Christian humanism . . . including cultural anthropology with its positive discrimination in favor of the marginal and the local."[2] If anthropology can claim as much, how much more should theology, and therefore missiology, claim? The work and life of Louis Luzbetak are testimony to the validity of such a claim.

Jesus exemplifies *par excellence* the person who is relevant to ordinary people yet converses with experts and gives a life to extend the *missio Dei*. Jesus offers something new, exciting, life giving—not just by proposing a godly vision, but by eliciting people's deepest aspirations and bringing them to fulfillment. He did not come to add to religious restrictions but to manifest God's revelation and invite people to enjoy the freedom of God's children. Thus my reflections will be more about revelation than religion, more about faith than doctrine, and more about orthopraxy than orthodoxy. They will be focused through the twin lenses of theology and anthropology. Such a binocular enhancement—theological anthropology and anthropological theology—may bring both the divine and the human into sharper relief.

In various ways, we are called to a common vocation and sent on a single mission: called to come and to go, to gather and to scatter, to be filled and poured out for the sake of the *basileia*, God's reign. Yet there remain incompatible understandings and sometimes even violent disagreements about the nature of the theological project, the contours of the *basileia*, and the very identity and purpose of the church. Each of us is intimately and passionately concerned about the implications and the applications of the good news of Jesus Christ, in a world that has changed out of recognition not only from the years when Jesus walked in Galilee, but from the centuries when Christianity was transformed and deformed into Christendom. Thus today is as good a time as any for us to ask again, "Who do we think we are?" "What do we think we are doing?" "Where do we think we are going?"

Compromise or Cost Effectiveness

David Bosch and others have reminded us that, far from being incompatible, Christianity and crisis have an almost symbiotic relationship. Crisis is characterized by danger and opportunity, and it requires discrimination and decision. Not only was Christianity born in crisis, crisis is actually necessary, since true Christianity requires a free choice; it cannot be imposed or made compulsory. Jesus promised fire, called people to radical commitment, warned of persecutions, but never coerced or cajoled. The images he used—salt, light, and leaven—are images of scarcity-with-potential rather than of dominance-with-power. The "Jesus movement" was marginal and sectarian, with virtually no likelihood of becoming mainstream or significant. If ever it *were* to reach the ends of the earth, it would not be to dominate, but it would point like a finger or attract like a light for many to see but few to follow. If ever it *did* spread beyond its point of origin, it would have to negotiate (not to crush or obliterate) the challenge posed by non-Jews and people of other cultures and beliefs, as indeed it did in its first generation. The first fruits of the Council of Jerusalem were the thoroughgoing acceptance of local variations within the one community. Those who came to be called Christians no longer needed to be male, or Jewish, or circumcised; and the languages and customs—the actual cultures—of Greeks and barbarians were, in principle, accepted. This did not make Christianity socially significant, but it did make it revolutionary in its strange inclusiveness and paradoxical teachings.

For almost three centuries, crisis hung in the air, as Christians remained marginal, threatened, and periodically persecuted. The extraordinary social fact is that under those precise circumstances the community grew and spread. In a remarkable book, *The Rise of Christianity*, Rodney Stark charted the course of this phenomenon.[3] His wry subtitle puts it well: *How the Obscure, Marginal Jesus Movement Became the Dominant Religious Force in the Western World in a Few Centuries.*

His main points are these. First, Christians *expected* life to be difficult in a Roman Empire seeking to extend its influence, to control its subjects, and to standardize its practices (notwithstanding the tolerance the empire showed when it felt unthreatened). Second, Christians were *explicitly* committed to love of neighbor, but neighbors were not just those one knew, or even fellow Christians but, literally, anyone and everyone in need. Third, the first centuries of Christianity were marked by war, poverty, sickness, and plague, but while most people looked out for themselves, Christians specifically looked out for others as well.[4] Fourth, because of the powerful networks among Christians and between them and the broader community, the Christian survival rate turned out to be significantly higher than that of the wider population: in the teeth of sickness, famine, and war, those known as Christians actually grew in numbers relative to others. Fifth, Christians came to be known precisely *as Christians*, and their sense of community, solidarity, outreach, and embrace made them particularly attractive to pagans who sought incorporation into the community through baptism. And sixth, despite marginalization and the persecutions they suffered, the number of Christians grew and expanded exponentially.

Stark shows how Christian numbers grew at an extraordinary rate, from about 120 core disciples (intimated in Acts 1:14–15) to perhaps 1,000 in the year 40, and to 6.3 million by the year 300.[5] Even if these figures seem hard to grasp, the argument is nevertheless compelling, though we cannot pursue it here. Basically, however, Stark shows that this early Christian growth—about 43 percent per decade—is almost exactly the same as that of the Mormons during the twentieth century. What we can do is identify two crucial factors of immense importance for the subsequent development—qualitative, quantitative, universal, and local—of Christianity.

The Constantinian Compromise[6]

It is dangerously naïve to think that Constantine "saved" Christianity by making it official and banning paganism. Rather, he made "the Christian church *the most favored recipient* of the near-limitless resources of imperial favor"[7]; but by so doing, he set it on a perilous road to power, privilege, and compromise. Christianity should never have become the sponsor of Western civilization: this is entirely antithetical to the gospel of Jesus. And the church's undoubted responsibility to other people did not mean an *uncritical acceptance* of cultures. Christianity always carries a call to conversion, but this is incompatible, both with violence toward other people and with capitulation to their cultural forms. Christianity requires thoroughgoing encounters and dialogue, but it must present a clear invitation, and indeed a challenge, to follow Jesus.

From the early fourth century, Constantine, the Edict of Milan, and subsequent imperial decrees dramatically changed the religious and political map of the Western Empire and set the stage for the creation of Christendom. By facilitating the triumph of Christianity, Constantine undermined some of its most attractive and dynamic aspects, and contributed to turning a "high-tension grassroots movement into an arrogant institution controlled by an elite who often managed to be both brutal and lax."[8] Constantinianism was the transformation of pre-Christendom Christianity into full-blown imperial Christendom.

The fledgling church was now almost swept off its feet by a completely new kind of crisis, no less life threatening but now largely internal.

Protected by imperial power and promised respectability and privilege, Christians faced an increasing temptation to relax. They gradually came to see themselves not as fragile and marginal but as dominant and central. The attraction of spiritual power was fading before the seduction of political power. Theology was now being done, not from the bottom or the edges but from the center and the top.[9] Critically, mission, no longer perceived as constitutive of the church's identity, yielded to a commitment to the maintenance of the imperial church.[10] Now those seeking to be disciples would need to make new choices, new decisions. And those who did so would always be the minority as it was in the beginning: the light, the salt, or the leaven in the mass.

Others nominally Christians were of a different caliber. Some, particularly the ambitious, embraced Christianity because it offered attractive incentives; and some, particularly the common people, became Christian by birth and sometimes by coercion. Yet without a faith community, authentic, mature Christianity is not possible; and coercion can never convert. As Christianity became compulsory rather than voluntary (and coercion or convention supplemented or even replaced conviction), the quality of life and the level of commitment were inevitably modified. Whoever valued the faith would now need to make firm choices and hard decisions. Those willing to do as much thereby contributed to the tension on which the church thrives. They ensured the persistent, though sometimes virtually invisible presence and spirit of the primitive church, the church of prophecy, radical discipleship, and mission. But the imperial church, far from being invisible, was growing visibly stronger every decade. A philosophy of "the end justifies the means" and "error has no rights" gradually turned into a rigorous and abusive practice in the name of Christ and Christianity. Bishops quickly became civil servants with legal privileges and immunities, the church began to feel increasingly at home in imperial garb and trappings, and many of its leaders postured as prelates and potentates.

Patristic texts and teachings illustrate the effect of Constantinianism on Christianity, including Origen and Eusebius from the church in the East, and Tertullian, Cyprian, and Augustine from the church in the West.

Origen (185–254?) (*Contra Celsum*) maintained that God "had been preparing the nations for His teaching, that they might be under one Roman Emperor, [and] the unfriendly attitude of the nations to one another caused by the existence of a large number of kingdoms might not make it more difficult for Jesus' apostles to do what he commanded when he said 'Go!' "[11] Thus Origen saw the Roman Empire as nothing less than a providential instrument for Christian expansion and unity. Wherever the church appropriated this perspective, Christianity was thereby compromised and co-opted by empire.

Eusebius (220–339), reflecting on thirty years of Constantinian rule, wrote, "[Jesus Christ] . . . is the Lord of all the Universe; from whom and through whom the king, the beloved of God, receives and bears the image of His Supreme Kingship, and so steers and directs, in imitation to his superior, the helm of all the affairs of this world."[12] Such encouragement not only affirmed Constantine's status as deputy of Christ,[13] but also set in train the process that would bind church and state together, would legitimate imperial authorities, and ultimately produce the doctrine of the "Divine Right" of kings. Violence and the destruction of rivals were implicitly endorsed, and the Christianity of the margins was set free to develop into the "Catholic" universal church and to determine, patrol, and defend the boundaries of orthodoxy.[14]

Unsurprisingly, Constantine favored the version of Christianity found in Rome—the "Catholic" version—over its Marcionite, Montanist, and Donatist rivals. The Constantinian "adoption" of Christianity changed the identity of the Christian movement gradually and radically, as Christianity itself became increasingly imperialized[15] in a world (before Islam) without a dominant monotheism.

The Eusebian Accommodation, as it is known, provoked a number of critically significant developments, one of which directly impacts my thesis here. As the church gradually became Romanized (the process whereby "*Romanitas*" became equivalent to "*Christianitas*") and centralized, so its missionary dimension atrophied. Before the fifth-century revival, only those within the borders of the empire (and some already-functioning Christian communities beyond) were addressed. St. Patrick was the true pioneer here. Thanks to him, mission *ad extra*—*and specifically to and for non-Christians*—would again be seen as critically important to the church's identity.[16]

Patrick (after 431) was a true theological innovator. He traveled widely, and went where no Christian community existed and where no one had ever ventured to baptize. He was "a churchman who experienced a missionary vocation to take the faith to heathen barbarians"; "the first person in Christian history to take the [great commission] literally; to grasp the teaching that "all nations" *meant teaching even barbarians* who lived beyond the frontiers of the Empire."[17] Unlike Columba, Patrick was *the first cross-cultural missionary.*[18]

Despite mainstream developments both imperial and imperious, however, the more radical, fragile face of the church was never completely obscured, however. As the Constantinian church began a centrifugal movement to create and colonize Christendom, the nascent monastic movement provided a complementary and centripetal movement of asceticism and radical commitment.[19] The dangerous tendency—part of the "crisis" with which Christianity had to live—was that of a fissiparous church. Religious ascetics or professionals came to be perceived as superior to the rank and file and clergy superior to laity, while "orthodox" were opposed to "heretics,"[20] and an uneasy tension prevailed. Increasingly, the actual coercive power of the church—political and economic—was justified as being legitimate authority, divinely endorsed. From a Spirit-led church of the few and fragile faithful, a powerful, papal, patriarchal church was evolving, in grave danger of forgetting its accountability and moral responsibility.

Eusebius's idealized vision was wishful thinking: attempts by the imperial church to excise heresy and maintain orthodoxy and unity, whether by force, fear, or flattery, were only that: attempts. Woodhead says, "the 'early church' was no such thing." It was an amalgam, "an unregulated mix of all sorts of different religious and spiritual groups, all of whom looked back to the inspiration of Jesus Christ, but who interpreted his legacy in different ways, and constructed very different sorts of 'church' in the process. Among them was the embryonic Catholic church which would ultimately win out and destroy its rivals."[21] Paradoxically, perhaps, this (the reality of different sorts of "church" but without vindictive hegemony on the part of any one) is a perfectly good description and not of an aberration of a church that attempts to be both universal and local. It describes very well the existential circumstances from which every authentically inculturated church will be formed.

But if this church of the East, legitimated by Origen and Eusebius, developed a "political theology" of accommodation with the empire,[22] thereby becoming an imperial church, what of the church of the West, of Tertullian, Cyprian, and Augustine?

Tertullian (160–225?)—the same misogynist who refers to women as "the devil's gateway" and bringer of sin into the world—lamented that Marcionism "filled the entire world,"[23]and wanted to resist its allure. Marcion's was a form of radical Christianity and, as such, it attempted to be faithful to true, authentic discipleship. But although austere and God fearing, it soon hardened into intolerance and vindictiveness. Few would warm to Tertullian himself, whose spirituality is sparse and spare and who sees sin much more than grace abounding. Yet his commitment is to the cross-bearing, powerless marginal church rather than to the church of bombast and belligerence. Tertullian is now looking for personal and corporate self-sacrifice to replace bloody martyrdom, and thus prefiguring many of Augustine's thoughts.

Cyprian (200?–258) emphasizes that Christianity must be freely chosen: "the liberty of believing or not believing is placed in free choice."[24] This implies—critically—that the church of Jesus Christ can only be a voluntary association and not a superimposition. It therefore means that Christianity is "incompatible with force or compulsion,"[25] which in turn indicates that church cannot use the institutions of empire, and implies that it must, in fact, oppose empire.

Above all, as Richard Fletcher puts it, "Augustine was the discordant (radical) voice in the general chorus orchestrated by Eusebius in celebration of the Christian Empire."[26] For him, no state was to be identified with the Christian community or the City of God. The empire was *not* privileged, whatever Eusebius might claim. For Augustine (354–430) indeed, the true, authentic church may be the "invisible" but committed and potent church of the *Letter to Diognetus* of the second century. Augustine "thought that true Christians might make up as little as 5% of the visible church/world."[27]

If the voices of people like Tertullian, Cyprian, and Augustine were less arrogant and more sober than those of Origen and Eusebius, their sentiments were endorsed by those for whom Christianity was not so much a religion as a faith, not identified with privilege but with service, not with status but with discipleship. Those, by contrast, who sought to justify and impose authority and control, would find much consolation and support in Origen and Eusebius.

In the early years of Constantinian Christianity, the West could be antiworldly, rigorist, and separatist,[28] but also ascetical, generous, and cost effective in its understanding of discipleship. The face of the primitive church remains visible as it stands fast against the excesses of imperial Christendom. This is not to suggest that the Western church remained untouched by the Constantinian compromise: far from it. Christendom drove on like a gathering wave until it inundated Europe with the waters of baptism. But it could not sweep away all traces of what Richard Horsley calls the "little tradition," Kenelm Burridge the "Devotional" mode of being church, and Rodney Stark "the church of piety." This kind of church was the prophetic, radical community of believers, epitomized in monastic and missionary communities that never allowed the zeal to be eclipsed, the kind of community where the vision of a church, truly universal yet also truly local, continued to be fostered.[29] It was always set for a struggle with the imperial church, but it remained faithful to the critical intuition that the responsibility of the church is to incarnate the faith in the lives of the people of myriad cultures, and to endorse and support difference and sameness, many and one, universal and local, in equal measure.

The church of Constantine became both the church of Christendom and the church of compromise: "Two visible and separate entities, church and state, were fused."[30] The distinction between church and world was blurred. The dominant profile of Christianity became bloated by authoritarianism and blotched by corruption, though reforming movements[31] constantly attempted to keep the softer profile of service and piety visible.

The near identification of Christianity with imperialism and the nation-state has been nothing short of disastrous. It allowed Christians to treat the "other" or the "stranger" no longer as Christ in disguise but as "infidel," "barbarian," or "heretic," and took out a license to kill in the name of Jesus, the church, and the faith.[32] Yet even Luther's Reformation ultimately failed, as all reformations do, for the church needs continuous reformation: it is *semper reformanda*. Luther really aspired to articulating another call for primitive discipleship; but fatefully, between 1522 and 1525, the reformers failed to challenge the Constantinian settlement head on, and "abandoned many of the very things that had continued to distinguish the church from the world."[33] Such "things," however, still flourished in the softer profile of the Roman Catholic Church—the authentic *ministerium-cum-magisterium* of apostolic hierarchy, the blazing commitment, still identifiable in the monastic orders, and the commitment to universal mission. "Despite the Reformers' intentions, the autonomy of the state was furthered by what they said and did."[34]

Constantinian Christianity is still alive and well in "civil religion"[35] in the United States and among other "culture Christians"—those who think they can be true Christians simply by being law-abiding citizens. But many contemporary theologians and historians, far from bemoaning the demise of Christendom, are profoundly grateful that Christendom is moribund, because Christianity may at last, after sixteen centuries, be able to rise like a phoenix and be converted again to its original vocation.[36] Cynics may judge this as an attempt to make a virtue out of necessity, but it is much more. With the demise of Christendom, we are in a much better position to visualize Christianity again as a voluntary association, requiring free choice, stimulating a commitment to justice and to humanity, demonstrating a real respect for non-Christians, not to be taken for granted and certainly not easy, but nevertheless cost effective.

Now, all of the foregoing, though important to my purpose, is ultimately background, since my primary concern is neither structural nor historical, but rather theological and anthropological. I want to work to some conclusions or implications for ourselves today, disciples trying to live in and with the Spirit of Jesus in a world compromised by principalities and powers but also one filled with a single humanity whose seven (almost eight) billion members are also and necessarily multicultural and irreducibly different. In order to do this, it will be necessary to trawl through the depths of Christian history again in greater detail. But first I must explicate a particularly significant notion: cost-effective Christianity.

Cost-Effective Christianity[37]

Constantinianism tends to produce generic, "lowest common denominator" Christianity, and when it does not coerce, it coaxes or cajoles. With the "Christendom shift" effected by Constantinian Christianity, people were offered enticing incentives to conversion.[38] Alan Kreider says that they "became Christians for many reasons, but not least because it was the emperor's religion. Christianity now provides access to professional advancement. People of social eminence and economic power became Christian."[39] This is a complete reversal from the early church, and from cost-effective Christianity. Cost effectiveness is a function of the relationship between cost (or price) and quality (or value). Some things are expensive yet considered worth the cost and thus desirable. Other things are inexpensive but deemed cheap and tawdry, not worth having. Cost, plus quality, equals value or worth, but everything depends on one's perspective and judgment.

Originally, Christianity was costly, and clearly visible as such to non-Christians. The likelihood of committed Christians living a long and trouble-free life was virtually nil. Yet, not only did Christians relish and value their identity even to the point of dying for it "by dungeon, fire, and sword," but non-Christians were increasingly attracted to the new religion, the new community, and the way of living, despite enormous *disincentives* from without and within. Harassment, ostracism, and even execution could be expected; but "the church also imposed its own disincentives to cheap conversion; its lengthy catechetical program helped ensure that converts were genuine. Nevertheless, despite these deterrents, people persisted in becoming Christian at an astonishing rate."[40] Christianity remained highly cost effective: expensive *and* desirable. That is why it grew as it did, and why people could say "see how these Christians love one another."

Cost-effective Christianity is essentially what Bonhoeffer meant by "costly grace" as opposed to "cheap grace." He said, "we are fighting today for costly grace." Cheap grace is sold on the market at cut price: grace that is without cost, free, and already paid for. Cheap grace "means grace without discipleship, grace without the cross, grace without Jesus Christ living and incarnate."[41] It is costly, says Bonhoeffer, because "it calls us to follow . . . it costs a life; and it is grace because it gives a [person] the only true life. [But] as Christianity spread, the realization of the costliness of grace gradually faded. Grace became a common property. It was to be had at low cost, and it was disastrous, and the ruin of countless Christians."[42] Yet, Bonhoeffer also noted, "the church of Rome did not altogether lose the earlier vision. The monastic movement, on the outer fringe, was a place where the older vision was kept alive."[43] An important observation, this.

To summarize, crisis, tension, and challenge are constitutive of the church as it tries to find its way forward in specific times and places, with specific temptations and dangers. There will—there must—always be a struggle, from one generation to the next, between the two components of church that we have identified: the strong and the weak, the hard and the soft, the seeking to convert, and the seeking to be converted. There is a great deal at stake: faithfulness to Jesus; personal and social integrity; and the needs and rights of God's people—who are never generic but always specific, with cultural, gendered, and other differences, whether they are within the visible church or not.

Power and Piety

A structure built upon a fault line will require constant attention and perhaps reinforcement. From the very earliest years, such a line developed beneath the ground on which Christianity was growing. Jesus had warned his disciples not to act like potentates, pagans, or punctilious legalists: something new was in the air, calling for an inspired and imaginative response. Authentic *diakonia* and eschatological values were proposed.[44] But because life can only be lived in concrete circumstances, there would inevitably be tensions between the gospel values and those of the prevailing culture. Despite the teaching, the example, and the constant reminders, Christians have always struggled to pay appropriate tribute to Caesar and to God, to be in the world yet not to be compromised by it, and to live the paradox of first-as-last and leader-as-follower. So the tectonic plates of gospel and culture ground against each other, and the fault line became increasingly apparent. Two thousand years have seen the gap alternately open wider, then close, only to open yet again.

Tracking the myriad processes that produced Christianity is delicate. Different pictures will emerge from different perspectives: Eastern or Western, Orthodox or Catholic, patristic or medieval, mainstream or marginalized, a church becoming or a church in flux, or a church alternately formed, deformed, and reformed.[45] It can be very helpful to contrast two profiles or facets of the church. Religious sociologist Rodney Stark tracks the development of two major religious elements or "churches" in the first millennium, coexisting within the one institutional church: the *church of power* and the *church of piety*.[46] When they are misaligned, the fault line shows clearly. When the tectonic *power* plate grinds against the more fragile *piety* plate, a seismic disturbance results. Unless the lubricant of reform maintains each without destroying either, the friction will produce violence and destruction.

Crudely put, the church of power is represented by what would become the Roman Catholic Church in its institutional, authoritative, and authoritarian majesty and might. Developing gradually after the fourth century, it became thoroughly established as the church of Christendom. This power allowed the church first to define, and when appropriate to confront, heresy.[47] And then (thanks to an imperial structure, a succession of powerful popes, and the exercise of force and diplomacy), such power can extirpate heresy or drive it underground.[48] Having established hegemony, the church of power maintained it by a combination of what historian Ramsay MacMullen has called "flattery and battery."[49]

But the church also had another face or aspect: far smaller numerically and weaker politically was the church of piety, which was kept alive by the developing religious orders,[50] but sustained by support and endorsement from a wider constituency. It called the imperial institutional church to the radical simplicity of the gospel and, over time, would remind the institutional church of its missionary dimension and indeed its missionary nature.[51] Until the church of power became supremely self-confident but also morally challenged by the integrity of the church of piety, the latter could coexist quite peacefully as a "series of encapsulated sect movements"[52] constituting only minimal threat or inconvenience. But so long as the church of piety remained a faithful remnant, it would always constitute a challenge—prophetic or moral, rather than political—to the church of power. And if it refused to be marginalized, muzzled, or muted, then the church of power would ultimately be stung into reaction.

It is important for my purposes to try to chart the developing relationship between the church of power and the church of piety so that we may better understand both what the true church is called to and the temptations it has faced in the course of its history. This I will do—obviously in very summary form—in ten points:

1. Gradually, the church of power became more distinguishable from the church of piety: the main beneficiaries of Constantine accumulated increasing influence and wealth, while a small (reactive and radically gospel based) group refused to compromise or disappear. So how did the church of piety survive, and why did it not just fade away or become suppressed? It might have become an unsustainable sect, but it survived for two main reasons. First, committed to the moral vision of early Christianity, devotees of the church of piety embraced costly Christianity, sustained each other in communities, and created a solid institutional base in monasticism. And second, they received sufficient financial support from a minority of the growing nobility and upper classes.[53] Where mainstream Christianity risked being seduced by worldliness and the domestication of the radical gospel, monasticism was a "high intensity" movement embodying a visible and focal "contrast society."[54] Initially, monastics were tolerated by the church of power because, although perceived as sectarian, they were dispersed rather than centralized and thus considered marginal and powerless. But they would in fact prove to be a powder keg. By the

fifth century, there were thousands of monastics, enough to constitute a palpable counterexample to the dissolute clergy who might compromise the church of power.

2. From the fourth century onward, as the church infiltrated almost half the empire, the literate population generated priests and bishops with significant local power.[55] But papal power as such was hardly a scandal before the fifth century, though by the sixth there was a felt need for simplification. Thanks to a succession of monastic popes, a call for reform was sounded, and the visibility of the church of piety was again raised.[56]

3. Before Constantine, the church had made little impact on the countryside, but by the sixth century, the expanding boundary of Christendom had become increasingly visible: the whole social or cultural world was being "Christianized," even if it were not persuasively Christian. The real challenge now was to form Christians into free, mature, and committed followers of Jesus. But power and piety would always be in tension. Ecclesiastical power holders would justify unsavory methods in the name of God and salvation, while petty rulers and kings would accept Christianity because of promises of power sharing and prestige. If the church had not yet quite established a secure institutionalized power base, nevertheless it was tempted both by imperialism and by laxity. To become a Christian was by now quite easy, a very different reality from that of earlier centuries. Real conversion such as marked the early church and made it so visible and cost effective was increasingly rare. For very many people, Christianity became an "add-on" religion and was widely contaminated by incompatible cultural practices. Rather than heresy, the problem now was what was perceived as syncretism, polytheism, or paganism. Christianity in the West had become a "strange amalgam of [the] superficial."[57]

4: The great defender of the church of piety around this time is Pope Gregory the Great (590–604). He was also a shrewd ruler who held power and piety in tension by formulating "a highly influential ideal of Christian rule and submission."[58] His *Regula Pastoralis* (which would be given to every bishop and king and become highly acclaimed and widely distributed)[59] "outlined a sophisticated understanding of the use of power"[60] exercised with piety. He emphasized the importance of prayer and meditation, and offered his *Regula* to the secular clergy explicitly as a counterpart to the monastic Rule of Benedict. Commenting on 1 Timothy 3:1–2, which talks about the noble task of the bishop, Gregory says,

We must, however, observe that this was said at a time when who-soever was set over the people was the first to be led to the tortures of martyrdom. There was no doubt that [a bishop] would meet with the most severe sufferings. A man not only fails completely to love the office, but he is ignorant of it if, yearning for supreme rule, he feast on the subjection of others in the hidden reveries of his thoughts, is glad to hear his own praises, feels his heart surge with honor, and rejoices in the abundance of his affluence.[61]

But Gregory's reforms were to be undermined. At his death, "the Roman clergy's outraged *esprit de corps* and concern for career structure reasserted itself, the new pope replaced monks with secular clergy, and degeneration supervened."[62] And so it went as power and piety sparred, struggled, and alternately prevailed, at least for a time.

5. Prior to Gregory, indeed since 476 (the time of Patrick), there had been no Western emperor, and the center of the Roman Empire had moved to Constantinople. But under the (Western) Holy Roman Empire centralized under Charlemagne in 800 and growing imperiously thereafter,[63] whoever migrated onto erstwhile imperial soil was *ipso facto* converted to Christianity. But we should not imagine a single, mono-lithic, expanding, uniform church in the West. There were still very many churches.[64]

6. Can we characterize the church as it reached the landmark of half a millennium after Constantine, when the Roman Empire was thriving in the East and Christendom in the West? Some say that the church of piety had made its mark, for there was (after Patrick) a much greater sense of the church's missionary activity than at the time of Constantine and the early expansion of Christendom. Others aver that power is more in evi-dence than piety and that the Eusebian Accommodation was widely ac-cepted. Richard Fletcher argues persuasively that once the boundaries of Greater Christendom had been pushed beyond the Holy Roman Empire to the edge of the Muslim world, the subsequent diffusion of Christianity was due more to "seepage" than to direct evangelization.[65] Still, for almost half a millennium, the missionary movement, which now began to fade, had been growing since Patrick's initiative and the Irish monks' gradual transformation from *peregrinatio* to the more focused evangelization of pagans and barbarians beyond the former Western and the current Holy Roman Empire.

7. For most of the first millennium, the missionary impulse was neither a response to a perceived threat posed by Islam, nor a papal initiative to extend the power of the papacy. In fact, says Fletcher, "it is sheer fantasy to suppose that missionary expansion was deliberately engineered simply in order to inflate papal power."[66] It was indeed due to the resilience of the church of piety and a deep commitment to Christian discipleship and its extension into the wider world. This impulse was driven by an increasing response to the Great Commission and to an emphasis on the vocation of every Christian. Patrick had been a catalyst for the Irish religious diaspora,[67] which saw "Pilgrimage for Christ" develop into a more focused and organized missionary movement among the Anglo-Saxons under Augustine of Canterbury, and by Willibrord in Frisia, Boniface in Germany, and their successors, up to Cyril and Methodius among the Slavs.

8. The fact remains that the church of piety and the church of power are but two facets of one church, two profiles of a single face; so it is not surprising that some missionaries struck mutually beneficial bargains with local rulers. Others were indeed killed, whether due to their own rank insensitivity or to the genuine challenge of their witness. But many were indulged and privileged. Yet it would be a caricature to paint them as lackeys of, or partners with, royal personages or to charge them with abusing and betraying the lower orders.[68] However, missionaries did indeed operate on the assumption that Christianity could fulfill human and material needs better than any alternative, and to that extent, they sometimes dangled the promise of worldly prosperity before would-be converts. Bede's *History* illustrates this well.[69]

9. The ninth century saw the *Carolingian reform* (named after Holy Roman Emperor Charlemagne). More stringent demands would now be made of the laity, and new standards would be articulated for converts,[70] with some evident hope that the faith would truly be caught by, and not simply taught to, subsequent generations. But at the same time, Latin and Orthodox Christianity continued to move apart on different tectonic plates of their own and due, in no little measure, to the affront suffered by Constantinople at the papal indulgence of Charlemagne as Holy Roman Emperor. That is another significant missionary story but much too ambitious to try to recount here.[71]

10. What does need emphasis, though, is that as church turned into mission, so mission could also turn into church, bringing power and piety into a dangerously unbalanced relationship. An example is helpful here: by

780, Willehad had established a mission station in Bremen, but three hundred years later "the archbishopric of Bremen/Hamburg had become an institution of an almost unrecognizably different character: rich in lands, buildings and treasures; proud of its traditions; claimant to patriarchal rights over churches scattered from Sweden to Greenland; a power within the German monarchy. A mission has turned into a church."[72]

Let us summarize the first Christian millennium in terms of the fluctuating fortunes of the church of power and the church of piety. Following the twists and turns, advances and retreats, commitment and infidelities, conversions and falls from grace, we realize that all these are integral to the two-thousand-year-old story of the Christian church. They constitute the story of very fallible attempts by the church of piety to remain faithful to the Way of Jesus and of the church of power to act responsibly as the Body of Christ on earth. And throughout, movements of dissent and reform will prove alternately creative and destructive, sometimes healing wounds and sometimes exacerbating them, sometimes leading to mutual cooperation and sometimes to mutual mistrust.

For a millennium, then, the tectonic plates ground against each other as the church of power survived and consolidated itself. The fault line remained visible, and serious confrontation remained a possibility, and yet there was always hope that a spirit of reform would be the lubricant to assure the creative engagement of the church of power and the church of piety. Provoked by two eventualities, both stemming from the church of piety, this could well have happened: a series of reforming popes and a palpable atmosphere of zeal seemed to converge at just the right time. That the popes of the later eleventh century were all monks promised both authentic descending reform (from the top and down to the ranks) and ascending renewal (from the people to the potentates). For a too-brief period, there seems to have been real engagement at all levels. Tragically, the reforming monk-popes were followed by a line of degenerates, which explains both the increasing marginalization of the church of piety and its adamant refusal to disappear, as well as yet another seismic shift from life-giving possibility to life-threatening crisis.

Reform was never totally absent from the church, however, and in the eleventh century the Gregorian reform focused on the priesthood with the intention of improving both pastoral and personal standards. But—and this is of critical importance to the later history of Christianity—it also created a priestly caste.[73] Moreover, the outward focus also changed: given the advances of Islam at the time, and the centralized strength of the Catholic Church, it developed a crusading ideology both to "regain" the holy places and to restore a church fragmented by dissent and heresy. One result was that the dominant (though not always visible) paradigm of the first millennium—to bear faithful witness to the apostolic tradition with collegiality as the *modus operandi*—was thoroughly obscured in the second millennium by a paradigm of monarchical supremacy.[74]

Characterizing the church at the end of the first millennium, Richard Fletcher says that "by 1000, Christian communities had been planted from Greenland to China."[75] But he modifies this, saying that those communities were nevertheless essentially with *Romanitas*, which was not established in Lithuania until 1251 initially (and not finally until 1385), and never permanently among the Lapps.[76] Meanwhile, of course, Byzantium had withdrawn and followed a different agenda.

In the second millennium, the Christendom project would become more obviously confrontational and vindictive toward the last heathens and against the Muslims. Now is the era of Crusades and colonization. After 1200, the Gregorian reforms were more than a century in the past and less and less supported by a church losing its missionary urgency and becoming increasingly militant.

Without the constraint and discipline of monastic popes, the church of power could flex its authoritarian muscles and begin to designate reformers as heretics, claiming authorization for persecuting and executing them. Though physically and psychologically an excellent way to neutralize critics, such action would reap the whirlwind. Now mission and crusade form an unholy alliance. Even Bernard, the Cistercian monk (1090–1153), would preach the second crusade. He also addressed the newly founded Knights Templars in these—to our ears, chilling—words:

> The Knight of Christ kills in good conscience and dies in peace; in his dying he is working on his own behalf, but in his killing he is working for Christ. When he kills a malefactor, it is not "homicide" but—if I may say so—"malicide." When they move against the enemy, these men who are meeker than lambs become more savage than lions, and I do not know whether to call them monks or knights; perhaps they should be given both names, because they

demonstrate that they combine the sweetness of the monk with the courage of the knight. Such are the servants that God himself chose to guard the Holy Sepulchre.[77]

That crusading zeal strengthened from the late eleventh century, becoming a travesty of any authentic call to conversion or reconciliation and quite inconsistent with Christian respect for the other as sister or brother. Nor was it directed only externally against those vilified as infidels (Jews and Muslims), and who, for long periods, had been deemed unproblematic. Now it was focused internally against other Christians. St. Dominic preached the Albigensian crusade in the early thirteenth century, which put down the Cathars with unprecedented savagery. Twenty thousand people would be chased, hacked, and burned at Béziers and beyond by Christian forces led by a Cistercian abbot/archbishop. "Kill them all," he is reported to have said: "Let God decide" who is guilty or innocent. With tragic irony, then, it was not just the church of power, but also the church of piety—monks, friars, and patrons of orthodoxy—who preached the Crusades.[78] They continued until the fifteenth century as, in the West, the zeal of the church of piety shamefully justified indiscriminate barbarity in Christ's name. In all this, the church of power was also zealous—but particularly zealous consistently to exempt itself from reform, persistently to impose itself on others, and insistently to defend the territorial boundaries of Christendom.

The church is fallible in its members and thus always liable to be tempted and to fall from grace. In time, the church of power came to manifest a shocking vindictiveness, only exceeded by its scandalous lifestyle. The history of medieval popes (by no means only the notorious sixteenth-century Borgias, but of a majority from after the Gregorian reform in the early twelfth century through the Avignon papacy and into the fifteenth) is not only illustrative, but also provides ample endorsement of the legitimacy of the reformers' complaints. It is difficult to isolate one example of abuse: there are simply too many. But Pope Sixtus IV (1471–1484) will do: this Franciscan friar (thus, expected to profile the church of piety) was a blatant nepotist and dealer in indulgences. Creator of the Sistine Chapel and patron of the high Renaissance, he had a custom-made papal tiara that cost, in today's money, a little over two hundred million dollars![79] As David Edwards puts it laconically, "In the eleventh century, the papacy had been in the forefront of the campaign to end the scandal of simony. Now they presided over the system.[80]

It is not, therefore, only the church of power that can become corrupt, but also—tragically and ironically—the church of piety. History demonstrates that the church is always susceptible to corrupting forces. But if the church of piety should become vindictive and self–righteous, it will be no less culpable than the church of power. Attempts at clerical and structural reform are admirable; but misplaced zeal—whether on the part of piety or power—can so easily lead to further movements that prove, intentionally or not, exceedingly harmful to the integument of the Body of Christ. These may be movements against a variety of perceived threats, from Bogomils to Waldensians, Beguines to Brethren of the Free Spirit, Hussites to Lollards, and on to the cataclysmic confrontation between Rome and Luther, Calvin, Zwingli, and other radicals even less well known to most Roman Catholics. Previously tolerated nonconformity within the Christian family was liable to provoke preemptive or counterattacks, whenever the church of power[81] sensed that dissent or reform movements were gaining ground within the church, but in opposition to the hegemony of its Roman institutions and functionaries.

Is it tragic and reprehensible (or perhaps prophetic and admirable), and at the same time deeply ironic, that the true church of piety is to be found among some of the very people vilified, excommunicated, and marked as heretics by the church of power? Those whom Johannes Arndt identifies with "true Christianity" are as likely to be found calling for reform as among the fierce guardians of orthodoxy: among the Anabaptists, the Mennonites, and other reformers, as well as the so-called counterreformers.[82] The church of piety continues to be identifiable in the Bonhoeffers and Barths, the Francisco Clavers, Janani Luwums and Boffs, the Gutiérrezes, Vaniers, and Dorothy Days, as well as the Congars, Rahners, and Soelles of our time. It should be no less identifiable in each of us, because that is what Christian discipleship requires: risk as well as certainty, courage no less than obedience, loyal dissent as much as strict conformity. But it must never become self-righteous: the righteousness of God alone is to be championed. Unless the church of power can strive to listen and repent, and unless the church of piety can strive to avoid fission and maintain unity, the church of Jesus Christ (ostensibly marked by legitimate authority yet subservience to the Holy Spirit, and by charismatic piety and radical commitment) will suffer life-threatening disfigurements and amputations rather than experience the wholesomeness and unity that Jesus prayed for.[83]

The church of piety always remains vulnerable, but whenever it co-opts the coercive methods sometimes invoked by the church of power, its prophetic edge will be dulled and the Body of Christ will be even further debilitated. The church of power for its part has legitimate authority; but if it becomes authoritarian and vindictive, it betrays the very gospel it is pledged to serve. We must strive to become a church of piety but not self-righteousness, and a church of power but not hegemony, in order to be the one, true church of unity and not fragmentation. *Magi-sterium* (the matters of moment, the solemn invocation of legitimate authority) is part of the church's identity; but *mini-sterium* (the little things, the more inconsequential and less high-profile service) is no less essential. So we must struggle, seeking opportunity amid danger and identifying grace even where sin abounds. The church can never simply be identified with the church of power, but neither are all power holders irredeemably ambitious and wicked: that would be to paint a caricature. Without the church of piety,[84] sometimes almost suffocated but often tolerated, approved, and admired, the church is incomplete. Power without piety becomes arrogance, *hubris*; but piety without power as legitimate authority cannot fulfill its providential mission.[85]

An uncontested monopoly church will become impervious to voices within and without and therefore resistant to the Holy Spirit who wants to renew the face of the earth. A degree of pluralism—diversity in unity, or unity with diversity—is both necessary and consistent with Jesus and early church practice. When feeling safe and in control, it is of course much easier for the church to tolerate, endorse, and even welcome a diversity of forms,[86] from Gnosticism to monasticism to popular piety. But when under perceived threat, the tendency is to revert to authoritarianism, standardization, and centralization. Ultimately this produces a crippling uniformity if not dramatic fission. Pluralism is demanded, both because "in my father's house there are many mansions" and because human beings are formed in society, by culture, and are not uniform or generic. This brings us to two significant points for consideration: first, we must look at the relation between theology or the gospel ("faith") and the lives and contexts of those it encounters ("culture"); and second, we must explore the way in which the church, which is universal, encounters, interrelates with, and is in turn formed and reformed by, the local churches that constitute its very being.

This rather extended *excursus* into the historical development of the Christian church in the West has been primarily in order to alert us to the relationship between the practice of the faith and its cultural and historical contexts. To this we now turn.

Gospel and Culture

In its time, H. Richard Niebuhr's book, *Christ and Culture*, was highly influential. But fifty years have seen significant shifts in the anthropological understanding of culture and in the increasing sophistication with which theologians handle the notion. Max Weber gave us the "Ideal Type" or typification of notions such as "man," or "person"—and by extension "culture" or "gospel." This sociological tool is as helpful for coming to terms with complex notions like "politics" or "economics," "saints" or "sinners") as it is disastrous if it is reified and thereby comprehensively misunderstood: ideal types must not be confused with actual exemplifications, specific, concrete examples. There has always been a certain tendency to think of "culture" as an ideal type, but today culture is understood more as a process than as a fact, as evolving more than as evolved, and open-ended rather than as bounded, and thus as somewhat elusive rather than easily grasped, catalogued, and defined.[87]

Neither theology nor culture, then, should be hypostatized or treated as solid entities amenable to easy specification, definition, or comparison. They cannot be simply held up against the light or dissected on a laboratory table. "A culture" in the singular, is an amalgam; in the plural, it is a galaxy of amalgams. So is "theology" (in the singular or the plural, in particular or in general) or "faith." These are always appropriations, embodiments, and articulated very differently within or across communities worldwide. Notions such as culture, theology, or faith—or church or gospel—are irreducible. As a Beethoven piano sonata or a Chopin mazurka cannot be reduced to a written score but exists to be heard when piano and pianist produce a realization, a unique performance, so it is with culture. It cannot be reduced to a set of rules but is expressed as belief or behavior, ritual or reflection, and is sometimes sublime and sometimes rather ordinary. Reification or essentialization is very dangerous: a "culture" or "society" does not "think." "Theology" or "faith" does not "believe." In each case, it is human beings, singly or collectively, who are the subjects, the agents.

It is a long time since Clifford Geertz urged us to see culture in actual reality, as irreducible to psychological phenomena or cognitive structures (which are, in principle, universally the same) as is genetics.[88] But to understand culture—or faith, theology, or the challenge of the gospel—we need imagination as much as knowledge;[89] otherwise we will tend to reduce all of these to our own very limited grasp of their meaning and significance. The church's failure has often been born of a failure to imagine[90] other people, other realities, or other possibilities, and to take them seriously. But there can be no dialogue between "gospel" and "culture" that is not first between actual people; and it is not a *dialogue* unless they listen and respond to—and are some degree modified by—each other. Directives intended to make other people change their way of thinking or acting risk being coercive. Jesus calls people first to *imagine* the *basilea* or Realm of God—and provides numerous helpful similes—and *then* their thinking and acting will change. But, critically, they will do so within their own cultural circumstances and patterns of thought.

As John Paul II put it, "A faith which does not become culture is a faith which has not been fully received, not thoroughly thought through, not fully lived out."[91] Faith (or gospel) becomes culture, and vice versa, not by indoctrination or imposition but by internalization and assimilation. Consequently, both faith (or gospel) and culture must be understood primarily in terms of incarnation, not intellectualization. The only way people will believe they are being taken seriously is if those who presume to teach or prescribe for them are also committed to encountering and learning from them.

To use ideal types uncritically, then, is to be unsubtle or disingenuous, to oversystematize, and even to oppose and dichotomize entities rather than to relate them to each other. Better, with David Tracy, to employ the analogical imagination rather than the dialectical: to think in terms of both/and rather than always to opt for either/or.[92] That might help us better to appreciate that we are one church but many churches, one people but many communities and persons, and that there is one gospel but many evangelists, accounts, interpretations, and emphases. If "the gospel"—not as text but as hope and promise—is to be brought to and shared with every nation on earth,[93] it is critical that the bearers of that hope and promise are as attuned to the many contexts and cultures of the recipients as they are of the many layers and the various interpretations of the gospel itself. Translation is as important as hermeneutics and no less taxing.

In a stimulating book subtitled *A Theology of Culture*,[94] Timothy Gorringe makes three critical points. First, "culture is concerned with the spiritual, ethical, and intellectual significance of the material world; it is, therefore, of fundamental significance. Second, "the Gospel only exists institutionally; institutions are part of culture." Third, "theology is concerned with the whole of human endeavor."[95] These quotations underline the point that gospel and culture can, and indeed must engage in authentic dialogue, precisely in order that the good news can continue to be broadcast, received, and articulated on earth. But Gorringe makes a further, crucial point: theology or gospel (he simply speaks of "scripture") "functions uniquely as an ideological irritant, critiquing ruling systems of power."[96] So we must reassess whether and how every culture is called to bend the knee before God's revelation, and thus reassess the very meaning of mission itself.

Karl Barth declared that the gospel is both 100 percent human and 100 percent divine, both inextricably part of a culture and yet critical of, and a challenge to, ethnocentrism and cultural complacency.[97] Barth forges a potential link between theology and culture by identifying eschatology as theology's central category, for it is also, surely, culture's central category, though not in the narrow sense of the last things. Moltmann sees eschatology as "the hope that sustains": the *telos*.[98] In anthropologese, culture certainly involves fundamental values or questions: the meaning and purpose of life. Given the common ground on which anthropology and theology, culture and gospel, inevitably and unavoidably stand, there is an urgent need for more respectful, creative, and imaginative encounters between them, motivated not by a spirit of competitiveness or proselytism but by a conviction from both partners that the very best interests of everyone are thus served.

True dialogue changes both parties, and its outcome cannot be predetermined. It changes both parties by virtue of the fact that it introjects new information, new perspectives, new experiences; its outcome cannot be determined because its very progress is marked by each interlocutor's response to the unpredictable observations of the other. In the dialogue between theology and culture (strictly, between the human agents representing each) both parties can and must be changed. Conventionally, Christian theology—through its theologians—has defended the principle that it can effect change in cultures and societies. But since both "theology" and "the gospel" are carried in earthen vessels, as culture speaks to gospel so the gospel itself (specifically, those who articulate it from particular social and theological locations) is subject to rethinking, rearticulation, and reapplication. Just as cultures can be said to need the gospel, so the gospel needs cultures.[99] Every new encounter is a new opportunity for both parties to be challenged to conversion. Those who remain steadfastly attached to their provisional, bounded understanding of the gospel (or God, theology, faith, or church), commit idolatry.[100] Idolatry is uncritical worship of one's own ideas, schemes, paradigms, or models, whether in stone, or wood, or words.

For Gorringe, "a theology of culture is at the same time a theology of the Spirit," because it must be "about God active in the historical process." Critically, it must also be "a theology of diversity in unity, . . . of the valuing of real difference. At the same time it will have an underlying unity."[101] This might seem very ambitious, like a unified field theory, but Gorringe boldly and brilliantly lays out some of the work urgently needing attention and opens up a series of pathways linking the universal and the local, and the church's missionary vocation to that of its members. He also calls us to think seriously about the implications and the cost of responding to the challenge. Christian faith is no more uncritical of culture than people in society (culture) are uncritical of those who teach and purvey the Christian message: there must be a degree of "critical correlation" between faith and culture.[102] But mutual criticism that is not built on a foundation of mutual knowledge and respect will degenerate into rank condemnation of difference. The theological purpose of mutual critique is mutual clarification and collaboration.

Faith cannot exist in a vacuum. It needs cultural forms and expressions: cultural conventions and meanings are the *only* medium through which to express faith. Mutual critique should bring each party, in a fashion consistent with their own particular circumstances, to a more faithful following of Christ. Therefore, a church (which means its membership) that is not embedded and embodied in a culture—not complaisantly but critically—may be a Platonic form but can never be the Body of Christ incorporated on earth.

"Religion," said Wittgenstein, "is agreement in form of life."[103] A *form of life* implies a certain consensus, or the existence of social institutions (which anthropologists define as "standardized modes of co-activity")—in short, the cultural practice of the community. But faith is much more than religion. It is the risky, trusting conviction and commitment to the person on whom all religious formulations and prescriptions are predicated. Faith is not primarily intellectual assent (believing) but committed relatedness (belonging), and belonging can be justified culturally as well as theologically.[104] We must belong to each other, just as we belong to God. God is prior to the world and to the church, active in every culture both before and after the church arrives, and active in the church (in word and sacrament) before people of this or that culture assemble, believe, and act. But all of us, in virtue of our baptismal and cultural identities, must stimulate the relationship and dialogue between the two: between gospel (or church) and culture (local community). This imposes a missionary or missional responsibility on the church and all its members.[105]

There is always a danger that theologians and anthropologists (and their respective disciplines) take refuge or comfort in theory. It can become so neat, so wonderful to contemplate, so compelling. But it is never justifiable to theorize theology and culture at the expense of *people* of faith and *people* of culture. Neither theology nor anthropology can retreat into a pure "science of," at the expense of a committed "practice of," a disciple—a point consistently made by Geertz.[106] We need a practical theology that moves us between current experience and theory, between principles and agents, between the academy and the community, between the controlled environment and the real world—and back again—so as to serve and to generate the renewal of praxis, the name of which is conversion, piety, faith. This renewal starts with our own lives and encounters: it is the basis of all authentic evangelism. To paraphrase Cardinal Newman, no one will be converted by abstraction, by theory: only by encounter.[107] The church in what used to be Christendom will continue to make no headway if it is perceived as an abstraction, an irrelevance, and a deaf and distant moralizer.[108]

Local and Universal

A significant commonality shared by faith and culture is that each can be identified both in its broad or universal aspect and in its narrow or local form. Neither has an absolute priority: each depends on, and is related to the other. If culture is "the form of social life," then every person in society has culture. But everyone has language too; yet that does not mean that there is one universal language. Though language is universal, every language is particular. There are, of course, common features in languages: lexemes and morphemes (in common parlance, "words"), grammatical rules and constraints, semantic criteria, and all the rest. But the art-science of translation demonstrates very clearly that languages are also incommensurable. No language can be reduced to another, none can express all of perceived reality, and every language adds something to the universal phenomenon of language as well as to human comprehension of the world and its denizens.

As with culture, so it is with church. The church exists universally, yet there is no universal church *except as embodied and expressed in its multiple local forms*. Cardinals Ratzinger and Kasper had a lively debate on this subject, the former insisting that the universal church is prior to the local churches, the latter asking respectfully what that could possibly mean outside a world of Platonic forms.[109] But, as Rembert Weakland brilliantly observed, playing with words is just not good enough. If words have any common currency, the universal church *exists* in the local churches.[110]

There are, for us, two major implications. First, each local church has its own integrity and authenticity that absolutely must be respected. And second, if the universal church actually exists in its local manifestations, then each and every local church has something—something different and something unique—to contribute to the universal church.[111] It is not therefore a matter of some notional "universal church" tolerating local variations but all of us taking very seriously the image of the Body of Christ with its many parts, different from each other but organically related, united, and synchronized. The pastoral question is not whether universal *precedes* local, but how they coexist and relate.

Kathryn Tanner discusses theology as a cultural activity. Her argument develops in this way: theology is an activity done by theologians; theologians are people; and since theologians are people of culture and context, theology is inevitably colored by culture. But, she asks, is it culture specific? Is it something done *within* a specifically Christian culture, or at least within a Christian community or guild? In the final analysis she affirms that indeed it is.

Tanner cites Gordon Kaufman, who, emphasizing that culture is a human universal, seeks out cross-cultural commonalities as the basis for his theological synthesis. Not that he denies cultural specificity, but he tries to build a theology on cultural human universals. But anthropologists like to say that anything truly universal—like walking or talking, being happy or sad—is not particularly helpful in explaining human meaning and motivation, while anything that is a helpful cultural key to human meaning and motivation is not universal in its form. Even widespread belief in God or commitment to a creed tells us little about how such notions are actually understood.

Tanner points to David Tracy as one theologian attentive to human and cultural particularity. She might have identified anyone and everyone committed to the inculturation of the faith. But such attentiveness requires acknowledgment of, and engagement with anthropology's primary interest: cultural autonomy and cultural differences. Because there is no universal culture, anthropologists are perforce preoccupied with the particular—even as they seek to compare and generalize, though without reducing and standardizing. The social fact that culture is a human universal is less helpful to the anthropological and the theological enterprise than the empirical fact that humanity can only be encountered and studied locally, in its particularity.[112]

Cultural anthropology explicitly discloses the universal in the local and vice versa. It is committed to the notion that humanity is a single species but with infinite cultural variation that is not unimportant.[113] But the anthropological method also aims to disclose or expose what is common to humanity. Theology, or the church, however, has sometimes declared or imposed criteria and condemned whatever empirically failed to meet them. Thus it can speak about certain "intrinsically disordered" behaviors or states. But anomalies are always determined from particular cultural or theological perspectives and criteria. A daisy or a dandelion is neither a flower nor a weed until classified as such and until acknowledged as such by a community.

Hans Kohut and George Devereux contrasted "experience near" and "experience distant" concepts.[114] The former are derived from actual encounters and first-hand experience; the latter are declared or defined from a more distant, putatively objective perspective. If anthropology can be accused of being too "experience near" (and thus prone to relativism), theology may risk being too "experience distant" (and thus prone to be tempted by absolutism). A church committed to universalization and to articulating objective truth will find it rather more difficult to ask, seek, and knock, than to tell, require, and demand. But the integrity of the local will be thereby impugned and the enrichment of the universal compromised. The challenge posed by the local in the context of the universal, and the potentialities offered by the universal to the local, will only be met by those able to imagine "experience near" reality as "really real": as the sober experience of people seeking the inspiration of the Holy Spirit. This is one scale on which all efforts at inculturation will be measured.

The universal is not simply an aggregate of every local manifestation, though each and all of the locals together constitute the universal. To aggregate is to do violence to subjects, to individual agents.[115] Both the universal and the local have their own identity, just as every person with a U.S. passport is an American citizen; yet America continues to exist as new passports are issued and current passport holders die. Every American is unquestionably different; yet all Americans can and do share a common national identity—which is palpably real.

Between the local and the universal, tensions find a home. George Bernard Shaw recognized as much, and a dictum attributed to him observes that England and America are two nations *divided* by a common language. But tension is not all bad; where there is tension there is life. At least as much may be gained as lost by negotiating local and universal values, insights, and contributions. Why concentrate on impoverishment when enrichment is on offer? We are all different *and* all the same, and this is a godly gift. To standardize would be to coerce: and coercion is always immoral.[116] The universal will, and must, be modified by the local, or else the whole enterprise is just a charade.

The history of the expansion of Christianity discloses plenty of examples of the survival of the local,[117] but the renewed power of the church resulting from the Constantinian compromise ensured that the church's heavy hand could assure hegemony and enforce uniformity whenever deemed necessary. The Eusebian Accommodation provided theological justification for universal conformity and standardization. In Eusebius's words, "The Father is . . . like a supreme ruler" and "Jesus is the Lord, through whom the king . . . directs, in imitation of his Superior, . . . all the affairs of this world."[118] But, critically, local churches are *different* from each other, and difference is constitutive of their identity. If the faith is to be inculturated, the universal church must take local churches very seriously. The integrity of each is at stake. And to reiterate: the universal church actually *needs* local churches, as a body needs constitutive members. Greater unity is not assured simply through uniformity any more than it is by universalizing a single instance. *Cucculum non facit monachum*: the habit maketh not the monk, and the church is not an ecclesial cloning process.

To conclude this section with an ancient and modern observation: Gregory the Great (c. 600) said, "If there is any unity of faith, a difference of custom does no damage to the holy church"[119]—though the Fourth Lateran Council (1215) would beg to differ and indeed did so. Much more recently, Richard Fletcher put it this way: "The liberty to the convert of carrying a certain amount of traditional cultural equipment—as it were, a duty-free allowance—over the threshold of Christianity facilitated that transition for the individual. It also transmitted messages of reassurance to others. The shock of the new could be softened."[120]

Review and Preview

We may now recapitulate the argument and look to its outcome, in four points. First, Christianity began as a small and insignificant sect that did not have to worry about maintaining universal peace and order but could focus on the call to follow Jesus. Powerless and invisible, it grew from the bottom up, spreading largely through informal networks and it was valued as cost effective, though expensive. But the "Constantinian Compromise," "Constantinian Shift," or "Eusebian Accommodation" changed matters gradually but radically, and ensured Christian dominance (and its maintenance by the invocation of legitimate threat or force) in an operative world lacking a competing monotheism.

Second, before the end of the first millennium, Christianity (church of piety) was presenting another profile: the unmistakable church of power. Thereafter, one or other profile rather than the church's full face, would be more apparent, and the lines of tension would increasingly appear. When its authority was not perceived to be under threat, the institutional church of power would tolerate cultural and theological variation.[121] But if it felt threatened—by competing monotheisms (Jewish or Muslim) or by proto-reform groups from within—it would react with repressive power. Coercion was deemed essential for maintaining peace and order (religious tranquility). But the church of piety (more vulnerable and risk taking, prophetic and missionary) continued to embody an alternative ecclesial style. Tension remained, sometimes healthy and sometimes pathological, as the church established itself as coextensive with Christendom and strove to maintain and defend its monopoly. But ultimately, the whole "enterprise of Christendom was mistaken. It misidentified the nature of power according to the gospel."[122]

Third, "humanity" is a collective noun whose constituents are people, not generic but specific, individuated, culturally determined. So the legitimate universality to which the church aspires can *only* be realized in specific cultures and as a communion of local churches. Gospel must be "translated"—carried over—into the lives and languages of actual people, a process that demands of its bearers familiarity both with the deep meanings of the gospel (text and context) and the deep needs and aspirations of people of particular cultures.

Culture, too, must be understood in terms of actual people, which is why the following affirmation is so important: "Evangelization loses much of its force and effectiveness if it does not take into consideration the actual people to whom it is addressed, if it does not use their language, their signs and symbols, if it does not answer the questions they ask, and if it does not have an impact on their concrete life."[123] Actual people can and must become an authentic part of the dialogue, without which there is no true evangelization. Consequently, this whole agenda demands careful attention, on the part of theologians and pastoral agents, to local, cultural, and individual concerns, no less than to global, ecclesial, and evangelical values.

Fourth, to read church history as the story of the fluctuating relationships between power and piety can be illuminating in our own day. A church committed to defending its hegemony as the only way to maintain religious tranquility and exercise its divine mandate becomes counterproductive. Increasing internal fragmentation will result—and in a pluralistic world—the interreligious conflict characteristic of competing monotheisms will result as well.

These, then, are the broad lines of the argument. the final stage is to carry it forward into tomorrow's world, which can be done by building on four more principles.

In the first place, dissent is not necessarily disloyalty to the church and certainly not to God. Sometimes it is precisely the voice of dissent that calls the church and its members to greater faithfulness. The church of piety may find itself in dissent, as it tries to be faithful, but its own integrity demands that it remain faithful—to God and to Christ—in order to serve God's people.

Second, and conversely, to identify all dissent as insolence or heresy may be to perpetuate the fragmentation of the Body of Christ, when reconciliation and healing are called for.[124] A church tolerates dissonant voices and alternate views if it does not feel threatened or compromised thereby,[125] and a tolerant church is, by definition, open to variety. Perception of threat, and swift invocation of power and authority, should always be subject to review and reappraisal, for the sake of the unity (not uniformity) for which Christ prayed.

The third point is that if the theology and practice of inculturation is not to be permanently shelved or abandoned, then difference, dissonance, and a degree of dissent need to be negotiated through dialogue and not dealt with imperiously. Acknowledgment of, and respect for, interreligious pluralism—another social fact—seems the only way to a semblance of global tranquility. But intrareligious pluralism—pluralism within Christianity, including not only the acceptance of legitimate differences among various Christian bodies, but a real understanding of, and respect for, local churches within the Roman Catholic communion—constitutes a major part of a developing agenda.

Fourth, attention to this whole agenda demands a renewal of mission itself, as it—that is to say, the missionary church and the church in mission—engages with the social realities involved in inculturation, ecumenism, and interfaith collaboration. The totality of revelation by the one God extends far beyond the grasp of the Abrahamic religions and their historical and geographical boundaries. So culture and faith, dialogue partners for this enormous undertaking, must discover a more theologically informed anthropology and a more anthropologically informed theology. Its name is missiology, and it is a critically important assistant or midwife for a new creation being born of the Holy Spirit. But missiology without Johannes Arndt's "true Christianity" (practice and piety) remains theoretical and speculative.

Now, although these four things are mandatory, they are not new. They were always demanded of anyone committed to following Jesus, of true disciples.

The Place and Purpose of Mission

It is now a truism to say that mission is not simply a part of the church or its theology but that it is the church's *raison d'être* and the very action of the Triune God. But God the Creator made us all the same and yet all different, God the Son came to save humanity in its myriad particularities, and God the Holy Spirit inspires people of every nation, religious commitment, and good conscience. Gorringe describes the implications:

"A theology of the Spirit will be a theology of diversity in unity, of the valuing of real difference. At the same time it will have an underlying unity."[126] Meanwhile, Tanner, reflecting on humanity's inveterate cultural borrowing and *bricolage*, suggests that instead of trying vainly "to summarize the resemblances among all the different cases of Christian uses," we would be better served by acknowledging that "no pure Christian something exists."[127] Variation and difference describe humanity, and are therefore constitutive of Christians.

The point of mission is not simply to distance oneself from home but specifically to encounter humanity beyond one's familiar world, marked as it is by language, nationality, and religion. The purpose of mission, in fact, is to engage with God's own purposes, and therefore it can never be achieved by coercion or proselytism but only by a commitment to understanding and loving others better. In a world blighted by hostility where hospitality should reign, driven by the homogenizing tendencies of globalization at the expense of mutual respect and encounter with alterity, and seduced by a gospel of self-interest and consumerism rather than committed to a creed of altruism, the countercultural spirit of true Christianity, of true mission, is critically needed by women and men, poor and rich, deprived or privileged, whether Christian, God-fearer, agnostic, or atheist.[128] The stimulus or dynamo for such mission has always been, and remains, the church of piety.

Tragically, the church's mission, promised by the resurrection and born at Pentecost, has been historically compromised by ecclesiastical power seekers, by reduction of the *evangelion* to the semi-Pelagian pursuit of individual salvation by avoidance of actual sin, and by the development of elitist, exoticized, and very narrow understandings of mission itself.[129] But mission is neither controlled by nor reducible to the church. The church is servant, mission is God's, and those who forget this will inevitably reduce mission to "dangerous exclusivism and fanaticism."[130] The counterpart to hegemony is service; to good works, faith; and to elitism, inclusion. The best traditions of monasticism and mission are the major underwriters of ecclesial and social renewal. Far from there being no place for mission in a postmodern world, a rediscovery of its most authentic characteristics is as critical for human survival in a disoriented and self-destructive world as it proved vital and life giving in the world of the Roman Empire, long before Christendom and the Constantinian compromise. What does this entail?

It is easy to plot the history of Christian mission as a series of waves and to see what stimulates a new wave and what causes its collapse. Such an enterprise is only an approximation, one of several possible ways of modeling mission. But if in the past, missionary methods have been open to charges ranging from expansionism or confrontation to a spirit of competitiveness—not to mention coercion and crude proselytism—even that is still not sufficient reason to abandon the project. Rather, it could and should be a call to the conversion of the missionary and a rediscovery of the true dimensions and demands of mission.

Clifford Geertz, as he so often does, expresses the anthropological dimension beautifully, and Aloysius Pieris the theological. Geertz says that

> to see ourselves as others see us can be eye-opening: to see others as sharing a nature with ourselves is the merest decency. But it is from the far more difficult achievement of seeing ourselves amongst others, as a local example of the forms human life has locally taken, a case among cases, a world among worlds, that the largeness of mind—without which objectivity is self-congratulation and tolerance a sham—comes.[131]

This identifies the missionary challenge in terms of encounter and dialogue; but what of the outcome? Pieris (in Timothy J. Gorringe's words) says that "Asia will never be 'Christian' in the same sense that Europe was 'Christian.'"[132] Pieris himself says that, rather than baptizing Asia, the church itself must "be baptized in the Jordan of Asian religiousness."[133]

Before the consolidation of Christendom after the fifth century, there was no formalized "mission theology" as such.[134] Initially, the church was an insignificant sect. Yet even as it struggled to survive, it understood itself as having a centrifugal as well as centripetal dynamic. Tension, as we saw, was of its nature. The church gathered to scatter, just as the scattered church gathered. The missionary dynamic was embedded in the practice of the faith. But, as early mission theologies became more systematized, they were, as Luzbetak noted, "from above.[135]

The tension between centripetal and centrifugal forces and between gathering and scattering endures today in theologies from above and theologies from below. As the contemporary church explores the *sensus fidelium* in a post-Christendom, multicultural church marked by a huge variety of human experiences, it finds itself in acute tension with a theology from above. Tension can be resolved by submission or capitulation, or extended by dialogue or by loyal dissent. Christian mission, which serves God's vision (wider than the church's), and the inculturation of faith in myriad cultures and persons, both demand, as we noted, imagination as much as obedience, and an analogical imagination that is freed for both/ and possibilities rather than confined to either/or solutions. Now that we have considered the relationship between faith and culture, the universal and the local, similarity and difference, power and piety, and theology and anthropology, perhaps we are, at last, better placed to undertake a more imaginative—but certainly not risk-free and not blindingly clear—approach to mission.

To a reflective and responsible Christian, mission is mandatory but governed by rules, and not simply rules of doctrine but rules of humanity and charity. It cannot be based on coercive power, and it demands of the missionary true piety (Arndt). If it produces a local church, that church must be identifiably local, though part of, and in communion with, the universal church. But even before a local faith community has been formed, Christians who represent the church must show respect and graciousness; rudeness and bad manners are never justifiable. If the faith is to be taught and caught, it must be an inculturated faith, a faith that bonds with and is expressed in cultural terms, without violence and manipulation. Christians who deliberately try to *follow* the Spirit and to "learn of" Jesus can be a healing force in the world. But the tension between power and piety has tended, historically, to be addressed and resolved in favor of power, notwithstanding cyclical reform movements. In our own day, secular values of hegemony, triumphalism, and even Constantinianism still prevail.[136] In the contemporary church, the Enlightenment promise of freedom, distorted into self-centeredness, has produced the bitter fruit of alienation and meaninglessness in so many lives.[137]

Above all, perhaps, the missionary call challenges us to a more public (not "civil") religious practice or, more properly, to faith-in-action. The early second-century anonymous *Letter to Diognetus* (dated by scholars between 120 and 150) speaks of the self-effacing commitment of Christians, whose only power base is piety. They do not

> lead a life marked out by any singularity, [but] display to us their wonderful and confessedly striking life. Every foreign land is to them as their native country, and every land of their birth as a land of

strangers. Christians are known as such in the world, but their godliness remains invisible. Christians, though subjected day by day to punishment, increase the more in number. God has assigned them this illustrious position, and they are not at liberty to forsake it.[138]

After almost two thousand years, that near-invisible church of piety, having once swollen to a highly visible church of power,[139] has gradually become again a near-invisible church of privatization in many places. But a dispirited and attenuated church that has become a purely private matter will have ceased thereby to be the church of Jesus Christ.[140] Christian discipleship and Christian mission are needed in order to sustain a church community in communion with other communities. Otherwise, the church in some of its local incarnations will die, as indeed it has, throughout two thousand years.

A putatively universal church suffering from local paralysis or necrosis is barely recognizable as the Body of Christ. The universal church—specifically in its local incarnations—needs Christians with creative imagination, vibrant faith, and undimmed hope. This is a very tall order, and fewer and fewer people seem to have the fortitude, whether due to personal limitations or external constraints. But I conclude that authentic discipleship and significant Christianization can come only through true piety and deep commitment to personal conversion and ongoing reform. Some scholars say that true Christianity came only through the Reformation and its aftermath;[141] others say that it has not happened for sixteen centuries.[142] But it was not only the Reformation of the sixteenth century that contributed to a recovery of true Christianity, but both the reforms before it and those it provoked and has inspired ever since.

Power, Piety, and Paradox

We all like some degree of clarity and control, if not certainty in our lives, even though we know how unrealistic this can be. The promises of Christianity—that "all will be well, and all manner of things will be well"[143] or that "those who persevere will be saved" (Lk 21:19)—nevertheless coexist with a set of paradoxes: "now we see, but as in a glass darkly" (1 Cor 13:12); the *basilea* is "already, and not yet"; and so on. Paradox is an apparently absurd or contradictory thesis that may nevertheless contain deep truth, and it is a characteristic of religious verities that they be expressed in paradox. Paradox may bring us close to the mystery, though some see only the absurdity.

Certainly the Christian story abounds in paradox. As Christians called to have the Spirit of Christ and sent to share it with others, we should not fear paradox but learn to live with some "hard sayings" (Jn 6:60). After all, we are a people of hope, and hope is founded on commitment to the promises of the unseen God. Where everything is evident and unequivocal, hope would be redundant. Here, then, are seven paradoxes or aspects of paradox that challenge us. Each illustrates some of the tension and even the crisis we are called to embrace as people of faith. Some we have already identified, but now we can consider their cumulative force.

1. A church called to be truly universal yet created and crafted out of local materials is called to embrace that very paradox, to live with the tension, and to strain to focus through a binocular rather than a tunnel vision of reality. Likewise, a church sent into the whole world and yet called to respect people in their particularity must struggle with the mystery. But a church that promotes the good news of salvation by promoting crusade and justifying mortal violence must surely look at the scandal and destruction it creates, and must repent before it makes matters worse.

2. The central anthropological paradox, to which we already referred, but that has immediate implications for theology and mission, is that human beings are all different yet all the same. Human differences *are* deep and should not be trivialized or dismissed; yet human similarities are substantial and not accidental. Literary critic Lionel Trilling makes this point and draws a compelling conclusion: "The similarities between ourselves and others removed in place or period, are so much more profound than are the surface differences separating us from them, that their imaginative products can be put at the service of our moral life."[144] Similarly, our own imaginative products—our creative initiatives and responses to common human problems—can likewise be put at the service of their moral life. This is central to the missionary vocation.

But we must not overlook the real differences between ourselves and other people: the paradox is not to be resolved but engaged. Likewise, the mystery within the paradox remains. Geertz gets it right: "We are left," he says, "with the irresistible riddle that the significant works of the human imagination [he then identifies Kabuki theatre or Monteverdi opera; we might add the Tridentine Liturgy or the RCIA] speak with equal power to the consoling piety that we are all alike, and to the worrying suspicion that we are not."[145] This pushes us once again to address the missiological questions.

3. The faith is a treasure of which we are justifiably proud; as Christians we are called to share the treasure; and one of the purposes of mission is to assure that this sharing takes place. But God's gratuitous gift and our generous commitment to its distribution can never justify the use of force or fear. However well intentioned, the Crusades were unjustifiable and sinful fruits of a Christian practice compromised by Constantinianism and of a Christian piety contaminated by Christian power. Attempting to justify the means by appeal to the intention or the end is a contradiction of basic principles of civilized behavior. If, to reiterate a memorable phrase of Gorringe, "power is the thread that stitches the seams of the cultural garment,"[146] the church must be exceedingly wary, lest it become compromised by a particular culture and betray its first loyalty to the gospel. The paradox is that the church is called to be in the world but not of the world, and to use legitimate power even though power tends to corrupt.

4. A further paradox is that the very monastic foundations that, from the sixth century onwards had initiated and carried forward both reform and mission, had, by the thirteenth century, been at times compromised by splendor, wealth, and their own commercial success. Piety had made unholy alliances with power. Cluniacs had collapsed under the weight of liturgical splendor, Cistercians had become the merchants and entrepreneurs of prosperous Europe, and Benedictines luxuriated in the resources furnished by monastic industry and the generous sponsorship of the laity.[147] Abbot prelates now enjoyed the trappings of royalty and the favor of princes. And this paradoxical situation generated others: the paradox of a church that had lost a sense of mission, of a church calling people to reform but in dire need of reformation itself.

5. Jesus calls for "reversals": the first must become last; adults must become as children; mature people must be born again; to live you must die. These are all paradoxical notions. Each encapsulates tension and embraces mystery. Each requires a response; yet the process and final outcome remain unclear. These "reversals" must be addressed, not by choosing between and then excluding but by choosing among, and including. Thus we are called not to be *either* first *or* last but to a delicate integration, not to be *either* children *or* adults, *either* alive *or* dead, but to be something of each, a little of both, and always in the process of conversion. In a similar

fashion, we should not polarize or flatly oppose "faith" and "culture" because they too have a symbiotic relationship.[148] A pathological condition results when one or the other is insufficiently cherished or challenged or where one is exclusively privileged.[149] There will always be tension, though the simple fact of tension is quite insufficient as an indication of good health.

6. Here is a rich paradox: Jesus prays that they all may be one (Jn 17:21) and that disciples should be born again (Jn 3:3); yet despite that, as Stark points out, "sects and reformations are *inevitable phenomena*, because, even if there is One True God, there can never be only One True Church."[150] This implies that the inveterate differences between people, and their own human weakness, mean that even though humanity and the truth are one, humanity will continuously realign itself and contest different understandings of truth, just as it will fall from grace or judge others as falling from grace. This human weakness produces sectarianism and a never-completed conversion, necessitating a never-ending series of reformations.[151]

7. Given Jesus' teaching on servanthood, or Paul's on weakness, should we conclude that Christians must always eschew power? Is hegemony always negative, and is countercultural Christianity always antihegemonic? Again, there is paradox here. We distinguish "power," the simple ability to act upon someone or something, from "authority," understood as the legitimate, legitimated, authorized use of power under particular circumstances and by appropriate persons. Authority ultimately belongs to God, and—classically—human authority purports to derive from it. So, "power" in the sense of "legitimate authority" is surely consistent with the gospel. "Hegemony" understood as domination is unjustifiable. If Christianity is truly countercultural, it must therefore be antihegemonic.[152] But in the sense that Christianity aspires to build a new social order, it has the opportunity to demonstrate a more authentic form of the freedom of individual conscience.[153] Such hegemony, paradoxically perhaps, might enable the (single) leadership and rule of Christ without standardizing the response or dissolving the differences between human beings.[154]

Peter Phan raises some critically important questions for the church in the United States. It is, he says, "embedded in this superpower [U.S.]," so "how can it credibly preach Jesus' teaching on non-violence?" Furthermore, "how can the church, whose hierarchy is still dominated by whites, relinquish its eurocentrism and accept other cultures as valid ways of living the gospel?"[155] He is putting a finger on the paradox of a church of power and piety and a church both universal and local. The undoubted power that the Catholic Church still wields in the United States comes with great responsibilities. A truly cost-effective church would be seen to be publicly committed to justice and peace—everywhere and for all, both within and beyond its own community boundary. This, Phan reminds us, is constitutive of authentic Christianity. But Constantinian Christianity is very much alive in the United States and elsewhere, and a church that acknowledges its own privilege but fails to be prophetic—a church that fails to speak truth to power—is a church still some way from its own conversion. Again Phan notes, there was

> a massive failure of leadership of the American Catholic church in the recent presidential election [2004]. The bishops remained mute . . . as the country was inflicted with an immoral war, lack of healthcare for the poorest, massive tax cuts for the wealthy, naked violation of human rights, refusal to establish effective policies to protect the life of the unborn . . . and the imposition of unconscionable economic burdens on future generations through a colossal federal debt.[156]

All of this is true: but it does not fall only upon the bishops but upon each and every one of us. This is the missionary challenge, and it should leave none of us unaffected, even in the midst of the pursuit of theological insight!

Reform and the Future of Missionary Christianity

Despite his good intentions for Christianity, Constantine succeeded in undermining one of its characteristic features: its voluntary nature.[157] Gradually, informal but effective "Christian missionizing" broke down in the fourth century, leaving much of Europe unchristianized. By degrees, the church of power became the dominant force—and force is the operative word here—in Christendom. As Stark says, "the laxity of the church of power was seen as nothing less than sinful heresy from the perspective of the church of piety."[158] Until the late sixth century, it would be the church of piety that kept the flickering flame of mission alive in the church.

Gerald Arbuckle writes, "With the peace of Constantine, the church's leadership uncritically acculturated itself to the courtly and hierarchical ways of the imperial system. Bishops now used the power symbols of royalty, in dress and title. Priests accepted authority over people and downplayed their role as servants."[159] He quotes Yves Congar: "There existed an imperialism which tended to confuse unity and uniformity, to impose everywhere the Roman customs and rites: in a word, considering the universal church as a single extension of the church of Rome."[160]

But this needs to be nuanced, for the church of piety remained as a prophetic witness to such creeping imperialism. Moreover, at least initially, the imperial, acculturated profile was more evident in the Eastern church; in the West, simplicity and discipleship remained more visible as the church strove to remain separate from the principalities and powers, to survive as antiworldly and radical. But unquestionably, tension rumbles through the subsequent social evolution of the church, erupting periodically down to our own day.

To conclude and to close with one of Gorringe's many trenchant comments: "Constantinianism has to be disavowed. The total identification of a political goal with the will of God always unleashes demonic powers."[161] Many agree with this assessment, and yet there is more to be said; for having identified the project as a failure and sometimes reprehensible, hope remains. The hope is that, in a postmodern world, where Christianity poses no threat and holds no promise, Christians can again explore the cost-effective potential that has been latent for so long.[162]

The saga of Christianity is not simply the history of Christianity so far. Nor is it to be identified with the history of Christian theology. As Peter Berger said, it is the history "of a particular kind of religious *experience* and religious *faith*. Consequently, the future of Christianity will not depend on any theological program. If Christianity has a future, it will be in the resurgence of Christian experience and faith in the lives of people who have never read a theology book. Yet what theologians do is not irrelevant."[163]

For those of us here today, and many others further afield, the history of Christianity is still unfolding towards its *telos*, its end point in Jesus Christ. Those who do read theology have a critical role in midwifing the new creation of new ecclesial communities, of local churches, of inculturated faith. Theology, and theology books, are part of our journey and part of our lives. But in the final analysis, what we cling to and what we seek more intensely is what Berger identifies as the priority and what Johannes Arndt identified four hundred years ago as the "true Christianity" of piety and practice. It is the experience that comes only from encounter with real people, and from an abiding faith in the one who called us to be followers, and in order to send us forth.

Notes

1. Johannes Arndt, *True Christianity* (Mahwah, NJ: Paulist Press, 1971 [1606]).

2. Jonathan Benthall, Editorial, *Anthropology Today* 21, no. 2 (2005): 20.

3. Rodney Stark, *The Rise of Christianity: How the Obscure, Marginal Jesus Movement Became the Dominant Religious Force in the Western World in a Few Centuries* (Princeton, NJ: Princeton University Press, 1996).

4. Where people were more "selfish" and concerned for their own survival, they would be unlikely to find assistance in their need, since everyone else would be looking after their own welfare. But Christians actually sought out people in need, and made a virtue of tending the sick and the destitute.

5. Stark, *The Rise of Christianity*, 5–7.

6. Rodney Clapp prefers "Constantinian Shift," quoting John Howard Yoder: "The most 'pertinent fact' of the Constantinian Shift was not that the church was no longer persecuted but that the two visible realities of church and world were fused." See Rodney Clapp, *A Peculiar People: The Church as Culture in a Post-Christian Society* (Downers Grove, IL: InterVarsity Press, 1996), 23. Clapp leans heavily on John Howard Yoder, "The Otherness of the Church," *Mennonite Quarterly Review* 35 (October 1961): 212. The essay has also been published in Michael G. Cartwright, ed., *The Royal Priesthood* (Grand Rapids, MI: William B. Eerdmans, 1994), 53–64.

7. Richard Fletcher, *The Barbarian Conversion: From Paganism to Christianity* (New York: Henry Holt, 1997), 190.

8. Rodney Stark, *For the Glory of God* (Princeton, NJ: Princeton University Press, 2003), 33.

9. Doing theology as a way of life in the early church would have been very challenging, and not for the last time. Apart from examples from our own time, we can note that with the rise of the universities after 1200, "theology became the revolutionary—the most high risk—discipline" in the church (Stark, *For the Glory of God*, 62, with further references). Theologians no less than others are challenged to live a cost-effective Christianity.

10. Alan Kreider, "Beyond Bosch: The Early Church and the Christendom Shift," *International Bulletin of Missionary Research* 29, no. 2 (April, 2005): 62.

11. Quoted in Fletcher, *The Barbarian Conversion*, 24.

12. Quoted in Linda Woodhead, *An Introduction to Christianity* (Cambridge: Cambridge University Press, 2004), 9.

13. For historian C. N. Cochrane, Constantine was "the one human being to have enjoyed the distinction of being deified as a pagan god while, at the same time, he was popularly venerated as a Christian saint" (C. N. Cochrane, *Christianity and Classical Culture* [Oxford: Oxford University Press, 1944], 12).

14. Woodhead, *An Introduction to Christianity*, 11.

15. See ibid., 43–55. For Eusebius, orthodoxy is prior to heresy, and heresy is a later deviation or "innovation." Historian Walter Bauer, says Woodhead, asserts the opposite; out of "heresy" or "opinion," "orthodoxy" is formed. See ibid., 59. But once "orthodoxy" has been defined and defended, authorities that perceive dissent as a threat (see Stark, *For the Glory of God*) label it heretical and attempt to suppress it. Consequently, some legitimate reform movements will inevitably encounter opposition from a centralized church of power.

16. See Fletcher, *The Barbarian Conversion*. Fletcher brilliantly establishes this. During the Roman Empire there is *no* example of a bishop being appointed *ad extra*, for mission to the barbarians, as it was later understood. The exception is here an *existing* (fledgling) Christian community has been founded and requests a bishop. Such persons included Frumentius of Axum (Ethiopia), Theophilus the Indian (Arabia), Ninian and Palladius (England), and Ulfila (Goths). But these went as bishops of existing communities, even if beyond the imperial frontier. If "*Romanitas*" equaled "*Christianitas*," everyone within the empire in principle belonged to the church, and everyone outside it did not. This establishes a Christian polity (25). "The conversion of the heathen was not perceived as the church's main function" (76).

17. Fletcher, *The Barbarian Conversion*, 78, 85, 86. Before the Roman withdrawal from Britain in the fifth century, there were Christian enclaves in Galloway (Scotland) and Ireland. But Patrick was the first deliberately to venture beyond the borders of empire.

18. Columba was a monk who crossed the sea but remained within his own linguistic and cultural milieu. His was a life of pilgrimage ("*peregrinatio propter Christum*") rather than mission in the classical sense. But Columba's activities, as he renounced his homeland, "merged insensibly into mission" and the network of monasteries became "mission stations" (Fletcher, *The Barbarian Conversion*, 94, see also 94–96).

19. Woodhead, *An Introduction to Christianity*, 12.

20. Already, in 180, when the Christian population was only about one hundred thousand, Irenaeus lists nearly two dozen "heretical" groups. Hippolytus, a little later, counted almost fifty. See Stark, *For the Glory of God*, 117.

21. Woodhead, *An Introduction to Christianity*, 11.

22. Fletcher, *The Barbarian Conversion*, 24.

23. Cited in Woodhead, *An Introduction to Christianity*, 33.

24. Cyprian, *Ad Quirinum* 3, 52.

25. Kreider, "Beyond Bosch," 63.

26. Fletcher, *The Barbarian Conversion*, 28.

27. Clapp, *A Peculiar People*, 25.

28. Fletcher, *The Barbarian Conversion*, 28.

29. Richard Horsley, *Sociology and the Jesus Movement* (New York: Crossroad, 1989), 58; Kenelm Burridge, *In the Way: A Study of Christian Missionary Endeavors* (Vancouver: University of British Columbia Press, 1991), 59–72; Rodney Stark, *One True God: Historical Consequences of Monotheism* (Princeton, NJ: Princeton University Press, 2001), 159–62.

30. Clapp, *A Peculiar People*, 25.

31. "Many reform movements arose because the church failed to reform, while insisting on its absolutely religious monopoly"—and often overreacting by the imposition of coercive power. Stark counters those who claim that heretical movements were largely about class conflict and power struggle. They were not materialistic but moral, and the emphasis was on authentic form (Stark, *For the Glory of God*, 60).

32. Clapp, *A Peculiar People*, 25.

33. Ibid., 27.

34. Ibid., 28.

35. Clapp quotes J. D. Hunter, who says that Constantinian civil religion in the United States "has been enlarged from evangelical consensus to Protestantism-in-general, to the Judeo-Christian-tradition-in-general, to deism-in-general"—with a sprinkle or topping, we might add, of Gnostic, privatized, "me-and-Jesus" spirituality to taste (Clapp, *A Peculiar People*, 31, quoting James Davison Hunter, *Culture Wars: The Struggle to Define America* [New York: Basic Books, 1991], 69).

36. We must not make such a strong contrast between the pre- and post-Constantinian church as to suggest they are polar opposites. Since Pentecost, the church has lived in tension. But the pre-Constantinian church "did not see itself as sponsor of the world," while Constantine himself "made his aim the legislation of Christ's millennial kingdom in a generation" (Clapp, *A Peculiar People*, 23, 24, citing Cochrane, *Christianity and Classical Culture*, 211).

37. See Stark, *For the Glory of God*, 17–20. The idea is an application of Max Weber's notion of "cost effectiveness."

38. Ibid., 24.

39. Kreider, "Beyond Bosch," 62.

40. Ibid., 62.

41. Dietrich Bonhoeffer, *The Cost of Discipleship* (New York: Touchstone, 1995), 35–36.

42. Ibid., 45–46.

43. Ibid., 36–37.

44. "You have heard it said . . . but I say to you"; "The first shall be last and the last, first," and so on.

45. For a helpful summary of polarities and paradigms (including David Bosch and Andrew Walls), see Kreider, "Beyond Bosch," 59–68. Kreider avers that compulsion is not simply a feature of the "Western" or "Catholic" church. It is indissolubly linked with the Christendom phenomenon. Thus the demise of Christendom may well be the door to a renewal of authentic piety and appropriate authority.

46. Stark, *One True God*.

47. Heresy is "socially constructed": it is not "given" but must be identified by someone and from some perspective. What distinguishes a heretical position from one accepted as a legitimate development or reform depends on who has control (power).

48. The masses were only "slightly" Christianized. Their religion was characterized by popular piety rather than by orthodoxy. They were minimally sacramental, and the higher clergy and papacy were widely effete or corrupt. This picture, as with most generalizations, needs to be nuanced but provides a valid contrast with the *Church of Piety*. See Stark, *One True God*, 159, and Michael Singleton, "Let the People Be: 'Popular Religion' and the Religion of the People," *Pro Mundi Vita Bulletin* 61 (July 1976).

49. Ramsay MacMullen, *Christianizing the Roman Empire* (New Haven, CT: Yale University Press, 1984), 119.

50. Religious life could be a potential or actual challenge to a lax church or a threat to current orthodoxies. Stark claims that variations or differences within religious orders were much greater than those among the laity or ordinary clergy. But religious life was a way of challenging energies, thus preventing the multiplication of sects, but always at the possible cost of challenging the church of power and the unity it attempted to broker and maintain.

51. True "mission"—in the sense of formal or systematic outreach *beyond* the confines of institutional Christianity *and to* and *for* the unbaptized—developed only in the fifth century, probably with St. Patrick, as developed above.

52. Stark, *One True God*, 160.

53. Stark, *For the Glory of God*.

54. "A 'contrast society' or 'alternative community' [is] counter-intuitive and requires a process of re-education, escaping hegemony. Did Paul intend to replace the hegemony of the *Pax Romana* with the *Pax Christi*? I think he

did, but through the agency of the whole 'contrast community.' The vision (1 Cor 12) was lost in the Christendom situation which, in the distinction between priest and lay, instituted precisely that distinction between expert and everybody else which [is] the mark of an alienating hegemony" (Timothy J. Gorringe, *Furthering Humanity: A Theology of Culture* [Aldershot, England: Ashgate, 2004], 145).

55. Woodhead, *An Introduction to Christianity*, 51.

56. Yet, consistent with the cyclical nature of reform, even the ascetic and monastic witness came to be seduced or softened by the lure of the church of power. Courageous, prophetic women disciples were reined in and controlled by an increasingly patriarchal hierarchy (Woodhead, *An Introduction to Christianity*, 56–57).

57. Stark, *For the Glory of God*, 40.

58. Woodhead, *An Introduction to Christianity*, 93.

59. "Augustine brought [the *Regula Pastoralis*] to England [598 A. D.]; [King] Alfred [c. 900] had it translated; every bishop in England was instructed to have a copy; it was widely disseminated in the Carolingian church for the education of priests, and given to every bishop at consecration" (Henry Davis, ed., *St. Gregory the Great, Pastoral Care, Ancient Christian Writers*, vol. 11 [Westminster, MD: The Newman Press, 1950], 11.

60. Woodhead, *An Introduction to Christianity*, 93.

61. Davis, ed., *St. Gregory the Great*, 35–36. Fourteen centuries later, Pope John Paul II said something remarkably similar to his bishops: "Experience shows that when priority is given to outward stability ["power"], the impetus to personal conversion, ecclesial renewal and missionary zeal ["piety"] can be lost and a false sense of security can ensue. Bishops need to be esteemed as successors of the Apostles not only in authority and sacred power, but above all by their apostolic life and witness ["piety"]." Quoted in Rocco Palmo, "New Model Bishops," *The Tablet*, June 25, 2005, 21.

62. Stark, *For the Glory of God*, 41–44.

63. The Holy Roman Empire would extend from Brittany to Croatia, and Holstein to Catalonia. For the conversion of the West, including the best of mission and the worst of coercion, see Fletcher, *The Barbarian Conversion*, 97–222. "Charlemagne made the link between secular and spiritual imperialism even closer . . . with a hitherto unmatched brutality. For the first time in Christian history a state-sponsored mission used the faith quite unabashedly as an instrument for the subjugation of a conquered people [the Saxons]" (Fletcher, *The Barbarian Conversion*, 194–95).

64. Ibid., 92. Fletcher also makes the point that there never was a "Celtic" church *as opposed to the Roman*. Such terms are too monolithic and polarizing.

65. Ibid., 229.

66. Ibid., 229–30.

67. Ibid., 231

68. See ibid., 231–44.

69. The Venerable Bede, *A History of the English Church and People* (New York: Dorset Press, 1985).

70. Fletcher, *The Barbarian Conversion*, 273.

71. See ibid., 329–65.

72. Ibid., 451.

73. England was evangelized by Augustine of Canterbury around 600. Remarkably, by 630, priestly ordinations proceeded apace as a native clergy was created, thus setting the priest *among* the people. But "a prime aim of the Gregorian Reformers [1073–1085] was to set the priesthood apart from the secular world as a separate, disciplined, and above all celibate caste. These measures were intended to improve standards of ministry" (Fletcher, *The Barbarian Conversion*, 464).

74. Hermann Pottmeyer, *Toward a Papacy in Communion: Perspectives from Vatican Councils I and II* (New York: Crossroad, 1998), 14. See also 25–33.

75. Fletcher, *The Barbarian Conversion*, 1.

76. Ibid., 502–6.

77. Quoted in Laurent Theis, "Les Templiers," *Le Point*, May 11, 2005, 54. My translation.

78. Stark, *One True God*, 161.

79. Stark, *For the Glory of God*, 68.

80. David Edwards, *Christianity: The First 2000 Years* (Maryknoll, NY: Orbis Books, 1997), 255. Reforms were talked about at the Council of Vienna (1311); but there was no ecumenical council in the fourteenth century (*Christianity*, 253). The papacy increasingly dominated. Gregory VII (Hildebrand, the reformer, 1073–1085) supported an absolutist, monarchical papacy: "The pope can be judged by no one; the Roman church has never erred and will never err" (Gerald Arbuckle, *Violence, Society and the Church* [Collegeville, MN: Liturgical Press, 2004]). Innocent III (1198–1216) claimed that the pope alone represented Christ. The fact that from 1159 to 1303 every pope was a lawyer is not inconsequential here (Woodhead, *An Introduction to Christianity*, 112–17).

81. See Stark, *One True God*, 162. Michel Foucault also develops the notion of power, but his usage is different. He contrasts "strong power" (the noncoercive power of attraction) with "weak power" (the coercive power that is invoked when strong power fails). For him, hierarchical imposition of authority is "weak" and degenerate. Authentic reformation is through "strong power"—very close to our use of *piety* here.

82. Woodhead points out that early "desert Christianity" may have been part of a "heretical" tradition but was co-opted by Catholicism. See *An Introduction to Christianity*, 53–55.

83. See Stark, *One True God*, 219–59, esp. 219–22.

84. Many authors identify (and oppose, contrast, polarize, or dichotomize) these two aspects. Woodhead favors "high power" and "low power," showing how both were combined in Jesus who was both divine and human. She also identifies "power from above" (hierarchical) and "power from below" (the power of kenotic discipleship), showing the historical tensions between the two. Like any heuristic device, this contrast can harden into a false antithesis. Part of the paradox or scandal of Christianity is its combination of power and powerlessness. Kenelm Burridge contrasts the "Devotional" and the "Affirmative" modes of being church, also complementary: the former emphasizing asceticism, sacrifice and surrender to God ("piety"), the latter emphasizing engagement in culture and improving social conditions ("power") (Burridge, *In the Way*, 59–70 and passim). But the affirmative mode is as ambiguous and packed with contradiction as "power" is. Richard Horsley talks of the "little tradition" ("piety"), a counterpoint to the magisterial power. In contrast, Michel Foucault speaks of strong and weak power: the former is authentic, true, and biblical ("piety"); the latter is bogus and backed by coercion. See Margaret Miles, *The Word Made Flesh: A History of Christian Thought* (Oxford: Blackwell, 2005), 212, 305.

85. John Milbank and others seem to *oppose* "power" and "piety" rather than seek a relationship of complementarity (see Kathryn Tanner, *Theories of Culture: A New Agenda for Theology* [Minneapolis, MN: Fortress Press, 1997], 97). In *A Spirituality of the Road*, David Bosch argues that Jesus epitomizes the complementarity, and that we must follow him in this (David J. Bosch, *A Spirituality of the Road* [Eugene, OR: Wipf and Stock, 2001 (1979)]).

86. Stark, *One True God*, 220; Singleton, "Let the People Be"; Anthony J. Gittins, *Bread for the Journey: The Mission of Transformation and the Transformation of Mission* (Eugene, OR: Wipf and Stock, 2001), 132–48 (on popular religion).

87. One of the best anthropological discussions of cultural anthropology as *interpretative* ethnography is by Clifford Geertz (see *The Interpretation of Cultures: Selected Essays* [New York: Basic Books, 1973] and *After the Fact: Two Countries, Four Decades, One Anthropologist* [Cambridge, MA: Harvard University Press]). A recent discussion of theology and culture is by Kathryn Tanner (*Theories of Culture*).

88. Geertz, *The Interpretation of Cultures*, 12–13.

89. Einstein declared that "imagination is more important than knowledge." See George Silvester Viereck, "Interview with Albert Einstein: What Life Means to Albert Einstein," *Saturday Evening Post*, October 26, 1929.

90. This imaginative engagement produces *empathy*: a capacity to resonate with other people and their experiences, *not* by thinking we completely understand or have experienced what they experience, but by making imaginative connections between (our limited comprehension of) their (unique) experience and our own analogous experiences. The basis of empathy is common humanity, not identical experiences.

91. John Paul II, Address to the Italian National Congress for the Ecclesial Movement for Cultural Commitment, *L'Osservatore Romano*, Eng. ed., June 28, 1982, 7.

92. See David Tracy, *The Analogical Imagination: Christian Theology and the Culture of Pluralism* (New York: Crossroad, 1981).

93. Notwithstanding Jesus' other injunctions *not* to broadcast the "messianic secret" (Mt 16:20).

94. Gorringe, *Furthering Humanity*.

95. Ibid., 3, 23, 102.

96. Ibid., 105–6.

97. See ibid., 102.

98. Quoted ibid.

99. This leads logically to a consideration of the relationship between the universal church and its local incarnations, the topic of the next section.

100. A point made by Walter Hollenweger and Wilfred Cantwell Smith. See Walter Hollenweger, "Evangelization in the World Today," *Concilium* 114 (1979): 40–41, and Wilfred Cantwell Smith, "Idolatry in Comparative Perspective," in *The Myth of Christian Uniqueness*, ed. John Hick and Paul Knitter (Maryknoll, NY: Orbis Books, 1987), 53–68.

101. Gorringe, *Furthering Humanity*, 102.

102. Paul Avis, *A Church Drawing Near: Spirituality and Mission in a Post-Christian Culture* (Edinburgh: T & T Clark/Continuum, 2003), 170–71, 187.

103. Quoted in Avis, *A Church Drawing Near*, 184.

104. Avis, *A Church Drawing Near*, 184. See also Geertz, *The Interpretation of Cultures*, 175–76, on Bali and internal conversion. "The Balinese seem much too busy practicing their religion to think . . . very much about it."

105. Avis, *A Church Drawing Near*, 188, 36–40. A recent neologism, the word "missional" is intended to identify a boundary-breaking dynamic that will characterize every authentic Christian and Christian community. Avis quotes Erik Erikson and identifies quest, content, and meaning as constituting identity, which is located both "in the core of the individual and in the core of his [or her] communal culture. But quest is assisted by encounter, content is informed by culture, and meaning is accumulated in narrative. This scheme neatly gathers the themes of missionary outreach (encounter),

dialogical engagement (culture), and the gospel (narrative)" (Avis, *A Church Drawing Near*, 39. See Erik Erikson, *Identity: Youth and Crisis* [London: Faber and Faber, 1968]).

106. Clifford Geertz, *Local Knowledge: Further Essays in Interpretive Anthropology* (New York: Basic Books, 1983), 10–35.

107. Mission must "be offered on as broad a front as possible, through a multiplicity of points of access. The church must draw nearer than it often does to human needs, questions and aspirations—and it must be seen as doing so" (Avis, *A Church Drawing Near*, 199).

108. Ibid., 198.

109. For an excellent summary of the debate, with a bibliography of the articles that both Ratzinger and Kasper wrote in dialogue with one another, see William Clark, *A Voice of Their Own: The Authority of the Local Parish* (Collegeville, MN: Liturgical Press, 2005).

110. I cannot, unfortunately, retrieve the original source for this important observation.

111. Cultures need not to be cut off at the root. This is necessary both for their own survival and because the universal church can forever learn from new examples of how humanity exists and persists in society. See Geertz, *The Interpretation of Cultures*, 189.

112. Tanner, *Theories of Culture*, 63–67.

113. Geertz quotes Lionel Trilling: "One of the significant mysteries of [human] life in culture [is]: how is it that other people's creations can be so utterly their own and so deeply part of us?" (*The Interpretation of Cultures*, 54).

114. On Devereux, see Joan Cassell, book review essay, "Authenticating (and Inauthenticating) Local Moral Worlds: Ethnologies of Interpersonal Experience," *American Anthropologist* (2000): 619. For Kohut, see Geertz, *The Interpretation of Cultures*, 57.

115. Geertz, *The Interpretation of Cultures*, 21–22.

116. This may sound harsh. Was not the liturgical calendar formalized and standardized without coercion? The answer is complex. The imposition of uniformity certainly helped oust paganism and heresy, but many local churches remain deeply dissatisfied, and attempts at "liturgical inculturation" continue to be stymied. See Woodhead, *An Introduction to Christianity*, 39, 45.

117. Stark says, "It is far less the case that Christianity 'Romanized' the Germans than that the latter 'Germanicized' Christianity. The subsequent addition of Greco-Roman learning was more decorative than fundamental" (*For the Glory of God*, 134). Fletcher says, "The conversion of 'barbarian' Europe brought all manner of Roman and Mediterranean customs" (*The*

Barbarian Conversion, 1). Nevertheless, Rome would tolerate what was not threatening but confront what was, as with the Synod of Whitby in 664.

118. Woodhead, *An Introduction to Christianity*, 44, 9.

119. See Arbuckle, *Violence, Society and the Church*, 59.

120. Fletcher, *The Barbarian Conversion*, 520.

121. Stark, *One True God*, 220.

122. Gorringe, *Furthering Humanity*, 173.

123. Paul VI, *Evangelii Nuntiandi*, 63. The same paragraph also warns of the danger of compromising the gospel by uncritically favoring local culture.

124. In a somewhat more restricted context, but with obvious applications, Walbert Bühlmann said, "Third World theologians must be granted the 'right' to risk 'heresy'; it has been a constituent part of history. Mistakes will probably be corrected by the *koinonia* of other theologians and bishops. . . . Outright denial of a dogma of faith is one thing, but exploration, the discovery of hidden dimensions, is something else. If Christology could make use of 'pagan' Greek concepts, how can the use of Hindu philosophy be excluded *a priori*? No one who understands the genius of Hinduism would think to question the orthodoxy of a Christology incorporating Hindu elements" (*The Church of the Future*, 156–57).

125. Stark, *One True God*, 46.

126. Gorringe, *Furthering Humanity*, 102.

127. Tanner, *Theories of Culture*, 147–48.

128. Because of the demise of Christendom, "mission no longer originates with a Christian world, so neither does it continue to address a 'pagan' world. It addresses a world that God so loved" (Lucien Legrand, *Unity and Plurality: Mission in the Bible* [Maryknoll, NY: Orbis Books, 1990], xii).

129. Gorringe, *Furthering Humanity*, 256.

130. Legrand, *Unity and Plurality*, 5.

131. Geertz, *Local Knowledge*, 16.

132. Gorringe, *Furthering Humanity*, 207.

133. Aloysius Pieris, *An Asian Theology of Liberation* (Edinburgh, Scotland: T & T Clark, 1988), 53. "Cosmic [*local*] religions postulate a Transcendent Reality. Once a metacosmic [*universal*] religion has taken root, history shows that one metacosmic religion cannot be dislodged by another except through force" (Gorringe, *Furthering Humanity*, 207). Korea is cited as a partial exception; relations between Christianity and Islam are confirmation.

134. There was no *systematic* missiology in the Patristic period. Only rustics (within) and not barbarians (without) were considered. But Chrysostom, Augustine, and Gregory the Great—and the anonymous writer around 440 have proto-theologies of mission. The latter-mentioned is "the first work

. . . concerned with infidels" (Fletcher, *The Barbarian Conversion*, 33. See also Luzbetak, *The Church and Cultures*, 15, 115, and 163).

135. Ibid., 199, 115. It is well known that the earliest expansion of Christianity was a popular ("lay") rather than a hierarchical ("clerical") movement.

136. And this, despite clear warnings articulated for Matthew's community in the very early years. See the "seven woes" in Matthew 23, especially verses 11–12.

137. Stanley Hauerwas and Will Willimon, *Resident Aliens: Life in the Christian Colony* (Nashville, TN: Abingdon Press, 1989), 50 and passim; Viktor Frankl, *Man's Search for Meaning* (New York: Simon and Schuster, 1984).

138. James A. Kleist, trans. and annotated, *The Didache, The Epistle of Barnabas, The Epistles and the Martyrdom of St. Polycarp, The Fragments of Papias, The Letter to Diognetus*, Ancient Christian Writers, 6 (Westminster, MD: Newman Press, 1948), extracted from chaps. V and VI, 138–40.

139. John Milton excoriated the pretensions of the seventeenth-century Church of England in his poem *Lycidas*: "The hungry Sheep look up, and are not fed./But swoln with wind and the rank mist they draw,/Rot inwardly, and foul contagion spread."

140. Robin Horton and Bryan Wilson have argued separately that "religion" before the Enlightenment or as found in more "traditional" societies can be seen to have four functions: explanation, prediction, control, and community-building and sustaining. With post-Enlightenment seculariztion, the first three functions have been co-opted by other institutions, leaving religion either with a crucial community-building function, or with very little else other than self-defeating privatization (Robin Horton, *Patterns of Thought in Africa and the West* [Cambridge: Cambridge University Press, 1993]; Bryan Wilson, *Religion in Sociological Perspective* [Oxford: Oxford University Press, 1982]).

141. Stark, *For the Glory of God*, 77; Hauerwas and Willimon, *Resident Aliens*, 167–68; Clapp, *A Peculiar People*; Fletcher, *The Barbarian Conversion*; Woodhead, *An Introduction to Christianity*; and Gorringe, *Furthering Humanity*. Stark notes that a single exception is southern Europe.

142. Hauerwas and Willimon are among the number, but others, such as Stark, Clapp, and Avis (*A Church Drawing Near*) imply as much.

143. Julian of Norwich, *Showings*, chap. 27, in *Classics of Western Spirituality*, ed. Edmund Colledge and James Walsh (New York: Paulist Press, 1978), 225.

144. Cited in Geertz, *Local Knowledge*, 41.

145. Geertz, *Local Knowledge*, 41.

146. Gorringe, *Furthering Humanity*, 105.

147. Fletcher, *The Barbarian Conversion*, 519–20.

148. "Culture cannot be discussed without taking account of power. What allows us to speak of 'revelation' with regard to the Christian scriptures is their continuing capacity to challenge our taken for granted pieties. . . . If Scripture fails to do that, if it consistently failed to do so, then we might argue that the church of that period had been colonized by culture, [and] we could no longer speak of revelation" (Gorringe, *Furthering Humanity*, 119).

149. "If mission brings a 'gospel' then it can change a culture, but culture can also radically change the gospel. [Pope John Paul II fails to see that] the theology in Europe [USA] might be purely 'indigenous' and stripped of any true link to Christ" (Gorringe, *Furthering Humanity*, 179).

150. Stark, *For the Glory of God*, 119.

151. Reformations—or reforms—(typically by the church of piety) can be seen as expressions of cost-effective Christianity: people cherished their faith to the point of sacrificing their lives. "Each Reformation exhibited a courage and vitality which astonish us as we remember how much power—physical, emotional, and intellectual—had been wielded without much confidence by the authorities of medieval Catholicism. A claim made at the time was accurate: not only Europe but also Christianity was being renewed" (Edwards, *Christianity*, 281).

152. For an excellent and wide-ranging discussion, see Gorringe, *Furthering Humanity*, 129–46.

153. "When Christianity was a minority religion, the fourth century convert Lactantius wrote, 'religion cannot be compelled. The whole thing must be done with words, not whips, so that it be voluntary.' . . . Augustine defended correction, not destruction of the heretic. . . . [But] Thomas Aquinas asked, 'Should heresies be tolerated?' He answered No. True, God was always ready to forgive, [but] 'The Church cannot imitate this'—perhaps the most chilling line in Thomas" (John T. Noonan, *A Church That Can and Cannot Change* [Notre Dame, IN: University of Notre Dame Press, 2001], 151–52).

154. "The new hegemony of which Jesus speaks is called 'subalternity.' Liberation theology is built on the fundamental biblical insight of the priority of the poor, to argue that a new society (hegemony) must be built from the bottom up, not the top down" (Gorringe, *Furthering Humanity*, 146).

155. Peter C. Phan, "Where Are We Going? The Future of Ministry in the United States," *New Theology Review* 18, no. 2 (May, 2005): 6.

156. Ibid., 9.

157. Stark, *One True God*, 61.

158. Ibid., 220–21.

159. Arbuckle, *Violence, Society and the Church*, 59.

160. Ibid., quoting Yves Congar, "Christianity as Faith and as Culture," *East Asian Pastoral Review* 18, no. 4 (1981): 310. This "simple extension of the church of Rome" is what Lamin Sanneh characterizes as the "global church," rather than the "world church" that would be extended throughout the world, not in universal uniformity but with appropriate diversity. See Lamin Sanneh, *Whose Religion Is Christianity? The Gospel beyond the West* (Grand Rapids, MI: William B. Eerdmans, 2003), 22–23.

161. Gorringe, *Furthering Humanity*, 253.

162. "Constantinian Christendom seems to be definitively ending, and reshaping of ecclesial thought and practice greater than those of the Reformation and comparable, perhaps, to the fourth century, may well be unavoidable" (George Lindbeck, "Scripture, Consensus and Community," *This World* 23 (1988): 16–17, cited in Clapp, *A Peculiar People*, 214, note 12).

163. Peter Berger, *The Heretical Imperative: Contemporary Possibilities of Religious Affirmation* (New York: Doubleday Anchor, 1980), 171.

7

Ghana's Witches: Scratching Where It Itches!

Jon P. Kirby, SVD

Dr. Kirby's provocative lecture begins with a description of "witch camps" in northern Ghana that sequester (mainly) women who have been accused of witchcraft. He then analyzes the phenomenon of witchcraft and locates it within the economic development of women in Dagomba (northern Ghanaian) society and the jealousy that such development engenders. The lecture was delivered on October 16, 2006.

I am visiting Fr. Joseph, the Catholic priest at Ngani, northern Ghana. Elderly women have gathered at the church compound and are enjoying themselves drumming and dancing. It is their annual Christmas celebration. It would all seem quite festive if it were not for one sobering thought. They have all been accused of witchcraft and have been forced to live out the rest of their days at Ngani, one of the so-called witch camps of northern Ghana. Without a doubt this is the happiest day of the year for them. They will have a full meal, share the local strong drink, *pito*, and they will laugh, dance, and sing. For one day in the year, they are human again.

This presents an immense contrast with the rest of their year, which is bleak and without hope. Just two hundred meters away, across the road from the church, is the witches' quarters, a warren of mud hovels with knee-high walls that deny even the slightest hint of privacy or human dignity. Here there is no dancing, no singing, no laughing or feasting. There is only inhuman suffering and misery. Their situation denies them even the most basic of human necessities, food and water, shelter and clothing, but most of all human recognition, companionship, and love.

189

Northern Ghana is celebrating one hundred years of Christianity this year (2006). The lengthy celebrations, elaborate activities, honorifics, and awards tend to emphasize the great progress that has been made in education, health care, and in Christian life. But some areas of life have been almost completely neglected. Witchcraft is perhaps the most problematic of these, not only in northern Ghana, but also throughout Africa. This is therefore a fitting topic for this year's Luzbetak lecture.

Even since I first visited him at the Center for Applied Research in the Apostolate in 1969 while I was studying in Washington, DC, Fr. Luzbetak has been an inspiration for me. Louie was, above all, a practical anthropologist with the common touch. Two of his sayings hover in the air whenever I think of him: (1) knowing the "mind of the people," which means doing the necessary digging, making use of the human sciences, especially cultural analysis; and (2) "scratching where it itches," or offering culturally appropriate responses to peoples' problems. These have led me along paths that were not well trodden and on others that I have had to forge for myself.

Inculturation and Africa

We theologians and missiologists are often quite glib in accepting inculturation as normative for today's ministries. Seeking the insider's cultural knowledge in order to offer culture-specific responses are the hallmarks of incarnational ministry, contextual theology, and they are the backbone of inculturation. Yet, in the two generations that have passed since Vatican II, very little of this has actually been done in Africa. Inculturation has stalled in Africa and elsewhere because so few know what they are doing.

The real work of inculturation, the actual digging into the meanings of the people, has been especially neglected. Theologians have not been equipped to do the digging for one thing, nor have they interpreted things from the people's perspective—preferring what they know from their training to be God's perspective—so, in most cases they have not taken the mind of the people very seriously. The two main reasons for this, I believe, are naïve realism (what we see is really what is there) and ethnocentrism (what I see is more real than what you see). Africans no less than Europeans fall prey to these fundamental blocks to learning. Today we need ministers who are "crossers," who are able to cross over

and act as bridges to other "minds." Thus they need to be practical anthropologists who know how to put the human sciences, especially anthropology and cross-cultural psychology, to work for them.

However, not all who chant "inculturation" will enter the mind of
the people. It doesn't just happen. Inculturated ministries need to be uncovered by crossers. The process is very simple, and it is the same for any
crosser—to be open, honest, and loving. But it involves a lot of digging,
searching, learning, and scratching. To defy naïve realism and ethnocentrism, we must first take the absolutely realistic posture of a learner. This
is (1) that the other has something valuable we need to learn, (2) that we
don't already know it, and (3) that we can only learn it from the people.
Then we need to be evangelized by the Spirit already present and working within their world. They will teach us their mind, and the Spirit
will teach us where to "scratch." Only after we actually start appropriate
Spirit-led "scratching" and see the fruits of the Spirit can we speak theologically about it.

My aim here, then, is twofold: to do some inculturation and to reflect
on the process. The doing involves seeking the "mind of the people"
about witchcraft, being attentive to what real people say and do, and
honestly understanding their knowledge, and the way the Spirit of the
gospel is already in dialogue with this knowledge, in order to arrive at
loving ways to enhance the work of the Spirit. The reflecting is to stimulate among ministers and theologians, especially in Africa, an appreciation
for the overall process of adapting ministries to cultural contexts before
reflecting on them theologically.

Cultural analysis is always tied to real case studies, the experiences and
the understandings of real people. We will therefore focus on the phenomenon of witchcraft in the kingdom of Dagbon in northern Ghana,
where I have been digging and learning for more than thirty years. We
will try to locate "the mind of the people" in their worldview, as it has
been contextualized in the past and the way it interprets the present. Although it is a particular place, the learning process itself, as well as many
of the particular findings, apply quite broadly across Africa.

There are four witch camps like Ngani in northern Ghana. All of
them are situated in Dagbon, the kingdom of the Dagomba people, except the camp at Gambaga among the Mamprusi people who are their
direct cousins. We shall focus on the camp at Ngani and compare it with
the camp at Gambaga as the need arises. Although little is known of their

exact origins, we do know that these two go back to precolonial times and that they arose as a more compassionate response than execution. To Western sensibilities, the camps are hardly compassionate. But even the slightest probing reveals a startling truth; as bad as their condition is, none of the women wishes to go back home, for that would mean certain death. These women are outcasts, banished from their communities, cut off from their people like a cancer. A deeper look reveals that what appears to be the offensively cruel and heartless treatment of elderly women is, from the people's perspective, motivated by a genuine drive for self-preservation, the quest for life, and the attainment of life's goal. It is not just the life of an individual that is at stake but also that of the community and, indeed, the very principle of life itself. To better understand how and why this is the case we need to examine their worldview.

The African Worldview

If the African is "incurably religious," as Mbiti says,[1] then witchcraft is at the very heart of this religion and worldview. Before going any further, then, it will be necessary to outline this worldview. We will examine it in terms of four presuppositions: the unity of the seen and unseen worlds, their interconnectedness, a hierarchy of being, and an internal dynamic.

Basic Understandings of Witchcraft

To the Western mind, beliefs about witchcraft are superstitious and irrational—not to be taken seriously by educated people. Yet, when I asked Simon Atunga, the head of the Gambaga Outcasts Project of the Presbyterian Church, and a quite educated man, if he believed in witchcraft, he responded, "Yes, here in Ghana, everyone believes in it. If someone tells you they don't believe, they are lying." Simon is not alone in his view. Almost two generations ago, Jahoda's study of Ghanaian university students showed a widespread belief in witchcraft regardless of educational level, and a more recent study shows little has changed.[2]

We might rather ask why it is that the Western mind doesn't accept witchcraft and has roundly rejected African presuppositions concerning the unseen world while not examining its own presuppositions. Witchcraft proceeds out of a collectivist cultural grounding of relationships. It occurs where people experience themselves as inherently connected to others and to the unseen world. The primary experience of oneself as connected to others and as the "objects" of others' attention leads to the presupposition of personal causality. If bad things happen, it is because of their attention. So where people are group oriented, such as in Africa, it is far from being irrational or superstitious. It is simply "their reality," just as the primary experience of unrelated individual selves provides the basis for the presupposition of nonpersonal causality and a nonexistent unseen world in the West.[3]

In the West, witchcraft may be benign and trendy, but in Africa there is nothing more sobering than the threat of witchcraft. In the light of the interconnectedness of all things, it is any serious threat to life or any life-negating thought, intention, or action. Wherever the principle of life is threatened, especially in cases of untimely deaths and misfortunes that block the primary goal of life—becoming an ancestor—witchcraft is always present.

This is not to say that the internal workings of the phenomenon do not change. In fact we have been witnessing quite momentous changes over the past two decades including socioeconomic, political, and familial changes, and we shall take these up below, but the belief itself is not fading away. On the contrary, the underlying conceptions not only persist, they are the filter through which the various imported institutions, arrangements, and facts associated with modernity, are colored, interpreted, judged, given new meanings, and dealt with.[4] I am sometimes asked by well-meaning Westerners, "When will Ghanaians stop believing in witchcraft?" To this I can only reply, "When will the Western world begin to take seriously African philosophical, social, and psychological orientations?"

The "Seen" and "Unseen" Worlds

The first unshakable presupposition is that the African world occupies two dimensions, the seen and the unseen. The unseen or the spirit world is so closely linked to the seen—the physical and material one we see about us—that it is conceived to be all part of the same reality. One routinely sees trees next to family compounds that are "clothed" with a band of traditional woven cloth because a diviner has revealed them to be ancestors "come back" to protect the house. To the question "Where are the ancestors?" one usually hears the response, "They are sitting right here among us." All of creation participates in relationships extending in two dimensions—horizontally among the living in the visible, material world and vertically between them and the agents of the invisible world.

Interconnectedness of All Things

The second presupposition is the interconnectedness of being. The unseen world is connected with the seen, the vertical dimension with the horizontal. All things are connected in a great chain of life. Whatever happens in the seen world affects relations in the unseen world, and vice versa. When relations are broken in one dimension they are broken in both and need to be reestablished in both. Both vertical and horizontal mediation are needed.

Hierarchical Order

The third presupposition is the hierarchy of being.[5] The uncreated God, source of all life, is at the top of the hierarchy, followed by the created world with the divinities and earth spirits, or "God's children." This is followed by the ancestral spirits, nature spirits, and errant "bush spirits" who inhabit the unseen world. This is followed by the seen world beginning with humans, animals, vegetation, and insensible matter in the seen world. The errant bush spirits include disembodied humans who did not become ancestors but who embody, as we shall see, the power of witchcraft.

The hierarchical order of life dictates the rules of subsidiarity for propitiation and mediation, and establishes a hierarchy of problems and of problem solving. God relates to problems proper to God or those associated with the overarching sky, that is, transterritorial problems such as worldwide drought, epidemics, and disasters. The earth spirits and divinities relate to territorial problems such as localized drought, epidemics, and disasters. The ancestors deal with problems of the household or extended family such as quarrels, poverty, illness, famine, and infertility. The tutelary or guardian spirits relate to problems affecting individual destiny such as "bad death," bad destiny, ill health, infertility, and other personal misfortunes. Witchcraft can be the cause of problems at any of these levels. In its broadest conceptualization it is simply the blocking of life's goal.

Dynamic Universe

The fourth presupposition is that the world is dynamic, that being is in flux. Life is conceived of as a problematic passage or cycle. An Anufo elder once explained it to me thus:

When a new child is born the naming ancestral spirit (guardian spirit or tutelary spirit) approaches God and tells God that he/she will go into the world as a new child and then tells all that will happen during life. God puts His seal of approval on this and the new child is born. As life progresses it gradually becomes clear whether the child has a good or bad destiny. Life moves ahead until the person completes life becoming an ancestor or fails to become an ancestor, thus living an incomplete life.

The goal of life is to complete the "life cycle"—from the domain of the ancestors and God through life's difficulties and back to the ancestors and God. The objective is to accrue life in the seen world in order to achieve fullness of life in the unseen world. Thus the older and closer one is to the ancestors, ideally the more life filled one becomes. Ancestors, who have already achieved "abundant life,"[6] are appealed to for help in this passage. Mediators such as diviners, earth-priests, and the elders also assist in this.[7] Successful strategies always involve both the horizontal (seen) and vertical (unseen) relations.

God and Evil

Evil, or that which blocks abundant life, is a result of human choices, not God. African etiologies about the origin of evil always involve the disobedience of humans (usually women) and a choice that is at the same time both for "life" and against "life." Among the Bulsa of northern Ghana, God allowed all the soup ingredients but forbade the use of pepper. One day a woman decided to try putting pepper into the soup—and so evil entered the world. Among the Akan, God was thought to be quite close at first, and evil came about when a woman who was pounding the basic staple food called *fufu* kept knocking God with her pounding stick thus forcing God to move further away.

Divination

The system needs diviners who can look into the unseen world to see the connections with the seen and thereby determine the source of misfortune, the witch, or other blocks to life. Thus, diviners are "misfortune tellers" who are more concerned with the past—why relations have broken down and resulted in misfortune—than the future. They try to discern the causes of life negation. Once the cause is found, the problem is solved either by substitution, propitiating the particular agent responsible, by "putting food into the mouth of trouble," or by seeking protection against the source, for example, witchcraft. In either case appropriate sacrifices or "gifts" are required in order to reestablish a life-affirming state.

Life-Negating Forces

Evil is any personalized force that stands in opposition to life and to those striving to accrue it. Because of African collectivist values, good and evil are always contextualized in terms of relations with others. The primary reference point is not "I think therefore I am," as in the West, but "We are, therefore I am." It is not the existence of good and evil per se that is relevant, as it is in the West, but rather its presence in people. In Africa, we are what we do. Good exists as a result of what good people do, and evil exists as result of the evil people do. In Africa, therefore, misfortunes are never by chance or of themselves, the witch is evil incarnate, and "once a thief always a thief." Evil persons lurk behind evil deeds.

Since the seen and unseen are joined, evil exists in both. The many misfortunes and evils that do not seem to have any visible person as their immediate cause must therefore be caused by unseen agents and the bad intentions of others. The saying "You will see!" is an example of the power of such evil intent. It is a powerful curse that, in effect, declares spiritual warfare, and it is always taken very seriously. If something bad happens, for example, a lorry accident or illness, it is believed that the person uttering the curse has caused it, and he/she is held responsible—he/she is the witch.

Death per se is not "life-negating" but merely a transition in the life process leading to fullness of life among the ancestors. But some forms of illness and death are "life-negating" in that they block this end or cut destiny short. The clearest example is "bad death" (lit. "bad corpse"), which refers to such antisocial ends as the death of a woman in child-birth, suicides, and death alone in the bush. It can also include victims of witchcraft, who need special rituals to wash them of the taint of this unfulfilled-destiny.[8]

The Earth Shrine as the Key

Life-negating forces are not only a danger to individual lives, but they also defy the collective life of families, communities, and the very principle of life itself. They defy the unity and integrity of life in both its horizontal and vertical, physical and spiritual dimensions. At the community level, witchcraft, and certain other life-negating acts,[9] break the vertical relationship between the seen and unseen worlds and threaten the horizontal relations among the people and their environment. A state of ritual pollution ensues.[10] If nothing is done to correct it, things begin to die. Nothing grows. People fall victim to unlikely accidents and misfortune. When the vitality and fertility of the earth is killed, only pain and suffering are harvested. War, in particular, causes this perilous state of pollution. For the peoples of Dagbon, the earth needs to be ritually restored.[11]

At the family level, untimely deaths, particularly of children, "spoil the house" or destroy the life principle within the extended family unit. These require rituals directed to the ancestors to restore the connection with the life-principle at this level. But if witchcraft is involved, it is always considered a potential threat to the whole community. "Spoiled house" can quickly advance to "spoiled earth" because of the contamination involved. Earth shrines act as key junctures for the maintenance and renewal of relations between the seen and unseen worlds at the community level, and this accounts for the earth's ultimate responsibility for the control of witchcraft—and thus for the fact that all witch camps are located within the premises of an earth shrine.

Oracles and Rites of Control

The various oracles or divinatory practices that form part of the apparatus of earth shrines to discern the presence of witchcraft are all functions of the shrine's life-enhancing/death-defying power. The process of discernment usually requires the accused to take a "drinking oath," which is also called the "washing of the stomach" (lit. insides). Through these rites the accused are "put into the shrine" or under its power, and witchcraft is thereby nullified. Those accused persons lose their power and become "servants" or "wives" of the shrine.

The ritual restores vertical integrity—at least as long as the "witches" are "covered by the shrine"—but not the horizontal. Both vertical and horizontal healing is required in order to restore the full harmony and unity of life. The accused persons can be ritually cleansed and their witchcraft nullified by the earth-priest, but horizontal mediation is also necessary—acceptance by the community is also needed. It takes time for trust to be reestablished. Essentially it involves taking back the spoken word, the "curse" of accusation, which when spoken takes on a life of its own in the community. Among small, isolated homogeneous societies the earth-priest performs this role but in larger state societies such horizontal mediation can only be done by chiefs.[12]

History of the Dagbon

We now turn to the history of Dagbon, especially slavery and its effect on the peoples' understanding of themselves and their relationship to one another. We will try to connect the past with the present in order to gain some insight into their understanding of the camps and witchcraft in general.

Since precolonial times, the most powerful chiefs of the North have been those of Dagbon, the centralized state of the Dagomba people.[13] Over five hundred years, they gradually gained control over most of the territories and peoples of what is now northeast Ghana. Today, with a population of around one million, Dagbon is bordered in the north by the kingdom of Mamprusi, on the west and south by that of the Gonja, and on the east by the Togo border. The language, called Dagbanli, is a member of the Gur or Voltaic family, and their culture is a mixture of the original Voltaic raiders and that of the Konkomba groups that they raided and incorporated.[14]

The Konkomba

The Konkomba (*kpankamba*), who have a segmentary-lineage type of sociopolitical organization,[15] live in the eastern side of Dagbon. They were in precolonial times, and in many ways still are, subservient to the Dagomba. Konkomba have no chiefs but organize themselves politically around clan or lineage heads and religiously around earth-shrine custodians. They are completely autonomous and greatly value their freedom—so much so that they are intensely resentful of any expression of authority and meticulously avoid the show of any authority over others. Regarding this, and other fundamental values, they are diametrically opposed to their overlords the Dagomba. These opposing cultural pathways are the essential ingredient for the periodic conflicts that occur between the Dagomba and Konkomba peoples.[16]

The Witch Camps

Ghana's four established witch camps[17] are all associated with earth shrines, and three are located in eastern Dagbon. The camp at Gambaga, in the neighboring Mamprusi area, is the fourth. It serves both western Dagbon and the Mamprusi traditional kingdom from which the Dagomba peoples migrated in the fifteenth century to establish their own satellite kingdom thirty kilometers north of Tamale.

Ngani is a town of about two thousand inhabitants (five hundred Dagomba, fifteen hundred Konkomba), which is located fifty kilometers east of Yendi next to the Oti River. It lies along the major precolonial east-west trade route from Yendi to Hausaland, and it marked the eastern outpost of the Dagomba kingdom and the frontier with Konkombaland. The town is divided into two parts—the Dagomba section along the main road and the Konkomba section to the north, toward Konkombaland proper. The "witch camp," which is simply referred to as "*ten*" (earth), has its origins in the precolonial period.[18] It is located within the precincts of the earth shrine in the Konkomba section and counts as its inhabitants about five hundred persons (two hundred men and three hundred women). Some of these are family members who have accompanied the accused. Like the town, the camp is also divided into Dagomba and Konkomba sections.

One is immediately struck by the prominent, parallel divisions. The population of the town is split—Dagomba vs. Konkomba—and the offices of life over vertical and horizontal mediation are also split—Konkomba earth-priest versus Dagomba chief. This runs contrary to their understandings of their world. Why this should be so requires further explanation.

Dagomba Domination

The expansion of Dagbon took place in two stages. In the first stage, in western Dagbon (1500–1700), Dagomba warriors killed the Konkomba earth-priests and usurped their roles.[19] As they expanded eastward, they gradually assimilated the indigenous Konkomba peoples. The second stage (1700–1900), in eastern Dagbon, was quite different. Due to the Asante conquest of Dagbon (1742–72) and the increased demand for tribute in the form of slaves (one thousand to two thousand per year), domestic animals, and foodstuffs, their "benevolent" raiding turned predatory with little assimilation of people or earth-priests. The Konkombas were pushed further and further eastward and northward.

When the British took charge in 1900, they put a stop to the raiding, but with the institution of "indirect rule," they put Dagomba chiefs in charge of the Konkomba and the other groups without chiefs, making it possible for them to continue extorting labor, wives, foodstuffs, and animals. The Dagomba status as chiefs, royals, and commoners at the upper levels of the state hierarchical ladder and the Konkomba place at the bottom as little more than slaves, "*grundo*,"[20] became fixed. Dagomba chiefs maintained political powers while Konkomba earth-priests retained ritual powers, which were made subordinate to the political.

This separation of roles, status, and identities was reinforced and continued after Ghana's independence and found its way into successive governments. Political patronage maintained and widened the split between Dagomba political authority and Konkomba ritual authority, and between the chiefly and nonchiefly groups in general. In 1979, the new constitutions made northern lands the property of the chiefs, who hold the land on behalf of their people. But this excluded the Konkomba and other nonchiefly groups who form the majority and alienated their lands. These unequal relations were challenged by a series of ethnic conflicts with the government always on the side of the chiefs. In 1992 the constitutions were challenged but the law remained in force. This led to the devastating 1994 civil war in which the entire north was embroiled. As noted above, widespread conflict indicates that witchcraft is abroad.

During the colonial era the development of the North had been purposely retarded by the British who saw the North as only a labor pool for the mines and cocoa farms of the South. The first schools in the North, in the 1930s, were limited to children of the chiefs. Although, with the tacit approval of the British administration, the Missionaries of Africa, or the "White Fathers," had been working in the areas bordering on Burkina Faso already from 1906, missionaries were officially excluded until the 1950s, when they opened schools and literacy programs for all, including the Konkomba and other acephalous peoples. Soon the Bible and other publications emerged in these languages and gradually, with more education, the people became conscious of their ethnic identity and denied rights. By the late 1970s, education led to new awareness that, in turn, led to the series of ethnic conflicts over identity, dignity, land, and political representation.[21] Thus the churches played an important role in conscientizing the oppressed non-chiefly groups.

Witches, Chiefs, and Earth-Priests

The political divide between the Dagomba and Konkomba peoples, originally brought about by slave raiding and reinforced through the colonial era into the modern, also brought about a split in mediation between vertical and horizontal mediation, but only in east Dagbon. This is the reason that all the witch camps are in east Dagbon,[22] and there are no camps in west Dagbon. In west Dagbon the earth-priest, who is also a chief, combines the two roles needed for this dual reintegration. Here, the traditional system is able to provide the appropriate solution. As earth-priest, he administers the "washing of the stomach" of the accused and reestablishes relations with the "unseen" world. Then as chief, he provides the impetus needed for acceptance by the community.

The effects of this dual role are clearly evident in the handling of accusations by the earth-priest chief of Yongduni, a town in west Dagbon ten kilometers northwest of Tamale. The "drinking oath" normally taken to abjure any connection with witchcraft becomes a two-edged sword in his hands. The accused is brought before the chief by his/her accusers. He/she either admits to being a witch, and is subjected to a ritual that nullifies the "witch medicine," or swears that he/she is not a witch, and the shrine is expected to kill the accused if he/she lies. If the oracle shows that the accused is not a witch, the accuser must recant and the accused is accepted back. If there is any more trouble or if the accuser(s) refuse to accept the person back, then the accuser(s) themselves become a source of disunity within the community—in effect they become the "witches."

Thus the repair system that aims at restoring unity of being is able to function moderately well in west Dagbon. It helps keep accusations in check and offers some protection for the weak. Even so, the system is not perfect, and it is always the weak who suffer.[23] Accusations are a factor of the political power and influence that the accuser versus the accused exercise in the larger community. A powerful accuser can insist on another trial by ordeal, but a weak accused must submit to whatever "they say" about him/her. In the end, it is the social dynamics of power in the community that finally determines whether or not the horizontal integration takes place, and although the chief normally has the most weight, when the community is adamant the accused is sent to the camp at Gambaga. But even this is temporary.

It is clear then that "witch camps" are as a whole intended as sanctuaries, not prisons. They serve an important function in society. Witches are accused in the heat of anger. People need time to cool down and trust must be reestablished. The full solution can only be one that harmonizes both vertical and horizontal relations, bringing about complete reintegration into the community. This is possible in west Dagbon because of the dual role of the earth-priest chief. But in the case of east Dagbon, this is prevented by the continued separation of the offices themselves, which is reinforced by the separation of their respective ethnic groups—Dagomba have only chiefs (horizontal mediation), and Konkomba have only earth-priests (vertical mediation).

This insight leads to a further distinction in the types of camps—permanent (those in east Dagbon) versus temporary (Gambaga). In east Dagbon, the witches cannot go back, but at Gambaga the "Outcasts Project" has successfully helped more than fifty to return. East Dagbon suffers from the separation of the vertical and horizontal mediation and is incapable of healing itself. Thus a split in the two authority roles brings about and maintains a split in the two unified dimensions of their worldview—the seen and unseen worlds. This is, in turn, maintained and aggravated by the ethnic division. The witches are only the tip of the iceberg. The issue is not how to return the women but the inability of the system to reconcile peoples or their broken worlds.[24] This is where we must do the "scratching."

The Present: A Time of Change

We now turn to life in Dagbon today. We will be especially intent on the changes that have had an effect on understandings of witchcraft.[25]

In the 1950s, the anthropologist David Tait found seven factors related to the rise of witchcraft accusation in Dagbon: (1) seasonal rainy season famines, (2) tensions in the house, (3) women's leisure, (4) men's frustrations, (5) general insecurity, (6) economic deprivation and food insecurity, and (7) availability of an easy solution.[26] We will try to examine the major changes in the light of these factors.

Ghana was virtually bankrupt from 1978 to 1988. But throughout the 1990s, due to economic recovery programs driven by loans from the big donor countries, the World Bank, and the International Monetary Fund, the national economy and the flow of goods and services between north and south greatly expanded.[27] Northern improvements included the completion of the north-south highway, electrification and general face lifts in the major northern cities, and the nongovernmental organization (NGO) boom. As never before, commodities flowed to the North, including bicycles, motorcycles, and vehicles of all sorts, building materials, farming supplies, and implements. But besides these general goods, a special category of goods also increased. It included enamel bowls and serving ware; women's clothing; wax prints; head scarves; cosmetics like oils, creams, lipstick, nail polish, and hair dressing supplies; jewelry; and all manner of goods that were simply referred to as "women's things." These were stockpiled in sideboards and megasuitcases in women's rooms. From the 1990s onward, the only pause in the flow of these goods was occasioned by the lack of cash to buy them, but the vast bulk of these goods remained inert and simply gathered dust in women's rooms. Here, quite ironically amidst the appearance of plenty, we find "economic deprivation," one of Tait's causes.

Much of the NGO boom was development and aid money intended to launch production, but this did not happen. Although northern production of maize and livestock marginally increased, most of the production went to the South for cash. The cash paid for the improvements. During the 1980s, people had reverted to a subsistence economy where cash was needed only for salt. One decade later, cash was needed for everything: school fees, hospital fees, medicines, fertilizers, pesticides, fuels, water from boreholes, electricity and the use of all the new utilities, and above all taxes. These far exceeded the average person's modest earning power and because most of these new expenses were in the public sphere, for services used by the family or the whole community, the obligation to pay for them fell to the men. This has led to a feeling of generalized frustration and insecurity especially among the men of the community, which confirms two more of Tait's major causes of witchcraft.

Increase in Accusations

Over this same time period, accusations against women increased alarmingly. Most of the cases I interviewed in some way fit into the profile of economic change described above coming into conflict with the traditional rules governing the division of roles and responsibilities. In almost every case of accusation there was tension in the household, which confirms another of Tait's observations. We offer details of one such case.

Pagkpiema is a Konkomba married to a Dagomba. She says she left her Dagomba husband because after her first child, her other children kept dying (this is already an indication of witchcraft). She went to her home village and became an additional wife of a Konkomba man. She had five more children with him. Listen to her story:

> What made me to come here is that the son of my husband want-
> ed to take another wife. But my son also wanted to take a wife.
> The son [of the Konkomba man] needed money to buy things for
> his wife. He came to me and asked but I told him that I had no
> money because I had given it all to my other children. The way I
> made the money was from making shea butter. So I told him to go
> to the father and ask him for the money to buy the things. When
> my son went to the father he said he had no money because he
> used it to get a new wife for himself . . . So I said that I will not al-
> low my husband to take that particular woman because I know she
> is "not good" and I did not want her to come to live in our house
> . . . I told my husband that he should go and build a new house
> for the new woman to move in but I am not leaving my children
> or the house . . . And this new woman had a son. So the son got
> sick and died and my husband's brothers accused me of killing her
> son because they knew I didn't want her to come and she came.

Pakpiema has a private income from shea butter. She clearly feels she has the right to dispose of her personal income as she sees fit. But jealousies have been aroused by her wealth. This is evident in that one of her sons asks her for money to buy things for his future wife, and he would not have asked if he didn't know that she has it. In any case, this is not the traditional way of getting a wife among the Konkomba, and the elders are uneasy about women bringing wealth into the marriage because "it causes quarrels." Among the Konkomba, marriages are traditionally made by arrangement between families. As a marriage prestation, the father offers the labor of his son to the family of the bride for seven years. Thus Pakpiema rightly feels she is not obliged to provide her son with a wife. This is the duty of fathers who pass it on to their sons. So she says that she has given it to her other children. This would especially be directed to her daughter but might also include things that she feels are important but that her husband simply may not be able to pay for such as sending the children to school. This means two things: (1) the son does not want to give the seven years' work (or doesn't want to wait the seven years) but wants a shortcut; and (2) he goes to the mother simply because he sees that she has the means, and the father would tell the boy that "quick marriage" is your own responsibility.

From the people's perspective she oversteps her bounds in two ways: (1) when she criticizes her husband for taking a second wife whom she has called "bad" or a "witch," and (2) when she tries to force her husband not to accept his new wife by demanding that he build a separate compound for her. An important measure of a man's success (abundant life) is the number of wives and children he has. But if her husband is in the wrong, it is the role of his brothers and the elders to decide, not hers. The fact that he builds another compound means he has left her to her fate. They now are living in disunity, and she is already a "witch" waiting to be accused. This happens when the untimely death of her rival's son "proves" that she is killing by bad intentions, and it is the brothers of her husband who are her chief accusers.

The factors of change related to the 1990s boom account for all of Tait's seven factors, but times and conditions are different from the 1950s, and overall they suggest a different interpretive pattern. Four areas of major change are all closely connected to the traditional division of labor: (1) the accumulation of "untouchable" wealth by women called "women's things"; (2) family breakdown brought about by the switch from bride-wealth to dowry or from men's control over reproduction to women's control; (3) the enormous infusion of development money and cultural propaganda, which has the effect of shifting wealth from the public sphere and from the group to the private sphere and the individual; and (4) the women's leisure that has resulted from labor-saving innovations has not led to more production but instead has led to more women's leisure activities like gossiping and thus witchcraft accusations. Another factor related directly to the third factor but affecting all four of these changes is cultural propaganda and the media that, as Akosah-Sarpong describes it, "drives the culture of rights." The popular press has sanctified Western notions of individual rights, especially women's rights, over the traditionally prescribed common good.[28]

Women's Wealth and the Breakdown of the Family

Today women are perceived as accumulating wealth in the form of "women's things" that are private and over which they feel they should have sole rights. Until very recently, such "things" consisted of clay pots, bowls, dishes, and traditionally woven cotton cloth. Their cash value was negligible, and they were not durable, so they couldn't accumulate. Nowadays the goods are considerable and durable, they amount in many cases to thousands of dollars, and they are highly visible. When a situation arises in the extended family where cash is needed, the rules of the society are conflicted—solidarity is challenged by the tacit rule of women's rights in "women's things."

Although "women's things" is an untouchable category, their use is moderated by the group's expectations. Women who choose to use them in a way that breaks family unity, for example, by setting themselves up with a business in town, defy the group's expectations of unity. If they give goods to their daughters, the wealth leaves the house, and it may be perceived as betraying the family. Both of these break conventions and can be extremely disruptive (especially among the Konkomba). Alternatively, women could choose to invest their earnings into animals, which are regarded as common property, but human nature intervenes. "Why should we?" they will ask. "This is men's work!" So they invest in untouchables that remain as an inert security blanket. But the rest of the community perceives it as bordering on witchcraft.

Such women's wealth contrasts dramatically with the extreme poverty of northern households as a whole. Eighty percent of the people of the North are rural farmers who are living at little more than subsistence levels. But there is now pressure on northern men to produce food for the whole country. They have replaced the sturdy Sahelian domesticated millets and sorghums with maize, which is not suited to northern conditions but is suited to southern palates. This means crops are more susceptible to drought and require costly fertilizers. The traditional mixed cropping has given way to monocropping, and most of a farmer's crop is converted to cash. But production levels are not much greater because few have bullocks, and almost no one has a tractor. Although marginally more food is produced, they consume less, and a steady diet of maize is not nutritious. When they run short, as usually happens in the rainy season, they must pay dearly for food and must use up some of their hard-earned cash that is badly needed for other things.

In the end, the men feel that they are working harder for less, and they actually are. Their wealth and security seem to be diminishing, and their ability to provide for their families is reaching the danger point. The greatly increased cash expenses are never recovered by their modest earnings, and the slightest misfortune brings matters to a head. When illness strikes, when an expensive funeral must be organized, or even when the predictable droughts, famines, pests, and flooding arrive, there is never any reserve, and they depend on their links in the community to help them. At such times, the untouchable wealth in the women's rooms becomes an obscene source of "antilife."

The basic rule regarding property, which is built into the worldview, is that of solidarity: "from those that have to those that need." The difficult question is, who is in greater need? This is always negotiable because understandings of need depend on those judging and the circumstances. Furthermore, they change over time. Ideally, all wealth is public. Women's private wealth is a kind of fiction invented to keep peace in polygamous households. And it is only permissible when it is negligible, short term, and invisible. As visible wealth becomes durable and increases, it automatically becomes less private and more public, and thus seemingly available to those in need. When it continues to be used for private interests or hoarded, it is identified with witchcraft. This is the crux of the problem.

Hoarding wealth runs solidly against the primary values of solidarity and interdependence. But if holding such wealth is an unforgivable offense, using it in the two preferred way—either setting oneself up as an entrepreneur or giving it to daughters as dowry—constitutes witchery. In the latter case, it not only sends wealth out of the house, it also jeopardizes relations with other extended families, which are absolutely needed when misfortune comes around. Good relations with other families are established over time by marriage exchange. Wealth that empowers a woman in marriage is often an underlying cause for divorce, for it acts to make women independent and jeopardizes relations among families that are controlled by men.

Today Konkomba youth are seeking "fast" marriages of elopement. Their model for this is Dagomba marriage where the locus of exchange is between young men and their future wives and mothers-in-law rather than between families. It also encourages elopements, which are a modern version of wife-theft. In former times, the Dagomba stole their wives from the Konkomba. A Konkomba youth might seek cash employment on southern farms. Then he would use the cash to buy "women's things" to give to his girlfriend and her mother. By doing this, he is dodging work responsibilities at home. Then the girl's mother privately arranges an elopement, which in effect steals the woman from her arranged husband. This destroys the relations between three families—the groom's, the bride's, and the eloper's. But this "fast" way rarely lasts. When the young couple meets with any misfortune, the woman usually leaves the man, taking her wealth away with her. But she is not easily accepted back into her family, and getting a second husband will be difficult. She and her husband become social outcasts. Meanwhile, the jilted husband must find another wife, and he too looks for a "short-cut," thus perpetuating the cycle.

"Wicked wealth" and the cycle of family breakdown described above are tremendously aggravated by Western development and aid that is individual oriented and thus favors individual entrepreneurs, especially women. The naïve realist presupposition of the West is that the African system is basically the same as that of the West but less developed. Thus it is usually taken for granted that "if you develop a woman you develop the whole family." Thus women's entrepreneurial projects are favored over those that are thought to benefit only the men. What actually happens is the private sphere is empowered to the detriment of the public sphere. The final result is that development money produces witches.

As noted above, women's leisure is also increasing. Development initiatives have brought in many labor-saving devices and services that help the women but make things more difficult for the men. For example, in towns and cities charcoal and cooking gas, paid for by men, have taken the place of firewood that is collected by women. Similarly, electricity paid for by men is used for appliances like refrigerators, cookers, water heaters, and machinery that make women's work easier. Grinding mills, a public investment, have replaced the women's grinding stone. Piped water and nearby boreholes have ended the women's long treks to the river, but men must pay the rates. Cement bought by men has replaced the mud plastering formerly done by women. All of this seems to have made the women's lot easier at the cost of the men's. All of this leads to frustrations, especially when the men are unable to provide for their families, for this means "they are not men." This and infertility are the major causes for women leaving their husbands. All of these changes in some way break the rule of solidarity and interdependence. If wealth is there, it must be shared. In the final analysis, these changes are experienced as going against life itself, in other words as witchcraft.

The development objective is that women's leisure will lead to more production. If this would actually happen, the profits would immediately be put into more "women's things" where they would sit and arouse envy. But more often than not, women's leisure simply leads to less time at work and more time doing what women always do with their leisure—socializing, sitting around with other women, and talking. Tait cites women's leisure and men's frustration as the most prevalent causes of witchcraft accusation.[29] Both of these have seen dramatic increase since the 1990s.

Overall, we can say that modern life is perceived as empowering women but disempowering the men. If this were simply the battle of the sexes it would be fair play. But what brings the antilife quotient into the picture is that public wealth is being diverted into untouchable private vaults, and the only way to put it back subverts life. It is interesting to note here that when entrepreneurial women are accused of witchcraft and either killed or sent to Ngani, their wealth goes "back to the house."

Difficulties from the Media

The greatly increased power of the media adds to these difficulties. It seeks out the exotic stories, and it promotes Western values of individualism over collectivism, independence over solidarity, and progress over tradition. It is slanted against African tradition that is always backward and oppressive, especially toward women. There have been dozens of newspaper and journal articles,[30] numerous film documentaries,[31] and television programs[32] about the oppression of women, most of which focus on the exotic and sensational, and especially on incidents or practices that are perceived as abuses. One film on the Gambaga camp interviews a woman who claims she was "tied to a log and tortured for three months."[33]

The media focuses strongly on human rights: "Enhanced by the swelling democratization of communications, the mass media is ever more becoming aware that human rights and journalism are intrinsically entwined and brutally inseparable—that each drives the other."[34] But their interpretation is always highly individualistic.

African "tradition" is described as "backward" and "oppressive" and as suppressing women's rights and progress. Witchcraft is seen as part of a "traditional superstitious worldview" that needs to go. It needs to be replaced with the enlightened Western view, where human rights, equality, and freedom, are interpreted primarily in terms of freedom from male domination and repression. "Older women are 'accused of using' witchcraft to cause illness and almost always subjected to various forms of abuse that includes physical attacks, humiliation in public, destruction of property and ostracization."[35] "It is a way of persecuting older women who have become superfluous to the community."[36] Or it is interpreted as a perverse resistance to women's empowerment: "I didn't realize how much people hated my independence."[37] Or it is portrayed as outright male domination: "Violence against women is a particular problem in Africa where women are often expected to be in total submission to their men."[38] In response, the Ghanaian journalist Akosah-Sarpong proclaims, "progress is on the ascendancy especially from . . . superstition, malevolence and unreason."[39]

Response toward Outcasts

Fr. Joseph, the pastor of Ngani Catholic Church, complains that the social services of Ghana and the various NGOs with projects at Ngani simply don't do their job. We must remember that the witch is first and last an outcast. The media make them out to be poor women, but nobody believes that—not even the accused. Because the accused are felt to be a source of perilous danger to the community, all the considerable supportive powers that exist in collective societies are suddenly reversed to cut off the offending party completely. Outcasts must not be helped. NGOs and governmental institutions that offer social services do not officially recognize the existence of witches, but those who perform those services do. The social services in northern rural towns, such as Ngani and Gambaga, are almost nonexistent anyway. But it is not unusual for their functionaries to become lax in their duties when it comes to helping "witches." Nobody really expects them to help. Rather the opposite is expected—to give food to "witches" rather than to the normal, more worthy, people who are also in need would be considered quite inappropriate if not anti-social "witchery."

Fr. Joseph cited four examples of this at Ngani: a grinding mill, a bore hole, a school, and a toilet that were to help the witches but somehow ended up helping someone else or no one. The grinding mill was operated by the chief's sons who charged the women and pocketed the money. The witches were too poor to use it. When it broke down, no one took charge, and so it remains broken until now. The bore hole was taken over by the sons of the earth-shrine custodian, who said that it produced too little to be helpful for the witches. It was chained up and used only by them. Because water is such a serious problem, Fr. Joseph distributes drums of water to the most destitute of the witches every Saturday. Word is that money was given by an NGO for a school, but how can the children of the witches have a better school than the townspeople? Only a shed stands where the school should be. A communal toilet was also supplied by an NGO but was commandeered by the townspeople. After it was burnt by bushfires a few years ago, it was left for the witches.

Acknowledging Witchcraft

We have gotten some insight into the "mind of the people" and some grounding of the witchcraft phenomenon in the local context. Now let us consider the scratching, the appropriate responses. First of all we must take the African worldview, the symbolic forms, and the understanding of life as the appropriate theological grounding. The primary concern is for the preservation and fulfillment of life. Witchcraft is an antilife force and thus patently bad. This is our starting point. This does not mean Christians must be resigned to evil or to the traditional methods for dealing with it. But these need to be recognized and to become the launching pad.

In the mind of the people, appropriate scratching took the form of prevention and substitution. But how does the good news of Jesus relate to the preservation and fulfillment of life? Mainline churches have not touched this because of the appalling Western associations—"Good Christians" shouldn't talk about it. But many African Independent, Pentecostal, and Charismatic churches do. They have responded with a Christian preventative action: "I am covered with the blood of Jesus." The true power of Jesus becomes just another "protective medicine" to add to their traditional stockpile. This is good tactics, not "good news." The "mind of the people" should be informed that the blood of Jesus not only protects, it also enlivens and fulfils our quest for abundant life. It transforms us, vanquishes fear, and makes us free to love, so much so that that protection is no longer necessary.

As far as substitution goes, the Charismatics quite rightly insist that we no longer need "something to put into the mouth of trouble" because Jesus is the eternal sacrifice. But they sell God short by settling for Western values, namely, prosperity or simply money, when they could have had what their fathers longed for, "abundant life." The really good news gets trampled in the rush. Because Christ's life is forfeited for the lives of all, all lives have already been fulfilled in the life force of his Spirit. In our ancestor Jesus we are all swept up into the fullness of life that is the reign of God.

Our digging into the history and contemporary situation in Dagbon has yielded a number of factors that support and maintain witchcraft. First, a history of slavery and oppression not only sustains disunity in eastern Dagbon, it also blocks the traditional ritual and horizontal mediation needed for its restoration. This state of disunity is manifested in permanent witch camps like Ngani and in a series of ethnic conflicts. More recently, it has also manifested itself in a murderous conflict between the royal families of Dagbon over competition to their highest office, the Ya Na. Witchcraft threatens the political life and security of Dagbon. Second, the modern influx of goods and a channeling of wealth to empower women have favored the private sphere over the public, which has created a disharmonious, "antilife" environment that in turn produces witches. These are experienced at different levels (individual, family, community, world) and in their economic and social life. An appropriate ministerial strategy must take these dimensions into consideration.

"Scratching" at the Witch Camps

The camps are part of the traditional response to the threat of witchcraft. So they need to be regarded not as a problem in themselves but as imperfect solutions. Permanent camps, like Ngani, lack the means (earth-priest chief) for reunification. Gambaga camp, on the other hand, which serves west Dagbon, effectively reintegrates women back into their communities because it has such a combined religious-secular authority figure in the earth-priest chief. Each requires a different approach.

The Presbyterian "Go Home Initiative" at the Gambaga camp viewed through the eyes of faith reveals the life-giving presence of the Holy Spirit leading us on. The project is on the right track, though perhaps for the wrong reasons. It has offered credible help and true reconciliation, in contrast to the work of governmental services and well-meaning NGOs, because it has been able to adjust to this basic dual schema—albeit without explicit awareness of this.[40] In effect, the project's dedicated caregivers have extended the chief's horizontal role. Simon Atunga says, "The Gambaga chief supports our efforts and we do press the villagers, but we must also be very sensitive to their feelings. If we try to press too strongly they will turn on us and there will be no cooperation after that." Their prayers[41] and assurances of God's support are also effectively extending the earth-priest's vertical mediation. These combined efforts are, indeed, bringing about some measure of reconciliation and enabling reintegration.

In east Dagbon, however, the problem is much more serious. Here the "witch camps" are but one of the many by-products of the former slave raiding and present injustices that undergird periodic ethnic conflicts. The final solution can only be an integration of the two ethnic groups, at least at the level of mediation. But we are far from this at present. In fact, the main issues of land, identity, and chieftaincy remain untouched, and both groups are moving further apart. Millions has been spent on "peace-building," but these efforts have not even brought about a reintegration of the Konkomba into Tamale and Yendi, the major cities of Dagbon.

This is not surprising. The issues are tough. Chiefs cannot become earth-priests, because, as the Konkombas say, "the earth knows its people!" And the chances of earth-priests becoming chiefs is curtailed for two reasons. Dagomba are willing to appoint Konkomba as subordinate chiefs but not as equal (paramount) chiefs. The Konkomba, on the other hand, want their own paramount chief with title to their own land.[42] Differences such as these brought about the fierce 1994 conflict that was called by some "the final solution."

Although there is no war at present, all of Dagbon is internally conflicted. The "witch camps" are increasing in size, and new "camps" are being formed.[43] The legacy of slavery has produced disunity in the communities, permanent witch camps at the territorial level, and the "witchery" of civil war at the transterritorial level. The need for a better solution—one that responds to the humanitarian concerns as well as to the deeper systemic causes—has become critical.[44] In east Dagbon what is needed is nothing less than an integrated peace-building vehicle that builds on traditional pathways in order to transform them. We have such a vehicle in "culture-drama."

Culture Drama and Peace-Building

Peace-building has become one of the largest industries in northern Ghana. NGOs dispense millions for peace-building workshops, seminars, projects, and infrastructure, but virtually none of this considers local cultural pathways. With so little effort in this direction. I set out to do something myself. In 2001, with a grant from Catholic Relief Services-Ghana, I spent a sabbatical year doing a cultural analysis of chiefly and nonchiefly pathways. Four cultural themes emerged in which the values, expectations. and behavior of each group were shown to be diametrically opposed to the other.[45] To bring about an integration of these pathways I then made use of a new therapeutic enactment genre and peace-building vehicle that I and a psychodramatist colleague[46] stumbled upon called "culture drama."[47] A one-week workshop in March 2003 involving ten Konkomba and ten Dagomba produced astonishing results. The level of mutual trust, the common vision of a new peace culture, and the confidence that they could actually work it out together reached by the end of the workshop went beyond my highest expectations.

Two things emerged from this effort: the therapeutic genre empowered them to trust one another, and through this mutual trust, they gained the insight that they actually needed one another to build a peaceful and nurturing environment, in short a "peace culture." By acting out a series of conflict scenarios in reversed roles, they gradually came to discover their own pathways and those of the other and how they both came into conflict with one another. Furthermore, they discovered that if they acknowledged their pathways and tried to bring about an integration, then, with each other's help, they could solve their problems and live together in harmony. They now have a vision of what a peace culture is like. They know how to build it together, and they know it can actually be done because they did it once. This is a tremendous step forward, and it was acknowledged by all.

One of the scenarios constructed in the drama concerned the realignment and unity of earth-priests and chiefs. Within the drama itself, the earth-priest and chief began to share roles, and each was empowered by the other. I believe that this is the key to empowering the system to change permanent camps to temporary camps and to reintegrate the accused back into society. But the vision still needs to become a reality.

Responding to Imbalanced Division of Labor

The so-called division of labor between men and women in Africa includes far more than labor. It is better to speak of the public versus private divide. Our analysis indicated that if the people's ideal is solidarity and interdependence, then at some point there is going to be a clash with the individualism and entrepreneurial spirit of Western-initiated development and globalization. Unless it is carefully contextualized, it acts against life as the people understand it and thus produces witches. Agents of globalization need to begin to obey the "do no harm" warning at the conceptual level not just that of implementation. This means looking deeper into the "mind of the people" and letting that be one's guide. African churches have a special role to play here. Indeed, they have a mandate from the Spirit to put local culture first. Part of the "scratching" means extending this mandate to the avalanche of secular "crossers" in today's globalized context so that they may be fully authentic, fully open, honest, and loving.

Regarding the disastrous new alignments in the division of roles and responsibilities, we need to seek a more open and fluid medium of exchange. The division of roles needs to become more open and flexible. Facilitating this is not easy. Women will not easily spend their "hard-earned cash" on what they regard as "men's responsibilities." And if women do work hard to produce more, they won't easily give it over to the whole "house," which includes their cowives (rivals) and their children. Many of those accused at Ngani fit into this category. They tried to favor their own children over the "children of the house."

Nevertheless, there are ministerial possibilities here. Northern women can be made more aware of their coresponsibility in the public sphere. Grassroot discussion groups, the "Christian Mothers," and various guilds and tribal associations are quite effective at this. Leisure can be a source of creativity and social improvement rather than gossip, but it requires sensitive leadership and a community will. A project in the town of Sirigu was recently adopted to encourage the women to continue their highly creative traditional designs in house decoration. The aim is not to produce for money but for "life."

An Equitable Distribution of Wealth

There are three "jealousy factors" that govern witchcraft accusations associated with private wealth. These are the amount, its visibility, and the level of communal need. There can be progress only if these are carefully balanced. Women can claim private rights only to the extent that these do not jeopardize the life of the community, for example, when the refusal to help (by buying medicine and so on) *"causes"* death. Economically speaking, the biggest problem in the North is too little production. Virtually everyone is either a subsistence farmer or petty trader. The market is filled with girls trained as seamstresses and hairdressers, but they are not earning a living or producing anything substantial. No one can afford such luxuries. Small-scale productive industries are needed that can offer on-the-job training and that can produce jobs and affordable goods. Until the situation in the North becomes more stable, people will continue to hold collectivist worldviews where solidarity and interdependence are the rule. And until there are real jobs, real production, and real incomes, the levels of access to wealth and opportunity will be imbalanced. People will keep privatized wealth from entering the public sphere, leading to more accusations and to more witch camps.

What is the role of the churches? Is it to facilitate the flow of wealth and empowerment back and forth across the public-private divide or to facilitate love and let the people find a way to do this? We need to ask how the wealth of the North can be distributed more equitably and to find a balance between the new individualist and the traditional collectivist values. We need to let Christian charity and traditional hospitality engage one another. Charity presupposes private ownership and the gift, whereas hospitality presupposes that those in need have the right to what is given them. The Akan of Ghana say, "*Sie ne kegya nni aseda*" (the anthill and the *kegya* plant don't thank each other because they are indispensable to each other).

We have seen how the services NGOs offer the accused are being selfishly diverted. Facilities and institutions are used according to the expectations of the people. These, even for Christians, are the socially approved ways of behaving toward witches. At Ngani, the earth-priest and chief are at loggerheads, and, rather than offer the healing mediation that is the purpose of their office, each tries to get whatever he can from the situation. Because of the divide in ethnicity and authority roles at Ngani, the Catholic priest is very limited in his response. The church can only help to serve and empower local institutions if they are healthy. Fr. Joseph is caught in between. Anything he does is suspect by one or the other. One of the accused explained: "Here at *Ten* you can't go out at night [for night prayers]. When it is night time the shrine goes out and if you also go out you might meet it [and die]. Are you under the shrine or under the Father?"

Nevertheless, as Fr. Joseph shows us, a good deal can be done. A Christian response—demonstrating God's love—starts from the heart. It starts with Christmas parties, drums of water, and roofing grass given with love. It brings joy to the disheartened and humanity to those disowned by humanity. It brings hope and the will to go on. It is all part of the rehabilitation—not just of the witches but of the entire community; after all, it is perhaps the only place in Dagbon where the Konkomba and Dagomba can have fun together.

There are, of course, national and international connections also built into these issues. The old discrepancy of finished goods against raw materials assumes many forms. The infrastructure improvements, like roads, electricity, and most recently, cell-phones, are both a boon and a burden. The bottom line is that goods and services need to be affordable. This is not simply a question of international justice. Even if national debts of impoverished African countries like Ghana are canceled, there is no assurance that the savings will be passed on to the people by corrupt politicians. Here ministries of justice need to be engaged. It is all part of the scratching that is needed when considering the broad parameters of witchcraft.

Postscript:
Highlighting the Dark Side of Globalization

We are living in a global era, and our mission vistas have broadened "elephantly," as we say in Ghana. Now the world's most visible "missionaries" are the secular benevolent institutions and their agents: from "Band-Aid" to the World Bank and the United Nations; from movie stars, like Angela Jolie, and pop singers, like Bono, to dilletantes and professionals, "gap year" students, and volunteers of every description imaginable. If these are the new missionaries, then the new role of the missionary anthropologist is "highlighting the dark side of globalization."

Building the reign of God now means keeping these agencies on track and keeping the media culturally attuned and "authentic." Bernard Lonergan succinctly identifies our common human path as being fully authentic, which is to be fully attentive, intelligent, reasonable, and responsible.[48] These are the criteria for building the reign of God. They are the same for everyone. In our age, more than any before us, this means everyone is called to be a "crosser." Being able to cross over is the survival gene for the twenty-first century. Mission applies to everyone, not just to Christians. Religion must once again embrace the secular. If they are not against us, they are with us! Places like the Tamale Institute of Cross-Cultural Studies (TICCS) in northern Ghana, which facilitates cross-cultural learning, are needed to direct the tidal wave of human crossings. Any adequate ministerial response in our age to any issue, including witchcraft in far away northern Ghana, must embrace the enormous potential of the secular "crossers" and the constraints of their prejudices. Mission needs to embrace world development efforts and help create awareness of the absolute importance of culture and peoples' pathways.

If our local objective is empowering appropriate ministries based in the mind of the people, which take their lead from an authentic local spirituality that is open, honest, and loving, then we are also on the way to producing a grounded African theology.

Notes

1. John S. Mbiti, *African Religions and Philosophy* (London: Heineman, 1969).

2. See G. Jahoda, "Supernatural Beliefs and Changing Cognitive Structures among Ghanaian University Students," *Journal of Cross-Cultural Psychology* 1, no. 2 (1970): 115–30; and G. Adams, "The Cultural Grounding of Personal Relationship: Enemyship in North American and West African Worlds," *Journal of Personality and Social Psychology* 88 (2005): 948–68.

3. See Adams, "The Cultural Grounding of Personal Relationship."

4. Various contemporary authors are beginning to account for the durability of such "irrational beliefs" by expanding the orthodox parameters of traditional Western disciplines like philosophy (e.g., K. Wiredu and K. Gyekye, eds., *Person and Community: Ghanaian Philosophical Studies* [Washington, DC: Council for Research in Values and Philosophy, 1992], and P. Geschiere, *The Modernity of Witchcraft: Politics and the Occult in Postcolonial Africa* [Charlottesville: University Press of Virginia, 1997]); social psychology (Jahoda, "Supernatural Beliefs," and Adams, "The Cultural Grounding of Personal Relationship"); health care (Jon P. Kirby, "White, Red and Black: Colour Classification and Illness Management in Northern Ghana," *Social Science and Medicine* 44, no. 2 [1997]: 215–30, and Sjaak van der Geest, "Dying Peacefully: Considering Good Death and Bad Death in Kwahu-Tafo,

Ghana," *Social Science and Medicine* 58, no. 5 [2004]: 899–911, and "Respect and Reciprocity: Care of Elderly People in Rural Ghana," *Journal of Cross-Cultural Gerontology* 17 [2002]: 3–31); and religions (B. Meyer, *Translating the Devil: Religion and Modernity among the Ewe in Ghana* [Edinburgh, Scotland: Edinburgh University Press, 1999], Abraham Akrong, "Neo-witchcraft Mentality: A Scheme of Interpretation in Charismatic Churches," in *The Witchcraft Mentality Seminars: Applications to Ministry and Development*, ed. Jon P. Kirby [Tamale, Ghana: TICCS Publications, 2004], 50–58, R. Van Dijk, *Christian Fundamentalism in Sub-Saharan Africa: The Case of Pentecostalism* [Copenhagen, Denmark: Centre of African Studies, 2000], and P. Gifford, *Ghana's New Christianity: Pentecostalism in a Globalizing African Economy* [Bloomington: Indiana University Press, 2004]) to include Ghanaian perspectives and meanings.

5. See Laurenti Magesa, *African Religion: The Moral Traditions of Abundant Life* (Maryknoll, NY: Orbis Books, 1997), 61.

6. See Magesa, *African Religion*, for this concept.

7. See E. Tengan, *Land as Being and Cosmos* (Frankfurt am Main, Germany: Peter Lang, 1991) for elaborations of this worldview as it connects with the earth.

8. Certain forms of "bad death" (war victims, by drowning, by witchcraft) are redeemable by a ritual called "turning the corpse" (see Jon P. Kirby, *God, Shrines and Problem-Solving among the Anufo of Northern Ghana* (St. Augustin, Germany: Collectanea Instituti Anthropos 35, 1986). See also Van der Geest, "Dying Peacefully," on good death and bad death among the Akan.

9. These include sex in the bush and the spilling of human blood in homicide or war. Even worse, ritual contamination was thought to result from spilling a witch's blood. In the South, early sources (B. Cruickshank, *Eighteen Years on the Gold Coast of Africa*, vols. 1 & 2 [London, 1841, reprinted 1966], 177–79, J. Beecham, *Ashanti and the Gold Coast* [London: 1841], 214–15) speak of witches being executed through strangulation and drowning to avoid this. In the North they were (and are) beaten or stoned to death to avoid having their blood touch the earth.

10. Various authors (see David Tait, *The Konkomba of Northern Ghana* [London: Oxford University Press for the International African Institute, 1961]; R. S. Rattray, *The Tribes of the Ashanti Hinterland*, vol. 1 [London: Oxford University Press, 1932], 258; Jean-Claude Froelich, *La tribu Konkomba du Nord-Togo* [Dakar, Senegal: Mémoire I.F.A.N., 1949], no. 37, and Kirby, *God, Shrines and Problem-Solving*) have described in detail these acts of desecration that unleash chaos or a state of "ritual pollution" on the ecosystem.

11. Thus there is a great urgency for this restoration. Rattray quotes one informant as saying, "the land is a bitter thing, it will cast out, finish, your

house (if you refuse to purify it)." To address this situation and to revive the earth, the elders, chiefs, and people must call upon the earth-priest (*ten'daana*). Harmonious relations can only be restored by a ritual of purification called the "burying the blood" or "smoothing of the land" (Rattray, *The Tribes of the Ashanti Hinterland*, 258).

12. Drucker-Brown puts greater emphasis on the separation and opposition of these roles in Mamprusi, and while there too the secular chiefly office dominates the ritual office, they nevertheless have managed to combine the complementary roles of chief and earth-priest. See S. Drucker-Brown, "Mamprusi Witchcraft: Subversion and Changing Gender Relations," *Africa* 63, no. 4 (1993) 531–49.

13. M. Staniland, *Lions of Dagbon: Political Change in Northern Ghana* (Cambridge: Cambridge University Press, 1975).

14. For a linguistic account demonstrating Konkomba origins in west Dagbon, see P. D. Strevens, "Konkomba or Dagomba: A Linguistic Corollary to History and Social Organization," *Transactions of the Gold Coast and Togoland Historical Society* 1 (1955): 211–16.

15. Tait, *The Konkomba of Northern Ghana.*

16. Jon P. Kirby, "Peacebuilding in Northern Ghana: Cultural Themes and Ethnic Conflict," in *Ghana's North: Research on Culture, Religion and Politics of Societies in Transition*, ed. F. Kroeger and B. Meier (Frankfurt am Main, Germany: Peter Lang, 2003), 168–79.

17. Gifford (*Ghana's New Christianity*, 88, note 14) mentions six "camps" including Duabone in the South and Tendang in the Upper West citing *Mirror*, May 5, 2001, 19 and *Mirror,* August 5, 2000; *Graphic*, June 29, 2000, 32; *BBC Focus on Africa,* October–December 2000, 24–25. Naboli emerged after his research. I concentrate on these four "camps" because they are linked historically and culturally.

18. Ghana National Archives: Yendi District Office Records (Informal Book), ADM 67/5/1, 10/8/16-10/2/30 Signed: AWL 1917, GNANI.

19. A. W. Cardinall, *The Natives of the Northern Territories of the Gold Coast* (London: Routledge; New York: Dutton, 1920 [reprinted by Associated Negro Press, Chicago, 1960]), 16.

20. A general appellation given by Dagomba to all those formerly raided for slaves.

21. H. A. S. Pul, "Exclusion, Association and Violence: Trends and Triggers of Ethnic Conflicts in Northern Ghana" (M.A. thesis, Duquesne University, 2003), 6, counts eight major conflicts involving the Konkomba and Dagomba (and/or other chiefly peoples of the northern region) from 1981 until 1994. The 1994 Northern Conflict was Ghana's most extensive and

destructive conflict ever, bordering on civil war, and with estimates of from 2,000 (officially) up to 20,000 (unofficially) dead, and 200,000 refugees (see J. Katanga, "Stereotypes and the Road to Reconciliation in Northern Ghana," *Uhuru* 6, no. 9 (1994): 19–22, and "An Ethnographic History of the Northern Conflict" [unpublished manuscript, 1994]; Ada Van der Linde and Rachel Naylor, *Building Sustainable Peace: Conflict, Conciliation and Civil Society in Northern Ghana,* Oxfam Working Papers and A. Bogner, "The 1994 Civil War in Northern Ghana: (Oxford: Oxfam, 1999); The Genesis and Escalation of a 'Tribal' Conflict," in *Ethnicity in Ghana: The Limits of Invention*, ed. C. Lentz and P. Nugent [London: Macmillan, 2000), 183–203.

22. From 2002 to 2004, the author intermittently conducted research at the village of Yongduni, eight miles north of Tamale, where a prominent earth shrine is maintained by an earth-priest who is also a ranking chief in Dagbon.

23. Drucker-Brown ("Mamprusi Witchcraft," 546) refines this idea saying that although it is the junior wives who accuse the senior wives in Mamprusi, it is only those seniors who do not have familial or local support that end up being accused.

24. For more about this see Jon P. Kirby, "Mending Structures for Mending Hearts in Dagbon," in *The Witchcraft Mentality Seminars: Applications to Ministry and Development*, ed. Jon P. Kirby, rev. ed. (Tamale, Ghana: TICCS Occasional Papers in Cross-Cultural Studies, no. 1, 2004). Here the author attempts to explain the insecurity of Dagomba women and high incidence of accusation in terms of the master-slave relations between the Dagomba and Konkomba.

25. The author recently encountered in Accra the use of an electronic device called "computah"—ostensibly a black box with lights inside—which was reputed to be able to "eat witchcraft medicine." Drucker-Brown ("Mamprusi Witchcraft") mentions the switch from the witches being transformed into various animals, etc., in the 1960s to the transformation of the victims into various insects or "bush meat" in the 1990s. Gifford (*Ghana's New Christianity*, 83–90) argues that dimensions of traditional religion including witchcraft, spiritual causality, and destiny have been transferred to Christianity in the contemporary charismatic phenomenon. This peculiarly Ghanaian form of Christian expression provides deliverance from all evils—especially poverty.

26. Tait, *The Konkomba of Northern Ghana.*

27. See the discussions in R. J. Sandbrook and J. Oelbaum, *Reforming the Political Kingdom: Governance and Development in Ghana's Fourth Republic* (Accra, Ghana: Centre for Democratic Development [CDD], 1999); E. J. Aryeetey and M. Nissanke, *Economic Reforms in Ghana: The Miracle and the Mirage*

(Oxford: James Currey, 2000); and N. Van de Walle, *African Economies and the Politics of Permanent Crisis 1979–1999* (Cambridge: Cambridge University Press, 2001).

28. K. Akosah-Sarpong, "The Dawn of the 'Culture of Rights'," April 26, 2004. http://www.expotimesonline.net/index.php?option=com_content&view=article&id=47:the-dawn-of-culture-of-rights&catid=42:arts-a-culture-&Itemid=57.

29. David Tait, "A Sorcery Hunt in Dagomba," *Africa* 33, no. 2 (1963): 136–47.

30. M. Adinkrah, "Witchcraft Accusations and Female Homicide Victimization in Contemporary Ghana," *Violence against Women* 10 (2004): 325–56; Y. Badoe, "Women Spellbound: Ghana's Witches Find Sanctuary," *New Internationalist,* September 2005, 382; K. Palmer, "Accused of Witchcraft, Women Banished Far from Home," *Toronto Star,* October 31, 2004, 31. http://karen-palmerinafrica.blogspot.com/2005_08_01_karenpalmerinafrica_archive.html.

31. A. Berg, "Witches in Exile" (film, 24 min) http://www.girlsclub.org/special/Film%20Fest%202002/film/intro.html and www.metroactive.com/papers/sonoma/09.20.04/myff-0440.html.

32. A. Mahama and K. Hackman, Women's Hour—BBC 4, 2005.

33. Badoe, "Women Spellbound."

34. Akosah-Sarpong, "The Dawn of 'Culture Rights.'"

35. Ibid.

36. Mahama and Hackman, Women's Hour—BBC 4, 2005.

37. Badoe, "Women Spellbound."

38. African Women's Development Fund, "The Witches of Gambaga: A Documentary by Yaba Badoe." http://www.awdf.org/browse/1497; http://www.youtube.com/watch?v=iFhHX7CJSes.

39. Akosah-Sarpong, "The Dawn of 'Culture Rights.'"

40. Although this is, in fact, the case it is not the specific goal of the program or of the Presbyterian Northern Mission Fields as such.

41. Prayers are always acceptable to Christians, Muslims, or Traditionalists, regardless of the religion of the one offering them. Not to accept would be to curse oneself.

42. Under the present constitutions, the land is held by the paramount chiefs on behalf of their people.

43. Underlining the trend toward separation, a new "camp" was established at Naboli in 2002 for only Konkomba. The Konkomba complained that they didn't want their "witches" to be slaughtered ever again as they were at Kpatinga during the 1994 war.

44. The peace-building authority, John Paul Lederach, urges a four-tiered

approach toward peace-building. His crucial third and fourth levels—the systemic (including culture) and the envisioning of a "peace culture"—have not yet been applied by peacebuilders to the Ghanaian scene. See John Paul Lederach, *Building Peace: Sustainable Reconciliation in Divided Societies* (Washington, DC: United States Institute of Peace, 1997).

45. Kirby, "Peacebuilding in Northern Ghana."

46. Dr. Gong Shu is a specialist in psychodrama and art therapy who came to Ghana in 1989 at the invitation of the Major Religious Superiors of Men to investigate conflicts arising in religious communities at that time. She discovered that the members of these communities were healthy individually but that the Ghanaian cultural pathways were in conflict with those of the Europeans. Together we worked out a method for integrating cultural pathways that I baptized "culture drama."

47. Jon P. Kirby, *Culture Drama and Peacebuilding: A Culture-Drama Workbook* (Tamale, Ghana: TICCS Publications, 2002).

48. Bernard J. F. Lonergan, *Insight: A Study in Human Understanding* (New York: Philosophical Library, 1957).

8

Mission and Culture:
A Historical Theologian's Perspective on
Twentieth-Century U.S. Catholic Mission

Angelyn Dries, OSF

Professor Dries reflects on the theme of mission and culture through the lives of three U.S. Americans who lived in the first half of the twentieth century: Joseph J. Williams, John Montgomery Cooper, and Anna Dengel. The lecture was delivered on October 15, 2007.

Louis Luzbetak's major professional interest lay in providing students with a background in cultural anthropology for the purpose of being better missioners. His *The Church and Cultures* (1963) and its revision in 1988 is a testimony in that direction. Luzbetak had to buffer the hostility of some anthropologists toward missionaries and convince future missioners that anthropology was an important tool for mission. In 1985, he proposed a possible synthesis of the differing worldviews of missioners and what he called absolute cultural relativists, a point that Sjaak van der Geest made a few years later in "Anthropologists and Missionaries: Brothers under the Skin."[1] Luzbetak was firmly situated in a religious community wherein Wilhelm Schmidt and the *kulturkreise* circle had offered a substantial theory of anthropology around issues related to humanity's origins and related questions.[2]

I would like to explore the "Luzbetakian theme" of mission and culture as seen through the lives of three American Catholics whose work expands over several decades in the first fifty years of the twentieth century. The three knew each other through the Catholic Anthropological Conference, but each had a particular way of relating science and religion, and culture and mission, with a different inflectional use of the theological framework of the period. I will provide a brief biography for each person, suggest the perspective they took on the relationship between science and religion, and examine the effect on the theological foundations upon which they drew. Each employed the then new sciences of ethnology and anthropology against the background of a traditional theological stance. But all stretched their theological framework in order to provide a more positive "reading" of science for purposes, ultimately, of evangelization. In the end, their use of the sciences contributed toward an expanded theological position.

The persons I will focus on are Joseph J. Williams, SJ, a New England Jesuit with mission experience in Jamaica; Catholic University Professor John Montgomery Cooper, the architect of the Catholic Anthropological Conference; and Anna Dengel, a medical doctor in India and foundress of the Medical Missionary Sisters.

Theological Climate in the United States, 1890–1945

First, I provide a brief reminder about the theological climate in the United States in the first half of the twentieth century. The emergence of so-called modern times brought great challenges for Catholics and Protestants around issues of authority, revelation, reason, and church/state relations. Pope Pius IX's *Syllabus of Errors* (1864) identified eighty theses that Pius considered to be wrongful thought premises of the time. Pope Leo XIII's propagation of Thomism and an apologetics based upon that philosophic system was meant to provide Catholics with the intellectual tools to combat the "Modernists." Pope Pius X's *Lamentabili* and *Pascendi Dominici Gregis*, both published in 1907, highlighted several of the same themes, among them the relationship between science and religion.[3] This emphasis was particularly noted because of the infusion of Darwin's theory of evolution and natural selection. The theory affected the fields of biology, sociology, and history, as well as broached some attendant possible theological implications of scientific premises. While Modernism was largely a European phenomenon, American Catholicism had its own share of the Modernist spectrum or "trajectory,"[4] ranging from the Paulist William L. Sullivan to John R. Slattery (1851–1926), a Mill Hill missionary to African Americans. Ecclesiastical figures such as Paulist founders Isaac Hecker, Walter Elliot, John J. Keane, and Denis J. O'Connell emphasized more the democratic and "American" characteristics suitable for the modern age. Holy Cross priest and scientist John A. Zahm (1851–1921) became a well-known speaker, elucidating the compatibility of modern science and Catholicism.[5] However, by 1898, his book *Evolution and Dogma* was withdrawn from sales. The answer to the prevalent question of the last half of the nineteenth century, "How does the Church relate to the Age," appeared to be, at least in relation to science, either ambivalent or hostile.

In the early twentieth century, there was a kind of fluidity to the relatively new academic fields of anthropology and ethnology,[6] but both disciplines were immersed in the larger philosophical battle between science and religion. In this intellectually turbulent time, it was feared that perhaps science would even win out over religion in the Western world. While Roman Catholics were more concerned with the effects of science on dogmatic truths, Protestants were affected especially when they considered the impact of Darwin's thought upon the inerrancy of scripture. The well-known drawing that featured the "Descent of the Modernists" (a parody of Darwin's "Descent of Man") captured the "backsliding" that would take place if Christians were to accept the theory of evolution.

Humankind's origins and related scientific theories were again the topic in 1950 in Pope Pius XII's *Humani Generis*. While the document indicated a positive regard for certain aspects of the theory of evolution, it still maintained that "the faithful cannot embrace that opinion which maintains that either after Adam there existed on this earth true men who did not take their origin through natural generation from him as from the first parent of all, or that Adam represents a certain number of first parents." That view, said Pius XII, undermined the Catholic Church's teaching on original sin, "which proceeds from a sin actually committed by an individual Adam and which, through generation, is passed on to all and is in everyone as his own."[7]

A variation of the science/religion, mission/culture theme was found when the religious intellectual culture of the world was on display at the 1893 World Parliament of Religions, held in Chicago. Organized mainly by Protestant missionaries, the gathering was meant to be a *tour de force* in support of the value of religion in just such a climate by including speakers from many religions around the world, including those from ancient civilizations. The argument was that religion was part of the fabric of ancient cultures in China and Asia, civilizations that were religious and sustained great artistic and literary treasures into modern times.[8] John J.

Keane, a representative of Catholics at the Parliament and soon to be-come the first rector of the Catholic University of America, emphasized the worth and dignity of all persons, especially in view of theories of evolution and comparative religions. He highlighted a universal craving for union with God, which presupposed a teleological orientation for all humanity.[9] Thus, in science and in what would become the field of com-parative religion, similar issues were at play. This, then, is a brief overview that forms the theological background for our three protagonists in the conversation about mission and culture.

Joseph J. Williams, SJ, (1875–1940) in Jamaica

Born in Boston, Massachusetts, Joseph J. Williams entered the Jesuits fol-lowing his first year at Boston College. After two years of scientific and philosophy studies at Woodstock College, he was assigned to Jamaica, where he spent a deeply formative year from 1906 to 1907. Not only the experience of a particularly devastating hurricane on the island but interaction with people in the "bush," as he called it, left a deep-seated impression on him.[10] He earned a doctorate in ethnology at Woodstock and was editor of *America* from 1910 to 1911. He then spent five years in Jamaica and returned there several times over the years, considering himself an "exile" when he left the island.[11] During his Woodstock years, the Jesuit became intrigued with rural black folklore and spirituals he heard near the college. In Jamaica, he played those remembered tunes on a harmonica and after people's curiosity drew them near, Williams provided a simple sermon.

The missionary's personal and academic interests came together as he began to collect books (over ten thousand), maps, lithographs, engravings, and woodcuts related to African and Caribbean cultures and Judaism. Items from his collection and objects from Asian and Native American origins formed the center of a small archaeological museum at Boston College in the former Stinson mansion.[12] His lectures in the graduate school beginning in 1932 and a journal, *Anthropological Series of the Boston College Graduate School*, became the foundation of the college's anthropol-ogy department.

Williams engaged in two major ethnology projects, one to investigate monotheism among African tribes and the other to examine the worldview of Jamaicans, centered around narratives associated with a spider. In his early career, Williams examined "Hebrewisms," wherein he sought to trace and compare the language for God found in Semitic literature and the language found among African tribes. In correspondence with British Captain R. Sutherland Rattray, at the time an Ashanti district commissioner and editor of a volume of African proverbs, the Jesuit ethnologist explored questions such as whether African tribes had learned "god" or a monotheistic vocabulary from Jewish tribes or whether Jewish tribes had learned "god" vocabulary from Africans.[13] For this project, Williams relied upon the writings and research of many field reports, which sources became the foundation of his considerable library.

While in Jamaica, Williams collected versions of the Anancy stories, Afro-Caribbean tales about a clever spider and its interaction with animals and humans. The Jesuit included a drawing of the spider in his somewhat autobiographical *Whisperings of the Caribbean*. The great household spider was common in Jamaica and, while the arachnid appears rather ominous, people considered it helpful because the spider killed cockroaches. Williams asked five thousand junior high students to speak to their grandparents and record their memories of the stories that sprang up around the helpful invertebrate. The students wrote down the narratives, often embellishing the paper with hand-drawn pictures and melodies. Williams observed the value of the ambiguous and the grotesque rather than the linear and logical as important features of the narrative.

Given the value the American School of Anthropology placed on finding facts, rather than starting with theory, Williams noted the value of the missioner in the process of obtaining information. He pointed to the difference in how tourists, the colonial elite, and the missionary in the "bush" obtained facts and narratives from indigenous people. Tourists and the elite, he noted, captured a "studied" view, specifically projected for them by Jamaicans. Or, one might find that Jamaicans presented tourists with stories having moral endings for Sunday school or tales learned in an English textbook. To get the "authentic" story, it was important to be as close as possible to the people, and "even after years of residence in the 'bush' itself, in closest contact with its people," Williams said, "It is not easy to follow the narrator, when one has chanced to overhear an Anancy Story in the telling." He concluded, "The native power of imagery, replete with proverb, and peculiar intonation where a shade of inflection changes 'yes' to 'no,' and especially the fascinating *patois* with all its disregard for person's gender, tense or case, completely mystifies and makes one doubt whether one has grasped the true meaning in the end."[14]

Intersection with Anthropology

Williams generally favored the "American School" of anthropology, especially the principles devised by Franz Boas of Columbia University. Unlike the British and German anthropologists who used a "comparative" approach to anthropology, that is, the application of a hypothesis to the facts that surfaced in the field to discover a "uniform history" of development, Williams preferred an inductive process from the facts, whereby "the actual history of definite phenomena" could be written.[15] Williams's two projects argued from "facts" as reported by field sources, a number of whom were missioners.[16] In a 1936 article in *Thought*, Williams paid homage to Boas's view of evolution, especially in relation to the historical development of culture. The question in this regard was "whether or not cultural development had been in conformity with the a priori postulates of the general scheme of evolution."[17] In other words, was culture, and its expression in history, simply a matter of certain laws of evolution, progressing from the most primitive to the most advanced of civilizations? Did historical development of culture follow certain fixed laws that could be applied everywhere? Boas presented evidence that cultural phenomena could appear in a variety of ways, a position that, for Williams, supported theological premises about the specialness of human origins.

With respect to a more positive approach to evolution, Williams, as had the censored John A. Zahm before him, reminded American Catholics that while it might appear startling, earlier churchmen, such as Gregory of Nyssa and Thomas Aquinas, had "in some sense" been evolutionists. If anything, Williams noted, "Evolution, as formally enunciated by Darwin, was in the main a recrudescence of an old theory. What was actually original in his system was the formulation of the principle that higher species were to be explained solely by evolution from lower species through . . . Natural Selection."[18] For many Catholics of this time, these ideas would have been surprising indeed.

Translation to Spirituality and Evangelization

The Jesuit missionary's ideas about the interactive relationship between mission and culture contained some theological assumptions and translated into his presentation of an enriched spiritual life. In several of his scientific explanations, Williams used a methodology of similarity, the point of which was to link similar experiences between groups. For example, he described African spiritual entities found subservient to any type of supreme being as "messengers," rather than as "minor deities," for the latter term could give the impression that they share "in the Divinity by their own right," thus being thought of as inferior, polytheistic gods. When represented symbolically, they "appeal to the imagination, even as the spirit-messenger or angel is represented in Christian art by a human body with a pair of wings attached." Williams concluded that "there is no more intention of real anthropomorphism than there is in the artistic concept of the painter."[19] Similarly, Williams compared ancestral spirits of indigenous tribes with veneration of deceased persons in the Western world in the form of monuments to national heroes.[20] Christianity had its own spirits, the saints, as did the country in such figures as Washington and Lincoln whose pictures or statues were meant to evoke action toward noble and worthy lives. Williams thus sought to provide a more hospitable connection between American Catholics and African groups.

His anthropological research also affected the direction of his first two books on the spiritual life. *Keep the Gate* and *Yearning for God*, retreat talks based on the Ignatian Spiritual Exercises, began with several incidents from his experience in Jamaica as example and motifs for retreatants, thus providing another worldview for their consideration.[21]

John Montgomery Cooper (1881–1949)

The Catholic University of America and the Catholic Anthropological Association (1926)

John Montgomery Cooper was born in Rockville, Maryland. After his education at Saint Charles College in Ellicott City, Maryland, and the North American College in Rome, he was ordained for the Baltimore Archdiocese in 1905. He served as assistant pastor at

St. Matthew's Parish in Washington, DC, until 1918 and taught part-time in the Department of Apologetics at the Catholic University of America. In 1923, Cooper became a full-time faculty member in the theology and sociology departments at the university. He had been trained as a moral apologist and, though his theology remained traditional, he wove insights from anthropology into religious education courses for college students. He became nationally recognized for that work in his *The Content of the Advanced Religion Course* (1924) and his four-volume *Religion Outlines for Colleges* (1924–1930). Labeling college religion textbooks as "vest pocket" editions of manuals written in Latin for future confessors and as small tomes exuding "arctic temperature," the educator inquired, how could students "warm their hearts and hands over such icy pages"?[22]

Having taught for many years, the author observed students' "'passive' resistance to subjects that lack vital interest or essential value to them."[23] His *Outlines* began with the "moral ideal"—love of God and neighbor. In the first volume, topics included racism, labor (women in industry, living wage), means of preserving peace, and the effect of monotony in the modern world. He named his pedagogical principle that of "correlation," leading a person from the known to the unknown rather than beginning with the logical or theological.[24] The educator further noted that current college texts did not take into consideration local situations and cultures, a perspective gleaned over the years from his observation of Native American tribes in New York, Montana, and Quebec.

In his student days in Rome, he had become interested in archaeology. Upon his return to the United States, the priest undertook field trips to various Native American communities, working in conjunction with the Smithsonian's Bureau of American Ethnology. Through that institution, Cooper published his *Analytical and Critical Bibliography of the Tribes of the Tierra del Fuego and Adjacent Territory* (1917). There was a sense of urgency among anthropologists in obtaining information about tribal people all over the world—a kind of salvage ethnography, as it was called—because there was a consciousness following the First World War that Euro-American culture was flooding the rest of the globe and that it resulted in a loss of material from which to reconstruct the unwritten culture of humankind along with answers to the questions of origins of the human race. Cooper felt this to be true among the Native American tribes he investigated. The priest established the Department of Anthropology at the Catholic University in 1936 and continued his fieldwork into 1941, when a heart attack prevented him from further trips.

Inauguration of the Catholic Anthropological Conference

In a growing trend among American Catholics to organize national Catholic societies in the early twentieth century, Cooper initiated the Catholic Anthropological Conference in 1926. The conference and its journal, *Primitive Man*, "hatched" in New Haven, Connecticut, when Cooper and Maryknoll Father Leo Tibesar attended a convention of anthropologists at Yale University the previous year. After lunch at the Hofbräu nearby, the idea arose to begin an association of Catholic anthropologists. The plan was to have well-prepared missioners contribute to a journal along the lines of the *National Geographic* magazine.[25] While *Primitive Man's* appearance was more prosaic, Cooper edited the journal until his death.[26] The first issue furnished an overview of the spirit and trends in anthropology, and each issue provided reviews of scholarly books on various aspects of the field. The conference published periodic monographs, including one on the Apinayé, which Cooper translated along with Boas-trained Robert H. Lowie (1883–1957), a professor of anthropology at the University of California, Berkeley.[27]

Cooper's interest in the relationship between mission and anthropology was expressed in the aim of the conference: "the advancement of anthropological science through publication by Catholic missionaries and specialists, and through the promotion of ethnological training for missionary candidates."[28] In an issue of *Missionary Academia*, Cooper cast slight aspersions on Fordham University psychologist James J. Walsh's popular book, *The Thirteenth, the Greatest of Centuries* (1907), by reminding seminarians and clergy that they were living in the twentieth century, and that they were challenged to make original scientific contributions to human knowledge and not to fall back on an imagined glorious past. Missionaries in the field had "thousands of laboratories," but anthropology needed missionaries who knew how to gather the information. Cooper had urged a program to include this mission emphasis in 1938, but it wasn't until 1958 that an interdepartmental graduate program in mission studies was approved by the Catholic University of America faculty.[29]

Though a self-taught anthropologist, Cooper read widely and cor-responded with others in the field. He was a critic of the *Kulturkreise* school[30] and, like Joseph Williams, tended toward the American school of anthropology. Cooper emphasized observation, firsthand experience, the accumulation of facts, and awareness that "religion" infiltrated all elements of the cultures anthropologists studied.[31] But he also identified the rac-ism that undergirded some theories of culture. In an *Ecclesiastical Review* article, Cooper suggested that Native Americans, often considered as hav-ing a "lower culture," "have been taken too much *en bloc*."[32] When one examined particular tribes, one noticed not only degrees of culture, but one could also observe their complexity. In another case, when Cooper distinguished some of the "primitive" cultures, he suggested use of the term "non-literate," which he saw preferable to "savages, barbarians, and uncivilized."[33] This attitude further reflected Cooper's basic understand-ing of the unity of the human family, which put all groups on a relatively equal footing.[34]

Anna Dengel and the Medical Missionary Sisters

Born in Austria, Anna Dengel's (1892–1980) interest in mission was en-gaged after she read a Franciscan Missionaries of Mary pamphlet describ-ing their work. The young woman matriculated at a missionary nurs-ing school in Lyon, France, and corresponded at length with Dr. Agnes McLaren from Scotland, who had begun a small hospital in Rawalpindi, India.[35] After studying medicine at Cork University, Dengel went as a lay mission doctor to that hospital. Four years later, Dengel returned to Eu-rope, exhausted from the demanding work. She realized that missionaries needed a community base for social and spiritual support in the ministry. During a retreat, she resolved to begin a religious congregation for the express purpose of medical missions. Anna was keenly aware of the influx and influence of Protestant medical missionaries around the world, es-pecially in India, and knew about global medical issues learned firsthand and from reading Protestant medical mission material.

To obtain financial assistance for the mission, the young doctor toured the United States in 1924, along with Pauline Willis, a native Bosto-nian and foundress of the Catholic Women's League in that city. When the women arrived in Washington, DC, they met with Michael Mathis (1885–1960), a Holy Cross priest with experience in India and the superior of the Holy Cross Foreign Mission Seminary in the nation's capital. With the help of Mathis, Dengel, Dr. Joanna Lyons, and two nurses founded the "Pious Society" of Catholic Medical Missionaries in 1925. Their aim was to bring professional medical assistance to the most needy people, without respect to the "color or creed" of the person.[36]

However, a church sanction against women religious becoming surgeons and obstetricians prevented them from becoming a "full-fledged" religious community. Dengel and Dr. Agnes McLaren had lobbied several times in Rome to change this pattern, as did Cardinal Dougherty of Philadelphia, who later welcomed the Society of Catholic Medical Missions into his archdiocese.[37] Finally, in 1936, a Vatican decree, *Constans ac Sedula*, removed the barriers to the women becoming professional surgeons and obstetricians and the society was approved as a religious congregation.[38] One wonders whether Propaganda Fide was cajoled into action by the fact that the India government had begun health programs in addition to significant numbers of Protestant medical missionaries who were training local medical staff.[39] The society was asked to undertake dispensaries, hospitals, leprosaria, sanitaria, training schools, maternity and child-welfare centers, and native nurse-midwife programs. The community remained in Washington, DC, until 1939, during which time Dengel became well acquainted with some of the faculty at the Catholic University, particularly John Montgomery Cooper and William Kerby (1870–1936), the inspiration behind the university's School of Social Service.

Theoretical Foundation for the Interaction of Science and Culture

Dengel, who was on the board of the Catholic Anthropological Association for several years, was not an anthropologist by training, but as a physician she had developed astute powers of observation. The vast suffering she had seen in India and later encountered in Africa touched her deeply. She noted that adverse religious and cultural practices particularly affected women and children. Social customs that prevented women from fresh air, light, and clean surroundings led to tuberculosis, bone disease, and death in childbirth. Unsafe obstetrical practices frequently maimed women. Women in Muslim and Hindu countries could not be seen or treated by male doctors. While she sought to bring skilled medical care to relieve people's suffering and to "bring people to a knowledge and appreciation" of the Christian faith, at the same time, she also insisted that "people must never get the idea that conversion and baptism are necessary to reward your devoted care."[40]

From her experience and pioneering efforts in the foundation of a Catholic medical mission congregation, her continual reading in multiple subjects, and her personal appropriation of mission, Dr. Dengel wrote a cameo book, *Mission to Samaritans*, wherein she presented her theological foundation for medical missions, portrayed the history of Christian medical missions, and reviewed the major medical problems throughout the mission world. Simply put, she provided three reasons for medical missions: the Good Samaritan is the model of how Christians need to "go and do in like manner"; Christ was a healer, a physician, and "Christlike charity means giving the best we have"; and finally, and certainly perceptively for her time, she noted that medical missions were "a work of restitution. . . . It is the tremendous debt which we, the white race, owe to the peoples subjected and exploited by our forefathers."[41]

Dengel and the Medical Mission Sisters faced many of the same issues as did the anthropologists: aboriginal family structures, social practices, religious rituals, and especially by the 1950s due to mass movement to the cities, the disintegration of the structures of daily life. Dengel approached these situations by personalizing the issues and indicating the effects of technology and globalization on an underreported group in anthropology—women and children. She fought for their professional health care, and toward this end, the sisters began women's medical training programs in India and Africa.

In 1927, just as the Catholic Anthropological Conference journal was launched, Dengel inaugurated a mission magazine of her own, *The Medical Missionary*, and remained its editor until 1959. Dengel's direction of the magazine differed from the ideas of Father Michael Mathis, who wanted to become the editor and to steer the magazine in a strictly scientific direction.[42] *The Medical Missionary* noted important local customs, especially those that involved women, family, and health. The magazine portrayed the role for women in African medicine and presented the African understanding of the relationship between medicine and religion. In the 1950s, the magazine identified the effects of globalization and the intervention of the West upon changing social and economic structures. Dengel had no doubt about the importance of medical science for the women's well-being and felt that science *and* religion were to interact with each other to the benefit of both. The cover of *The Medical Missionary* in the 1930s clearly expressed this as seen in their community symbol, which fashioned science and charity (mission), soul and body, each surrounding Mary and the child Jesus. Science and religion were at each other's service when they met in the person of an ill human being. As Anna wrote on the occasion of the final authorization of her community in 1937,

> In a Catholic mission hospital, love and sympathy must be a testimony . . . that there is a God of love who cares for all His creatures; that all men of all races, of all conditions, are brothers in Christ. . . . But this testimony will only find a favorable echo if it is coupled with professional competence and skill. This requires dedicated, devoted, professionally trained missionaries; long and strenuous years of spiritual preparation and professional studies are necessary, to be able to function in a far away non-Christian country as a representative of Christianity, a representative of the Divine Physician, Who has not left us His power of miracles but has put into our hands wonderful remedies and means of healing and easing the ills of mankind.[43]

Mission, Culture, and Liturgy

Anna reflected another expression of the interaction between mission and culture in her emphasis on liturgical life as a source of mission for her community. Growing up in the beautiful Tyrolean Alps, she possessed a kind of natural mysticism and an appreciation of the land, values she carried with her throughout her life. Her father had designed and sewn liturgical vestments. Her home parish articulated a vigorous liturgical life, celebrating with full color and sound the Rogation Days, processions, and Sunday Eucharistic liturgies. An appreciation for the elements and significance of ritual provided an experiential platform for the knowledge that Michael Mathis later imparted concerning liturgical developments in Europe and the United States in the 1930s and 1940s.[44] Mathis's idea was that one did not simply study the liturgy, one *did* it.[45] Liturgy and missionary life became interwoven for the Society of Catholic Medical Missions from its inception. The liturgical emphasis went hand in hand with study of the scriptures, or, as Dengel noted, "We should be actually steeped in the gospels. Otherwise . . . we will never really have fundamental and basic attitudes [for mission]."[46]

Anna's appreciation of the deep elements and patterns of ritual, which she had witnessed in Hinduism, Islam, and in tribal religions, also sensitized her to a rich liturgical practice, in such things as the "dialogue Mass" or "missa cantata," where *all* the people responded to the prayers, more frequent communion, the celebration of liturgical seasons of the year, and a movement from liturgy toward the reconstruction of society.

The Medical Mission Sisters read the scripture and liturgy books authored by Pius Parsch (1884–1954), one of the founders of the liturgical movement in Europe. Johannes Hofinger's significant book, *Worship: The Life of the Missions* published under the influence of Mathis's Liturgical Institute, also reflected these developments.[47] In a profound way, anthropological processes of *communitas* and *liminality* would later surface as a background for appreciation of the process underlying the reinstituted Rite of Christian Initiation of Adults in 1972.

Implications of Their Work and Thought

With an eye to the first half of the twentieth century, we have looked at three Catholics who applied anthropological and scientific perspectives with an explicit direction for mission and evangelization. What conclusions might we draw from their experience? What did they bring to the theological table? In the long run, did it matter to theology? Did it matter to mission?

To answer these questions, we might note some similarities among our three protagonists. First, Williams, Cooper, and Dengel held to a positive view of the human person and recognized in a significant manner the worldview of religious and racial groups with an effort to understand the implications of the intersections of these worldviews with the gospel.

Second, they used their scientific expertise for theology and/or mission: Williams for retreats and spiritual direction, Cooper for catechetical material for college students, and Dengel for provision of resources for the care of body and spirit as well as for a liturgical foundation for the sisters' life and ministry. Scientific method was a sign of "modern" times. Anthropology, ethnology, and medicine were the scientific tools that all three viewed as valuable sources to understand the groups they studied. Each of our subjects was actively "redeeming" science in interaction with mission and evangelization.

Third, the three scientists observed that thought and cultural patterns were indicative of a complex worldview. Questions about the origin of humanity and about how humans relate to a transcendent being were not simply intellectual assertions. Doctrine interfaced not only with science, but also with visual, ethical, and ritual differences among people. A forum opened in theology beyond debates on the origins of humankind and turned toward ideas about revelation and the process of Catholic faith meeting inculturated religions. The themes eventually surfaced in "accommodation" theories in the early part of the century and then in "inculturation"—motifs that reflected mission theory and liturgical development by the 1970s.[48]

We might also mention an unforeseen consequence of missionaries' use of science to understand culture in the period we have viewed. Theology's prevalent scholastic methodology employed a hypothesis that was then deductively applied to various cases or situations. This was the same methodology used by the "comparativist" anthropologists, an approach that Williams and Cooper decried, saying that "facts" were the basis of arriving at a theory. Inductive, rather than deductive, thinking gave a clearer view of the truth in science. Because Darwin's ideas were a theory, the theory could be refuted by facts. Furthermore, vicarious experience lagged behind personal observation and experience, and, therefore, missioners, who were "outsiders" but who had the advantage of daily close observation of people's customs, could be tapped to gain "facts" upon which a scientific theory could be built.

This approach also opened new possibilities for theology. Discussion around issues of mission and culture provided theology with the suggestion of a mental framework that included imagination, inductive reasoning, and experience. The use of narrative to learn the cosmic and spirit world of Jamaicans, as in Williams's case, Cooper's utilization of student daily life situations as the start of theological inquiry, and Anna Dengel's alleviation of adverse health conditions that were often the effect of social and religious structures, reflected a theology that emphasized connections, relationships, and what we would today term "incarnational" theology.

In the end, the scientific methodology the three people emphasized gradually eroded traditional neo-Thomist deductive methodology. Williams, Cooper, and Dengel employed one approach in theology and an opposite method in science in academic fields where both areas had been intersecting for some time. Theoretically, they could have held apart the scientific and theological worlds, but, in fact, they did not in their effort to link life and God, culture and mission. They used traditional theology but were creative and inductive in method. Anthropology and ethnology provided theology with the suggestion of a different mental framework to approach questions about the relationship between mission and culture, a framework that included imagination, inductive reasoning, and experience. While an examination of cultural elements showed up anomalies and incongruities that were easier to see in other religions than in one's own, the application of scientific approaches to benefit mission and evangelization provided another way to "do" theology.

Second, Williams, Cooper, and Dengel, while important in their own scientific and mission worlds, illustrate the ongoing transoceanic conversation that involved not only Europe and North America, but that included the "mission countries" in Africa, the Caribbean, and Asia. The geographic location from which Darwin materialized his nineteenth-century theory was the Galapagos Islands, but by the third and fourth decades of the twentieth century, anthropological discoveries in eastern Africa shaped the conversation in new ways. The pope who wrote *Humani Generis* in 1950 wrote *Fidei Donum* in 1957. The encyclical, addressed to bishops around the world, drew attention to the growth of the church in Africa. Missionaries witnessed a huge growth in adult converts, especially in eastern Africa, where Richard and Mary Leakey uncovered important anthropological evidence about humanity's origins. But the same missionaries questioned the effectiveness of traditional apologetics and catechetical presentation (which often relied upon an actual or quasi-scholastic framework), when African Independent Churches held strong appeal and where Protestant missionaries were showing up in greater numbers than before.

Maryknoll men in Tanzania, for example, looked to the social sciences and specifically to the work of François Houtart of the Center for Socio-Religious Research in Louvain to find new ways to address the formation of converts rather than to anthropology. Catechumens in Africa and Asia were not necessarily using the philosophical systems or mind-set underlying existentialism, immanentism, idealism, or materialism, warned against by the pontiff in *Humani Generis*, but they were engaged heavily in ritual and symbol and the worldview represented thereby.

In spite of the efforts of the Catholic Anthropological Conference, the Fordham Mission Institute[49] in the 1950s and early 1960s, and the work of the Society of the Divine Word[50] to engage U.S. Catholic missionary interest in an investigation of mission and culture by way of anthropology and ethnology, Americans generally favored the *social* sciences in addressing mission questions in that period. Among the reasons for this, aside from Americans' penchant for pragmatism, we see the rise of lay involvement in mission through Catholic Action. Based on a theology of the Mystical Body, the movement grew rapidly from the 1930s into the 1960s and spread with Canon Joseph Cardijn's popular methodology of "observe, judge, act."[51] Groups in France, the United States, and even in Eastern Africa, avidly applied the method to their particular circumstances through the Young Christian Workers, the Young Christian Students, and eventually the Christian Family Movement.[52] The method was at the foundation of what became liberation theology.

The issues raised in *Fidei Donum*, did not further address the theory of evolution, but rather Pius XII noted the problems raised with African migration to the cities and the eagerness Africans had "to lend an ear to the fallacies of that species of civilization known as technological." This was quite a different kind of "modernism," one related not to philosophical issues but to rising social concerns created by globalizing companies. While Pius called for more missionaries for African countries, he also called for the development of a Catholic "elite" and well-trained Catholic action groups to address a rapidly changing sub-Saharan continent.[53]

While Williams, Cooper, and Dengel by themselves did not create a "paradigm shift" in theology, their endeavors became part of larger movements in liturgy, scripture, and catechetics, which in the end did alter the relationship between theology and science, culture and mission. At the present time, when we see in some ecclesiastical places a trend toward what cultural anthropologist Mary Douglas would call "high role definition," and the standard of "loyalty" as a primary ecclesiastical value, it is worth recalling the work of our three protagonists, who sought to relate experience, culture, mission, and the gospel.

Notes

1. Louis Luzbetak, "Prospects for a Better Understanding and Closer Cooperation between Anthropologists and Missionaries," in *Missionaries, Anthropologists, and Cultural Change*, ed. Vinson H. Sutlive et al. (Williamsburg, VA: College of William and Mary, 1985), 1–54; Sjaak Van der Geest, "Anthropologists and Missionaries: Brothers under the Skin," *Man, New Series*, 25, no. 4 (December 1990): 588–601. See also Fiona Bowie, Debra Kirkwood, Shirley

Lardner, eds., *Women and Missions: Past and Present: Anthropological and Histori-cal Perceptions* (Providence, RI: Berg, 1993).

2. Louis Luzbetak, SVD, contributed the entry on Wilhelm Schmidt, SVD, to Gerald H. Anderson et al., eds., *Mission Legacies: Biographical Studies of Leaders of the Modern Missionary Movement* (Maryknoll, NY: Orbis Books, 1994), 475–85.

3. For a recent collection of articles on North American, English, and European rejoinders to Modernism, see the entire issue of *U.S. Catholic Histo-rian* 25, no. 1 (Winter 2007): *Pascendi Dominici Gregis: 1907–2007: Centennial Essays on Responses to the Encyclical on Modernism.*

4. F. Scott Appleby has suggested the term "trajectory of modernism" to indicate the varieties of responses unfolding in Catholic theological circles of the time. See F. Scott Appleby, *"Church and Age Unite!": The Modernist Impulse in American Catholicism* (Notre Dame, IN: University of Notre Dame Press, 1992).

5. John A. Zahm, CSC, *Evolution and Religion* (Chicago: D. H. McBride, 1896). The lecture that he gave in several places and drew national attention, "The Church and Modern Science," was given initially at the cathedral in Denver, Colorado, in 1883. On Zahm's life and the context for his approach to evolution, see Ralph Weber, *Notre Dame's John Zahm: American Apologist and Educator* (Notre Dame, IN: University of Notre Dame Press, 1961). Appleby included a chapter on Zahm in *"Church and Age Unite!": The Modernist Im-pulse in American Catholicism.*

6. In the early twentieth century, ethnology was a branch of anthropology that examined the origins, characteristics, and distribution of races. Anthro-pology included an examination of groups' social customs and beliefs.

7. Pope Pius XII, *Humani Generis*, 1950, para. 37. Evolution remains a current topic of interest, seen, for example, in recent state court cases sur-rounding teaching about evolution, creationism, and intelligent design in grade and high schools. See Avery Cardinal Dulles's McGinley Lecture on the topic at Fordham University in April 2007 and the popularity of Kenneth R. Miller's, *Finding Darwin's God* (New York: Cliff Street Books, 1999).

8. For the talks at the Parliament, see John Henry Barrows, *The World's Parliament of Religions*, 2 vols. (Chicago: Parliament, 1893). For American Catholic attitudes and involvement, see Angelyn Dries, "American Catholics and World Religions: Theory and Praxis: 1893–1959," *American Catholic Stud-ies* 113, no. 2 (Spring–Summer 2002): 31–50.

9. John J. Keane, "The Ultimate Religion," in *The World's Parliament of Religions: An Illustrated and Popular Story of the World's First Parliament of Reli-gions, Held in Connection with the Columbian Exposition of 1893*, ed. John Henry Barrows, 2 vols. (Chicago: Parliament, 1893), 1331–38.

10. The Jesuit wrote about the 1907 Jamaica hurricane in several places, including Joseph J. Williams, *Whisperings of the Caribbean: Reflections of a Missionary* (New York: Benziger Bros., 1925). The English Jesuits had turned over missionary jurisdiction of Jamaica to the New York/Maryland Province in 1894.

11. Robert J. Stewart, "The Contributions of Joseph John Williams, SJ, 1875–1950, to the Study of Religion in the History of Africa and the Caribbean," a paper presented in March 1991 at the annual conference of the Association of Caribbean Historians (Joseph J. Williams folder, reading room desk, John J. Burns Library, Boston College). I have relied on Stewart's paper for several points in Williams's biography. See also Robert J. Stewart, *Religion and Society in Post-emancipation Jamaica* (Knoxville: University of Tennessee Press, 1992), esp. 136–38, for aspects of Williams's view on Afro-creolization.

12. A similar museum was begun at the Catholic University of America around 1925 in McMahon Hall, though its collection was broken up after offices were changed in the building.

13. Joseph J. Williams, *Hebrewisms of West Africa: From Nile to Niger with the Jews* (New York: L. McVeagh, Dial Press, 1930). The Jesuit missionary gave a paper at the 1937 Catholic Anthropological Conference, "The Idea of God among the Ashanti," though *Primitive Man* cites it as "The Idea of God in Primitive Culture" (Joseph J. Williams, SJ papers, Box 2.6, Burns Library, Boston College, Boston, Massachusetts). Quite a large amount of his *Anthropological Series of the Boston College Graduate School* was the venue for his research on Africans and "primitive religions."

14. Williams, *Whisperings of the Caribbean*, 206. For Williams's description and analysis of what he heard and saw in Afro-creolized religion, see Joseph J. Williams, SJ, *Psychic Phenomena of Jamaica* (New York: Dial Press, 1934). Williams further provided descriptions of the Jamaica Maroons, the group formed by ex-slaves in the eighteenth century. They worked the sugar plantations and provided a threat to the British colonial government.

15. Williams quoted Boas on the point in Williams, "Boas and Ethnologists," 201.

16. The method is also observed during the same time period in Saint Louis University anthropologist, Albert Muntsch, SJ (1873–1967), *Evolution and Culture: Their Relation in Light of Modern Ethnology* (St. Louis, MO: B. Herder Book Co., 1923).

17. Joseph J. Williams, SJ, "Boas and American Ethnologists," *Thought* 11, no. 2 (September 1936): 194–209, at 196. For Williams's advocacy of the American school, see Joseph J. Williams, SJ, "Rejection of Cultural Evolution by American Ethnologists," *Anthropological Series of the Boston College Graduate School* 4, no. 4 (December 1939): 189–209.

18. Joseph J. Williams, SJ, "Thoughts on Evolution," *Anthropological Series of the Boston College Graduate School* 4, no. 1 (1939): 3–43, at 5.

19. "The Idea of God among the Ashanti," 6 (Joseph J. Williams, SJ papers, Box 2.6. John J. Burns Library, Boston College, Boston, Massachusetts). Williams concluded that the Ashanti had a basic monotheistic belief and practice, "though not in as pure a form as it existed during the earlier periods of tribal existence before outside contacts tended to accentuate the animist phases of local culture" (Williams, *Thoughts on Evolution*, 12).

20. Ibid., 10.

21. Joseph J. Williams, SJ, *Keep the Gate: Guarding the Soul against Sin* (New York: Benziger Bros., 1923). Joseph J. Williams, SJ, *Yearning for God: The Path to Peace of the Soul* (New York: Benziger Bros., 1924).

22. John M. Cooper, *The Content of the Advanced Religion Course* (Washington, DC: Catholic Education Press, 1924), 15.

23. John M. Cooper, *Religious Outlines for Colleges*, vol. 1 (Washington, DC: Catholic Education Press, 1924–1930), v.

24. Ibid., vi, iii.

25. Leo T. Tibesar, MM, "Dr. Cooper Initiates the Catholic Anthropological Conference" (Creative Works/Papers Box 28.5 Leo Tibesar, Maryknoll Fathers and Brothers Archives, Maryknoll, New York). Part of the paper appeared in *Anthropology Quarterly* after Cooper's death. Father James A. Walsh, Maryknoll co-founder, had asked Tibesar (1898–1970) to teach a course in cultural anthropology at the Maryknoll Seminary in 1924. Tibesar contacted Cooper to obtain a list of books for the course, and the two became friends. Tibesar was on the board of the Catholic Anthropological Association and its vice president for a few years, even though he was assigned in 1926 to Fushun and eventually worked with the Maryknoll Japanese mission in Los Angeles and Seattle. He was on the executive board of the Catholic Anthropological Association in 1941. He returned to Japan in 1946. He contributed an article, "Japanese Religion," to *Primitive Man* 10, no. 2 (April 1937): 17–24.

26. The journal continued as *Anthropological Quarterly* in 1950. In the first issue, Cooper provided an overview of the field. See John M. Cooper, "Present-Day Anthropology: Its Spirit and Trend," *Primitive Man* 1, no. 1 (January 1927): 3–5.

27. Curt Nimuendajú, *The Apinayé*, trans. Robert H. Lowie and John M. Cooper (Washington, DC: Catholic University of America Press, 1939).

28. Cooper, "Present-Day Anthropology," 1.

29. John M. Cooper, "Primitive Religions," *Missionary Academia* 2, no. 5 (February 1945): 7–22. *Worldmission* replaced *Missionary Academia* in 1950. Prior to this, Fordham University, through anthropologist J. Franklin Ewing,

SJ, became the home of an anthropological approach to mission through various workshops for returned missionaries and mission seminarians to examine mission possibilities for anthropology. Ewing weighed in on evolution a few years after *Humani Generis*, in J. Franklin Ewing, "Human Evolution—1956," with an Appendix, "The Present Catholic Attitude Towards Evolution," *Anthropological Quarterly* 29, no. 4 (October 1956): 91–135. He provided a version of the history of preliterate humanity's history and works from the nature of the evidence and the "reasonableness" of methods used to identify the story.

30. The Culture Circle Theory or Cultural-Historical Method of Ethnology was advanced by Wilhelm Schmidt, SVD (1868–1954) and Franz Graeber.

31. J. Montgomery Cooper, "Anthropology and the Missions," *Ecclesiastical Review* 75 (November 1926): 507–14, at 507. For an excellent analysis of Cooper's anthropology in the context of the field in his time, see Elizabeth McKeown, "From *Pascendi* to *Primitive Man*: The Apologetics and Anthropology of John Montgomery Cooper," *U.S. Catholic Historian* 13, no. 2 (Winter 1995): 1–22, and Elizabeth McKeown, "Tribal Encounters: Catholic Approaches to Cultural Anthropology," in *American Catholic Traditions: Resources for Renewal*, ed. Sandra Yocum Mize and William L. Portier (Maryknoll, NY: Orbis Books, 1997), 210–21.

32. John M. Cooper, "Higher Culture of Early Man," *Ecclesiastical Review* 60 (September 1914): 259–83.

33. Cooper, "Primitive Religions," 7. McKeown notes that Cooper and John A. Ryan left the American Eugenics Society in protest of the racism underlying the organization (McKeown, "From *Pascendi* to *Primitive Man*," 2).

34. Cooper, however, also retained belief in the original couple, Adam and Eve. Other missionaries highlight the theme of the unity of the human family, including J. H. Oldham and John J. Considine, MM, who, having read Oldham, found an important source for his analysis of racism (Sr. Xavier O'Donnell, MM, and Leo T. Mahon, in *A Catechism of the Family of God* [Maryknoll, NY: Maryknoll Publications, 1965]), use the theme in their bilingual catechetical text with the first chapter proceeding from the *Genesis* story in the Old Testament.

35. A pamphlet, "The Catholic Medical Mission of St. Catherine of Genoa," that described the Rawalpindi mission is found in Pauline Willis to P. C. Hayes, c. November 1924, Q9 (1924) Correspondence to [Patrick Cardinal] Hayes, Archives of the Archdiocese of New York, New York, New York.

36. Anna Dengel, "The Society of Catholic Medical Missionaries," in *The Mission Apostolate* (New York: Society for the Propagation of the Faith, 1942):

179–86, at 182. In 1942, when Dengel wrote the paper for the SPF, there were one hundred sisters in the society. Biographical details and reflective chapters on Dengel are found in Medical Mission Sisters, *Fire and Flame: The Legacy of Anna Dengel* (Philadelphia: Medical Mission Sisters, 1998). See also Katherine Burton, *According to the Pattern: The Story of Dr. Agnes McLaren and the Society of Catholic Medical Missions* (New York: Longmans, Green and Co., 1946). For an overview of Dengel's mission perspective, see Angelyn Dries, OSF, "'Fire and Flame': Anna Dengel and the Medical Mission to Women and Children," *Missiology* 27, no. 4 (October 1999): 495–501.

37. Margaret Mary Reher, "Denis J. Dougherty and Anna M. Dengel: The Missionary Alliance," *Records of the American Catholic Historical Society* 101, nos. 1–2 (1990): 21–33.

38. The Medical Mission Sisters received their medical education in places like Trinity College, Providence Hospital School of Technology, and Georgetown. A few received degrees in anthropology. When the mother-house moved to the Philadelphia area, the sisters' junior college, St. Therese's Institute, offered courses in missiology and missiography and by 1960, classes in the world's great religions, world culture regions, and oriental civilizations.

39. One can draw that inference from the papal instruction issued to approve the society on February 11, 1936. The first perpetual vow ceremony for the sisters took place on August 15, 1941.

40. Anna Dengel, *Mission for Samaritans, a Survey of Achievements and Opportunities in the Field of Catholic Medical Missions* (Milwaukee, WI: Bruce, 1945), 3–4. The pioneering book preceded missiologist Pierre Charles's (1883–1954), *Medical Missions: The Necessity for Medical Missions, Their History, Development and the Many Obstacles to Be Overcome in Their Fulfillment* (New York: America Press, 1949). See also Pierre Charles, "Medical Missions," *Missionary Academia* 6, no. 5 (January 1949). Dengel was further influenced by Catholic University of America Professor William Kerby's thought. Dengel remained the superior general of the Medical Mission Sisters until 1967.

41. Dengel, *Mission for Samaritans*, 2, 5. John M. Cooper wrote an introduction to the book. William Kerby, *The Social Mission of Charity: A Study of Points of View in Catholic Charities* (Washington, DC: Catholic University of America Press, 1944) has a chapter on "Good Samaritans," but uses the term in a different fashion than does Dengel.

42. In 1928 Michael Mathis, CSC, read a paper at the third Catholic Anthropological Conference, on "Some Values of Anthropology for the Foreign Mission Student."

43. Medical Mission Sisters, *Talks and Writings of Mother Anna Dengel*, compiled and indexed, Archives of the Society of Catholic Medical Missionaries, Fox Chase, Pennsylvania.

44. Mathis severed his formal connection with the Medical Mission Sisters in 1938 and went on to found the Liturgical Institute at the University of Notre Dame in 1947.

45. Author interview with Medical Mission Sister Jane Burns, January 1998, Philadelphia, Pennsylvania. Burns received her master's degree in liturgy from the University of Notre Dame.

46. Medical Mission Sisters, *Fire and Flame*, 112. A. G. Hamman, *Liturgie et Apostolat* (Paris: Les Editions du Cerf, 1964) represents the vast amount of literature that developed in the 1950s and early 1960s on the relationship between mission and liturgy. The liturgical/mission emphasis in Dengel's community is found more recently in the Medical Missionary Society's, *Spirit, Life, and Mission: The Synthesis of Membership Reflections, Sector North America, September 2000* (Medical Mission Sisters, privately printed, 2000).

47. Johannes Hofinger, *Worship: The Life of the Missions* (Notre Dame, IN: University of Notre Dame Press, 1958). On the same topic, see also Johannes Hofinger, SJ, *Liturgy and the Missions: The Nijmegan Papers* (New York: Kenedy, 1960).

48. See, for example, Gustav Voss, "Missionary Accommodation," *Missionary Academia* 4, no. 2 (October 1946): entire issue. For a brief history of the term in relation to inculturation, see Karl Müller, SVD, "Inculturation," in *Dictionary of Mission: Theology, History, Perspectives*, ed. Karl Müller et al. (Maryknoll, NY: Orbis Books, 1997), 198–201. In 1982, the Gregorian University in Rome began the journal *Inculturation*. For about ten years, starting in 1986, the Society of Saint Columban published a journal in Korea, *Inculturation*, edited by Sean Dwan, SSC, as an attempt to have missionaries make the connection between Korean culture and Christianity.

49. The mission secretariat at its October 1951 meeting endeavored to enroll experienced missionaries into a body called Worldmission Institute, with Bishop Fulton J. Sheen, national director of the Society for the Propagation of the Faith, at their head. Fordham University and the Worldmission Institute jointly sponsored the first gathering. The mission institute met from 1953 though 1962, with published proceedings from six of those years. J. Franklin Ewing, SJ's "For a Better Missionary" outline of a formation program for missionaries had both an anthropology and sociology emphasis as part of a master's degree. The program was initiated in 1958 but closed just two years later from lack of participants (J. Franklin Ewing, SJ, "For a Better Missionary," M.A. Program for Missionaries, Fordham University, 1958, J. Franklin Ewing Papers, Archives Fordham University, New York, New York).

50. On the development of the Catholic mission schools in the Chicago area, see "Introduction," in *Mission in the 70s: What Direction?* ed. John T. Boberg, SVD and James Scherer (Chicago: Chicago Cluster of Theological

Schools, 1972), 7–15, and Paul Bechtold, *Catholic Theological Union at Chicago: The Founding Years* (Chicago: Catholic Theological Union, 1993).

51. For some of Cardijn's speeches, see Eugene Langdale, ed., *Challenge to Action: Addresses of Joseph Cardijn* (Chicago: Fides, 1955).

52. On various lay groups influenced by Mystical Body theology with the encouragement of the papacy, see Georges Vromant, *De fidelium associationibus, de actione catholica, de legione Maria: ad usum utrius clergy, praesertim missionariorum* (Paris: Desclée, De Brouwer, 1955). Vromant attempts to define their place canonically. A parallel discussion ensured as clergy sought to find a "place" in that system. See, for example, Dennis Sanders, *To Build Together: The Role of the Priest in the Lay Apostolate* (St. Louis, MO: Resurrection Press, n.d.); and Pope Paul VI, *The Role of Priests in Catholic Action* (Washington, DC: National Catholic Welfare Conference, 1966).

53. Pope Pius XII, *Fidei Donum*, 1957, paras. 21, 26, and 65.

9

Weapons of the Weak: Cultural Forms of Resistance and Their Implications for Missionary Theology and Practice

Gemma Tulud Cruz

Dr. Cruz argues that even the weak and vulnerable have powerful weapons of resistance in such practices as stories, songs, dance, and jokes. In this way, even those with little power can name injustice, express dissent, and point to solutions for a more just society. Dr. Cruz speaks out of and to the experience of Asian and African American women, and reflects on the implications for missionary engagement. The lecture was delivered on October 6, 2008.

Unpacking the Weapons of the Weak

In his insightful books *Domination and the Arts of Resistance* and *Weapons of the Weak*[1] Yale professor and anthropologist James Scott talks about the ways in which subjugated peoples refuse to give in to their oppression. Drawing primarily from the more than a year and a half he spent listening, asking questions, and trying to understand the issues that animated and plagued the peasant village of Sedaka in Malaysia, Scott argues that the oppressed have strategies that, at first glance, may look negative, passive, or weak but that are actually quite potent.

Scott calls these strategies "hidden transcripts" or "weapons of the weak" as the title of his second book aptly trumpets. By hidden transcripts or weapons of the weak Scott refers to a politics of disguise and anonymity among subordinate groups that is partly sanitized, ambiguous, and coded. He says this is often expressed in rumors, gossip, folktales, jokes, songs, rituals, codes, and euphemisms that usually come from folk culture. These, according to Scott, do not contain only speech acts but a whole range of practices that contravene the public transcript of the dominant group.[2]

Stories, Songs, and Dance

So what specifically are these weapons of the weak? How do they become forms of resistance that are culture-based? Let me begin with stories, songs, and dances. Stories, songs, and dances may look harmless. Some may even characterize the telling of stories or the singing of songs or the performance of dances as mere products of a wild imagination or as acts of people who are just letting off steam. In the world of the oppressed, however, stories, songs, and dance can serve as moving and powerful ways to name injustice, express dissent, and point to solutions for addressing social problems. Stories, songs, and dances become, in other words, the most available means for the oppressed to preserve their identity as well as to struggle for some semblance of decency and integrity in a life that is otherwise marked by difficulty, misery, and inequality.

Stories

Let us begin with stories. Stories or narratives, as we know, constitute a basic component of the identities of peoples and communities. Missiologist Tom Steffen contends that "symbol-based narrative serves as the primal foundation of worldview and social structure."[3] As N. T. Wright also rightly points out, "people live by stories—they use stories to organize and store cultural traditions."[4]

But how do stories concretely become acts of resistance and storytelling a transforming activity for people on the periphery? Let us take the story of the early Christian communities. The early Christians were, at first, a persecuted minority. But they survived, thrived, and even turned Christianity into a religion of the empire by holding on to the message in the story of Jesus and keeping it alive by telling the story of Jesus over and over again in their communities and in places in and around the entire Roman Empire. Thus, Christianity was able to survive the persecution by the Romans as well as by the Jewish community. The story of Jesus kept the early Christians going. Jesus, who was a marginal Jew himself, used stories as a means of protest against the inequities of his time. His stories drew attention to the outcasts of Jewish society, from the story of the publican to the Good Samaritan, Lazarus, and the rich man. Klyne R. Snodgrass highlights this in relation to the parables in his recently released book *Stories with Intent: A Comprehensive Guide to the Parables of Jesus*.[5]

Turning to examples in Asia, I would add that stories are not only important, but also vital to Korean women's theologies that emerged from the interweaving of Korean life stories and the interpretation of the experiences of *minjung* or oppressed women. The *minjung* themselves prefer stories rather than abstract logic that is fabricated from the desk of an elite culture. They have difficulty believing in an abstract God since their indigenous myths and stories tell them that the deities were previously human beings who did noble things for their fellow beings, went through suffering, and come out victorious from life-risking ordeals.[6]

Then there are the stories that courageous victims of armed conflict and violence tell. For many of these victims, telling the story, though painful and difficult, is probably their best possible or most available way of starting to seek redress and healing from a traumatic experience. To be sure, these stories are valuable to a theology that is missionary as these stories can shift the cultural and theological discourse by focusing on the contradiction between the lived experience of survivors' agency and the discursive theological meanings that negate such agency.[7] In the struggle of ordinary oppressed peoples, telling the story is key to bringing attention to their plight, raising awareness of it, and possibly convincing people to sympathize, join, or help alleviate their suffering. For example, in *The Shape of Water*, a recent documentary that chronicles the multifaceted struggle of women all over the world, there is a scene of a group of Indian village women each telling a story and then collectively singing a song about their struggle against the building of a dam.[8] Another segment shows a group of three young Senegalese women first telling a story and then singing a song about their struggle against female genital mutilation.

Songs

This brings me to songs, the second cultural form of resistance in the trilogy of stories, songs, and dances. Like stories, songs can be seen as insignificant. As the language of the soul, however, songs can speak the unspeakable. They expose the shadows and name the truths we often could not say in ordinary, conventional conversations and interactions.

They express what we think and feel deeply in our hearts. They reflect our joys and sorrows, our hopes and dreams for ourselves and the world. Mary's song, the *Magnificat*, is a classic example of the song as a possible means for the powerless and voiceless in society to articulate not only what ought to be celebrated, but also what needs to be mourned and corrected in the world.

The Filipina domestic workers in Hong Kong who suffer multiple forms of oppression[9] have a few interesting ways in which they utilize songs as a form of resistance. On some Sundays, for example, they serve as accomplices to their cash-strapped compatriots who sell the illegal *halo-halo* (a concoction of fruits, milk, sugar, and shaved ice) by providing the vendor with a human camouflage every time the Urban Services Guard passes by. When one of these food sellers is caught for illegal hawking by the patrol, the cluster of Filipina customers suddenly sing "Happy Birthday" and instantly transform the activity into one of many birthday parties celebrated in the square.

In another instance, in 1994 when a notice was posted by the management of a condominium chastising Filipina maids washing their feet after washing their employer's car, the DHs (as they are more popularly known) came up with a song to express their disapproval at the rude notice.[10] The song has the following lyrics: "Washing car is little fun. Rub and scrub in morning sun. Water flooding down the street. Maid wash car but not her feet." The song has the tune of *"Magtanim ay di Biro"* (Planting rice is never fun). The choice of *"Magtanim ay di Biro"* is significant as it is a Filipino resistance song against planting rice,[11] an agricultural work that American colonizers tried to inscribe on Filipinos by peddling the idea that the Philippines is better off as an agricultural country.

In the United States, African Americans' use of spirituals to deal with and struggle against their oppression, particularly during the antebellum period, has been well documented. In her book *Quest for the Living God*, for example, Elizabeth Johnson contends that no other legacy from this bleak period in American history does a better job of passing on the idea of God as breaker of chains than this religious music that was fashioned by the slaves themselves. The spirituals explicitly named the suffering that the slaves endured as well as how the slaves did not allow their suffering to break their spirit but enabled them to resist and struggle against it instead with the help of their faith.[12] In fact, many spirituals have double meaning. Johnson points out: "In a powerful way characteristic of the music of the oppressed people, some spirituals conveyed veiled social commentary and criticism. Themes of freedom and going home frequently appear, longed-for goals that were not just reserved for a future in heaven but could be gained even now through struggle and escape."[13] Diana Hayes gives us examples of these double meanings in spirituals, as when, for example, the slaves sang of Canaan and ran away to Canada. They sang "Steal Away to Jesus" while they stole away North, and they sang "Wade in the Water" while they walked across the Ohio, the Delaware, and the Mississippi Rivers.[14]

Dances

Spirituals that combine African rhythms, chants, and patterns of lament with biblical themes can be accompanied by rhythmic hand clapping, foot stomping, and ring dancing, pointing to the last member of the trilogy of stories, songs, and dance. Dance communicates truths through the body. Like stories and songs, dance can be a means of releasing pent-up sorrows and hopes, pointing to life's tragedies and victories, and expressing longings and visions. Together with stories and songs, dances are also utilized in the midst of actual protests. To the disengaged, storytelling, singing, and dancing in the context of a protest could be strange. But Maria Corazon Manalo clarifies in "Dance: A Woman's Way to Peace" that just as dance may create moods and provide a sense of context that frames, prolongs, or may even cut off communication, dance can also enhance (or destroy) life.[15]

In *Jesus for Asian Women* Muriel Orevillo-Montenegro goes even further and describes song and dance as "expression of resistance," particularly in the Filipino context. She avers that "Filipinos use songs and dances to tell their stories, their dreams, and their everyday struggles . . . religious and cultural rituals, as well as their connectedness with their communities and nature."[16] And this is true not just among Filipinos. A 2008 issue of *Studies in World Christianity* (vol. 14, no. 1), for example, is devoted to how music, song, and dance are cultural sources not just for expressing the Christian faith, but also for struggling against oppression or fighting for change, particularly in Africa, Latin America, and the Pacific.

In an article in that issue titled "Sounds of Change and Reform: The Appropriation of Gospel Music and Dance in Political Discourses in Kenya," Damaris Seleina Parsitau writes about how gospel music and dance are used to usher in or clamor for social change and reform, particularly in contemporary Kenyan politics.[17] Kelly Johnson-Hill, in the meantime, explores the theological significance of the Tongan words *mafana* and *heliaki*.[18] *Heliaki*, for example, is a common, layered linguistic pattern of communication between Tongans that involves alluding to a truth without stating it directly. Tongans, for instance, will say "The sun has set" when in reality they are referring to the fact that a high chief or the monarch has died. Johnson-Hill points out that this cultural practice stands in contrast to the Western modes of communication of calling a spade, a spade or speaking in plain terms. True enough, these subtleties of Tongan metaphorical speech were not appreciated by the majority of early missionaries. As a result, Tongans increasingly resorted to practicing *heliaki* by applying it to song lyrics and choreography, which missionaries still largely failed to take into account. Johnson-Hill articulates what was lost in the process: "With their limited linguistic and cultural knowledge, they (missionaries) failed to perceive the potentially transformative role *heliaki* could have played in the spread of the Gospel. Had the Gospel been communicated orally, in sung poetry and in dance, contextual interpretations of the Gospel message could have been transmitted in Tonga."[19]

Cláudio Carvalhaes explores a similar experience in Brazil in an article titled "'Gimme de kneebone bent': Liturgies, Dance, Resistance and a Hermeneutics of the Knees," which delves into how colonial Christianity disrespected, pressured, and stiffened Brazilian people's knees and, consequently, the significance and power of dance in Brazilian life. Carvalhaes says that for Brazilians, who are known for their love for dancing (as shown in their carnival and the samba), this was tantamount to taking away part of their identity. Citing Nancy Pereira Cardoso, Carvalhaes contends that Brazilians need to engage in the de-evangelization of Brazilian knees and proposes, as Cardoso recommends, a feminist hermeneutic of the knees as a way of helping Brazilians to move forward and dance to their heart's delight once again. This, of course, is in view of what Carvalhaes perceives as the ways in which Christian liturgical (grid/order/proper) faith provided/allowed patterns for us to move accordingly within very specific limits (the "please stand/please sit" kind).[20]

Parsitau, Johnson-Hill, and Carvalhaes insist that dance is central to the culture of Kenyans, Tongans, and Brazilians. They illustrate the reality that song and dance are not just windows into peoples' cultural expressions of faith, but also ways in which they resisted evangelization that did not take into account local customs and traditions.[21] Most of all, song and dance also give us a glimpse of how oppressed peoples draw from cultural traditions to struggle against death-dealing situations. The expression "gimme de kneebone bent," for example, is found in a song sung by African slaves in the United States. Jacqui Malone speaks of the origins of this expression as follows: "Africans brought to North America were no doubt affirming their ancestral values when they sang a slave song that urged dancers to 'gimme de kneebone bent.' To many western and central Africans, flexed joints represented life and energy, while straightened hips, elbows, and knees epitomized rigidity and death. The bent kneebone symbolized the ability to 'get down.'"[22] She explains,

> The ability to get down does not mean surrender or subservience but rather an assurance that the body had strength to move, to twist, to shake, to hold an energy that was like a belief. If the body was alive, they were alive. The knee bent was a certainty that final death was not close by, and that even the rigidity of the social system demonstrated through exploitation, violence and death could not hold back the aliveness of those bending knees. Moreover these bending joints, these fighting knees that along with the movements of hands, arms, hips, torso, head, and foot, would bring about changes in culture and would write and change history.[23]

Humor and Laughter

Humor and laughter are also cultural forms of resistance. In a presentation on women and globalization, for example, a student of mine showed video footage of a center in Nepal that provides shelter and helps women victims of trafficking who are ashamed of returning to their families. What struck me in the video was how the women were laughing and making fun of themselves in the midst of the tragic situation they were in.

One might wonder, why the laughter? What is humorous about their situation? Doesn't it reek of pain and oppression that one couldn't help but sulk and be angry most, if not all, of the time? The Filipina domestic helpers in Hong Kong who suffer multiple forms of oppression[24] even use jokes, complete with an iconic caricature (Maria the stupid DH), to combat their oppression. The DHs have jokes that not only get back at their oppressive employers, but also poke fun at themselves and the problematic conditions they encounter because of gendered migration, gendered transitions, and gendered violence. One joke speaks of a *promdi* (a pejorative for rural-born and bred DHs who are supposed to be less sophisticated). The joke has it that upon arrival in Hong Kong, a small prosperous Chinese city that one can travel by car from one end to another in a matter of hours, the DH found out that

> No one is there to meet her so she gets (back) in line at the ticket counter. The person at the counter says, "Your ticket was coming to Hong Kong, right?" She answers, "Yes, but no one was here to meet me." So she asks directions to the domestic airport. He tells her that there is no domestic airport in Hong Kong. She answers, "I have to go to the domestic airport because I am a domestic helper."[25]

At first glance, laughter could be seen as a form of toleration of one's oppressive situation. It could also be construed as making light of the situation in order to make it more bearable. In other words, it could be perceived as escapist. But laughter is also upheld by folk wisdom as a means of resistance.[26] Filipina feminist journalist Rina Jimenez David, for instance, points at how obstinate cheerfulness serves as a personal bulwark against the vicissitudes of loneliness and alienation, particularly of migrant life.[27]

Gerald Arbuckle affirms humor as means of resistance in *Laughing with God: Humor, Culture, and Transformation*. Although humor is a non-confrontational style of critiquing an oppressive situation, Arbuckle insists it is effective as it is often able to portray fraud, hypocrisy, and injustice far more powerfully and emotively than the written word.[28] In fact humor's subversive quality, Arbuckle says, is its most important function as it "deflates pomposity and undermines the rigidity of the status quo. When humor pokes fun at the oppressive stringencies and conventions of society, people have the chance to re-imagine alternative ways of behaving."[29] Humor then is prophetic in that it breaks the mold of thinking and provides a designated radically new alternative behavior pattern.

Like humor, laughter is also undervalued in theology. Augustine and Chrysostom, for example, consider laughter as derisive and inessential to faith.[30] Jacqueline Bussie, in her study of what she calls "the laughter of the oppressed" as expressed in the classic texts of Elie Wiesel (*God's Mistake*), Shusaku Endo (*Silence*), and Toni Morrison (*Beloved*), offers interesting theological reflections on laughter.[31] Arguing for a theology of laughter Bussie contends that laughter increases our consciousness of faith since faith is born of the very stuff that also engenders laughter, namely, contradictions, incongruity, and paradox. Bussie also argues that laughter reflects and heightens our consciousness of hope. She says "life is a conflict between two narratives: the narrative of reason/reality and the narrative of faith, the narrative of facts and the narrative of longing. This collision can lead to despair or hope, but when it leads to hope, that hope is heroic but appears to many eyes as madness. We hope because it is absurd."[32]

This ridiculous hoping against hope that is expressed in laughter among the oppressed actually underscores the notion that redemption's "already" aspect is as real as redemption's "not yet." It drives home the point that the divine is both present and absent, and life is both horror and love. It highlights the cries of the oppressed for recognition of the "doubleness" of their experience as both children of God and the rejected of humanity. By taking laughter into account, theology recognizes and holds in awesome wonder the deep complexity of human experience.[33] Ultimately, laughter creates a new space within theology for reconsidering the work and importance of critical doubt as an element within faith, for laughter itself exposes the fact that faith is partly contrarational and metaempirical.

Silence

Let me note one hidden transcript that is usually labeled as submission to oppression but I think could also be categorized as a weapon of oppressed people, especially in the Asian and Asian American context. I refer here to silence. Let me offer one or two examples. In the Philippines there is the legendary protest of the Cordillera women in defense of their ancestral land from the government's plan to build a nuclear power plant on it. Patria Agustin describes this protest:

> In one of the dramatic protests, the women, *not* the men, opened their wrap-around skirts, boldly facing the government engineers in their nakedness. This humiliated the government functionaries, causing them to run away. The second occurred with the arrival of trucks hauling the equipment to start work on this project. The mothers, carrying their babies, came down from their houses with their young

children. Silently, they positioned themselves around and under the trucks, blocking the unloading of the equipment. The women and children did not move away from where they stood. Only when there was an understanding that the truck would go back with the equipment did the women and children withdraw.[34]

As explicitly stated by Agustin above, the protest is clothed in silence. There was no need for words. This very absence of words, I suspect, made the protest more eloquent. Many of us know that silence does not enjoy a significantly respected place in traditional liberationist discourses, including feminist theology. This is mainly due, I believe, to the tendency to associate silence with passivity and lack of agency. This is especially true in Western (including feminist) thinking, which, in my opinion, accounts for the diminution of silence.[35] In the Western mind-set, the emphasis is on self-assertion and active protest against oppression. Consequently, silence becomes the opposite of words and protest, and is then reduced to cowardice, passivity, and invisibility, even when one is attempting to communicate through it. It is also construed as withdrawal, absence, a sign of shame and dishonor, acquiescence to injustice, or resignation to oppression. Obviously, one problem theologians have with silence, especially in the Western context, is that it is devoid of words. Words in the Western context are *the* mode and language of resistance. Silence allegedly does not speak, and hence it is not resistance.

But is there really nothing significant about silence? Is there nothing at all that could be gained from it? Is it irredeemable from a feminist theological perspective? Renowned Filipina feminist theologian Mary John Mananzan herself speaks of the above-mentioned dramatic silent protest by the Cordillera women as an example of a transformative action in the face of the destructive effects of globalization. Moreover, Rita Nakashima Brock argues that silence speaks and that it may also be an *active* strategy. Brock contends that the power of silence lies in its capacity to nurture presence, [and] the power of the semiotic, as well as in how it creates spaces squeezed out by words.[36]

Another possible problem theologians have with silence, particularly feminist theologians, is when it is a response by women to gendered physical violence. As one who has done research and written on wife battery, I recognize the problem posed by silence in such a context. I am uncomfortable, however, with the proclivity to conflate silence with gendered physical violence. The problem with entirely lumping or exclusively associating silence as a response to physical violence is that this strips and denies silence of its theological possibilities. Brock herself points to "the complexity of silence: its freezing of memory in inaccessible mystery, its signal of a stubborn refusal to speak, its indication of truth suppressed by fear, and its *revelatory power beyond words*" (emphasis mine).[37] She goes on to say that "the healing of relationships can [even] be known in silence" for "silence is not always the absence of communication, but can be a deeper interrelational connecting. Silence allows many things to coexist without eliminating each other; it makes space for emotional complexity and ambiguity."[38]

The Malay peasants that Scott wrote about in the two books of his that I mentioned earlier exemplify the use of silence by the oppressed as a means of resistance. Scott submits that the peasants' response of silence or their conspiracy of silence in the face of (possibly) oppressive situations constitutes an act of resistance. Scott submits that critics will probably say that these are individual responses or a self-indulgent, less-principled act. Scott argues, however, that it is misleading and naïve to insist upon distinguishing "self-indulgent" individual acts, on the one hand, from presumably "principled," selfless, collective actions, on the other, and excluding the former from the category of *real* resistance. Scott goes on to say that to insist on such distinctions as a means of comparing forms of resistance and their consequences is one thing, but to use them as the basic criteria to determine what constitutes resistance and to ignore the self-interested element is to miss the very wellspring and determinate context not only of peasant politics, but of most lower-class politics.[39] Edward Said, in his review of Scott's *Weapons of the Weak*, affirms that noncommunication and other resistance strategies by the peasants that are clothed in silence like footdragging and arriving late for work are strategies of noncompliance to power.

Arguably silence as a response to oppressive conditions is more strongly associated with Asians and, to a certain extent, with Asian Americans. This is especially true for Asian and Asian American women who are persistently stereotyped in the mass media as silent and silenced or as the "long-suffering, passive, submissive, needing to be saved" women. More and more scholars, however, are disputing these claims and are providing a more critically nuanced picture as far as Asian women are concerned. In "Myths of Asian Womanhood," for instance, Susan Mann argues that these images of Asian women are partly a Western creation peddled out of ignorance and colonial purposes.[40] In "Unbinding Our Feet: Saving Brown Women and Feminist Religious Discourse," Kwok Pui-lan even takes Mary Daly to task for her (Daly) uncritical (to the point of racist, colonialist, and imperialistic) treatment of Chinese women with regard to their response to the practice of footbinding in China. In this essay, Kwok also points out that the colonial construction of brown or Asian women as pitiful victims played into the superiority complex of Western audiences and that this condescending attitude remains deeply lodged in Western women's minds even to the present.[41]

As can also be seen with Brock, even Asian women or women of Asian descent are increasingly reframing silence by presenting other ways in which they (Asian women) understand and use it as a form of resistance. Nantawan Boonprasat Lewis, an Asian American feminist theologian, describes silence as a new meaning to (Asian) resistance and liberation. Lewis contends that there are Asian cultural expressions, such as silence, that have been understood as indications of submissiveness, subservience, and obedience, and that this has been questioned by feminist scholars as a misreading of the "hidden transcripts" that some women have used as resources for survival. She cites Jung Ha Kim's study of the participation of Korean American women in the church. Kim's study revealed that "churched" Korean women, contrary to public perception, are not "all passive and victimized" and that they utilize silence as a tool to resist a church that regards them as secondary to men and systematically excludes them from power structures. Lewis explains,

> [T]he women's understanding and use of silence not as a self-internalized expression of submission but as a means of resistance has allowed them to experience a sense of freedom and liberation. They interpret their silence as disagreement and as resistance to the treatment they receive in their church. This comes about as a result of not finding a channel in which to raise their concerns in church, whether at Sunday worship services or as members of the decision-making body of the church. Consequently, learned silence as adopted by "churched" Korean women needs to be understood not in terms of submission but rather in terms of resistance, and as a strategy of survival.[42]

Ultimately, as Brock says, understanding silence in the context of resistance amounts to recognizing the fact that

> moments of resistance to oppression and healing come in the midst of the puttering and sputtering. Silence that creates prisons must be shattered. The silence of listening must be respected. . . . To heal is to speak and work against injustice *and* to listen to silence. The work of spiritual healing is grounded, finally, both in the solidarity of silence and in the words and actions that convey our vision of justice and wholeness.[43]

Ecumenical Association of Third World Theologians (EATWOT) Asian women theologians themselves show an example of this when they employed silence as part of their resistance to the marginalization of women within EATWOT. Mary John Mananzan shares,

> [T]he women members felt that although there has been significant progress on the awareness of the gender issue, the feminist perspective was still left to the Women's Commission. The theological production of the male theologians was still oblivious of the feminist perspective. In one plenary session, the women addressed this problem and announced to the men that all the women delegates were leaving the plenum to give time to the men to reflect on the issue. And the women walked out. It may be due to this symbolic gesture that the assembly in its final resolution decided that there would be a gender dialogue in the next five years . . . that a compilation of the writings of the EATWOT women theologians of the four regions would be compiled and sent to all members; and that the male theologians would take seriously the inclusion of the feminist perspective in their theological production. The general assembly elected the first woman president of EATWOT, Mercy Oduyoye, and four women and three men in the executive committee.[44]

In summary, I do think we can, indeed, find something significant about silence, even from a feminist theological perspective. I believe that when one thoroughly scrutinizes the various ways in which silence is utilized by the oppressed, including Asians and Asian Americans, one can see that it is has a role to play in resistance.

Implications for Missionary Theology

On the surface, the above-mentioned culture-based hidden transcripts do not fall simply, neatly, and clearly into the resistance category. Some may even see these as strategies that accommodate oppression. While there is truth to this, I think rather that categorically labeling these as accommodation or submission constitutes an impoverishment of theology. I think these strategies offer something valuable in articulating the struggle of oppressed peoples for liberation. Unfortunately these potentially liberating strategies have been rendered less effective today because of their enmeshment in a patriarchal system.[45] This is particularly true of the strategy of keeping silent. Theology's overemphasis on metaphysics and its marginalization of aesthetics has kept the strategy of silence from being accepted as a *real* strategy of resistance. Arguably what has been traditionally accepted as valid, authentic, real theology are approaches that engage in what may seem to be like intellectual gymnastics. Official theology has tended to become an overintellectualized, overconceptualized, cerebral, abstract, dogmatic form of religious practice to the neglect, even diminishment, of the more intuitive, more imaginative, and more creative forms in which we can understand or make sense of our faith.

Muriel Orevillo-Montenegro, for example, writes about a Filipino male theologian who did not recognize *In God's Image* (IGI)—the first and only feminist theological journal in Asia—as a "scholarly" journal because its format resembles that of a magazine (each issue usually contains women's essays, poetry, songs, and art illustrations of Asian women). What he failed to see, according to Orevillo-Montenegro, is the way (1) the creativity of Asian feminist theologizing is expressed in the journal, (2) it popularizes theology through a variety of forms of expressions, and (3) it is not stuck to the traditional format of dense words and high language that is not accessible to the ordinary person.[46]

In *Introducing Liberation Theology*, Leonardo Boff and Clodovis Boff maintain that ordinary, oppressed people, like those in small Christian communities, primarily express their faith and resistance, and hence their theology, orally and sacramentally. Their theology, Leonardo and Clodovis Boff write, is more than speech but a sacramental theology expressed in gestures and symbols. The members of one small Christian community, for example, depict capitalism as a tree with rotten fruit and poison dripping from its branches. Another brings gospel scenes to life through dramatic presentations. The Boffs elaborate,

> [D]uring a course on the Apocalypse, [members of the group] prepared their morning prayer by devising a silhouette show of a dragon with seven heads confronting a wounded lamb. They invited those present to give names to the dragon's seven heads. Men and women came forward and wrote, as best they could: "multinationals," "Law of National Security," "foreign debt," "military dictatorship," and names of various government officials held to be against the people. And below the lamb someone wrote: Jesus Christ, Liberator." And a woman came forward and added: "The people of the poor."[47]

Leonardo and Clodovis Boff insist that this is critical theology because it is clear and prophetic. Its root is evangelical faith, and its objective is the liberating practice of love. African theologians themselves acknowledge the theological significance and challenges inherent in the oral form of theology that is very much part of the life and witness of many ordinary African Christians. Philip T. Laryea, for example, points to how ordinary African Christians are beginning to set the parameters and framework for doing theology in a new key through their reflections on the gospel that can be discerned in their prayers, songs, testimonies, and so on.[48] Tongan theologian Winston Halapua even goes so far as to question whether Oceanian theologians are actually contributing to a process of dehumanization of Oceanian peoples when they continue to overlook or disregard indigenous symbols as irrelevant to doing theology.[49]

Cultural forms of resistance obviously challenge theology to see resistance as a continuum or a spiral to give oppressed people's (cultural) hidden transcripts their rightful place. As I see it, they also challenge theology to value and engage the aesthetics of human existence and to desist thinking in terms of extremes or in framing discourses in opposing categories. To do theology justly, it would be best if theologians see life and reality in its full spectrum and complexity, particularly by not thinking in terms of either/or but in terms of both-and. "Both-and," as a form of holistic thinking, is a good way to see cultural forms of struggle as embedded and hence part of the same reality of resistance and struggle for liberation. The Bible itself is punctuated with silence, dotted with humor and laughter, interjected with song and dance, and filled with stories.[50] Jesus himself used humorous stories to criticize the injustice in his time. In his parables the marginalized ridiculously take the center stage and become protagonists, exposing the incongruities of Jewish society in the process.[51]

Indeed, dichotomous thought and practice stand in need of interruption. Silence, humor, laughter, stories, songs, and dance—unsilenced as they are by action and unfettered by contradictions—are placed in a unique position to provide such an interruption. A theology that is mission conscious needs to take these cultural practices seriously if theology is to confess its own inadequacies and sustain a hermeneutics of rupture. In so doing, it resists the perennial danger of domesticating negativity or disingenuously dismissing seemingly weak cultural practices.

Most importantly, a theology that takes these practices seriously rightly gives a much deserved place to the "theologically oppressed," the everyday theologians, the people in the trenches who are struggling to live real lives amidst the incongruities and injustices. The Boff brothers eloquently capture the significance of doing this with their conviction that ordinary people's "celebrations, popular dramatizations, ritualization of sacramental life, and its whole variety of religious creativity . . . give symbolical expression to the liberation already experienced by the people—fragile, certainly, but nevertheless true and anticipatory of the full liberation to come in the final kingdom of God."[52]

Implications for Missionary Practice

So what are the implications of these cultural forms of resistance for missionary work? How are they relevant to Christian life and witness? I would say that these cultural forms of resistance, first and foremost, offer us clues on how to proceed and engage in mission work given the sociocultural, religious, economic, and political contexts of the places and people we are trying to accompany, help, or work with.

In Tonga, for example, where Catholic missionaries are particularly aware of and sensitive to dance as an integral part of Tongan culture, dance is included in certain Catholic worship events, such as dances that tell the stories of the Exodus and the grief of Mary. Tongan dance is also included among other Oceanian dance forms in worship at the Roman Catholic Pacific Regional Seminary in Suva, Fiji. According to Johnson-Hill this was not the case especially among the early Protestant missionaries whose Victorian baggage with regard to sexual modesty and religious piety made them suspicious of Tongan dance to the point that dance, particularly in the context of worship, was considered pagan and offensive. In the process, the Tongans' ability to theologize was also seriously affected since, in many cases, dance performance is the only avenue through which they are able to theologize using indigenous modes of communication.[53]

In Latin America the recognition, engagement, and practice of these cultural forms of resistance has become a means of liberating evangelization for the Latin American church as a whole, as roles and styles of pastoral ministration and missionary work have been redefined. This inculturated way of witnessing to the Christian faith did not only draw more Latin Americans to Christianity, but it also encouraged ordinary people to more fully embrace and participate in the evangelizing mission of the church. It allowed, for instance, the small Christian communities to take on the task of evangelization in a way that is most meaningful and truthful to them, their culture, their concrete realities, and their struggle. In "The Use of the Bible in Christian Communities of the Common People," for example, Carlos Mesters points to how the common people in Latin America make up their own version of the "Bible of the poor" by resorting to songs and stories, pictures, and little plays, not just because these are the cultural forms and expressions they can most relate to, but primarily because many of them do not know how to read.[54] Singing, storytelling, and acting in plays in this case then become not just means of expressing the Christian faith with a Latin American face, but also in fighting against their inability to read in order to be literate in the faith. Mesters says that thanks to songs, many people who have never read the Bible know almost every story in it.

Stuart Foster, who has served as a missionary since 1986, describes something akin to this in the case of the Lomwe people in Mozambique. Summarizing and reflecting on the key themes of more than 263 original songs that he collected from Lomwe-speaking Protestant churches in northern Mozambique, Foster contends that discerning the Lomwe's reflections on the gospel and their faith through their songs is a method for missionaries like himself to listen to a people who have a lot to say but who tend not to write much down.[55] And this is not just for cultural reasons, but also for economic reasons. When the Lomwe learn or practice a song in groups, repetition is important because most people do not have the notebook where the lyrics of the song are scribbled. Only the leaders have the lyrics scribbled in notebooks, hand copied (not even photocopied) from one group to another.

Arguably marginalized peoples' cultural forms of resistance also offer us windows into cultural forms and expressions in which the Christian faith could be most meaningful and effective. Missionaries could then benefit by being aware of these forms and designing or organizing liturgies, programs, and activities around them. The collaborative work that Ronan White, a Spiritan priest, did with the Macua youth in the city of Nampula in Mozambique is an example. HIV/AIDS is a serious problem among the youth there, so to raise awareness White created a program that involves a number of diverse activities considered to constitute key components of both local and global youth culture. Theater, for example, is a form of expression that young Macua people find irresistible, so he made the performance of plays by each parish on the topic of HIV/AIDS the central part of the Archdiocesan Day of Youth. Cognizant of the fact that music and dance play a central role in youth culture, the Youth Commission that he coordinates came up with an annual interparochial dancing competition. Each parish is requested to compose three songs for the contest that must be sung in traditional choral tones and be accompanied by traditional Macua instruments and dancing. In doing these activities on top of the usual reflections, workshops, and sports activities, White got a broad spectrum of youth across the archdiocese to participate. In addition, he said that these activities also offered him a window through which he has been able to observe both the thinking and behavior of the young people, especially in relation to HIV/AIDS.[56]

Missionary practice in view of the cultural forms of resistance then entails reexamining and reevaluating traditional forms of doing mission. It might mean not just, or immediately, resorting to the usual lectures and group discussions as tools for evangelization or, in parish work, conducting meetings and deliberations to tackle social issues or to find solutions to community problems. It could mean having games, conducting plays, singing songs, or having an art contest. For those working on social problems, it might mean doing something within the confines of the parish or community hall and not always through the so-called parliament of the streets. It might mean dispensing with the placards and the slogans, the chaotic or peaceful march, or the angry mob, and doing a silent protest or instead protesting through art or an art festival. Remember that culture is not only about race or ethnicity, but also about age, gender, and all the other factors that constitute our identity markers, the boundaries of which are shifting and oscillating.

Ultimately doing mission is really about telling the story of Jesus in word and in deed. And this becomes more effective when it is done not just through prayer, but also with humor and laughter, especially with simple folks. In this day and age, which is marked by violent conflicts, stories and storytelling also take center stage as a strategy for doing mission. In a way, the choice of healing and reconciliation as the central theme for doing mission today in the reflections of the 2005 Conference of the Commission on World Mission and Evangelism of the World Council of Churches points to this critical role of stories and storytelling in missionary practice, particularly in places ravaged by violent conflicts. The setting up of a Truth and Reconciliation Commission in South Africa to deal with the devastating effects of apartheid also serves as a telling example of this approach since storytelling is part and parcel of truth telling.

Cultural forms of resistance, in other words, give us a glimpse not just into the cultural practices of people, but, in many cases, also their concrete political-economic realities, whether in the past or the present. The extent that we are aware of and appreciate these cultural forms of resistance will be the extent to which we can engage in that meaningful synthesis between faith and culture that is inculturation. Moreover, the extent to which we are aware of how these forms are rooted in or connected to other vital aspects of human life such as history, politics, and economics or how they point to pain, suffering, injustice, and the need for compassion will be the extent to which we can make possible an integral liberating evangelization.

Conclusion

Recognizing culture as a site of struggle and as the context for doing mission then demands that we engage in the recognition and recovery of cultural practices, for example, stories, songs, and dance, which continue to be subjected to "institutional forgetting." Insisting on our ways and imposing our cultural practices is tantamount to a form of control of memory and history. Theological integrity requires that we do not fear the scandal of theorizing and making affirmations on cultural practices that are devalued by or contradict the dominant consciousness. Missionary theology and practice, in other words, must be imaginative. In doing so, theology and mission do more than pay lip service to diversity. They celebrate otherness with a steadfast refusal to conflate diverse experiences into false synthesis.

Truly, there is sound in silence, sacred anger in humor and laughter, and resistance in stories, songs, and dance. Silence speaks, humor and laughter destabilize, while songs, stories, and dance narrate, mourn, and celebrate life's triumphs and tragedies. They are ways of questioning, finding, celebrating, and insisting on the sacred in our life experiences. They offer us windows not just into the beauty of our humanity, but also into what is tragic in people's lives and history. Our theology and way of life is, therefore, missionary to the extent that we are able to appreciate this beauty, recognize the inequity, and, at the same time, listen to the outrage and plea that is behind the silence, the humor and laughter, as well as the stories, songs, and dance of those whose lives hang in the balance. As I see it, every Christian's missionary calling is expressed in the following personal musing: "In the beginning is listening."

Notes

1. See James Scott, *Domination and the Arts of Resistance* (New Haven, CT: Yale University Press, 1990) and James Scott, *Weapons of the Weak: Everyday Forms of Peasant Resistance* (New Haven, CT: Yale University Press, 1995).

2. James Scott, *Domination and the Arts of Resistance*, 14–15, 19.

3. Tom A. Steffen, "Foundational Roles of Symbol and Narratives in the (Re)construction of Reality and Relationships," *Missiology* 26 (1998): 477, 480.

4. N. T. Wright, *The New Testament and the People of God, Vol. 1 of Christian Origins and the Problem of God* (Minneapolis, MN: Fortress Press, 1992), 77.

5. See Klyne R. Snodgrass, *Stories with Intent: A Comprehensive Guide to the Parables of Jesus* (Grand Rapids, MI: William B. Eerdmans, 2008).

6. Muriel Orevillo-Montenegro, *The Jesus of Asian Women* (Maryknoll, NY: Orbis Books, 2006), 92.

7. Elisabeth Schüssler Fiorenza, "Ties That Bind: Domestic Violence against Women" in *Women Resisting Violence: Spirituality for Life*, ed. Mary John Mananzan et al. (Maryknoll, NY: Orbis Books, 1996), 52.

8. Gabriele Dietrich, "People's Movements, the Strength of Wisdom, and the Twisted Path of Civilization," in *Toward a New Heaven and a New Earth: Essays in Honor of Elisabeth Schüssler Fiorenza*, ed. Fernando Segovia (Maryknoll, NY: Orbis Books, 2003), 407–8. Dietrich shares a similar scene (young and old women dancing to the songs and slogans of struggle) in relation to the struggle of the Adivasi people in India against the building of Sardar Sarovar Dam.

9. I have written about this elsewhere. See Gemma Cruz, "Gendering the Quest for Global Economic Justice: The Challenges of Women Labor

Migration to Christian Theological Reflections" *Voices from the Third World* 28, no. 1 (June 2005): 128–46.

10. The notice is as follows: "Washing oil or dirt off a Mercedes is OK, but not off a maid's feet." See "Atin-Atin Lamang," *TNT Hong Kong* 1, no. 3: 23.

11. See the similar explanation by Orevillo-Montenegro, *The Jesus of Asian Women*, 117.

12. In the spirituals the slaves expressed their pain (Sometimes I'm up, sometimes I'm down, Sometimes I'm almost on de ground), their condemnation (Were you there when they crucified my Lord? . . .), their lament (O my Lord delivered Daniel, O why not deliver me too?), their identification with the suffering God (Nobody knows de trouble I've seen, Nobody knows but Jesus . . .), their hopes (O Mary, don't you weep, don't you moan. . . . Pharaoh's army got drowned, O Mary don't you weep), and their vision (Slavery chain done broke at last, broke at last, broke at last. . . . Going to praise God til I die). See examples cited in Elizabeth A. Johnson, *Quest for the Living God: Mapping Frontiers in the Theology of God* (New York: Continuum, 2008), 118–22.

13. Ibid., 118.

14. See Diana Hayes, *And Still We Rise: An Introduction to Black Liberation Theology* (Mahwah, NJ: Paulist Press, 1996), and Diana Hayes and Cyprian David, eds., *Taking Down Our Harps: Black Catholics in the United States* (Maryknoll, NY: Orbis Books, 1998).

15. Maria Corazon Manalo, "Dance: A Woman's Way to Peace," *Religious Studies De La Salle Journal* 19, no. 2 (December 1996): 77–78, as cited in Orevillo-Montenegro, *The Jesus of Asian Women*, 116–17.

16. Orevillo-Montenegro, *The Jesus of Asian Women*, 117.

17. See Damaris Seleina Parsitau, "Sounds of Change and Reform: The Appropriation of Gospel Music and Dance in Political Discourses in Kenya," *Studies in World Christianity* 14, no. 1 (2008): 55–72.

18. Kelly Johnson-Hill, "Inner Exhilaration and Speaking the Truth through Metaphor: An Exploration of the Theological Significance of *Mafana* and *Heliaki* in Tongan Dance," *Studies in World Christianity* 14, no. 1 (2008): 19–34.

19. Ibid., 24–25.

20. Cláudio Carvalhaes, " "Gimme de kneebone bent': Liturgies, Dance, Resistance and a Hermeneutics of the Knees," *Studies in World Christianity* 14, no. 1 (2008): 1–18.

21. Robert Farris Thompson even goes as far as saying the African religion is a "danced belief" or a form of worship that is visible and inherently

attached to bodily action. See John Miller Chernoff, *Rhythmen der Gemeien-schaft: Musik und Sensibilität im afrikanischen Leben* (Wuppertal, Germany: Peter Hammer, 1999), 1712, as cited in Andreas Heuser, "'He Dances Like Isaiah Shember!': Ritual Aesthetics as a Marker of Church Difference," *Studies in World Christianity* 14, no. 1 (2008): 35–54, at 35.

22. See Jacqui Malone, *Steppin on the Blues: The Visible Rhythms of African-American Dance* (Urbana: University of Illinois Press, 1996).

23. Carvalhaes, "'Gimme de kneebone bent,'" 15.

24. I have written about this elsewhere. See Cruz, "Gendering the Quest for Global Economic Justice," 128–46.

25. Nicole Constable, *Maid to Order in Hong Kong* (Ithaca, NY: Cornell University Press, 1997), 175.

26. The Filipino proverb *tawanan mo ang iyong problema* (Laugh at your problems) reflects this.

27. Rina Jimenez-David, "Why Filipinos are happy," http://www.inq7.net/archive/2002-p/opi/2002/jan/11/opi_rjdavid-1-p.htm (accessed October 31, 2003).

28. Arbuckle says humor may be a legitimate way for people who have little political power to draw attention to oppression (Gerald Arbuckle, *Laughing with God: Humor, Culture, and Transformation* [Collegeville, MN: Liturgical Press, 2008], 12).

29. Ibid., 13.

30. For example, Augustine says "Human beings laugh and weep, and it is a matter for weeping that they laugh" while John Chrysostom thinks, "Truly it is not for us to pass our time in laughter" (as quoted in Jacqueline Bussie, *The Laughter of the Oppressed: Ethical and Theological Resistance in Wiesel, Morrison, and Endo* [New York: T & T Clark, 2007], 1, 9).

31. Wiesel, Endo, and Morrison's texts tackle three of the most tragic events in history, namely the Holocaust, Hiroshima bombing, and slavery in North America.

32. Ibid., 184.

33. Ibid., 186–87.

34. Sr. Aurora Zambrano, "Women in Tribal Filipinos, Their Land and Cultural Heritage," *Kalinangan* (March 1985), cited in Patria Agustin, "Women and Politics in the Philippines" *Journal of Feminist Studies in Religion* 3, no. 2 (Fall 1987): 117–18.

35. In Mary Daly, *Gyn/Ecology: The Metaethics of Radical Feminism* (Boston: Beacon Press, 1978), 340. For example, Mary Daly urges women to be active voicing agents, implicitly labeling silence as a nonvalue. Exceptions include Christin Lore Weber, *Woman Christ* (San Francisco: Harper and Row,

1987), 17, cited in Naomi F. Southard, "Recovery and Rediscovered Images: Spiritual Resources for Asian American Women," in *Feminist Theology from the Third World: A Reader*, ed. Ursula King (Maryknoll, NY: Orbis Books, 1994), 382. Southard argues, "Ebbing has been called weakness, but perhaps we will discover in it a new kind of power. Perhaps there is power in all that we have associated with the ebb side of the cycle: silence, waiting, emptiness, darkness, receptivity, detachment, aloneness, and death," and Janet Walton who asserts "silence and lament are partners in the struggles toward truth . . . silent time is fertile space, necessary for attentiveness, dreaming, and imagining. . . . Our silence and laments are deeply engaged and wide-reaching. They are another source of power" (Janet Walton, *Feminist Liturgy: Matter of Justice* [Collegeville, MN: Liturgical Press, 2001], 40–41).

36. Rita Nakashima Brock, "Interstitial Integrity: Reflections toward an Asian American Woman's Theology" in *Introduction to Christian Theology: Contemporary North American Perspectives*, ed. Roger A. Badham (Louisville: WJK Press, 1998), 192–93.

37. See Shirley Geok-lin Lim, "Asian-American Daughters Rewriting Asian Maternal Texts," in *Asian Americans: Comparative and Global Perspectives*, ed. Shirley Hune et al. (Pullman: Washington State University Press, 1991), 192, as cited in Brock, "Interstitial Integrity," 192.

38. Brock, "Interstitial Integrity," 193.

39. Scott, *Weapons of the Weak*, 295.

40. Susan Mann particularly criticizes one persistent Western image of Chinese women that feeds the long-suffering stereotype on Asian women: "Like Madam Roland, who quickly faded into obscurity in France but got a new life in modern China as the mother of the French Revolution, the footbound Chinese woman who dominates the Western historical imagination is a product of creative mistaking that has no place in the family album or storehouse of China's own cultural childhood. When women writers in Europe and North America reached for myths to explain the history of Chinese women, the creative mistaking becomes especially clear, for they tended to settle on a particular myth about Chinese women: the bound foot. . . . They selected the one aspect of Chinese womanhood that was never mythologized in history or fiction outside of the pages of erotic novels and 'spring pictures' used as guides and provocations for lovemaking. When footbinding was stopped in China, so suddenly that it left reformers and foreigners alike grasping in amazement, the shallowness of its cultural roots was clearly exposed. That many Westerners still cling to the myth of the bound foot as if it defined for all time the essence of what it meant to be female in 'traditional' Chinese culture tells us something important about the items in

the cultural storehouse of Europe and North America, especially the myths Westerners need to imagine an Asian other" (Susan Mann, "Myths of Asian Womanhood," *Journal of Asian Studies* 59, no. 4 [November 2000]: 857–58).

41. See Kwok Pui-lan, "Unbinding Our Feet: Saving Brown Women and Feminist Religious Discourse," in *Postcolonialism, Feminism, and Religious Discourse*, ed. Laura Donaldson and Kwok Pui-lan (New York: Routledge, 2002), 62–81.

42. Nantawan Boonprasat Lewis, "On Naming Justice: The Spiritual and Political Connection in Violence against Asian Immigrant Women," in Segovia, ed., *Toward a New Heaven and a New Earth*, 485.

43. Brock, "Interstitial Integrity," 94.

44. Mary John Mananzan, *Woman, Religion and Spirituality in Asia* (Quezon City, Philipines: Anvil, 2004), 18.

45. Southard, "Recovery and Rediscovered Images," 380.

46. Muriel Orevillo-Montenegro, "My Search for Asian Women's Voices," *In God's Image* 26, 4 (December 2007): 23.

47. Leonardo Boff and Clodovis Boff, *Introducing Liberation Theology* (Maryknoll, NY: Orbis Books, 2007), 16–17.

48. Philip T. Laryea, "Ephraim Amu as a Theologian in Song: The Impact of the Vernacular Apprehension of Christian Thought," *Journal of African Christian Thought* 5 (2002): 35, as quoted in Stuart J. Foster, "Oral Theology in Lomwe Songs," *International Bulletin of Missionary Research* 32, no. 3 (July 2008): 130.

49. Johnson-Hill, "Inner Exhilaration and Speaking the Truth," 25.

50. See 1 Kings 19:9–18 (God's silence), Genesis 18:9–15 (Sarah's laughter), Judges 5 (Deborah's canticle), Exodus 15:1–18 (Moses and the Israelites singing after crossing the Red Sea), Mark 6:17–29 (Herodias's daughter's dance), and Luke 10:25–37 (parable of the Good Samaritan).

51. This is a characteristic of Jesus' parables known as elements of reversal, which functions like the punch line of a joke. Parables that contain elements of reversal are among the most powerful instruments for change that Jesus used, for they force unexpected decisions and actions. The tax collector is righteous, not the Pharisee; the Samaritan is neighbor, not the Jewish elite (Klyne R. Snodgrass, *Stories with Intent: A Comprehensive Guide to the Parables of Jesus* [Grand Rapids, MI: W. B. Eerdmans, 2008], 19).

52. Boff and Boff, *Introducing Liberation Theology*, 60.

53. Johnson-Hill, "Inner Exhilaration and Speaking the Truth," 30–31, says that this is also partly a result of the early missionaries' failure to engage the significance of metaphor in Tongan communication. Johnson-Hill thinks that "the [Tongan] cultural practice of alluding to significant people, places,

and events—rather than referring to them directly was either unnoticed by early missionaries, or considered irrelevant to the task of conversion. Consequently, the Gospel was preached to Tongans in a direct manner. The wealth of metaphoric images which could have been used to present the Gospel in a uniquely Tongan way were [then] left to the arena of song, dance, and secular oratory."

54. Carlos Mesters, "The Use of the Bible in Christian Communities of the Common People," in *Liberation Theology: An Introductory Guide*, ed. Curt Cadorette (Maryknoll, NY: Orbis Books, 1992): 45–46.

55. One underlying theme in Lomwe songs, for example, is that of double contrast, for example, insiders with outsiders. This could give a more nuanced glimpse into the struggle of the group that, in turn, could be helpful to missionary practice. See Foster, "Oral Theology in Lomwe Songs," 130–34.

56. See Ronan White, CSSp, "Collaborating with Young People in the Fight against HIV/AIDS in Mozambique," *SEDOS Bulletin* 40, nos. 5/6 (May–June 2008): 139–43. Similarly in an article titled "A New Kind of Protest: Painting, Dancing, Singing," Kristine Alave describes how a public demonstration against the Philippine government that featured art works, dancing, and pop songs instead of the usual fiery speeches and chanting of slogans drew more than three thousand Filipino youth and encouraged them to join future similar protests because of the way in which the rally was conducted. A group of students interviewed, for example, said violent demonstrations that they see on television have scared them from joining and that protests that use creative means are better in that they are more peaceful. See Kristine Alave, "A New Kind of Protest: Painting, Dancing, Singing," http://newsinfo. inquirer.net/breakingnews/nation (accessed August 23, 2008).

10

Missiology's Future at the Intersection of the Intercultural and the Interreligious

Robert J. Schreiter, CPPS

Professor Schreiter reflects on missiology's work in the first decade of the twenty-first century, particularly its work in interpreting cultures, its participation in interreligious encounters, and how missiology today is engaged in the intersection of these two areas both as an academic discipline and as reflective praxis. Professor Schreiter delivered the tenth Louis J. Luzbetak Lecture on March 1, 2010.

It is a distinct honor to be asked to deliver the tenth annual Louis J. Luzbetak, SVD, Lecture on Mission and Culture. I came to know him in the mid-1980s as he prepared a revision of his classic work, *The Church and Cultures: An Applied Anthropology for the Religious Worker.*[1] As many of you know, his revision became a completely new book, *The Church and Cultures: New Perspectives in Missiological Anthropology*, appearing in 1988.[2] I had a small hand in helping him prepare this new edition. He was always overly modest about the contribution he had made to missiology—most notably, how we see the workings of culture in mission. Culture will be one of the major topics of this lecture in order to honor him, and the Society of the Divine Word, of which he was a member, which has done so much to promote an understanding of culture's role in the evangelizing mission of the church.

This is the tenth annual Luzbetak lecture. We are now a decade into the twenty-first century and into Christianity's third millennium. By now the prognostications made ten years ago can be examined as to what extent they were accurate; however, such a scrutiny will not be the object of what I have to say here. Although the word "future" appears in the title of this lecture, it will not be the principal focus of what I will be presenting. Rather I will be dwelling on three points. The first two are areas that have been embraced by missiology over the past thirty years: intercultural interaction and interreligious dialogue. I will be looking at a peculiar intersection of these two in missiology today. In light of that intersection, I will take on a third area, namely, missiology itself: both as an academic discipline and as a reflective praxis on the church's—and of course ultimately God's—mission in the world. How missiology is interpreting this intersection (or perhaps how it ought to be interpreting it) is crucial, I believe, for the future of missiology as an academic discipline and a reflective praxis.

The Contexts of Mission since the Second Vatican Council

In order to understand both the intercultural and interreligious dimensions of mission today, and how they have come to intersect, a brief reprise of mission history over the past half century is necessary. The documents of the Second Vatican Council, especially its Decree on the Missionary Activity of the Church, *Ad Gentes*, provided a new and potentially comprehensive theology of mission for the church. Moving beyond the debates over the primary intent of mission of the church before the Council—as to whether the principal purpose of mission was the salvation of souls or the instituting of the church in new places—mission came to be seen as the action of the Holy Trinity in the world, with the church as the instrument of God's action to achieve this new creation.[3]

This refreshing insight into mission, intended to reinvigorate missionary activity, had the unfortunate (or so it seemed at the time) luck of appearing just at the time when the whole missionary movement was being called into question. The decolonization that was taking place in Asia and Africa led to an incisive analysis of the complicity of much of nineteenth- and twentieth-century mission with the imperial ambitions of Europe. By the late 1960s, there were widespread calls for a moratorium on mission. Expatriate missionaries were to return to their homelands as the new local churches, especially in Africa, struggled to find their own identities apart from their colonial heritage.

As a consequence, mission thinking in both the Catholic Church and the mainline Protestant churches was thrown into disarray. Pope Paul VI's

1975 Apostolic Exhortation, *Evangelii Nuntiandi,* offered some light and direction for mission. But Catholic missiology did not really recover from its self-doubt about mission until 1981 when SEDOS, a mission think-tank in Rome, held a ten-day seminar that brought together missiologists, other theologians, men and women in religious orders responsible for carrying out the missionary charism, and missionaries on the ground to ponder just where mission was at that time. The result of that meeting was a reaffirmation of mission, seen now to be carried out in four distinctive but interrelated ways: direct proclamation, interreligious dialogue, inculturation, and the liberation of the poor.[4]

This fourfold scheme has had two effects on the subsequent theology of mission. First of all, it has encouraged missiologists, mission executives, and missionaries themselves to understand evangelization as an activity that has multiple modes of enactment—not just proclamation. This was already adumbrated in Paul VI's definition of evangelization in *Evangelii Nuntiandi.* It is evident in how mission has been construed since that time. For example, in their already classic theology of mission, *Constants in Context: A Theology of Mission for Today*, Stephen Bevans and Roger Schroeder point to six venues and modes of mission under the overarching theme of prophetic dialogue: mission as witness and proclamation; as liturgy, prayer, and contemplation; as justice, peace, and the integrity of creation; as inculturation and as interreligious dialogue; and as reconciliation.[5]

Second, seeing the multiplicity of forms of mission has helped nudge mission to a central place in the understanding of Christian faith as a whole: mission is central to our understanding of God and the place of the church within God's mission. While this second point has not yet achieved the visibility and the valence it deserves, the stage is at least set for this to happen.

Out of Bevans's and Schroeder's six forms of mission, I would like to select two—namely, inculturation and interreligious dialogue—and explore them further. All of the Catholic theologies of mission of which I am aware that subscribe to this understanding of mission in multiple forms include inculturation and interreligious dialogue. In what follows, I will select two issues each for inculturation and dialogue that represent the cutting edges of these approaches. Then I will concentrate on the points where inculturation and interreligious dialogue are intersecting today.

Inculturation

Inculturation has to do with how the gospel is brought to and received in a given culture. Systematic reflection on inculturation (in Protestant circles, the preferred term has been "contextualization") began in the 1970s. A focus on the methodologies began toward the end of that decade and has continued on up to the present time.[6]

In its initial stages, the focus in inculturation was on issues of Christian identity in non-Western cultures. These efforts coincided in many places with working to construct a postcolonial national identity apart from the history of European colonization. By the late 1980s, inculturation came to be seen as an important topic in other venues as well. For example, inculturation was also a way of revitalizing European and North American churches. This led to a number of projects to see more closely how Christian faith was to be expressed in increasingly secular contexts. More recently, greater attention has been paid to the social issues challenging societies and how these are given expression in specific contexts.[7] To an extent this most recent form of inculturation blends together the identity concerns of earlier efforts at inculturation with themes for the theologies of liberation. Some of this is going on in a second generation of postcolonial thinking.[8]

I would like to lift up two issues that represent cutting edges for theologies of inculturation today, at least from a methodological perspective. The first is the impact of globalization on our concepts of culture. The second is where we have come in developing an intercultural hermeneutics (that is, our methods of interpretation across cultural boundaries).

The Impact of Globalization on Concepts of Culture

It has become commonplace to suggest that there are three major ways of understanding culture that have grown up in the West over the last three hundred years. The first, often called the "classical" notion of culture, understands culture to be the most refined products in art, music, and literature that arise from a people. On this view, culture is something that the elites in a population have, but the uneducated masses do not. This view of culture continues to be of importance today. In the latter years of the eighteenth century, a second view of culture, usually called the "modern" sense of culture, emerged. The German philosopher Herder gave it its most well-known definition. Culture is the union of three things: language, custom, and territory. Culture in this sense is something that everyone possesses: we all have a (first) language, grew up in a network of values and codes of behavior, and lived with like-minded people in a given place. This is the understanding of culture that informs the social sciences.

In Catholic theology, both the classical and the modern senses of culture come into play. At times, culture refers to the highest achievements of humanity; at other times, it refers to ethnicity and belonging to a given group. These two understandings of culture were evident in the routine of Pope John Paul II's visit to a country: he would address the intellectuals and artists of the country, and would also address a beleaguered cultural minority that was struggling to maintain its own way of life.

More recently, a third understanding of culture has come into play. It is usually referred to as a "postmodern" sense of culture. I have also referred to it as a "globalized" sense of culture.[9] In this sense of culture, the trinity of language, custom, and territory breaks down. A bounded territory is missing for many people today, especially migrants and those living in large urban settings (which now accounts for slightly more than half the world's population). Customs and even language get intermingled with competing "cultures" in the urban setting. What then is "culture" in this setting? It is usually understood as a kind of force field wherein identities are constructed out of the fragments of custom and language that are at play in an urban setting or in refugee camps or camps of displaced persons. Identities are hybrid rather than integral and integrated, in the manner imagined in the modern concept of culture.

I prefer to call these concepts "globalized" rather than "postmodern," since the postmodern is usually associated with the West and those elites in settings outside the West. In globalization studies, four characteristics of how globalization is changing cultures are usually named. The first is *homogenization*, or the flattening out or erasure of local cultural identities by powerful global forces. Thus one talks of "McWorld" or the "coca-colonization of the world." What has become apparent is that the process of homogenization is not so simple as it first appears. Local cultures resist these incursions and make use of these outside cultural flows in ways of their own. Thus, homogenization can actually reinvigorate local cultures as they engage in acts of resistance. The second is called *hyperdifferentiation*, or a segmentation of society wrought by all the possibilities that are on offer. This is a phenomenon mainly in the wealthy parts of the world, where people can choose their sources of information or choose where they will live and with whom they will associate. The poor of the world do not have this luxury. The third is called *deterritorialization*, which means place no longer gives identity, and people find themselves disembedded and sometimes disoriented by the experience. This is experienced by people who are displaced in armed conflict, by migrants who must leave their homelands, and by urban dwellers whose location does not anchor their identity.

The fourth has already been mentioned; namely, *hybridity*. Hybrid identities—in which elements that were previously discrete are now mixed together through culture contact, multicultural societies, and acute displacement by war or natural disasters—are probably the rule rather than the exception in much of the world today. Inculturation is only beginning to catch up with this. The Abrahamic faiths, especially Christianity and Islam, tend to think of their faith in terms of purity and orthodoxy. Yet anyone who has been involved with inculturation knows that the reality is messier than that. Theology, at least from a missiological perspective, has come to accept folk religion or *religiosidad popular* as a legitimate site of Christian identity.

But how will it deal with the hybridities of, say, African Pentecostal churches flourishing in Europe or the United States, even attracting settled populations into its ranks? What is the "culture" of second-generation immigrants, caught between the identities of their parents' homeland and the place where they are now growing up? What of people who have come from a majority-religious identity when confronted with all the possibilities that are on offer in urban settings? These are of course hardly new problems. But we have sometimes essentialized the modern concept of culture, only to find it not very useful in the settings that I have been describing. From a missiological perspective, what does an inculturated theology look like in these places where hybridity marks most people's identities?[10]

Intercultural Hermeneutics

A second major set of issues for mission as inculturation has to do with the interpretation of meanings across cultural boundaries—otherwise known technically as intercultural hermeneutics. Efforts to develop intercultural hermeneutics grew in philosophy, psychology, and intercultural studies beginning in the early 1990s and moved into theology later in that decade.

One can discern three general approaches in intercultural hermeneutics. The first approach might be called a "universalist" one, in that it focuses upon commonalities between the two cultures under consideration. Comparative studies help locate the commonalities that are then theorized in an idealist or transcendentalist framework. This approach is particularly salient in the German-speaking world and connected with the names of Richard Schaeffler (on dialogue), R. A. Mall (comparative philosophies East and West), and Franz Wimmer (history of philosophy).[11] It seeks to harmonize traditions and meanings within cultures. It has seemed especially suited (especially in East and South Asia) to collectivist cultures. It works with more deductive methodologies.

The second approach might be called a more "particularist" one, inasmuch as it concentrates upon the differences between cultures rather than their commonalities. Here the methodology tends to be more empirical and inductive, and is found principally in the Anglophone world (Australia, North America, Europe). One finds this approach represented among postcolonial thinkers in philosophy, literature, and theology with their concentration upon the "other" and the "subaltern."[12] Another approach, mainly in the social sciences, concentrates on competence in intercultural communication and does research on levels of development of this competence.[13] The particularist approach favors the egocentric cultures that prevail in the West.

A third approach that shares ground with postcolonial thinkers is found in Latin America, where the study of *interculturalidad* focuses upon the unequal and violent encounter of the conquistadores with indigenous peoples, as well as the continuing consequences of this over half a millennium. This approach is especially attuned to questions of racism and of power.[14] It might be called an "oppositional" approach.

In the study of culture today, especially as it is present in mission, all three of these have something important to offer. The universalist approach, while it may seem to the particularists to erase or suppress difference, addresses the problem of how to create coherence in a pluralist situation without sliding into a mindless relativism. The second and third approaches (particularism and the concern for interculturality) address the importance of legitimate difference, especially when those differences are central to the identities of those made "other," but are marginalized by the powerful at the center of the culture. Theologically, the struggle to hold these three understandings in intercultural hermeneutics together is situated in the current discussion of catholicity—how the church maintains simultaneously its universality and its particularity, especially as a church of the poor.

In summary, these two issues in inculturation—what globalization is doing to the concept of culture, and the varieties of intercultural hermeneutics—are central ones for the conduct of mission today. Any attempt at understanding mission as inculturation has to be dealing with them.

Interreligious Dialogue

Dialogue has been a major feature of the church in the post-Vatican II era. Dialogue with other Christians and dialogue with other faiths were raised to the status of official policy by the decrees *Unitatis Redintegratio* and *Nostra Aetate*. Pope Paul VI, in his initial encyclical *Ecclesiam Suam*, made dialogue a hallmark of his papacy.

More so than ecumenical dialogue, interreligious dialogue was uncharted territory for the Catholic Church. By the mid-1980s, the Pontifical Council on Interreligious Dialogue was to define the church's efforts in this regard in a now-familiar fourfold manner: (1) the dialogue of life—the witness of Christian faith to others by one's way of life; (2) the dialogue of common social action—engaging in action with other faiths based on Catholic social teaching; (3) the dialogue of theological exchange—focusing upon commonalities and differences in doctrine; and (4) the exchange of mystical experiences—a dialogue carried on by spiritual adepts in the respective traditions.

Pope John Paul II was an enthusiastic practitioner of interreligious dialogue, whose actions in this regard sometimes outstripped a capacity to articulate them theologically. Pope Benedict XVI has shown more hesitation toward the dialogue of theological exchange and most recently pressed more in the direction of a dialogue of common social action.

Mission as interreligious dialogue was embraced especially by missionaries working in Asia, where Christianity remained a tiny minority among other religious traditions that had long preceded Christianity in those areas and, in the case of Hinduism and Buddhism, predated Christianity itself by centuries. The Federation of Asian Bishops' Conferences, knowing intimately the issues of interreligious relations in Asia, has, by and large, shared the missionary view that dialogue is the most effective form of witness, much more so than direct proclamation. This view has not been shared by sectors within the Roman Curia. The closer proximity and sustained contact of Christianity to these other religious traditions in Asia have opened up the question of religious pluralism in a highly neuralgic way.

I want to note two areas in interreligious dialogue that are pertinent here. The first has to do with how the interreligious is intersecting with the intercultural. The second is closely related to it, namely, the question of multiple religious belonging.

The Interreligious and the Intercultural

Formal interreligious encounters for Christianity have centered especially on dialogue as theological exchange, wherein Christians and those of another faith would discuss theological concepts that bear some resemblance across the two traditions. This was inevitably a dialogue of experts. It presumed that the traditions were best presented in terms of their doctrines and ideas. Because of this emphasis on doctrines and texts, culture was of itself of relatively little consequence. Second, in these exchanges, a Western concept of "religion" as a bounded set of doctrines and rituals was presumed as the point of departure for the discussion.

This concept of religion is relatively recent, even in the West. It dates back to the sixteenth-century European wars of religion, where Catholicism, Lutheranism, and the Reformed tradition were seen as "competing religions." In the Middle Ages, "religion" meant what we call "religious life," which was seen as a higher state of spiritual perfection than life as a lay person. Many languages of the world do not have a word for what Westerners call "religion." Indeed, in those settings, what Westerners call religion cannot be so easily abstracted from culture. This is certainly the case with small-scale societies where one is born into the religion of that culture. But it is also found in translocal traditions such as Buddhism, Islam, and Christianity that create something like "cultures" of their own. Pope Benedict's vision of a Christian Europe certainly supports this kind of coextensiveness of religion and culture.

But what happens when religion becomes disembedded from its customary cultures, as is happening with migration and urbanization? What does Moroccan Islam look like in the Netherlands or Belgium? Or the Christianity of Philippine workers in the Middle East? It is in such venues that one sees the confluence of the intercultural and the interreligious in the new social formations taking shape in the cities of the world. If the impact of globalization on culture has been to force us to think about culture in a nonessentialized way, what has happened to religion as it becomes disembedded from its familiar locales may end up giving us a less bounded notion of religion as well. This will have an impact on how we state and adjudicate truth claims, how we envision the boundaries of religious pluralism, and how we construe our own identities. Even as we talk about new forms of inculturation, we are uncertain of just how much any religious tradition may depend upon certain cultural forms for maintaining its identity. This may become even more clear as we come to realize how much of what we call "religion" is what we also call "culture" and vice versa.

As both culture and religion become for us less monolithic, we must try to discern if or how this represents the Triune God's *missio* in the world today. These are not just matters of our boundaries becoming fuzzy. They are questions as to how the interconnectedness that is fostered by one dimension of globalization is creating the conditions of possibility for convergences in culture and faith that we may not have anticipated. The intelligentsia of the respective traditions may be able to maintain discrete categories for all of this, but will that be the case for the great majority of adherents of those faiths? Part of the struggle within our own church about identity and engagement with the world and with the tradition is symptomatic of the playing out of these powerful social forces.

Multiple Religious Belonging

Multiple religious belonging—practicing and adhering in some measure to more than one form of religious faith—has been a problematic concept among the Abrahamic faiths. Although the boundary between Judaism and Christianity did not become firm in some regions for almost four hundred years after the time of Christ (and may have also been unclear between Christianity and Islam in the latter's early years), today it is generally regarded to have been clearly demarcated. Yet we also know that in the course of the history of Christianity, previous religious ways were not always eschewed with the embrace of Christianity, and a variety of identifications have been, and continue to be made.

The reasons for multiple belonging are several. At times, Christianity has been forced upon a population, and keeping the previous ways alive was a form of protest. Such was the case among many peoples in the

Americas.[15] At other points, the new religion does not deal as well with (often local) phenomena, so the old ways are maintained. One sees this especially in rites of healing and for caring for the dead. In yet still others, religions are not experienced as exclusive of one another. In Japan, one typically has more religious adherents than one has people in the population, since many Japanese feel that they can be part of different traditions at the same time. In the coronation rites for the king in Thailand, an overwhelmingly Buddhist land, the sovereign becomes a Hindu for about six weeks in the coronation process.

As the boundaries of cultures and religions have become more porous, believers find and develop new configurations. They participate in one another's practices, sometimes investing them with meaning of their own. Thus, there are groups of Christians in West Africa (in Ghana) whose fast during Lent closely resembles the practices of Ramadan. In Lagos, Musaddhin Saka, born a Muslim, has begun what he calls Chrislam, a mixing of Christianity and Islam that also has Pentecostal characteristics. There is a street in Mumbai that is home to two shrines: one to the goddess Kali, the other to Our Lady of Perpetual Help. On Tuesdays, the women of the neighborhood visit the shrine of Kali, and the same women appear at Our Lady of Perpetual Help on Thursdays. Are such things signs of a new tolerance, greater empathy, unreflective mixing, or dangerous syncretism? Such patterns of multiple belonging are not new, but they are likely to rise in number under the pressures of globalization, as people struggle in their own ways to overcome local differences or desperately seek out new avenues of divine assistance when human agency fails them. If identities become increasingly hybrid under the impact of globalization, can we not expect that this will also become evident in their religious behavior?

From a missiological point of view, we might ask the following questions: What do things like these, happening on the ground rather than in elite circles (a kind of vernacular cosmopolitanism, if you will) mean for our theologies of religious pluralism, our understandings of mission as inculturation and dialogue? How do we make claims of religious truth in the midst of such phenomena? As cultural practices have more impact on religious practices, how shall we interpret them? What kind of intercultural hermeneutics will be the most helpful in gaining insight into what people are experiencing? Should we remain with a universalist hermeneutic that has prevailed in interreligious dialogue to this time? Or should we adopt a more particularist or oppositional one?

Missiology and Its Future at the Intersection of the Intercultural and Interreligious

I have spent most of this presentation looking at some of the cutting edges in mission as inculturation and mission as interreligious dialogue. To a certain extent, the changes going on in those venues are driven by the forces of globalization and the consequences of globalization's impact on human life and religious belief and practice. In the title of this presentation, I have suggested that missiology's future is to be found at the intersection of what is happening in the intercultural and interreligious sectors. In this third and final section, I want to say a bit more about why I think this is where missiology—both as an academic discipline and as a reflective praxis of the church—might find its future. I take up the two dimensions of missiology—discipline and reflective praxis—consecutively.

The Future of Missiology as an Academic Discipline

The future of missiology as an academic discipline has been much debated in certain circles, especially in Europe.[16] On that continent, especially in the northern part, professorial chairs of missiology have been left vacant, have been fused with other, existing chairs, or discontinued altogether. The reasons given for this have been many. The connection of mission with colonialism has been a major one. Others have asserted that the concepts that underlie missiology have been superseded and are now obsolete. Others see the military metaphors of mission as offensive. Yet others think it is part of the shrinking of theological faculties in Europe as a result of continuing secularization.

One strategy to counteract this that is being used widely has been to rename missiology as "intercultural studies" or "studies in interreligious encounter." This renaming has also been followed widely in the United States, across the theological spectrum from evangelicals to Roman Catholics. "Mission" is deemed offensive because it is deemed proselytizing (in the face of interreligious dialogue), so it must give way to the more neutral-sounding "intercultural studies."

I want to raise just one point about this, regarding renaming as a way of saving an academic discipline. There has already been a considerable debate about whether missiology is a distinctive academic discipline with its own methodologies or whether it is a site of interdisciplinary study. I personally have found it hard to see missiology as a distinct discipline, despite efforts in some quarters to present it as such.[17] Whatever side of the debate one prefers, simply renaming missiology as "intercultural studies" is unlikely to assure its recognition as an academic discipline or assure its survival in the academy.

Many professors of missiology in the twentieth century were trained as historians and mainly pursued missiology as the history of Christian missions. With a few notable exceptions, the history written was indistinguishable in method from other accounts of church history. The notable exceptions have been attempts to recast the entirety of church history as a history of mission, as is found in Bevans and Schroeder's *Constants in Context* and the proposed two-volume work of Dale Irvin and Scott Sunquist, *History of the World Christian Movement*.[18] There one can make a case for a distinctive kind of history being written.

To shift missiology from being historical description to description of current intercultural and interreligious situations hardly makes a case for missiology to be a self-standing and self-sustaining discipline. Such description can already be done readily in departments of sociology and cultural anthropology or institutes of culture studies. If missiology is to be credible as an academic area of study, it must contribute to cultural studies in methodology and to the study of theology in a distinctive theological manner. The efforts at understanding contextualization did, in some measure, bring a methodological tone to missiology inasmuch as they helped theorize certain forms of cultural contact and processes of conversion. Theologically, inculturation has made arguments about the nature of theology as such and its occasional subservience to the academy at the cost of other important audiences, such as the church and society. It has argued for coming to understand the tradition in a different way and has given new confidence to the so-called younger churches in their attempts to do theology.

I have taken the time to try to lay out some of the growing edges in the intercultural and the interreligious in order to make the case that it is in those places that missiology as a discipline should be engaged. If what missiologists do makes no difference to what is happening in intercultural studies or studies of interreligious encounter, then it has little right to claim for itself academic standing.

Missiology as the Reflexive Praxis of the Church

If the mission of the church is to be at the service of the mission of the Triune God, the *missio Dei*, then missiology should be at those places where God's work is emerging into our awareness. The embrace of missiology of dialogue, inculturation, and liberation thirty years ago is an example of recognizing that certain practices of the church are part of God's mission to the world. If the church believes that God is active in the world, and goes before the church into the world, then dialogue, inculturation, and commitment to the poor have deep theological significance.

Perhaps another example would be useful here. Before inculturation came to be seen as an important theological practice, folk religion was seen as a Christian faith *manqué*, a phenomenon that showed a deficit of full evangelization. Today most thoughtful Christians would no longer say that *religiosidad popular* is an incomplete or immature response to faith. As interreligious and intercultural encounters converge, how are we to understand multiple religious belonging? Is it a natural stage in the inculturation process that is only overcome when no one remembers the historical origins of practices any more? If identities become increasingly hybrid, can religion escape this same process? And as hybrid religious identities become more prevalent, must not our definition of what religion is change? And, if it changes, how must we rethink our theologies of religious pluralism?

In the years ahead, the challenges that are likely to face us will create new hybrid identities but will also call for new forms of solidarity. We have to stand together to face global risks to the environment, to the security of food and water, and the uncertainties of global climate change. Conflicts that now appear to be driven by issues of identity will focus on food, water, and inhabitable and arable land. We will need to develop our universalist hermeneutics to find ways of building such solidarity that go beyond the impasses we have encountered in such universalizing projects as a Global Ethic. Our catholicity as a church requires nothing less than this. Where God is leading us, and where God wants us to go, will be of even greater importance for us as a church. Will a missiology that is willing to risk standing at neuralgic intersections be able to help us in that calling? I believe so.

Notes

1. Louis J. Luzbetak, *The Church and Cultures: An Applied Anthropology for the Religious Worker* (Techny, IL: Divine Word Publications, 1963). This edition is still in print through the William Carey Library.

2. Louis J. Luzbetak, *The Church and Cultures: New Perspectives in Missiological Anthropology* (Maryknoll, NY: Orbis Books, 1988).

3. For a recent commentary on *Ad Gentes*, see Stephen Bevans and Jeffrey Gros, *Evangelization and Religious Freedom: Ad Gentes, Dignitatis Humanae* (New York: Paulist Press, 2009).

4. The proceedings of that seminar were published as Mary Motte and Joseph Lang, eds., *Mission in Dialogue* (Maryknoll, NY: Orbis Books, 1982).

5. Stephen Bevans and Roger Schroeder, *Constants in Context: A Theology of Mission for Today* (Maryknoll, NY: Orbis Books, 2004).

6. Pincipal works have been Charles Kraft, *Christianity in Culture* (Maryknoll, NY: Orbis Books, 1979); Robert Schreiter, *Constructing Local Theologies* (Maryknoll, NY: Orbis Books, 1985); Aylward Shorter, *Toward a Theology of Inculturation* (Maryknoll, NY: Orbis Books, 1989); Stephen Bevans, *Models of Contextual Theology,* rev. ed. (Maryknoll, NY: Orbis Books, 2002 [1992]); Achiel Peelman, *Les nouveaux défis de l'inculturation* (Ottawa, Canada: Novalis, 2008).

7. See, for example, Jean Marc Ela, *Repenser la théologie africaine: le Dieu qui libère* (Paris: Karthala, 2003).

8. The leading figures here are Cuban-American exegete Fernando Segovia and Sri Lankan theologian R. S. Sugirtharajah.

9. In Robert J. Schreiter, *The New Catholicity: Theology between the Global and the Local* (Maryknoll, NY: Orbis Books, 1997).

10. I have tried to begin to address these questions in "Spaces for Religion and Migrant Religious Identity," *Forum Mission* 5 (2009): 155–70.

11. Richard Schaeffler, *Von Gott reden* (Freiburg, Germany: Karl Alber Verlag, 2006); R. A. Mall, *Philosophie im Vergleich der Kulturen* (Darmstadt, Germany: Wissenschaftliche Buchgeselleschaft, 2006); Franz Wimmer, *Interkulturelle Philosophie: Geschichete und Theorie* (Vienna, Austria: Passagen Verlag, 1990).

12. A postcolonial example in theology is the collection of D. N. Premnath, ed., *Border Crossings: Cross-Cultural Hermeneutics* (Maryknoll, NY: Orbis Books, 2008).

13. See, for example, Darla Deardorff, *The SAGE Handbook of Intercultural Communication Competence* (Thousand Oaks, CA: Sage, 2009).

14. One of the foremost figures in this is Raul Fornet-Betancourt, a Cuban now living in Germany. See, for example, his *Filosofía intercultural* (Mexico City: Universidad Pontificia de México, 1994).

15. For an account of this, see Manuel Marzal, ed., *The Indian Face of God in Latin America* (Maryknoll, NY: Orbis Books, 1996).

16. For my own contributions to this, see Robert J. Schreiter, "La missionología como disciplina academica del futuro," *Spiritus* 45, no. 4 (2004): 136–39; Robert J. Schreiter, "Verbreitung der Wahrheit oder interkulturelle Theologie: Was meinen wir, wen wir heute von Mission sprechen?" *Interkulturelle Theologie* 36 (2010): 13–31.

17. The Dutch missiologist Jan Jongeneel mounted a spirited defense of that some years ago as the future of his own chair at the University of Utrecht came under bureaucratic scrutiny. See his two-volume *Missiologie: I. Zendingswetenschap, II. Missionaire Theologie* ('sGravenhage, The Netherlands: Boekencentrum, 1991).

18. Bevans and Schroeder, *Constants in Context*, 2004; Dale T. Irvin and Scott W. Sunquist, *History of the World Christian Movement* (Maryknoll, NY: Orbis Books, 2001). The second volume is in preparation. One could make the case that Kenneth Scott Latourette's multivolume history of the church falls into this category. See also Heinzgünter Frohens, Uwe W. Knoor, and Knut Schäfdiek, *Kirchengeschichte als Missionsgeschichte* (Munich, Germany: Kaiser Verlag, 1979 [1974]), which only covers history through the early Middle Ages and was never completed.

11

Mission and Culture:
The SVD Connection

Philip Gibbs, SVD

Philip Gibbs, SVD, a long-time missionary and anthropologist in Papua New Guinea, challenges missiologists in general and members of the Society of the Divine Word (SVD) in particular, to reflect on their missionary work through the lens of a more postmodern, "globalized" understanding of culture. He offers examples from his own ministry of dealing with the closing of a local gold mine, witnessing the violence in a local election, and relating to a woman infected with AIDS. The lecture was given on October 11, 2010.

I have fond memories of the four years studying here at Catholic Theological Union (CTU) in the 1970s. At that time, Steve Bevans was teaching in the Philippines and Tony Gittins was, as he puts it, "beating about the bush" in Sierra Leone, and for two years my classmate Roger Schroeder was in Papua New Guinea. Bob Schreiter was rather new at CTU and working on his book *Constructing Local Theologies*. Under his guidance, I wrote my thesis—a theological reflection on a myth from Papua New Guinea, and when taking a break from studying Ricoeur's hermeneutics of the "text" and "metaphor," I read widely in the field of anthropology—scholars such as Claude Lévi-Strauss, Victor Turner, and Mary Douglas. The novel ideas in those days were from Clifford Geertz, who published *The Interpretation of Cultures* while I was here in Chicago in 1975.

I recall too how Louis Luzbetak lived with us in the SVD community on Woodlawn Avenue—just a few blocks from here—and it was at this time that he began working on a revision of *The Church and Cultures*. That opus would appear in its new form much later—in 1988. Louis Luzbetak was such a humble, hard-working confrere that I must admit that, to my shame and regret, in those days I did not realize his stature as a scholar, anthropologist, and missionary.[1] In terms of the latter—Louis, as a missionary *ad gentes*—I have since been fortunate to speak with people at Ambong—the outstation of Banz parish in Papua New Guinea, where he lived, worked, and studied from 1952 to 1956. The people remember him—not as a scholar but as a warm friendly missionary who was interested in their language and who liked to tell jokes and listen to stories.

Anthropos Tradition

There is a third strand to the thread of memories from my time in Chicago. As an SVD, I felt the benefit of a family link with the study of culture through what could be termed the "Anthropos tradition."[2] SVD founder Arnold Janssen had insisted from the beginning on the inclusion of academic sciences in the training of future missionaries. Wilhelm Schmidt took up the challenge in what was then called ethnology.[3] He began publication of the *Anthropos* journal in 1906, a journal still being published today, and he founded the Anthropos Institute in 1931.

Good ethnology depends on the data of ethnography, and Wilhelm Schmidt thought that missionaries could make an important contribution to ethnology through their cultural descriptions since many of them had lived for years with people, gaining their trust, and learning their language.[4] Louis Luzbetak, who later served as director of the Anthropos Institute, writes how Wilhelm Schmidt "was my mentor and constant inspiration in my attempt to serve faith through science."[5] Members of the Anthropos Institute focused on different areas of the world, Höltker and Aufenanger concentrated on Oceania, Schröder on China and Taiwan, Hermanns on Mongolia, Fuchs on India, and Saake on Brazil and other parts of South America. Paul Shebesta studied the life of the Mbuti Pygmies of Central Africa, and among his many studies, Martin Gusinde made four research trips to document the life of the indigenous people of Tierra del Fuego.

As an SVD having done postgraduate studies in anthropology through Sydney University, I was deeply impressed by the Anthropos tradition, not so much in Schmidt's culture-history method or his twelve-volume *Der Ursprung der Gottesidee*, but more because the tradition represented a special relationship between mission and culture. I spent my summers here in the United States studying linguistics with the Summer Institute of Linguistics: two summers at the University of North Dakota and one in Oklahoma, and had the first of my articles published in the *Anthropos* journal during the time here in Chicago.[6]

So it was with a sense of confidence that I returned to Papua New Guinea in 1979, with the intention of living with the people, learning their language, their values, and their worldview in order to be able to share the Word in a way that could be understood by the people. It was a noble ideal, possibly valid in its day—but in effect things turned out quite differently. I want to tell you how, and examine why, in three experiences associated with a gold mine, electoral politics, and the HIV epidemic. I have chosen these three because they involve the quality of our relationship with the environment, with society, and with fellow human beings—themes that are surely relevant globally and not to just one nation such as Papua New Guinea. I trust you will not regard my narrative style as simply anecdotal, because my purpose is to use narrative to share my personal insights into the context of mission and particularly the way it relates to the human condition.

A Gold Mine

My first assignment in Papua New Guinea was to Porgera-Paiela, a large isolated parish in the Highlands. In its remoteness at the very end of the five-hundred-mile Highlands Highway (think passageway), Porgera would have little of interest, except for the fact that gold was discovered there by the first Australian explorers in 1939. For the past twenty years, Porgera has been the site of one of the largest gold mines in the southern hemisphere, producing up to one million ounces of gold a year. It means profit for the multinational mining company but also cash for the local people, and there has been a steady stream of newcomers into the district, especially during the short-lived Mount Kare gold rush starting in the late 1980s when young children could earn up to $300 a day, and hiring a helicopter became the equivalent of someone in the United States hailing a taxi.

Concerned that influential outsiders might come with false claims as local "landowners," I worked with the local leaders to document exhaustive genealogies of the clans occupying land close to the mine-site. It was a fine study—but the problem was with the exceptions. People were not following the cultural "rules" as I understood them. The whole idea of "clans" is a central anthropological concept, but somehow it did not take into account improvisation and interested strategy. In the ambiguous rough-and-tumble of social interaction, I was forced to take a more constructivist perspective and to come up with a form of action theory that provided room for people as actors in these changed social circumstances.

When the local people from Porgera first encountered Australian explorers, they were not aware that they were being drawn into a historical context that was part of the colonial expansion of the world gold market. The Australian explorers referred to the Highlanders as "locals." So the global-local interaction commenced. However, as Marilyn Strathern has noted, typically Highlanders interpreted the newcomers as versions of familiar beings, first in spirit and then in human form.[7] They perceived the explorers as beings whom they could relate to even though they were from elsewhere; and the Australians were dreadfully conscious of being in a particular locality where they had never been before. So it is possible to cast the Highlanders' strategy as global, welcoming the strangers, and the Australians as local, away from the familiar within the confines of this new place.[8] In effect, that is what happened, and ever since the people of Porgera and the thousands of immigrants to Porgera from other areas in the Highlands have set out to devise ways to exploit possibilities for interaction in these changing circumstances.

The issue I had to face in this rather incoherent situation of rapid and chaotic cultural and social change was to find my place within this scenario. As Bob Schreiter reminds us, I had to "find ways of embracing both the global and the local if it is to be a faithful and credible voice for belief."[9] My education and past experience naturally cast me as a representative of the globalized world. Yet, at times I felt quite the contrary, as for example, recently when I struggled up a muddy path in Porgera hoping to meet and discuss local concerns with the chairman of the landowners' association only to be told that he was in New York presenting their views to the United Nations Forum on Indigenous Issues. They added that they could give me a cell phone number to contact him in New York if I wished.

Admittedly not everyone from Porgera is a "worldly 'native'"[10] traveling to the other side of the globe, but all, willingly or unconsciously, are now participating in a globalized world. In some ways they have reinvented themselves in local constructive efforts to indigenize exogenous elements. For example, people were willing to disregard their snake-ancestor Kupiane who lived in the mountain to be mined, only to reimagine the gold as the skin shed by their underworld snake ancestor.[11]

What is mission in that situation? I came with ideas of inculturation of the global Christian message into the local context. But this approach met with resistance because the local people were more interested in global citizenry and remaking themselves as global Christians. The majority found the millennial Seventh Day Adventist message more to their liking. It fitted more closely with the gold-mining developments and their desire to share in the benefits of modernity.[12] The fact that modernity in terms of wealth, harmony, and happiness proved elusive provoked frustration and resentment that only fueled the millennial vision.

How is one to accompany people who appear to be deluded in their millennial expectations? In Papua New Guinea, indicators, such as life expectancy, maternal mortality, nutrition, and health, are dismal. There are other dimensions of life more difficult to measure in terms of human well-being and dependency. I attended meetings in which people were consulted about the ecological impact of the mine, and they believed that it would be to their advantage in terms of "development" and said they were ready to pay the cost. But what is informed consent without experience? Did they truly realize what it would mean in terms of dependence on imported systems, goods, and ideas, including imported religion? Their children today cannot imagine what life would be like without the mine. They also appear to believe, not only in a Jesus who saves, but one who pays dividends, if not now, then soon in the imminent coming of the millennium, prefigured by the mine.[13] I perceived the situation as a religious attempt to deal with a cultural crisis, and the challenge is to find ways to work with these new identities and new logics to look for where God might be at work in this local-global complex.

An Election

Papua New Guinea achieved a peaceful transition to independence in 1975. Representatives are elected to a Parliament of 109 members, based on the Westminster system of government. The initial years of independence were relatively peaceful, but there was a flare up of violence and a gradual breakdown of law and order in the late 1980s. This was experienced particularly by the two million people living in the Highlands.

Elections in the Papua New Guinea Highlands are a form of investment, with successful candidates rewarding their supporters and disre-
garding others. I suppose this is typical of politics worldwide; however,
in the Highlands, the situation can be quite volatile, so much so that the
system has been labeled "gunpoint democracy."[14] People can go to the
extreme in their desperate desire to gain control of state resources and
services. The state, which has had a decreasing presence in more isolated
areas, finds it difficult to control the situation. In 2002 a "failed election"
was declared in six of the nine southern Highlands electorates. By August
that year thirty election-related deaths had been reported in the Highlands, including two electoral officials.[15] Fearing that this pattern might
spread, the electoral commission sought ways to control and monitor
future elections.

For the national elections in 2007, 2,700 candidates contested the 109
seats in Parliament in 9,100 polling places. I was asked through the National
Electoral Commission to form and lead a domestic observer team in the
Enga Province of the Highlands—a province known as a "hot spot" among
the nineteen provinces in Papua New Guinea. It might seem surprising
that they would request this of an expatriate missionary, but perhaps they
asked me because I had been researching and publishing on the political
culture of previous elections. I had noticed a renewed interest in power
and "religious" phenomena, particularly in the lead up to the year 2000.[16]

Forms of spiritual power were becoming more and more sought after
as people felt a need for personal and collective security in the face of
chronic political instability.[17] People are searching for solutions, and if
Christian churches are not part of the answer, they look elsewhere. One
recent study reveals that in the last ten years as many as five thousand
Papua New Guineans have converted (or as they say "reverted") to Islam.
Most of those converts had been Christian, and many had been Catholic.[18] Calls by some academics and church leaders to separate religion and
politics are met with incomprehension and resistance on the part of the
general populace. In Papua New Guinea, as in many other developing
nations, religion is part of life, which includes the social, the economic,
and the political.

An event in the national Parliament helps illustrate the holistic worldview. In the year 2000, the speaker of parliament, Bernard Narokobi had a
large cross mounted on top of the Parliament building. It was illuminated
so as to be visible at night throughout much of the city. In explaining

his action to the Parliament, Narokobi said that the cross is "the light of Calvary. With your concurrence I would ask that this cross remain. It is a memory of our hope in the future as Christians. This may not be the mountain or the hill of Calvary; however, the way we tend to crucify each other in here, we may as well nickname the hill on which Parliament stands, the Calvary Hill."[19] He explained further that Parliament makes decisions that are sacred because it is for the good of the people. This was an attempt by a devout Catholic to bring a symbol of Christian power into the very center of political power. Some people sensed a shocking conflict in bringing together these two powerful symbols, particularly those with a theology that sees an irreconcilable conflict between the reign of God and the realm of Satan. While Narokobi was absent from the chamber, a motion was passed to have the cross removed.

The incident described illustrates religious and political dimensions integrated in one worldview. To me the basic cultural issue is how such a view integrates a political culture based on strong-willed leaders who devise strategic alliances while competing for power, with money and guns as innovations on the traditional cultural practices. I ask myself, how can such a view be reconciled with gospel values? What is mission in this situation? Some Christians took what I call a spiritualist option, forming teams of "prayer warriors" to be positioned around election polling places to ensure that Satan could not enter and disturb the peace. That approach too easily allows a continuance of the status quo, which is basically unjust. There is little freedom of choice for the individual, particularly women, and often the electoral roll is grossly inflated with ghost names. In some communities people couldn't vote because the ballot papers were hijacked and sent elsewhere. What would be just in this situation? Am I trying to measure democracy using a yardstick from liberal democratic principles nurtured in the West?[20] Seemingly both democratic principles and Christian values have come from outside. Do they need to change in that new context?

The church cannot replace the state, but neither can it simply remain a spectator on the sidelines in what is clearly an unjust situation.[21] Political involvement is a duty. It is part of our mission to remind the political world of its real task, that is, the attainment of peace and justice and the development of a more human world. As more people are feeling frustrated and disenfranchised I am convinced that our mission is to help people view politics relative to the reign of God. What do I mean by that?

It would be to help people realize that it is not all about selling or trading votes to get access to money and what money can buy. It is also to offer a vision whereby they can claim a different future.

That may sound awfully idealistic in a chaotic context where wealth and power are so lacking and thus appear to be the solution. But the solution to being part of an abusive system is not to succeed in making it to the other side so the oppressed becomes an oppressor, but rather the transformation of the system itself in a way that ensures dignity for all citizens, where all can participate in society, including the political process. Some might think I am promoting socialism. I like to think that I am promoting a view of the world similar to that of Jesus who, quoting from the prophet Isaiah (Lk 4:18–19), spoke about liberty for captives and freedom for the oppressed, and then proceeded to put that vision into practice.

In that highly charged situation, I was aware of the futility of explicitly proclaiming gospel values associated with the reign of God. It would be like trying to talk about global warming to a crowd of supporters intent on watching a ball game—or maybe like Paul trying to speak at the Areopagus. What communication code might make sense? I noticed that people were using a metaphor associated with eating. They spoke in the local language about *nenge nanengepi*: those who eat and those who don't. It is a way of referring to haves and have-nots. If you support a winning candidate, you will "eat rice." If you lose you will get a five-year contract for sitting at home eating sweet potatoes from your own garden. In fact, the term is used in song as a protest against the politicization of the public service. Referring to the *nenge nanengepi*—eaters and noneaters, singers hope the situation will change and that the arrogant supporters of winning candidates will be brought down to a level where they can no longer boast about the privileges they enjoy.[22]

Roger Schroeder and Stephen Bevans, in a fascinating article on "Mission as Table Fellowship," show how Jesus' table fellowship with sinners, tax collectors, and other people marginal to society is an image of God inviting everyone to communion in the reign of God.[23] Could an image like that, linking with the metaphor of eaters and noneaters, be helpful for prophetic mission in the situation I have described, to help people come to new insights and a vision of alternatives to the present divisive political situation? I think that intercultural images such as the one just described can be helpful not only for developing ideas about God, but more importantly for witnessing to the reign of God in our midst.

An Epidemic

It is no coincidence that the countries struggling to face the HIV and AIDS epidemic today are the ones with a legacy of political, social, economic, and religious oppression in past centuries. This helps us realize that AIDS is not just a disease. It is a symptom of a cultural crisis: of dysfunctional political and socioeconomic structures, of lack of knowledge, and of things that have gone wrong in the way we relate to one another and particularly in the way we love one another.

Papua New Guinea is one of those countries. There are over thirty thousand people there who have tested positive for HIV/AIDS, but the number infected could be far greater because the majority of those infected don't know it.[24] Besides the *infected,* there are hundreds of thousands of people *affected*—searching for the resources to care for family members who are ill, or trying to cope without a husband, a wife, a mother, or father. In a country with no system for social security or old-age pension, the loss of a son or daughter is a severe blow to the security of parents in their advanced years.

In the last few years, my principal mission has been to research social and cultural factors that are contributing to the AIDS epidemic and to look for strategies that can help to alleviate it. "Going to church," prayer groups or Bible study groups have no necessary effect on reducing the epidemic.[25] In fact, some studies have found that attending church regularly may open new doors to relationships and consequent multiple sexual partnerships. Church rallies have been identified as "risk occasions" for youth in Papua New Guinea.[26]

Why would the church be so concerned about this situation when ministry to the sick has always been part of its mission? Perhaps it has something to do with HIV and AIDS being symbolic of frailties associated with our human condition that cries out for the love that we share through the church's ministry.[27] It also calls for special attention because so many people in our world, particularly the so-called developed world, do not realize its impact.

My principal experience in this field over the past few years has been a reflexive one. It has taught me a lot about mission because I have come to realize that I am the one who needs to be converted—in my attitudes, my values, and my openness to different cultural views of life and death, and ultimately to a new theological anthropology. Allow me to give just one example from many that I could relate.

Agnes (that is not her real name) is a young woman living in one of the settlements in a town in Papua New Guinea. She cared for her sister who died of AIDS, and Agnes is infected with HIV also. She has not been to school and can't read or write. But she works as a volunteer at one of the urban clinics, washing patients, talking with them, encouraging them. She has a small house in the crowded settlement, and she invites women—mostly those living with HIV—to come and stay with her and share what little food she has. I went and stayed there one night. Women came at different times through the darkness of the unlit settlement until there were eight of us sitting on the rough wooden floor around a kerosene lamp as they shared about what it was like, some having been cast out of their families due to stigma and discrimination. Surely for some, their only means of income would hardly square with official church moral teaching. However, what impressed me was the sense of community and the way they supported one another. By about 1:00 in the morning I felt tired and was shown a corner where I could sleep. As I lay there in the early hours of the morning, I could hear the others in the next room praying the rosary. You can imagine my mixed feelings, with these women from the streets conducting devotions while I, the missionary, lay in splendid isolation, secure under my mosquito net. I must have fallen asleep as they recited a litany from the movement for Divine Mercy.

Two weeks later, early one morning, Agnes called me on a borrowed cell phone:

"Father Philip?"

"Yes, Agnes."

"Scholastica died." (Scholastica was one of the women who had been with us that evening in the house).

"Oh, I'm sorry to hear that. What are you going to do?"

"I don't know. She is beside me now—she died."

"Are there some relatives?"

"No, they kicked her out."

"So, what can you do"?

"I'm going to bury her, but they want K30 for a place in the cemetery. Father, can you call me back, this phone is running out of units?"

After the call I sat there gazing at the computer screen in my room. I had just returned from saying mass at the nearby convent. The sisters had provided breakfast. I was safe, secure, well fed—but with some questions that troubled me. How can we understand the HIV epidemic in the light of the Christian mystery of life and death? Our response to such questions will affect the way we think about the epidemic and those affected by it.[28] If the life-giving Creator God is to be seen in the face of a human being living with HIV, then the Christian community has a responsibility to respond with the love and compassion. Our shared mission is found in promoting a new quality of life and meaning in life so that people will no longer think and talk about "dying from HIV," but rather "living with HIV." That is what Agnes and others like her are teaching me.[29]

A phrase came to mind: "The Word became flesh and dwelt among us" (Jn 1:14). Agnes could teach me a lot about what we call theological anthropology. Do we stifle Christ's incarnational presence in theological discourse remote from human experience? "Incarnation" is a technical word with Latin roots, but the important question is not the phrase itself, but rather "*What does it look like?*" I have a lot to learn from the many people like Agnes, witnessing to a culture of life, and revealing the love of Christ in very down-to-earth human ways. In its most fundamental sense, isn't that what mission is about?

The SVD Connection

I have chosen the three examples from many possibilities because I think they say something important about mission and the way we relate to people in the context of the crises of culture today. The lessons learned from those examples can have wider implications. Where does SVD fit into this and what might be some of the challenges in terms of mission and culture in the future? My focus is on the SVD—my own and Fr. Luzbetak's religious congregation—but I hope that what I say is in some ways applicable to every missionary congregation and in fact to everyone who accepts that as loving human beings, we are all called to be part of God's mission. I am proposing that we have something important to contribute to intercultural relations associated with globalization, democratic rights, the AIDS epidemic, and many other issues that are all part of a changing cultural context.

The SVD concern with mission and culture does not end with the Anthropos tradition. Scholars have observed the significance of the Vatican II Decree on The Mission Activity of the Church (*Ad Gentes*), having been written for the most part at the SVD house in Nemi near Rome, and how the SVD superior general at the time, Johannes Schütte, formerly missioned to China, chaired the commission in its later stages and acted as relator presenting the final schema to the Council.[30] After the Council Schütte noted how mission does not mean simply announcing the Good News, but a "new incarnation of Christ" in people's culture.[31]

Such ideas circulated within the SVD and eventually emerged in the 1983 revised Constitutions of the Society. Antonio Pernia, the present SVD superior general, points out how the 100s section of the Constitutions that presents the understanding of our missionary service has been greatly influenced by the Conciliar Decree *Ad Gentes*. Examples are Constitutions section 113 that treats the interaction of gospel, culture, and religion, and Constitutions section 114 that quotes from the Prologue to John's gospel and refers to the incarnation.[32]

SVD General Chapters since then have sought to deepen our understanding of the various ways we bear witness to the incarnation with debates on "passing over" to other cultures, to the poor and in dialogue with other religions and followers of contemporary ideologies (13th General Chapter, 1988). The idea behind the "passing over" concept was that missionaries should go to what were termed "frontiers" of faith and the margins of society. The chapter notes how this involves a "prophetic responsibility" to allow the unheard voices from the frontiers to be heard in the church and the world.[33] That prophetic responsibility has been treated further with the concept of "prophetic dialogue" introduced at the 15th General Chapter in the year 2000 and further developed in 2006.

The SVD adopted the term prophetic dialogue in an effort to bring together the Latin American concern for social justice and the Asian concern for dialogue. I wonder though where culture fits in. Could it be that prophetic dialogue is the method, and culture, wherever we are, is the context? In that case, how do we appreciate the intercultural dimension of our mission? I am concerned that prophecy and dialogue can get lost and confused if we don't take seriously the changing, deterritorialized, multidimensional, homogenized, hybrid, unbounded dimension that Stephen Bevans calls the "entire situation in which men and women live."[34] We need to reimagine the culture concept for today, and this will require a new recognition of the "Anthropos tradition"—not as a historical project, but looking to the future, including the development of what I am calling an "SVD tradition."

Conclusion

I would like to conclude with three points. First, the Anthropos tradition continues, but as Louis Luzbetak himself noted, while the Anthropos Institute can lead the way, it cannot produce a "cookbook" where one can find specific recipes. Learning spoken language and what he calls "the silent language" of culture is a learning process similar to learning to play the violin. You have to do it yourself. No one else can do the practicing for you.[35]

The SVD now has over six thousand members. It is part of the Roman Catholic Church, which is one of the largest multinational organizations in the world. At this time (2010) SVDs come from seventy-two different nationalities and work in seventy-two different nations—a happy scriptural coincidence (Lk 10)! I note too (depending on how one defines "continents") that SVD members are working on all seven continents. It is hardly surprising that the theme for the coming SVD General Chapter is from Revelation 7:9, "From Every Nation, People, and Language: Sharing Intercultural Life and Mission." The congregation hasn't fully realized the intercultural possibilities to date, but the potential is there. It is true, as Luzbetak said, if you are learning to play a musical instrument, no one else can do the practicing for you; but when you do play you will surely play with others, whether it be a quartet or an orchestra. Almost twenty years ago, Louis Luzbetak referred to the Augustinian image of a group of pilgrims walking together and singing a song of hope, "Thy kingdom come."[36] What tune or song is suitable for today? Would it be in harmony or discord?

Antonio Pernia gives an example of how the cultural makeup of the congregation can influence the way we do mission. He notes how the SVD mission in the twenty-first century will be carried out largely by missionaries originating from the third world, particularly from Asia.[37] From his own experience as Asian, he says that dialogue as a model of mission is one that accords with cultural dispositions from Asia: approaching mission from a position of humility, of contemplative presence, and as steward—not owner or master. One can only wonder at the combined contribution of cultural dispositions from the other five inhabited continents. That is the SVD connection—the long-term scholarly interest in culture coupled with living witness to the incarnation in flesh and blood internationalism.[38]

Second, after having just focused on the SVD, I wish to take a broader perspective, particularly with regard to the issue of theological anthropology. In the Luzbetak lecture of 2003 Darrell Whiteman refers to the incarnation and to people "embedded in their culture."[39] I agree with the concept, but from the examples offered today of the gold mine, electoral politics, and the AIDS epidemic, you will realize that I have issues with a culture concept that views people as "embedded" in their culture—when in so many places today reality appears quite the contrary. At this time, I take a less essentialist view of culture, and for that we have to look beyond what cultural or social anthropology have to offer. I agree with Bob Schreiter that we need a renewed *theological* anthropology.[40]

By theological anthropology I mean an understanding of what it means to be human from a faith perspective. Miracles in biomedical technologies, ecological awareness, and expanded reference to human rights are only some of the factors impacting on our understanding of what it means to be human. (I see now that in Germany access to the Internet is considered a "human right.") Theologians offer their views. Schillebeeckx refers to the "humanum"; Von Balthasar refers to a "being with finite freedom"; Panikkar writes about the "cosmotheandric." In recent papal encyclicals we hear of "transforming humanity from within, making it new" (*Evangelii Nuntiandi*), and more recently, there is the instruction on human dignity from the Congregation for the Doctrine of the Faith (*Dignitas Personae*). From my own study, I think the fundamental issue in the dispute between the Vatican Congregation for the Doctrine of the Faith and the liberation theologians was over how one understands humanity and whether we start our theological reflection with God or with the human condition. The same tension continues today with Jon Sobrino maintaining, "*Extra pauperes nulla salus*," putting the poor in the place of the church in the ancient saying according to which "outside the church there is no salvation."[41]

Consider again Luzbetak's analogy of learning to play a musical instrument. Music is universal to humanity; however, the form it takes and the instruments used are contextual. Here one enters the field of intercultural hermeneutics—do we link the "meaning" of the music to the composer, the performer, or the audience? Could the music be part of a protest and hence prophetic or counter-cultural?

How we understand what it means to be human is important because intercultural and interreligious dialogue are as much something we "are" as something we "do." Barbara Reid gives an account of the richly human experience of women's Bible study groups in Chiapas, Mexico.[42] I hope that the three examples I gave earlier in this lecture illustrate that point also. Pope John Paul II in his address to the United Nations in New York in 1995 said that "freedom" is the measure of human dignity and greatness.[43] I think we need to reflect in depth on anthropology in terms of what it really means to be human in the situations in which women, men, and children live today. Such a study presumes involvement in intercultural and interreligious dialogue that takes us beyond ecclesial circles such as in the three examples I have used in this presentation.

My third and final point is that we as people of faith have an opportunity to offer a new "grand narrative" to a world in which metanarratives have become lost to relativism in a fragmented sense of culture.[44] What we have to offer is not a theory, but rather a very human presence reflecting that "God is with us."[45] God is with us whether the tune is of joy or sorrow, triumph or protest. That presence harks back to a narrative that is close to the SVD tradition: "The Word became flesh and dwelt among us" (Jn 1:14). Here I base my presumption of what is human not on the Genesis account of creation and fall but more on the Johannine insight that the Word became flesh so that God who is love could enter into deep personal union with the world, the beloved.[46]

In her study of images and symbols in the Fourth Gospel, Barbara Reid shows how birthing imagery is woven throughout the whole of the Gospel of John. We read in John 1:12–13, "To all who received him, who believed in his name, he gave power to become children of God, who were born (*egennēthēsan*) not of blood or of the will of the flesh, or of the will of man, but of God." As Reid points out, these verses focus attention on the birthing of God's children through their faith in the *Logos*, using the verb *gennaō*, which in the Fourth Gospel evokes primarily the female imagery of birthing. The imagery continues through to the symbolic breaking of the amniotic fluid in the water and blood coming from Jesus' side at the crucifixion when the "power to become children of God" that was assured in the prologue is accomplished.[47]

We need to explore further such insights in order to enrich the symphony of the Good News that we share with "bold humility."[48] We need the contribution from scholars or from the "grass roots," and from the international SVD tradition, in order to imagine the world differently.[49]

- *What if* people at the mine site in Porgera could really sense that God is with them so that they don't have to be so concerned with a millennial Jesus coming at the end of the world?
- *What if* a realization that God is with us would empower people in electoral politics with a vision of the common good?
- *What if* we could realize that God is with us through the presence of people like Agnes and her friends?

That is what I mean by the importance of that life-giving grand narrative of the incarnation in mission today.

So, when I leave CTU a few months from now—thirty-three years after the first departure, how will it be different? We shall see; that is work in progress.

Notes

1. After studies for the priesthood at Divine Word Seminary, Techny, Fr. Louis Luzbetak studied in Europe for six years, obtaining degrees in Canon Law and Dogmatic Theology from the Gregorian University, Rome, and a Doctorate in Anthropology from Fribourg University in Switzerland. He served in Papua New Guinea from 1952 to 1956.

2. "Our Anthropos tradition is really a way of doing mission which considers an appreciation of people's culture as a necessary precondition for genuine evangelization. A way of doing mission whereby the gospel message is not simply parachuted from outside, but enters into dialogue with the culture of the people. And so, a way of doing mission whereby the missionary is ready not just to change people but to be changed himself, or as EN (e.g. no. 15) puts it, a way of evangelizing whereby the evangelizer not only evangelizes but allows himself or herself to evangelized" (Antonio Pernia, "Expectations of the Generalate of the Anthropos Institute," paper delivered at the Anthropos Institute—Europe meeting, Nysa, Poland, September, 14–20, 2003, 12). Pernia adds that "Without this tradition, something essential would be lost from our Society" (ibid., 13).

3. Ethnology analyzes data collected through ethnography. Schmidt as a culture-historian considered ethnology as *Geisteswissenschaften*, along with history, philosophy, and other social sciences. This was before Malinowski, Radcliffe-Brown, and Boas had combined both ethnologist and ethnographer in one and the same person. Ernest Brandewie notes how for Schmidt fieldwork was not a *conditio sine qua non* for one to become a good ethnologist. "To absolutely require this of someone doing culture-history would be the

same as requiring every historian to be actually present at that period of time or incident which he is describing, a principle which would quickly do away with history" (Ernest Brandewie, "Ethnology and Missionaries: The Case of the Anthropos Institute and Wilhelm Schmidt," in *Missionaries, Anthropologists, and Cultural Change*, vol. 1, ed. Darrell Whiteman and Frank Salamone [Williamsburg, VA: College of William and Mary, Studies in Third World Societies, 1983], 377, 379–80). James Clifford explains the change of view from the ethnographer-theorist to anthropological fieldworker, as with Malinowski and Mead (James Clifford, *The Predicament of Culture* [Cambridge, MA: Harvard University Press, 1988], 27–28).

4. Because of his interest in groups that were ethnologically "older" than others, Schmidt had encouraged fellow SVDs to study groups that were in danger of disappearing—such as the people of Tierra del Fuego or the Mbuti pygmies of Central Africa. The frontispiece of the *Anthropos* journal stated that it was published *unter Mitarbeit zahlreicher Missionare*—"with the cooperation of numerous missionaries." The phrase was omitted when the Anthropos Institute was established in 1931.

5. Louis J. Luzbetak, "My Pilgrimage in Mission," *International Bulletin of Missionary Research* 16, no. 3 (1992): 125. In one of several letters from Louis Luzbetak to Wilhelm Schmidt he apologizes, "I haven't forgotten you: I'm so taken up with my work now that I've given up practically all letter-writing" (December 9, 1953) (SVD archives, Collegio del Verbo Divino, Rome.)

6. Philip Gibbs, "Kepele: A Ritual from the Western Highlands of Papua New Guinea," *Anthropos* 73 (1978): 434–48.

7. It was a common occurrence for the Highlanders to view white explorers as spirits (see Bill Gammage, *The Sky Travelers: Journeys in New Guinea 1938–1939* [Calton, Victoria, Australia: Melbourne University, 1998]).

8. Marilyn Strathern, "The Nice Thing about Culture Is That Everyone Has It," in *Shifting Contexts: Transformations in Anthropological Knowledge*, ed. Marilyn Strathern (London: Routledge, 1995), 164.

9. Robert J. Schreiter, *The New Catholicity: Theology between the Global and the Local* (Maryknoll, NY: Orbis Books, 1997), ix.

10. Clifford's term referring to Squanto, a Patuxet "just back from Europe" encountered by the English Pilgrims on their arrival at Plymouth Rock in the New World (Clifford, *The Predicament of Culture*, 17).

11. The landowners association (*Kupiane Yuu Anduane*) is named after the snake ancestor. See Aletta Biersack, "The Mount Kare Python and His Gold: Totemism and Ecology in the Papua New Guinea Highlands," *American Anthropologist* 101, 1 (1999): 68–87; Richard Jackson and Glenn Banks, *In Search of the Serpent's Skin: The Story of the Porgera Gold Project* (Port Moresby, Papua

New Guinea: Placer Niugini, 2002); Jerry Jacka, "Emplacement and Millennial Expectations in an Era of Development and Globalization: Heaven and the Appeal of Christianity for the Ipili," *American Anthropologist* 107, 4 (2005): 643–53.

12. Ibid.," 645.

13. Jean Comaroff and John Comaroff, "Millennial Capitalism: First Thoughts on a Second Coming," *Public Culture* 12, no. 2 (2000): 291–343; Jacka, "Emplacement and Millennial Expectations."

14. Bill Standish, "Elections in Simbu: Towards Gunpoint Democracy?" in *The 1992 Papua New Guinea Elections: Change and Continuity in Electoral Politics, Political and Social Change*. Monograph 23, 277–322, ed. Yaw Saffit (Canberra, Australia: Research School of Pacific and Asian Studies, Australian National University, 1996).

15. Ron May, "Disorderly Elections: Political Turbulence and Institutional Reform in Papua New Guinea," State Society and Governance in Melanesia, Discussion Paper 2003/3 (Canberra: Research School of Pacific and Asian Studies, Australian National University, 2003), 8.

16. Christin Kocher Schmid, ed., *Expecting the Day of Wrath*, Monograph 36 (Boroko, Papua New Guinea: National Research Institute, 1999).

17. Pamela Steward and Andrew Strathern, "Money, Politics, and Persons in Papua New Guinea," *Social Analysis* 42 (1998): 132–49.

18. Scott Flower, *The Growth of Islam in Papua New Guinea: Implications for Security and Policy* (PhD diss., Canberra: Australian National University, 2010).

19. Papua New Guinea Parliament, *Hansard,* April 13, 2000, 2.

20. Philip Gibbs, "Democracy and Enga Political Culture," in *Politicking in the Highlands: The 2002 Papuan New Guinea Elections,* State Society and Governance in Melanesia, Discussion Papers, vol. 2004/1 (Canberra: Research School of Pacific and Asian Studies, Australian Catholic University, 2004), 2–15.

21. Ron May puts it well: "The problems that beset Papua New Guinea will diminish the state's legitimacy and eventually pose a threat to democracy that cannot be explained away as the result of a chaotic-looking but basically sound 'Melanesian Way' of doing politics" (May, "Disorderly Elections: Political Turbulence and Institutional Reform in Papua New Guinea," 164).

22. Philip Gibbs and Joseph Lakane, "Haves and Have-Nots: The 2002 Elections in the Enga Province, PNG," *Catalyst* 33, no. 2 (2003): 96–116.

23. Stephen B. Bevans and Roger P. Schroeder, "Mission and Table Fellowship: Mission in the Aereopagus of Today," in *Prophetic Dialogue: Reflections on Christian Mission Today,* ed. Stephen B. Bevans and Roger P. Schroeder (Maryknoll, NY: Orbis Books, 2011), 101–14.

24. *The 2009 STI, HIV and AIDS Third Quarter Surveillance Report, July–September, 2009*, Papua, New Guinea: National Department of Health, STI, HIV and AIDS Surveillance Unit, 2009).

25. Elizabeth Reid, "Pastoral Leadership and the HIV Epidemic," A Manual to Assist in the Formation of Priests, Religious, and Church Workers in PNG and the Pacific on the Pastoral and Ethical Challenges of the HIV Epidemic (unpublished manuscript, 2009), 124.

26. National HIV and AIDS Support Project (NHASP), *Situational Analysis for Strategic Planning at District Level: Simbu Province. Social Mapping Project* (Papua New Guinea: NHASP, 2005).

27. Robert Vitillo, "The Catholic Church Responding to AIDS as Teacher, Servant, and Pastor," Paper at Caritas Europa Conference, "Stigma or Solidarity? New Challenges for Church Responses to HIV and AIDS in Europe," Kiev, April 24, 2007.

28. Philip Gibbs, "Forces of Death and the Promise of Life in Papua New Guinea," *Australian E-Journal of Theology* 14 (2009).

29. Sadly, Agnes passed away in late 2010.

30. Heribert Bettscheider, "The Contribution of the Society of the Divine Word to the Elaboration of *Ad Gentes*," *Verbum SVD* 46, no. 4 (2005): 371–402.

31. "Missione non significa infatti semplicemente annuncio della Buona Novella di Cristo, ma una nuova incarnazione di Cristo e della sua Chiesa in un altro popolo, nella sua cultura e nella sua mentalitá" (Johannes Schütte, "I problemi posti dalla missione al Concilio," in *Il Destino delle Missioni*, ed. Johannes Schütte (Roma-Brescia: Herder-Morcelliana, 1969), 9–23, at 16.

32. Antonio Pernia, "Mission for the Twenty-First Century: An SVD Perspective," in *Mission for the Twenty-First Century*, ed. Stephen Bevans and Roger Schroeder (Chicago: CCGM Publications, 2001), 14–15.

33. *Nuntius Societatis Verbi Divini* XII, 5, 1988 (Rome: Generalate, 1990).

34. Stephen Bevans, "Inculturation and SVD Mission," *Verbum SVD* 42, no. 3 (2001): 260.

35. Louis J. Luzbetak, "Refounding Anthropos," Unpublished Position Paper (June 24, 2001), 8.

36. Louis J. Luzbetak, "'Inculturation': A Call for Greater Precision," in *Verbi Praecones: Festschrift für Karl Müller SVD zum 75. Geburtstag*, ed. Kurt Piskaty and Horst Rzepkowski (Nettetal, Germany: Steyler Verlag, 1993), 45.

37. Pernia, "Mission for the Twenty-First Century," 18–19.

38. I am proposing an ideal here. In a talk about developments with Anthropos International, Anthony Pernia challenges SVD missiologists to confront reality when he notes, "One can even wonder how many of our

students know that AI exists" (Pernia, "Expectations of the Generate of the Anthropos Institute").

39. See Whiteman's lecture in Chapter 3 in this volume.

40. Robert J. Schreiter, "A New Modernity: Living and Believing in an Unstable World," the 2005 Anthony Jordan Lectures, Newman Theological College, Edmonton, Alberta, Canada, March 18–19, 2005, 33.

41. Jon Sobrino, "Jon Sobrino al P. Peter Hans Kolvenbach," Letter, December 13, 2006. http://chiesa.espresso.repubblica.it/articolo/127601, para. 4.7.

42. Barbara E. Reid, *Taking Up the Cross: New Testament Interpretations through Latina and Feminist Eyes* (Minneapolis, MN: Fortress Press, 2007).

43. John Paul II, 12, address to the Fiftieth General Assembly of the United Nations. http://www/vatican/va/holy_father/john_paul_ii/speeches/ 1995/october/documents/hf_jp-ii_spe_05101995_address-touno_en.html.

44. Schreiter, *The New Catholicity*, 129.

45. "[W]hat revelation proclaimed, that God is with us to free us from the darkness of sin and death, and to raise us up to life eternal" (Vatican Council II, Constitution on Divine Revelation [*Dei Verbum*], para. 4). Significant elements of this text were introduced by the Indonesian bishops. See Philip Gibbs, *The Word in the Third World: Divine Revelation in the Theology of Jean-Marc Ela, Aloysius Pieris and Gustavo Gutiérrez* (Rome: Editrice Pontificia Università Gregoriana, 1996), 26.

46. Elizabeth A. Johnson, *Quest for the Living God: Mapping Frontiers in the Theology of God* (New York: Continuum, 2007), 40.

47. Reid, *Taking up the Cross*, 156.

48. "Bold humility" is a term used by David Bosch (*Transforming Mission: Paradigm Shifts in Theology of Mission* [Maryknoll, NY: Orbis Books, 1991], 489), which Bevans and Schroeder consider fits well with prophetic dialogue (Bevans and Schroeder, *Prophetic Dialogue*, 2).

49. See ibid., 116.

Contributors

JOSE M. DE MESA is professor of theology, emeritus, at De La Salle University, Manila, Philippines. He is the author of many articles and books, including *Why Theology Is Never Far from Home*, *In Solidarity with the Culture: Studies in Theological Re-Rooting*, *Doing Theology: Basic Realities and Processes* (with Lode Wostyn), and *Mga Aral sa Daan: Dulog at Paraang Kultural sa Kristolohiya*. He has lectured extensively throughout the world, especially in Asia, and has served several times as Visiting Louis J. Luzbetak, SVD, Professor at Catholic Theological Union, Chicago.

MARY DOUGLAS was, until her death in 2007, one of the most eminent anthropologists of our time. She taught at University College, London, and at Princeton and Northwestern Universities in the United States, and published many books, including *Purity and Danger: An Analysis of Concepts of Pollution and Taboo*, *Natural Symbols: Explorations in Cosmology*, and *Risk and Blame: Essays in Cultural Theory*. She was elected as a member of the British Academy in 1999 and was appointed Dame Commander of the Order of the British Empire in 2006.

AYLWARD SHORTER is a Catholic priest in the congregation of the Missionaries of Africa. He was the principal of Tangaza College in Nairobi, Kenya, and president of the Missionary Institute in London, and is the author of many articles and books. Among these are *African Christian Theology: Adaptation or Incarnation? Toward a Theology of Inculturation*, and *Cross and Flag in Africa: The "White Fathers" during the Colonial Scramble (1892–1914)*.

DARRELL L. WHITEMAN is currently vice president for mission mobilization and training and resident missiologist at the Mission Society of the United Methodist Church, USA. He worked as a missionary in Papua New Guinea; was professor of anthropology and dean at the E. Stanley Jones School of World Mission and Evangelism at Asbury

311

Theological Seminary, Wilmore, Kentucky; served for twelve years as editor of *Missiology: An International Review*; and is a past president of the American Society of Missiology. Among his books are *Melanesians and Missionaries* and *World Mission in the Wesleyan Spirit*, which he coedited with Gerald H. Anderson.

LINDA E. THOMAS is professor of theology and anthropology at the Lutheran School of Theology at Chicago. She has taught at Iliff School of Theology in Denver, Colorado, and at Garrett Evangelical Seminary in Evanston, Illinois, and has been guest professor at the University of Chicago, Vanderbilt University, and Drew University. She has published *Under the Canopy: Ritual Processes and Spiritual Resilience in South Africa* and edited *Living Stones in the Household of God*, a collection of essays about black theology in the new millennium.

ANTHONY J. GITTINS is a Catholic priest in the Congregation of the Holy Spirit (CSSp—Spiritans) and professor of theological anthropology at Catholic Theological Union, Chicago. He served as a missionary in Sierra Leone, and works with homeless women and men in Chicago. A well-known lecturer and retreat director all over the world, he is the author of, among many other books, *Gifts and Strangers: Meeting the Challenge of Inculturation*, *Reading the Clouds: Mission Spirituality for New Times*, *A Presence That Disturbs: A Call to Radical Discipleship*, and *Called and Sent: Co-Missioned as Disciples Today*.

JON P. KIRBY is a Catholic priest in the Society of the Divine Word (SVD). A long-time missionary in Ghana, West Africa, he is the founder and first director of the Tamale Institute for Cross-Cultural Studies (TICCS) in northern Ghana, and now resides in Los Angeles, California, where he writes and is engaged in mission animation. He has published extensively, including *God, Shrines and Problem-Solving among the Anufo of Northern Ghana*, *Culture Drama and Peacebuilding: A Culture Drama Workbook*, and he has edited *The Witchcraft Mentality Seminars: Applications for Ministry and Development*.

ANGELYN DRIES, a sister of St. Francis, is Danforth Professor in the Humanities at St. Louis University. She has served as associate editor of *Missiology: An International Review*, chair of the ASM Series Committee for the American Society of Missiology and Orbis Books, and as president of the American Society of Missiology. She has published *The Missionary*

Movement in American Catholic History and is currently engaged in writing a history of the Maryknoll Society for Orbis Books.

GEMMA TALUD CRUZ is currently senior lecturer at the Australian Catholic University, Melbourne Campus. She has also taught at Assumption College in Manila, Philippines, St. Ambrose College, Davenport, Iowa, and at DePaul University, Chicago. She has published *Into the Deep: A Theological Struggle of the Filipina Domestic Workers in Hong Kong* and *An Intercultural Theology of Migration: Pilgrims in the Wilderness.*

ROBERT J. SCHREITER is Vatican II Professor of Theology at Catholic Theological Union, Chicago. He is a Catholic priest of the Missionaries of the Precious Blood (CPPS). Schreiter has taught at the University of Nijmegen in Holland and at the Universities of Frankfurt and Erfurt in Germany. He is a past president of the Catholic Theological Society of America and the American Society of Missiology, and has received the John Courtney Murray Award from the Catholic Society of America. Among his many books are the groundbreaking *Constructing Local Theologies*, *The New Catholicity*, and *The Ministry of Reconciliation.*

PHILIP GIBBS is a Catholic priest in the Society of the Divine Word (SVD). Born in New Zealand, he has worked as a missionary in Papua New Guinea since 1978 and has taught at Holy Spirit Seminary, Port Moresby, PNG, Yarra Theological Union, Melbourne, Australia, the East Asian Pastoral Institute, Manila, and Catholic Theological Union, Chicago. He currently serves as an advisor for Caritas, Australia, and for peace and justice issues for the bishops of Papua New Guinea. He has published dozens of articles and, in 1996, published *The Word in the Third World: Divine Revelation in the Theology of Jean Marc Ela, Aloysius Pieris, and Gustavo Gutiérrez.*

Index

Previously Published in the American Society of Missiology Series

The American Society of Missiology Series, published in collaboration with Orbis Books, seeks to publish scholarly works of high merit and wide interest on numerous aspects of missiology—the study of Christian mission in its historical, social, and theological dimensions. Able presentations on new and creative approaches to the practice and understanding of mission will receive close attention from the ASM Series Committee.

1. *Protestant Pioneers in Korea*, Everett Nichols Hunt Jr.
2. *Catholic Politics in China and Korea*, Eric O. Hanson
3. *From the Rising of the Sun*, James M. Phillips
4. *Meaning Across Cultures*, Eugene A. Nida and William D. Reyburn
5. *The Island Churches of the Pacific*, Charles W. Forman
6. *Henry Venn*, Wilbert Shenk
7. *No Other Name?* Paul F. Knitter
8. *Toward a New Age in Christian Theoogy*, Richard Henry Drummond
9. *The Expectation of the Poor*, Guillermo Cook
10. *Eastern Orthodox Mission Theology Today*, James J. Stamoolis
11. *Confucius, the Buddha, and the Christ*, Ralph Covell
12. *The Church and Cultures*, Louis J. Luzbetak, SVD
13. *Translating the Message*, Lamin Sanneh
14. *An African Tree of Life*, Thomas G. Christensen
15. *Missions and Money* (second edition), Jonathan J. Bonk
16. *Transforming Mission*, David J. Bosch
17. *Bread for the Journey*, Anthony J. Gittins, CSSp
18. *New Face of the Church in Latin America*, Guillermo Cook
19. *Mission Legacies*, edited by Gerald H. Anderson, Robert T. Coote, Norman A. Horner, and James M. Phillips
20. *Classic Texts in Mission and World Christianity*, edited by Norman E. Thomas
21. *Christian Mission: A Case Study Approach*, Alan Neely
22. *Understanding Spiritual Power*, Marguerite G. Kraft
23. *Missiological Education for the 21st Century: The Book, the Circle, and the Sandals*, edited by J. Dudley Woodberry, Charles Van Engen, and Edgar J. Elliston
24. *Dictionary of Mission: Theology, History, Perspectives*, edited by Karl Müller, SVD, Theo Sundermeier, Stphen B. Bevans, SVD, and Richard H. Bliese